STATES AND REGIONS

HBJ

Harcourt Brace Jovanovich, Inc.

Holt, Rinehart and Winston, Inc.

Orlando · Austin · San Diego · Chicago · Dallas · Toronto

SENIOR EDITORIAL ADVISER

Dr. Phillip Bacon is a professor Emeritus of Geography and Anthropology at the University of Houston. Dr. Bacon has also served on the faculties of Columbia University and the University of Washington. Formerly Dean of the Graduate School of Peabody College for Teachers at Vanderbilt University, Dr. Bacon began his career in education as a teacher of elementary and secondary social studies. He is the author or editor of more than 36 books, including the *Life Pictorial Atlas of the World*. For 18 years, Dr. Bacon served as a member of the Editorial Advisory Board of the *World Book Encyclopedia*.

Among his numerous honors and awards, Dr. Bacon holds the distinguished titles of Fellow of the Explorers Club and Fellow of the Royal Geographic Society of Great Britain. He is a three-time recipient of the Teaching Excellence Award at the University of Houston. His biography appears in *Who's Who in America* and *American Men and Women in Science*.

ACKNOWLEDGMENTS

For permission to reprint copyrighted material, grateful acknowledgment is made to the following sources:

Brandt & Brandt Literary Agents, Inc.: From "Ode to Walt Whitman" in *Selected Works of Stephen Vincent Benét.* Copyright 1935 by Stephen Vincent Benét; copyright renewed © 1963 by Thomas C. Benét, Stephanie B. Mahin and Rachel Benét Lewis.

The Caxton Printers, Ltd.: Adapted from "Paul Bunyan in Puget Sound" in *Tall Timber Tales: More Paul Bunyan Stories* by Dell J. McCormick. Copyright 1939 by The Caxton Printers, Ltd.

Harcourt Brace Jovanovich, Inc.: From "Chicago" in *Chicago Poems* by Carl Sandburg. Copyright 1916 by Holt, Rinehart and Winston, Inc., renewed 1944 by Carl Sandburg.

Alfred A. Knopf, Inc.: "Puget Sound" by Harold W. Felton from *Legends of Paul Bunyan,* compiled and edited by Harold W. Felton. Copyright 1947 by Alfred A. Knopf, Inc., renewed © 1975 by Harold W. Felton.

Macmillan Publishing Company: From p. 67 in *Grasshopper Summer* by Ann Turner. Copyright © 1989 by Ann Turner.

National Geographic Society: From "Journey Up the Nile" by Robert Caputo in *National Geographic* Magazine, May 1985. Copyright © 1985 by National Geographic Society. From "Alone" by Robyn Davidson in *National Geographic* Magazine, May 1978. Copyright © 1978 by National Geographic Society. From "North Dakota, Tough Times on the Prairie" by Bryan Hodgson in *National Geographic* Magazine, March 1987. Copyright © 1987 by National Geographic Society.

G. P. Putnam's Sons: From pp. 7–13 in *Shh! We're Writing the Constitution* by Jean Fritz, pictures by Tomie dePaola. Text © 1987 by Jean Fritz; illustrations © 1987 by Tomie dePaola.

Viking Penguin, a division of Penguin Books USA Inc.: From *Along Sandy Trails* by Ann Nolan Clark. Text copyright © 1969 by Ann Nolan Clark.

Printed in the United States of America
ISBN 0-15-372623-7

PROGRAM ADVISERS

John F. Barbini, Ed.D.
Assistant Superintendent
School District 54
Schaumburg, Illinois

Willard Bill, Ph.D.
Chair, Social Sciences
International and Multicultural
   Division
North Seattle Community College
Seattle, Washington

Frank de Varona
Associate Superintendent
Dade County Public Schools
Miami, Florida

Paul S. Hanson
Principal
North Miami Beach Senior
   High School
Miami, Florida

William D. Travis, Ed.D.
Curriculum Director
Pittsfield Public Schools
Pittsfield, Massachusetts

Donald P. Vetter
Supervisor of Social Studies
Carroll County Public Schools
Westminster, Maryland

CONTENT SPECIALISTS

Irving Cutler, Ph.D.
Chairman Emeritus, Geography
   Department
Chicago State University
Chicago, Illinois

Donald O. Schneider, Ph.D.
Professor and Head of
   Social Science Education
University of Georgia
Athens, Georgia

Wm. Doyle Smith, Ph.D.
Associate Professor of Economics
University of Texas at El Paso
El Paso, Texas

Peter J. Stein, Ph.D.
Professor of Sociology
William Paterson College
Wayne, New Jersey

CHILDREN'S LITERATURE ADVISERS

Meridith McGowan
Children's Librarian
   and Consultant
Tempe, Arizona

Thomas McGowan, Ph.D.
Associate Professor
Curriculum and Instruction
Arizona State University
Tempe, Arizona

CLASSROOM CONSULTANTS

Joan Chambliss
Lead Teacher
Pine Tree Intermediate School
Longview, Texas

Anita T. Cummings
Teacher
Wesconnett Elementary School
Jacksonville, Florida

Joanne G. Gibson
Teacher
Noble Middle School
Wilmington, North Carolina

Kathyleen Guarnier
Teacher
Howe Elementary School
Schenectady, New York

John P. Hughes
Teacher
Thomas Jefferson Elementary School
Valparaiso, Indiana

Celia Ann Jeffers
Teacher
Sugar Creek Elementary School
Sugar Creek, Missouri

Dorothy Kueker
Teacher
Pinewood Elementary School
Rochester, Minnesota

Sarah Lee Little
Teacher
Our Lady of Lourdes School
Greenville, Mississippi

Dorothy Marcoux
Teacher
Adams Elementary School
Boise, Idaho

Elena M. Midolo
Teacher
W. A. Driscoll Elementary School
Dayton, Ohio

Judson A. Morhart
Coordinator of Instruction
Los Alamos Public Schools
Los Alamos, New Mexico

Marcia D. Muse
Teacher
Fair Oaks Elementary School
Highland Springs, Virginia

Molly Och
Teacher
Boone Elementary School
Alief Independent School District
Houston, Texas

Nancy D. Rodney
Teacher
Oliver Wendell Holmes
   Elementary School
Chicago, Illinois

Jerry Vitalis
Teacher
Webster Open School
Minneapolis, Minnesota

Dennis Wagester
Reading Specialist
Bailey Lake Elementary School
Clarkston Elementary School
Clarkston, Michigan

Wendell Gene Ward
Teacher
Bradley Elementary School
Columbia, South Carolina

Karen Tindel Wiggins
Director of Social Studies
Richardson Independent School
   District
Richardson, Texas

CONTENTS

UNIT REVIEW

61

UNIT TWO

THE SHAPES OF THE LAND

64

CHAPTER THREE

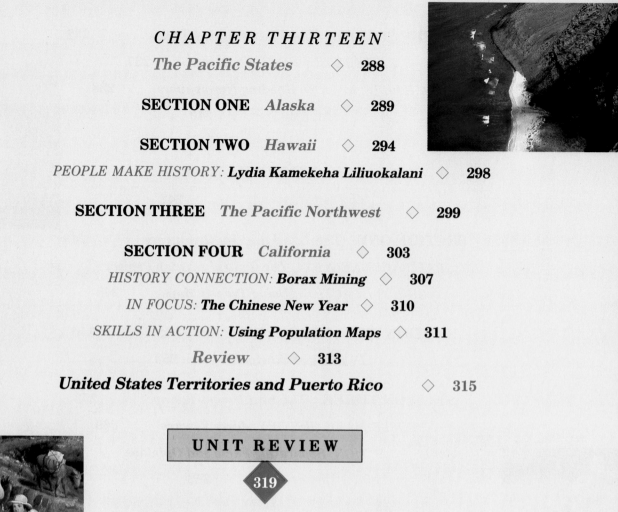

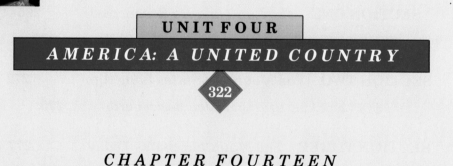

UNIT FOUR

AMERICA: A UNITED COUNTRY

322

xii

CONNECTIONS

SKILLS IN ACTION

READINGS

MAPS AND GLOBES

CHARTS, GRAPHS, DIAGRAMS, AND TIMELINES

xvi

Introduction

CITIZENS OF YOUR STATE AND COUNTRY

Suppose you know a girl named Ann. She is visiting another country. A new friend in that country asks Ann where she lives. Ann answers first by describing her neighborhood. Then she gives her address. But that does not help Ann's friend to understand where Ann lives.

Ann next describes her community. A community can be a town, a city, or a farming area. Ann explains that she and her family live in a housing development in a large city. But that still does not help Ann's friend.

"I live in Indiana, in the United States!" Ann finally says. Now her friend understands. Ann's community and many other communities are part of her **state.** Your state, like Ann's state of Indiana, is one of the 50 states in our **country,** the United States of America.

In this book you will read about your state and other states. You will also study the different **regions** of our country and the world. A region is an area with many things in common. The land, the water, and the people help to make each region special.

The picture of the waterfall shows a beautiful place on our planet Earth. The study of the Earth and its many kinds of places is called **geography.** The land and water a place has is an important part of its geography. You will discover that people are part of geography, too.

In this book you will read about the ways in which people in different places use the Earth. You will find out how people change the Earth as they use it. When people plant crops or build homes, for example, they change the land. People affect the Earth's water supply when they use water.

As you study geography, you will learn about many communities, states, regions, and countries. You will read about how people in all these places depend on each other. You will also find out how people work together.

Think about the many groups you belong to. You are a **citizen,** or member, of some larger groups as well. These are your community and your state. You are also a citizen of your country.

As a citizen, you are important to the place in which you live. You can learn how to keep your community and your state a good place to live.

1

USING YOUR TEXTBOOK

Your textbook is divided into several parts. Knowing about these parts will help you use this book.

The Contents

Near the front of your book, find the page labeled **Contents.** The table of contents tells where to find all of the book's parts.

Notice that the table of contents lists the book's **units** and **chapters.** After each title is a page number. That is the first page number of the unit or chapter. The table of contents lists other parts of the book, too. What are some of these?

Find Unit 1 in the table of contents. This unit tells about the people and the land of the United States. Unit 1 has two chapters. What are the titles of these chapters? On what page does Chapter 2 begin?

Chapters and Sections

Each chapter is divided into several sections. Each section has a number and a title. Above the title is a box labeled **Reading for a Purpose.** This box includes a list of important words and names, which are called **Key**

Words, People, and **Places.** It also includes three or four questions. These questions will help you focus your attention on the section's most important ideas. As you read, look for the answers to these questions.

You will see the important words and names again in the section. They are printed in a dark type called **boldface.** Sometimes a word in boldface is followed by a different spelling. For example, the word *plateaus* will be followed by (pla•TOHZ). This spelling tells you how to say the word.

When you see a boldfaced word, look for its meaning. Find each boldfaced place on a map. Knowing what these words mean and where these places are will help you understand the section. The boldfaced words will help you locate the answers to the questions in the **Reading Check** at the end of each section.

Other Parts of Your Textbook

If you do not remember the meaning of a key word, look for it in the **Glossary.** The Glossary lists the key words in ABC order. It gives their meanings and tells you how to say them. The Glossary is in the back of the book.

At some time you may need to review something, or you may want to read more about it. The easiest way to find any subject in your book is to use the **Index.** The Index lists subjects in ABC order, and it gives the page numbers where the information is located. The Index is also found in the back of the book.

Suppose you want to find information about China. You can find China listed in the Index under *C.* Look at the Index now. On what pages in the book will you find information about China?

The back of this book has other parts. One is called **Symbols of America**. It tells about some of our country's important symbols. The book also has an almanac called **Facts About the States**. It gives facts about each of the states in our country. The **Geographic Dictionary** describes different kinds of land and water. The **Atlas** provides you with maps of the United States, the world, and the continents. The **Gazetteer** (gaz•uh•TIHR) describes many of the important places named in your book. It also tells where you can find these places on maps in the book.

There is one more important thing to remember. Treat your

You can use the index to find any subject in this book.

textbook with care. Never write in it. Your book should be as clean for another student next year as it is for you this year.

Questions to Answer

1. What is Unit 4 about? On what page does it begin?
2. Find the first section in Chapter 2. What is the title of this section?
3. How can you find the meaning of the word *geography*? Give two ways.
4. On what pages will you find information on Missouri?
5. What does your book's Atlas include?

GEOGRAPHY: REVIEW AND PRACTICE

Imagine your neighborhood without any houses, streets, or signs. What can you say about the land? Is it flat? Are there hills or mountains nearby? These shapes of the land are called **landforms.**

Do you live near any **bodies of water**? Bodies of water include rivers, lakes, and oceans. Oceans contain salt water, which humans cannot drink. However, oceans provide us with fish and other seafood. Most lakes and rivers contain fresh water. We depend on fresh water for many of our needs.

Now think about the weather where you live. What is the weather usually like? Is it cold in winter, or is it warm all year? Does it rain a little or a lot? The weather a place has year after year is called its **climate.**

Your area also has **natural resources.** The word *natural* means "found in nature, not made by humans." Resources are things that people can use. Natural resources, then, are things found in nature that people can use. Water, forests, and soil are natural resources. How do people use natural resources?

You already know some of your area's geography. You know about its landforms, bodies of water, climate, and natural resources. These are its **natural features,** the things not made by humans.

Throughout this book, you will read about the natural features of different places. You will also find out how people use or change natural features. Special tools can help you as you study the geography of your state and of other regions of the country and the world.

Some natural features, such as this one in Utah, have unusual shapes.

Globes

One of the most important tools of geography is the **globe.** A globe is a model of the Earth.

Because the Earth has the shape of a **sphere,** or ball, a globe is also a sphere. Look at the drawing of a globe at the top of this page. Globes are the best models of the Earth that we have.

Find the **North Pole** on the drawing of the globe. The North Pole is as far north as you can go on Earth. The **South Pole** is as far south as you can go on Earth. The areas near the North Pole and the South Pole have very cold climates.

Look at the globe again. You will find a line that circles the globe halfway between the North Pole and the South Pole. This make-believe line is called the **equator.** Places near the equator generally have warm weather all year. Although you can see the equator on a globe, there is not really such a line on the Earth. The equator is added to globes to make them more useful.

The equator divides the Earth into a northern half and a southern half. You know that the Earth is a sphere. Half of a sphere is called a **hemisphere.** The equator divides the Earth into a **Northern Hemisphere** and a **Southern Hemisphere.**

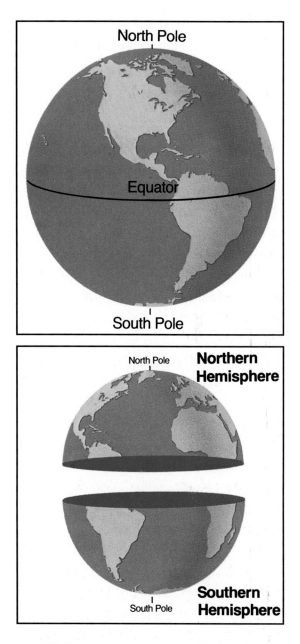

Globes are special because they look so much like the Earth. However, globes are not always easy to use. For example, you cannot see the details about a small place on a globe. You cannot see the whole Earth at one glance, either. Globes also are awkward to carry from place to

5

place. As you read this book, you will use another important tool of geography—maps.

Maps

A **map** is a drawing of a place. Maps can show many things. Unlike globes, however, maps are flat. They are not perfect models of the Earth. They cannot show the true shape of the Earth.

In the picture, you can see what happens when you try to flatten out the surface of a globe to make a map. The round surface will not flatten out perfectly. Look at the blank spaces near the poles. Mapmakers sometimes fill in the blank spaces with extra land and water.

Maps do not show land and water areas exactly. Even so, maps are very useful tools. Look at the map of the world. You can see all of the main land and water areas on Earth.

On most maps and globes, water is shown in blue. As you can see, most of the Earth is covered by water. In fact, more than seven-tenths of the Earth's surface is water.

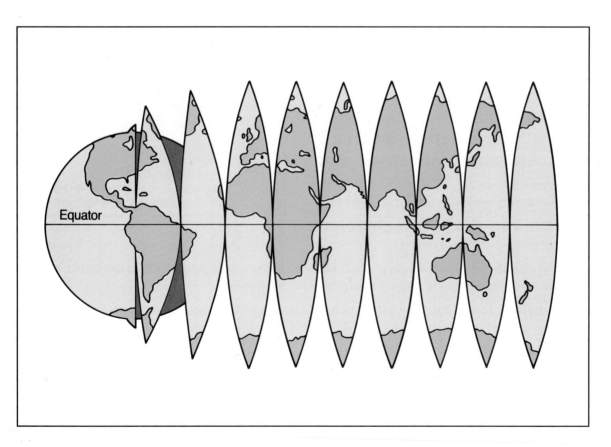

Equator

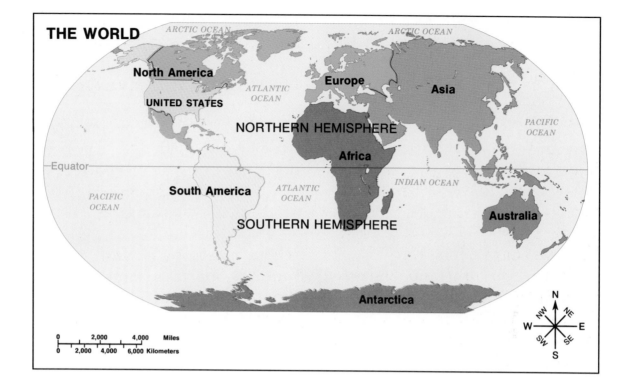

THE WORLD

ARCTIC OCEAN   ARCTIC OCEAN

North America   Europe   Asia

ATLANTIC OCEAN   PACIFIC OCEAN

UNITED STATES

NORTHERN HEMISPHERE

Africa

Equator

South America   ATLANTIC OCEAN   INDIAN OCEAN

PACIFIC OCEAN   Australia

SOUTHERN HEMISPHERE

Antarctica

N NW NE W E SW SE S

0   2,000   4,000   Miles
0   2,000   4,000   6,000   Kilometers

Oceans and Continents

Most of the Earth's water is in the oceans. If you look closely at the map, you see that all of the oceans are connected. Together, they make one huge world ocean.

Because the world ocean is so big, it is usually divided into four parts. From largest to smallest, these are the Pacific Ocean, the Atlantic Ocean, the Indian Ocean, and the Arctic Ocean.

On this map you can also see the **continents.** A continent is one of the seven main land areas of the Earth. The seven continents are North America, South America, Europe, Asia, Africa, Australia, and Antarctica.

Find Europe and Asia on the world map. Together they form a very large landmass. Europe and Asia are called different continents, though, because they are divided by mountains.

All of the United States, except for the island state of Hawaii, is in North America. There are other countries in North America, too.

Most continents have many countries. Australia is the only continent that is all one country. Antarctica has no countries at all. People do not make their homes on Antarctica because it is covered with ice and snow all year.

In what ways is this photograph of a farm like the map on the next page? In what ways is it different?

Reading Maps

Look at the photograph above. This photograph of a farm was taken from an airplane. You can see fields, buildings, and roads. You cannot, however, see what is growing in the fields. You cannot see which buildings are the houses and which are the barns.

The map on page 9 also shows what the farm looks like from above. The map helps you see some things that are hard to see in the photograph. Different colors and markings are used to show the four different fields.

Different shapes and colors show which buildings are the houses and which are the barns.

Colors, markings, and shapes on a map are called **symbols.** A symbol is something that stands for something else. A symbol on a map stands for something that is real on the Earth.

All maps use symbols. Some symbols are easy to recognize. For example, when you see the color blue on a map, it usually stands for water.

Other symbols can stand for many different things. For

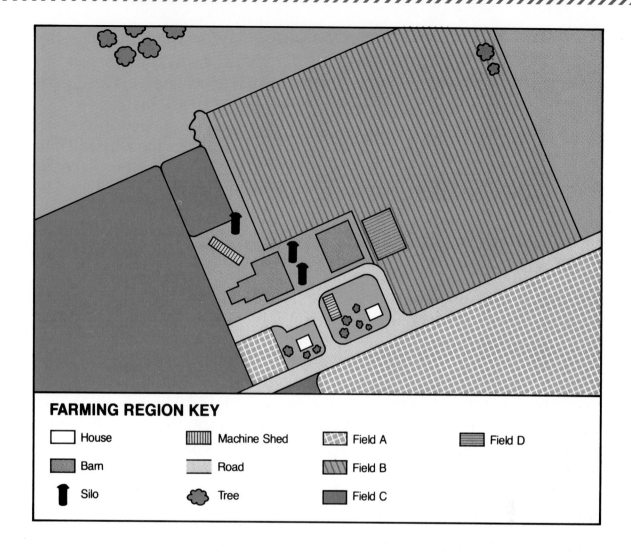

FARMING REGION KEY

- ☐ House
- ▨ Barn
- ⬛ Silo
- ⬚ Machine Shed
- ▨ Road
- ☁ Tree
- ▨ Field A
- ▨ Field B
- ⬛ Field C
- ▨ Field D

example, one map might use a line to stand for a road. Another map might use the same type of line to stand for the **border** of a state. A border is the outside edge of a place. You will see both borders and roads in the maps in this book.

To find out what the symbols on a map stand for, you need to use the **map key.** A map key shows the different symbols used on a map and tells what each one means.

Look at the map key for the map of the farm. What does the color white stand for on the map? What color is field C?

Symbols and map keys can help you see the natural features of a place. Which symbols on the map of the farm stand for natural features? Maps can also show you things made by people, such as buildings or baseball fields. Which symbols on the map of the farming area stand for things made by people?

How Far Is It?

As you know, a map can show a small part or a large part of the Earth's surface. Look at the two maps on page 11. The top map shows Lakeside Campsite. The bottom map shows Bear Lake Park, where the campsite is located.

The map of the campsite shows a smaller area than the map of the park. However, even the map of the campsite is not as large as the campsite itself.

Almost every map is smaller than the part of the Earth it shows. This means that the distance between two places on a map is shorter than the real distance between those places on Earth. To find out how far apart two places really are, you need a **distance scale.** A distance scale shows you that a certain length on a map stands for some longer, real distance on Earth.

Using Distance Scales

Look at the distance scale on the map of Bear Lake Park. You can see that the top part of the scale has the word *mile.* The bottom part of the scale has the word *kilometer.* Kilometers are part of the metric system. They are another way of measuring. You can find distances with either part of the scale. The top part will give the answer in miles. The bottom part will give the answer in kilometers.

You can use the distance scale on the map of the park to find out how far it is from one place to another. Measure the distance scale with a ruler. It is 1 inch long. Now read the number of miles. On this map, 1 inch stands for 1 mile on Earth.

If two places are 1 inch apart on this map, the real distance between them is 1 mile. If they are 2 inches apart, the real distance is 2 miles. If they are between 1 and 2 inches apart, you can estimate the real distance. Now use the distance scale to find the distance from the park office to the bridge.

Finding Your Way on Globes and Maps

To get from one place to another, you need to know more than the distance. You also need to know the direction, or which way to go.

North, south, east, and west are the main directions. They are also called **cardinal directions.** The word *cardinal* means "most important."

You already know how to find north and south on a globe. North

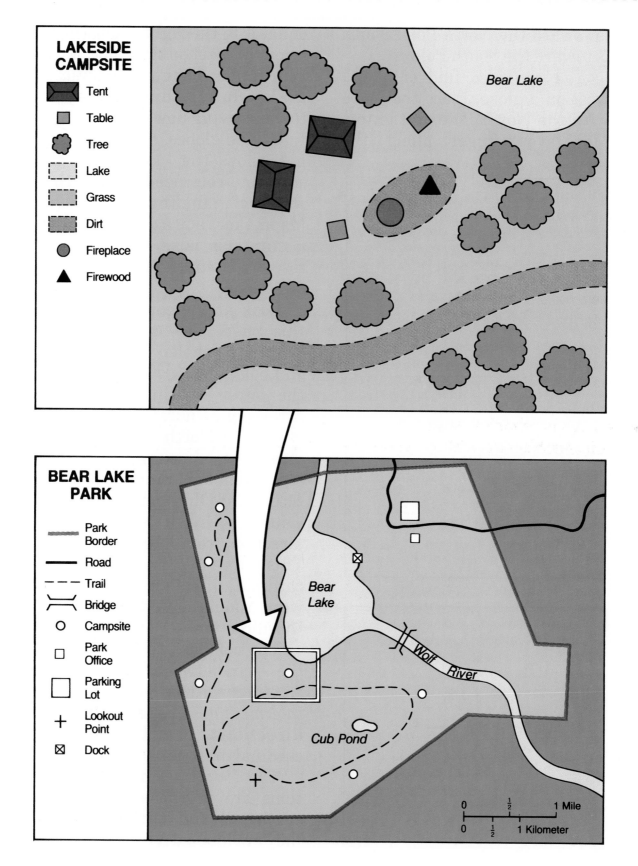

LAKESIDE CAMPSITE

- Tent
- Table
- Tree
- Lake
- Grass
- Dirt
- Fireplace
- Firewood

Bear Lake

BEAR LAKE PARK

- Park Border
- Road
- Trail
- Bridge
- ○ Campsite
- □ Park Office
- □ Parking Lot
- + Lookout Point
- ⊠ Dock

Bear Lake

Wolf River

Cub Pond

0	½	1 Mile
0	½	1 Kilometer

11

is toward the North Pole. South is toward the South Pole.

You can also find east and west on a globe. Place the globe with the North Pole on the top. Move your finger along the

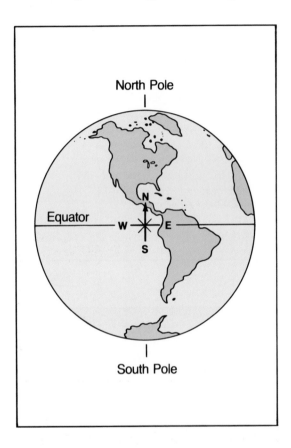

equator to the right. Your finger is moving east on the globe. Move your finger along the equator to the left. In what direction is your finger moving now?

Unlike globes, many maps do not show the poles and the equator. You need some other way of finding directions. Mapmakers add a drawing called a **compass rose.** The compass rose on a map shows you the directions.

Look at the compass rose on this page. The cardinal directions are labeled *N, S, E,* and *W.* Look at the arrow pointing to the letter *N.* On a map, this arrow points north, the direction of the North Pole. Four directions, however, are not always enough. Find the states of Maine and Ohio on the map. How would you tell someone the direction from Maine to Ohio? This direction is *between* two cardinal directions, south and west. You need another name for this direction.

The compass rose also shows the "in-between" directions. Another word for "in-between" is *intermediate.* The **intermediate directions** are between the cardinal directions.

The four intermediate directions are northeast, southeast, southwest, and northwest. Often they are labeled *NE, SE, SW,* and

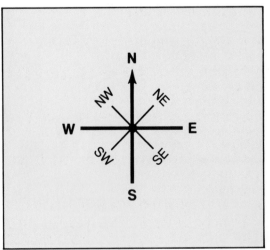

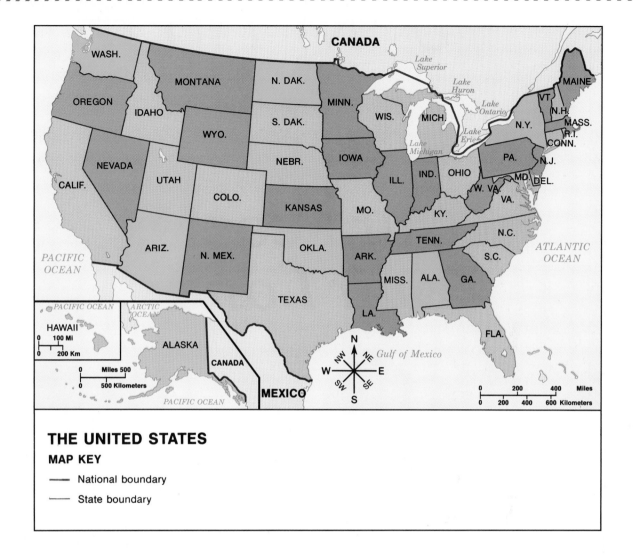

THE UNITED STATES

MAP KEY

— National boundary

— State boundary

NW. The names of the intermediate directions give you a clue for finding them. For example, *southwest* is between *south* and *west*. Where is southeast?

On a compass rose, the intermediate directions are often shown with lines between the main directions. Look at the line between *S* and *W* on the compass rose on this map. Which direction does this line show? In which direction would you go to get from Maine to Ohio?

Questions to Answer

1. Name four natural features of the Earth.
2. In which hemisphere is the United States?
3. How are maps different from globes?
4. What does a map key show?
5. In which direction would you go to get from Texas to Utah?

UNIT
1
Our People, Our Land

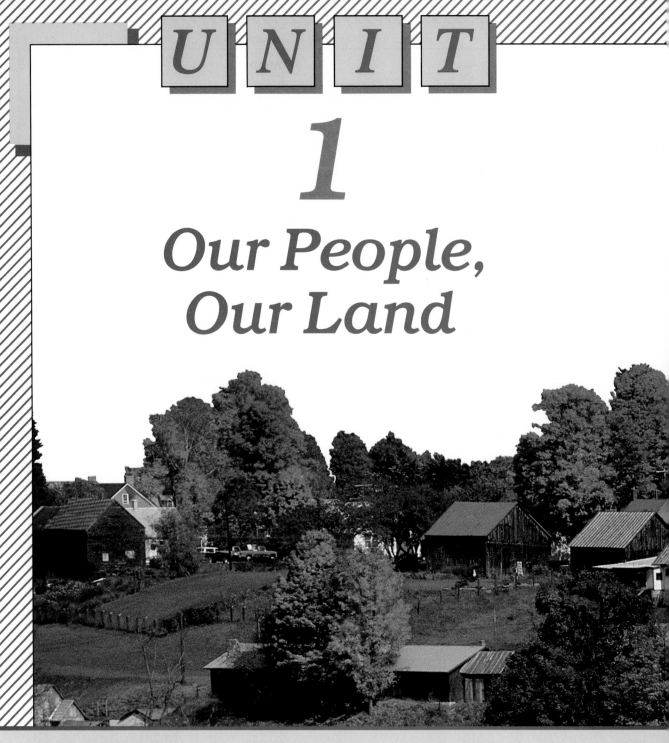

"The New Colossus," a poem by Emma Lazarus, was inscribed on a plaque in 1903 in the base of the Statue of Liberty. The poem describes how the Statue of Liberty, as a symbol of America's freedom, welcomes newcomers to our shores.

"The New Colossus"
by Emma Lazarus

Not like the brazen giant of Greek fame,
   With conquering limbs astride from land to land;
   Here at our sea-washed, sunset gates shall stand
A mighty woman with a torch, whose flame

The United States has people from countries around the world. They have different beliefs and ways of doing things, and they live in different kinds of communities. The United States has many different kinds of land, too.

In this unit you will read more about our country's people and land. You will learn why Americans are proud of their country.

Think Beyond   In what ways are the people who live in your community different from one another? How are they alike?

Is the imprisoned lightning, and her name
    Mother of Exiles. From her beacon-hand
    Glows world-wide welcome; her mild eyes command
The air-bridged harbor that twin cities frame.
"Keep ancient lands, your storied pomp!" cries she
    With silent lips. "Give me your tired, your poor,

Your huddled masses yearning to breathe free,
    The wretched refuse of your teeming shore.
Send these, the homeless, tempest-tost to me.
    I lift my lamp beside the golden door!"

CHAPTER 1

The American People

"No one wants to sleep tonight; everyone wants to stay awake to catch the first glimpse of America. By morning, all were dressed in their best outfits; but still no sight of land. As they watched for the promised land, the immigrants tried to envision what their futures would hold."

—from the book *Echo of Tomorrow* by Ida Richter

Look for these important words:

Key Words
- customs
- nation
- immigrants
- ancestors

- Vikings
- Pilgrims
- slaves
- slavery

People
- Christopher Columbus

Look for answers to these questions:
1. What groups of people came to live in America?
2. Why did people come to America?
3. Why do people still come to the United States today?

1 | *Americans Come from Many Places*

Cowboy hats, Easter eggs, Halloween pumpkins, the English language. Each of these things is different. Yet all of them have something in common. People brought them to our country from other places.

Americans came to the United States from all over the world. They brought their special ways of doing things. These special ways of doing things are called **customs** (KUHS•tuhmz).

Many American customs come from around the world. For example, do you carve pumpkins at Halloween? This custom comes from Europe, where Halloween began. Do you color eggs at Easter? People from Poland and Russia brought their custom of painting eggs to America.

Many of the things we use come from other places, too. The Mexican *sombrero* (suhm•BRAIR•oh), for example, became our cowboy hat. Different kinds of music and dance also came here from elsewhere. Even the languages that Americans speak were brought here by settlers.

People have moved to this country, or **nation,** for hundreds of years. For this reason, the United States is often called a nation of **immigrants** (IM•uh•gruhnts). Immigrants are people who move to a new country. Each year, many immigrants still come to start new lives in our country.

17

The first Americans traveled from Asia and went on to settle in different areas all over North and South America.

The First Americans

Thousands of years ago, a piece of land joined Asia to North America. People walked across this land from Asia. They were the first people to come to North America. These people were the **ancestors** (AN·ses·tuhrz), or early families, of the American Indians.

The First European Explorers

People from Europe reached North America much later. About 1,000 years ago, the **Vikings** reached North America. These explorers from Northern Europe only stayed a few years. In 1492 **Christopher Columbus** sailed

here from Spain. He was trying to reach China. There he hoped to trade for gold, spices, and silk. Columbus thought he could reach China by sailing west from Europe. Instead he found North America. He gave the name "Indians" to the people he met. Columbus believed he had reached the islands south of China called the Indies.

Columbus returned to Spain with gold. Hearing his stories, other Spanish explorers crossed the Atlantic Ocean. Among these explorers was an Italian living in Spain, Amerigo Vespucci (veh· SPOO·chee). Vespucci said that he had explored parts of what is now North and South America. He believed he had reached a "new world," not Asia. A German mapmaker thought the new land should be named after Vespucci. Soon all of Europe was calling the new land America.

The French and the English

Because of these early explorers, the Spanish later settled in southern and western North America. They were not the only ones interested in America, though. Columbus's discovery also brought the French and the English.

Traveling by river, the French explored the north and the center of our country. They saw beaver and other animals with valuable furs. Soon the French were buying furs from the Indians to sell in Europe.

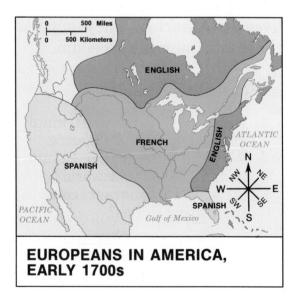

EUROPEANS IN AMERICA, EARLY 1700s

In the 1600s groups of English people settled in the eastern part of America. Some groups, like the **Pilgrims,** came here to find religious freedom. They wanted to have their own religion. In Europe they were not free to do so.

Many other people from Europe came to America. They wanted to find better lives for themselves. They wanted a chance to own land. They were willing to work hard to keep what they earned.

Slavery Begins and Ends

When our country was young, few people lived here. Needing workers for their large farms, some people bought **slaves.** A slave was a person owned by another person. Slaves could be bought and sold. They had no freedom.

Slaves came from Africa. In Africa, black people were taken from their homes and put in chains. Then they were locked up in ships. The ships carried them to many parts of North and South America. There they were bought by people who needed workers.

For years many Americans were troubled about **slavery,** or the owning of slaves. Though many people felt it was wrong, Americans were not sure how to end slavery. Finally, they fought

These immigrants from Asia are studying English and learning about American customs.

a terrible war among themselves. During this war, slavery was ended for all time. Freedom was now the right of all Americans.

The Land of the Free

Freedom is important to Americans. Through the years, the hope of freedom brought many people to America. They came from Europe, Africa, and South America. They came from Asia and Australia. Many came from other parts of North America.

Today, immigrants still come to live here. Like the immigrants long ago, they hope to find better lives in America. They hope to share in America's freedom.

Reading Check

1. Name two things that immigrants brought to America.
2. Why did Christopher Columbus sail to the new world?
3. Why have immigrants come to the United States?

Think Beyond How do you think slaves felt about coming to America?

20

IN FOCUS

AMERICAN FOODS

What are your favorite foods? Do you know where these foods came from?

When people came here from other places, they cooked foods they had enjoyed in their old countries. Other Americans tasted these new foods and liked them. Soon Americans were eating foods from all over the world.

Hamburgers got their name from Hamburg, a town in Germany. Another German food we eat is named after the town of Frankfurt. The Germans eat these sausages with sauerkraut (SOWR•krowt). We put them in buns and call them hot dogs.

From Italy came other foods Americans enjoy. Immigrants brought pizza along with spaghetti, macaroni, and ravioli. Spanish explorers planted the first orange trees in America. English settlers came here with apple seeds. Other immigrants brought us Mexican tacos and tortillas (tawr•TEE•uhz), Jewish bagels, Polish sausage, Swiss cheese, and much more.

Not all our foods came from other countries, however. The American Indians showed the Pilgrims how to steam clams and plant corn. Beans, tomatoes, and pumpkins are Indian foods, too. So are turkey and cranberries.

Think Beyond Why do you think there is such a variety of foods in America?

Tacos were brought to the United States from Mexico.

21

Look for these important words:

Key Words
- manufacturing
- goods
- service

Look for answers to these questions:

1. In what ways are Americans different from one another?
2. What kinds of jobs do Americans have?
3. How do Americans have fun?

2 *Americans Are Different in Many Ways*

Have you ever noticed how different Americans are? Each of us is different from one another in many ways.

Americans have come from all over the world. We have many different kinds of last names. Armas, Cerone, Lowenstein, Lucas, Jones, Rodriguez, Washington, Wong, Zisk—these are just a few names you might find in a phone book.

Americans are different in how they look and in what they do. Many Americans speak more than one language. We believe in different religions. Each of us has different talents and skills. Some of us are good in sports. Some of us sing well. Some of us know how to build or fix things.

Some Americans live in small towns.

Others make their homes in big cities.

22

Americans live in different kinds of communities. Many Americans live in great cities. Others live in suburbs outside of cities. Still others live on farms or in small towns.

Americans work at many different jobs. Some Americans are farmers. They grow wheat, corn, cotton, fruit, or vegetables. They raise dairy cows for milk or sheep for wool. They raise beef cattle, chickens, or hogs for meat.

Americans have many different jobs in **manufacturing** (man•yuh•FAK•chuhr•eeng). The word *manufacturing* means "making **goods.**" Goods are things people buy and sell, such as clothing, radios, and cars.

Americans have many different **service** jobs. A service is some activity that people do for others. When a waitress brings you food in a restaurant, she is providing a service. When your family gets mail, the mail carrier is providing a service. Teachers, doctors, writers, librarians, sales clerks, and truck drivers are just a few more people who provide services to many other Americans.

Americans may live in suburbs close to big cities. Many work in these cities during the day.

Our nation's farms provide food for people in our country's towns, cities, and suburbs.

Ballooning is one way Americans have fun together. It brings together many different kinds of people.

Americans enjoy many different ways of having fun. Millions of Americans enjoy sports like baseball, soccer, basketball, or swimming. Millions of others enjoy fishing, hiking, or camping. Some Americans enjoy flying in balloons, while others like movies, the theater, and concerts. Many Americans like taking pictures or reading. These are only a few ways Americans have fun. Each person's choice is different just as each American is different.

The United States is a mix of all these differences. Our people come from many places. We have many different customs and religions. We have different languages and different ways of living and working. All together, these differences make Americans special people.

Reading Check

1. Name three ways in which Americans are different from one another.
2. Name four different kinds of communities.
3. What is the difference between goods and services?

Think Beyond Think of a service you use. How would your life be different without it?

Look for these important words:

Key Words
- government
- laws
- republic

- voting
- democracy
- rights
- responsibilities

- culture
- heritage

Look for answers to these questions:
1. What do Americans have in common?
2. What is the difference between rights and responsibilities?
3. What are some parts of our American heritage?

3 *Americans Share Many Things*

What is an American? Ask a hundred different people, and you will get a hundred different answers. Yet in some special ways, Americans have much in common.

Americans share their country's past. Together we remember America's past on national holidays. These are days important to all our nation's people.

One of our most important holidays is the Fourth of July. Our country once was ruled by England. On July 4, 1776, America declared its freedom from England. Each July 4, millions of Americans celebrate this holiday. We fly our flag, have parades, and go on picnics.

Our people share a special way of life. We learn about one another from television and newspapers.

On the Fourth of July, fireworks light up the skies over our nation's capital, Washington, D.C., and over cities across the country.

25

Do you like baseball? If you do, then you are like millions of other Americans. In fact, baseball is so popular that it is sometimes called the national pastime.

Baseball as we know it began in the United States in the 1800s. However, baseball was developed from an earlier game called rounders. Settlers who came to America from England brought this game with them.

In rounders, players hit a ball with a bat and advanced around bases.

To make an out, however, fielders threw the ball at the runners! If the runner was off base and was hit by the ball, the runner was out.

Together we play and watch many sports. We eat American foods such as hamburgers and apple pie. All these things help bring us together as a people.

Our Government

One important thing Americans share is their **government.** A government is a group of people who lead a city, a state, or a country. One important job of leaders is to make **laws.** Laws are rules for all to follow.

The United States has a government called a **republic.** In the American republic, people are free to choose their leaders. We choose leaders by **voting** for them. To become a leader, a person must get the most votes. Our leaders must listen to the people who choose them. If our leaders do not do a good job, we can vote for new leaders.

Democracy

Americans also share many beliefs. Our most important belief is **democracy** (dih•MAHK•ruh•see). In a democracy people are free to make choices about their lives. They can choose the leaders of their government. They can choose where they live and how they earn a living. They decide what to think, say, and read. In many countries of the world, people are not free to make such choices. Why do you think this freedom is so important?

Rights and Responsibilities

In America's democracy, people believe in certain **rights** and **responsibilities.** A right is a freedom that belongs to you. We Americans believe in the right to choose our leaders. A responsibility is something that you should do. Americans have a responsibility to obey the laws. We have a responsibility not to harm other people. We have a responsibility to learn about our country.

Some of our rights were written down long ago. You can still read them today.

Our American Heritage

Americans share other beliefs. We believe in hard work and fairness. We believe in working together to solve problems. We also believe in doing the best we can. Americans have always come up with new ideas, new ways of solving problems. These beliefs have made the United States a strong country.

Finally, Americans believe in themselves. We believe in sharing our different ideas. By sharing them, we can find the best ways to solve problems. That is better than if everyone thought the same way.

Our **culture,** or way of life, and our beliefs make up our **heritage.** Our American heritage comes to us from our country's past. It comes from all the Americans who have ever lived. It is a heritage of which to be proud. It is a heritage that you will add to in the years to come.

Reading Check

1. Name four things that Americans share.
2. What kind of government do Americans have?
3. How do Americans choose their leaders?

Think Beyond Why do you think it is important for each person in a democracy to carry out his or her responsibilities?

People MAKE HISTORY

Trevor Ferrell
1972–

▶▶▶▶▶▶▶▶▶▶▶▶▶▶▶▶▶▶

Eleven-year-old Trevor Ferrell was shocked by the television report he had seen on homeless people. Trevor asked his father and mother to drive him downtown. He wanted to see how the homeless people of Philadelphia, Pennsylvania, lived. As Trevor and his parents walked out the door, Trevor grabbed a pillow and a blanket.

When they got downtown, Trevor saw a man sitting on the sidewalk. Trevor got out of the car and gave the man the pillow and blanket. This was the beginning of an organization known as "Trevor's Campaign for the Homeless." Today this organization helps hundreds of homeless people.

After that first visit downtown, Trevor decided he wanted to do more. Night after night the Ferrell family delivered blankets and food to the homeless. At first they used supplies from their own home. Then Trevor asked other people and businesses for donations.

A local business donated a 33-room building for use as a shelter. The first homeless people who lived at the shelter answered the telephone by saying, "Trevor's Place." Trevor's Place became the name of the shelter.

Trevor is now a busy teenager. He travels around the world, speaking to groups about his work with homeless people. Although Trevor is not sure what the future holds for him, he is certain about one thing. He says, "I want to help the homeless as long as I can."

Think Beyond Why is it important to help other people?

SKILLS IN ACTION

EXPLORING THE LIBRARY

Suppose you want to find out about American Indians. You would probably go to a library. Most libraries have a number of books about this **subject.** The subject is what a book is about.

Look at the picture on this page. All these books are about one subject. What is it?

Parts of the Library

Libraries keep their books in three different sections. One section is for **fiction,** one is for **nonfiction,** and one is for **reference** books.

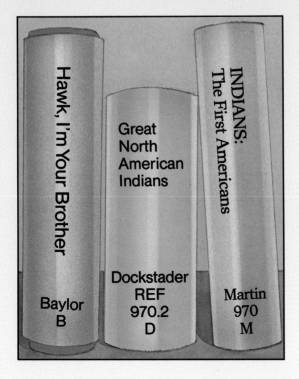

Hawk, I'm Your Brother

Baylor
B

Great North American Indians

Dockstader
REF
970.2
D

INDIANS:
The First Americans

Martin
970
M

Fiction books are made-up stories. *Hawk, I'm Your Brother* is a fiction book. It is a made-up story about an Indian boy who wishes he could fly like his hawk.

Find this book in the picture. You can see the spine, or backbone, of the book. The spine shows the book's title, the author's last name, and the letter *B*. The letter *B* is the first letter of the author's last name. What is the author's last name?

Now suppose you are looking for *Hawk* on the shelves. Fiction books are arranged in alphabetical, or ABC, order, by the authors' last names. Does this book come before or after a book by Mary Barton?

Nonfiction books give facts about real people and things. *Indians: The First Americans* is a nonfiction book. It describes how and where different Indian groups lived.

Look at the spine of this book. It shows the book's title, the author's last name, and the number 970. Nonfiction books are arranged in number order. All nonfiction books on the same subject have the same number. For example, 970 is the number used by the library for books about American Indians.

29

The card catalog lists all of the books in a particular library.

Reference books are collections of facts. Most libraries have encyclopedias, dictionaries, and atlases in the reference section. Reference books have a number and the letter *R* or *REF,* for *reference*, marked on them. You may not take reference books out. You have to use them at the library.

Finding the Book You Need

The **card catalog** can help you find books in the library. Each book has at least two cards in the card catalog. One is the **title card.** It has the book's title at the top. Another is the **author card.** It has the author's last name at the top.

All cards are kept in alphabetical order. Suppose you want to find the title card for *Hawk, I'm Your Brother.* You will look in the drawer marked *H.* This letter begins the first word in the book's title.

Suppose you have read several books by Miska Miles and want to find another one. The author cards will tell you the titles of her books. You use the author's last name to find them.

To find a nonfiction book, you need to know its number. The title card will give you the number of the book. The number is in the upper left-hand corner. Find the title card of *The Art of the North American Indian* on page 31. What is its number?

jF   Hawk, I'm your brother.
Baylor, Byrd. Illustrated by Peter Parnall. New York: Scribner, 1976.
48 p. illus.

jF   **Miles, Miska**
      Annie and the old one. Illustrated by Peter Parnall. Boston: Little, Brown, 1971.
44 p. illus.

30

970.6
G
The art of the
North American Indian.
Glubok, Shirley. New York:
Harper & Row, 1964.
48 p. illus.

973.1
B
INDIANS — AMERICAN
Baity, Elizabeth (Chesley)
Americans before Columbus.
Illustrated with drawings and
maps by C.B. Falls and with 32
pages of photographs. New
York: Viking Press, 1961, 1951.
272 p. illus., maps

Subject cards can also help you find books. All nonfiction books have subject cards. You look under "Indians—American" for any books about American Indians. These cards are in the card catalog drawer marked with the letter *I*. Each card has the subject at the top. Then it gives the author, title, and number.

Using Larger Libraries

Some libraries have put their card catalogs on **microfiche** (MY•kroh•feesh). Microfiche is a sheet of microfilm that lists thousands of books by title, author, and subject. Other libraries use computers to help you find books.

CHECKING YOUR SKILLS

Answer the questions below. Use the spines of these books to help you.

Pilgrim Thanksgiving
Hays
H

PILGRIM HOMES and How They Were Built
Bryant
REF
974
B

The Pilgrims Knew
Pine
973.2
P

1. What is the subject of these books?

2. Which book is nonfiction?

3. Which book cannot be taken out of the library?

4. Suppose you want to find a nonfiction book called *The Plymouth Thanksgiving*. What information do you need to find this book?

5. Suppose you want to find a book about the Pilgrims. How could you find books about them?

31

CHAPTER 1 REVIEW

Thinking Back

- People have come to live in America from all parts of the world. The first Americans came from Asia. Later, people came from Europe. Others were brought from Africa as slaves.

- Americans have different last names, appearances, languages, religions, talents, skills, and jobs. Americans also live in different kinds of communities and enjoy different activities.

- Americans have much in common. They share their country's past, a special way of life, and their government. Americans share a belief in democracy as well.

- Americans believe in certain rights and responsibilities. Americans also believe in hard work, fairness, working together to solve problems, and sharing ideas. These beliefs have made the United States a strong nation.

- Our culture, or way of life, and our beliefs make up our heritage. Our heritage comes from those Americans who lived before us. It is a heritage of which all Americans can be proud.

Check for Understanding

Using Words

Copy the sentences below. Fill in the blanks with the correct words from the list.

democracy
government
immigrants
manufacturing
right

1. People who come to a new country are ____ .
2. Making goods is called ____ .
3. People who lead a city, a state, or a country make up a ____ .
4. In a ____ people are free to make choices about their lives.
5. A ____ is a freedom that belongs to you.

Reviewing Facts

1. Which of these is a custom?
    a. carving Halloween pumpkins
    b. making cars
    c. voting
2. Where did the Spanish settle in America?
3. Why have immigrants come to America? Give two reasons.

32

4. Give an example of a service job.
5. Name two ways in which Americans share a special way of life.
6. How do Americans choose their government leaders?
7. What are some choices that Americans can make?
8. What are some responsibilities that all Americans have? Give three examples.
9. Why is it important for Americans to share their ideas?
10. What makes up our American heritage?

Thinking Critically

Imagine a place where everyone is the same. Describe the place. Would you like to live there? Explain why or why not.

Writing About It

Write a letter to an imaginary pen pal in another country. In your letter, explain what it means to you to be an American.

 ## Practicing Study Skills

Exploring the Library
Use the title card on page 31 to answer these questions.

1. What is the title of this book?
2. Who is the author?
3. What information on the title card will help you find the book in the library?

 # On Your Own

Social Studies at Home

Ask family members to help you cut out pictures from old magazines and newspapers that show people working at different kinds of jobs. Then label one-half of a large piece of cardboard *Manufacturing* and the other half *Services*. Take turns pasting pictures under the correct heading to make a poster about jobs.

Read More About It

Fireworks, Picnics and Flags by James C. Giblin. Clarion Books. The author tells about some of America's songs, flags, and holidays.

Libraries and How to Use Them by Jeanne B. Hardendorff. Franklin Watts. This book explains all about libraries and what they offer us.

Making a New Home in America by Maxine B. Rosenberg. Photos by George Ancona. Lothrop, Lee & Shepard. In this book you will read stories about children who recently have come to live in our country.

Poem Stew. Poems selected by William Cole. J. B. Lippincott. These poems describe the things we eat.

Steven Caney's Kids' America by Steven Caney. Workman. This book, drawing on America's history and customs, contains many ideas for fun-to-do activities.

CHAPTER 2

The American Land

"O beautiful for spacious skies,
For amber waves of grain,
For purple mountain majesties
Above the fruited plain!
America! America!
God shed His grace on thee
And crowned thy good with brotherhood
From sea to shining sea!"

—from the song "America the Beautiful"
by Katharine Lee Bates

Look for these important words:

Key Words
• boundaries

Places
• Rio Grande

• Gulf of Mexico
• Great Lakes
• St. Lawrence River

Look for answers to these questions:
1. What oceans reach the shores of the United States?
2. Which states do not touch any other state?
3. Which countries are our neighbors?
4. What other bodies of water form part of our borders?

1 *A Land Between Oceans*

The United States is a country of hot places and cold places, rainy places and dry places. Mountains, forests, and wide, open country stretch across the land. Rivers cut through the land, and oceans pound the shores.

The United States has so many different places because it is so large. It is the fourth-largest country in the world. The United States stretches east to the Atlantic Ocean and west to the Pacific Ocean. These two oceans form our nation's eastern and western **boundaries.** *Boundary* is another word for *border.*

The United States has 50 states, but only 48 are joined by their state borders. Each state touches at least one other. Two states, Alaska and Hawaii, stand alone. Alaska is far in the north. It is our largest state. Water surrounds Alaska on three sides. Hawaii, our fiftieth state, is far out in the Pacific Ocean. It is made up of more than 100 islands.

South of the United States is the country of Mexico. Part of our border with Mexico is a river, the **Rio Grande** (REE•oh GRAND). Rio Grande is a Spanish name meaning "Big River."

The Rio Grande flows into the **Gulf of Mexico.** This gulf is a body of water that is actually a part of the Atlantic Ocean.

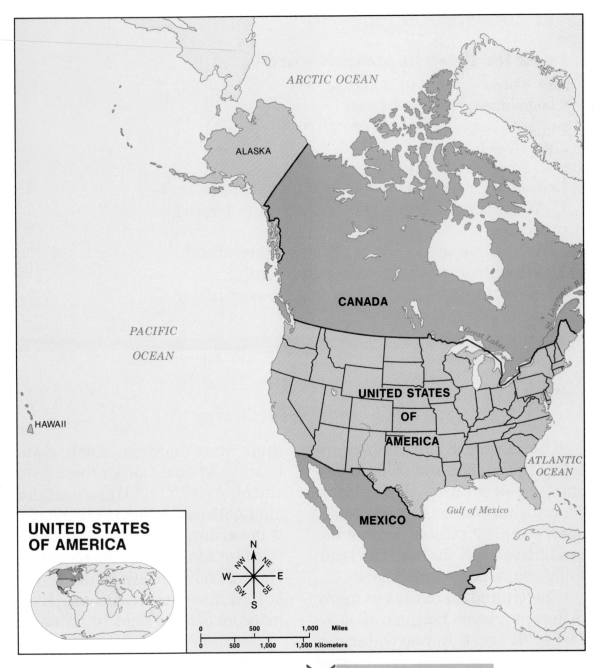

ARCTIC OCEAN

ALASKA

CANADA

PACIFIC

OCEAN

St. Lawrence R.

Great Lakes

UNITED STATES

OF

AMERICA

ATLANTIC
OCEAN

HAWAII

Rio Grande

Gulf of Mexico

MEXICO

UNITED STATES
OF AMERICA

N
NW   NE
W   E
SW   SE
S

0	500	1,000	Miles
0	500	1,000	1,500 Kilometers

The country of Canada is our northern neighbor. Our boundary with Canada is long. Four of the **Great Lakes** and part of the **St. Lawrence River** separate the two countries. Canada also shares a border with our most northern state, Alaska.

Reading Check

1. What is east of our country?
2. Which river forms part of our border with Mexico?
3. What forms part of our border with Canada?

Think Beyond How has our country's size helped it to grow?

36

Look for these important words:

Key Words
- skyscrapers
- coast
- capital
- plain
- harbors
- plateaus
- canyons

- desert
- basin
- wilderness

Places
- Washington, D.C.
- Coastal Plain
- Appalachian Mountains

- Interior Plains
- Mississippi River
- Rocky Mountains
- Great Basin
- Sierra Nevada
- Cascade Range
- Central Valley
- Coast Ranges

Look for answers to these questions:
1. Where are the plains in our country?
2. What mountains stretch across our land?
3. How are plateaus and plains alike? How are they different?
4. How is the Pacific coast different from the Atlantic coast?

2 *A Land of Many Lands*

Imagine that you are taking a trip across the United States. You board a plane at an airport in New York City. This is the largest city in the United States. After you take off, you fly over the **skyscrapers,** or tall buildings, of New York. Then suddenly the view changes. The land is now low, flat, and sandy. You are flying along the Atlantic **coast.** A coast is land next to an ocean.

Your next stop along the Atlantic coast is **Washington, D.C.** This city is our nation's **capital.**

A capital is a city where leaders make laws. Our leaders make laws for our country in Washington, D.C. The letters *D.C.* tell you that this city is in the District of Columbia. This area, or district, is not a state. It is a place of government buildings, a workplace for our leaders.

The Coastal Plain

As you fly out of Washington, D.C., you will see that the land around it is low and flat. This land is part of a long **plain** that lies

37

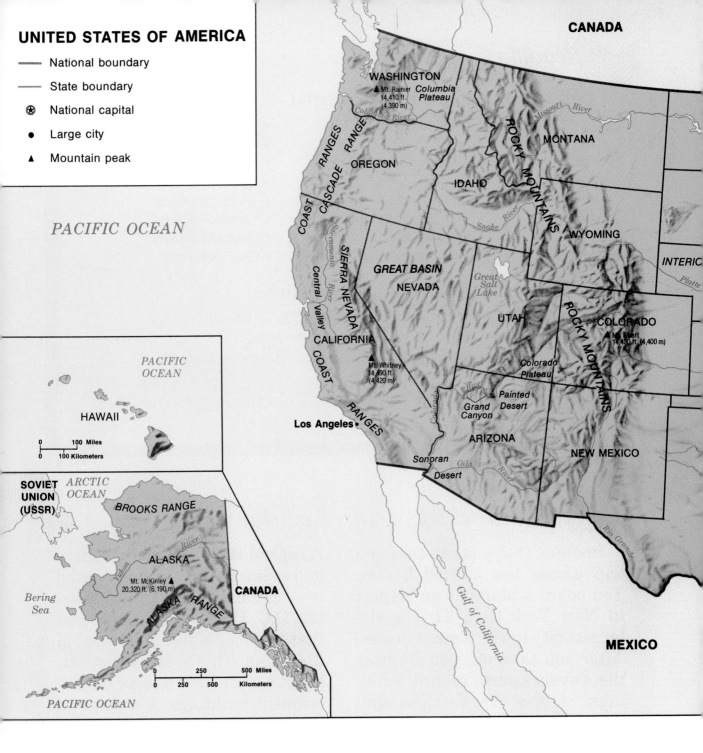

UNITED STATES OF AMERICA

- ——— National boundary
- ——— State boundary
- ⊛ National capital
- ● Large city
- ▲ Mountain peak

PACIFIC OCEAN

CANADA

WASHINGTON
▲ Mt. Rainier *Columbia*
14,410 ft. *Plateau*
(4,390 m)

Columbia River

OREGON

IDAHO

Snake River

ROCKY MOUNTAINS

MONTANA

Missouri River

WYOMING

INTERIC

Platte

COAST RANGES

CASCADE RANGE

SIERRA NEVADA

Sacramento River

Central Valley

GREAT BASIN

NEVADA

Great Salt Lake

UTAH

ROCKY MOUNTAINS

COLORADO
▲ Mt. Elbert
14,430 ft. (4,400 m)

Colorado Plateau

CALIFORNIA

COAST RANGES

Mt. Whitney
14,490 ft.
(4,420 m)

Colorado River

Painted Desert

Grand Canyon

Los Angeles ●

ARIZONA

NEW MEXICO

Sonoran Desert

Gila River

Gulf of California

MEXICO

Rio Grande

PACIFIC OCEAN

HAWAII

| 0 | 100 | Miles |
| 0 | 100 | Kilometers |

SOVIET UNION (USSR)

ARCTIC OCEAN

BROOKS RANGE

Yukon River

ALASKA

Mt. McKinley ▲
20,320 ft. (6,190 m)

ALASKA RANGE

CANADA

Bering Sea

PACIFIC OCEAN

| 0 | 250 | 500 | Miles |
| 0 | 250 | 500 | Kilometers |

along the Atlantic Ocean. A plain is a large area of flat, low land. Find the **Coastal Plain** on the map on this page. It begins on the coast of Massachusetts. Then it stretches from New York City to Florida, and on into Texas. In the north it is very narrow. In Florida it is more than 500 miles (about 800 km) wide.

Many important rivers cross the Coastal Plain and spill into

the ocean. Can you name some of them? Three of them are the Delaware, the Potomac, and the Savannah rivers. At many places where rivers meet the sea there are good natural **harbors.** A harbor is a place where ships can dock safely. The land around harbors protects the ships from storms and strong winds. A good harbor is deep so ships can come close to shore.

39

The beautiful Blue Ridge Mountains are part of the Appalachian Mountains.

The Appalachian Mountains

As you travel west across the Coastal Plain, the land begins to rise. The **Appalachian** (ap•uh•LAY•chuhn) **Mountains,** with their low, rounded tops, come into view. These tree-covered mountains stretch through the eastern part of our country.

The Interior Plains

To the west of the Appalachians, the land slopes down. The view ahead seems endless. Here in the center of the United States lie other plains. They are the huge **Interior** (ihn•TIHR•ee•uhr) **Plains.** The word *interior* means "inside." The Interior Plains are inside our country. They have some of the richest soil in the world. Much of our country's food comes from these plains.

Through the Interior Plains flows the longest river in the United States, the **Mississippi** (mis•uh•SIP•ee) **River.** Other rivers and streams flow into the Mississippi. Some of these are the Missouri, Ohio, Arkansas, and Tennessee rivers.

The Great Lakes are another water treasure of our nation's heartland. Look for these lakes on the map. They are the world's largest group of freshwater lakes. They have enough water to cover the whole United States to a depth of 12 feet (about 4 m).

The Rocky Mountains

Your plane is now flying toward the western edge of the Interior Plains. Out of the plains rise the snow-covered tops of the **Rocky Mountains.** These mountains cover much of the western United States. The Rocky Mountains are famous for their scenery. Thick forests, clear blue lakes, and rushing streams attract many visitors every year.

The Rocky Mountains are among the world's tallest mountains. The highest parts of the Rockies are covered with snow all year.

Deserts and Plateaus

Within our western mountain region you can see other landforms. Besides the mountains, you can find many valleys, **plateaus** (pla•TOHZ), and **canyons.** A plateau is high, flat land, like a table. A canyon is a narrow valley with steep sides.

After you cross the Rocky Mountains, the view changes again. Now the land is mostly dry, with few plants. It is the largest **desert** (DEZ•uhrt) area in our country.

In this desert area you will find the **Great Basin.** A **basin** is low, bowl-shaped land. The Great Basin is one of the driest parts of our country. The Great Salt Lake is here. This lake is very salty.

Mountains and Valleys

As you continue to fly west, you will see more mountains. Just inside California is the **Sierra Nevada.** *Sierra Nevada* means "Snowy Mountains" in Spanish. The snow in these mountains melts to form many lakes, rivers, and streams. To the north, in Washington and Oregon, is the **Cascade Range.**

Ocean waves pound the rough cliffs along California's northern coast.

Snow and ice glitter at the top of Mt. McKinley in Alaska.

To the west of the mountains are large valleys of rich farmland. The largest is the **Central Valley** of California. The word *central* means "in the middle." Farmers in the Central Valley grow fruits and vegetables for much of the nation.

All along the Pacific Ocean are the **Coast Ranges.** These mountains give much of the Pacific coast a rocky, rugged look.

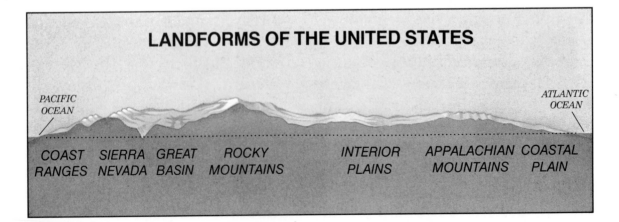

LANDFORMS OF THE UNITED STATES

PACIFIC OCEAN

ATLANTIC OCEAN

COAST RANGES   SIERRA NEVADA   GREAT BASIN   ROCKY MOUNTAINS   INTERIOR PLAINS   APPALACHIAN MOUNTAINS   COASTAL PLAIN

A chain of islands glimmering in the sun, Hawaii lies in the middle of the Pacific Ocean about 2,400 miles (3,862 km) from California.

Alaska and Hawaii

Your plane continues north along the Pacific coast to Alaska. Alaska, our largest state, has huge forests, open plains, wide valleys, and high mountains. Mount McKinley, North America's highest mountain, is in Alaska.

Summer months along Alaska's Pacific coast are fairly mild. However, snow and ice cover northern Alaska for most of the year. Thousands of animals roam free across this **wilderness.** A wilderness is land on which people do not live.

Flying south across the Pacific Ocean, you finish your trip in Hawaii. This state's islands are really the tops of mountains rising out of the sea. Hawaii is warm and green all year.

Reading Check

1. What kind of land is east of the Appalachian Mountains?
2. What is the Great Basin?
3. How is Alaska different from other states? How is Hawaii different from other states?

Think Beyond How might the kind of land in an area shape the way of life there?

43

RACING ACROSS ALASKA

The team of 16 dogs barks and whines excitedly. The dogs, Alaskan huskies, pull eagerly against their harnesses. However, it is not yet the team's turn to leave the starting line. It takes ten people to hold back the anxious dogs.

The sled driver, also known as a **musher,** speaks calmly to the dogs. As the countdown ends and the starting signal is given, the dogs lunge forward. There is no stopping this team or musher now! They have just begun the Iditarod (eye•DIHT•uh•rahd) Trail Sled Dog Race.

On the first weekend in March, dozens of men and women with their dog teams meet in downtown Anchorage for the race.

This team awaits the start of Alaska's Iditarod Trail Sled Dog Race.

Depending on weather conditions, it takes 11 to 32 days to finish the race.

Most of the mushers are from Alaska. A few are from other states and countries.

From year to year the race trail changes a little, but it is always more than 1,000 miles (1,609 km) long. During the race, mushers and their teams cross mountain ranges, frozen rivers, and miles of snow-covered land.

Preparation and practice for the race are very important. Many months before the race actually begins, each musher puts together about 1,500 pounds (675 kg) of food and equipment. These supplies are sent ahead to checkpoints along the race trail.

Mushers also prepare their sleds. Each sled must carry snowshoes, a sleeping bag, food for the driver and team, and booties to protect the dogs' paws from the cold. It can take up to four weeks just to make the 1,000 booties the dogs on one team will use during the race.

Mushers and dogs alike practice to be in good shape for the race. This is important because during a race, mushers sometimes run behind the sled. They do this to give their dogs a break. It is hard work to run in heavy clothes in the cold weather. The dogs must be physically fit, too, because they have to be able to run for long periods of time.

During the race, mushers stop at checkpoints along the trail. There they rest and eat the food they have sent ahead. They also cook meals for their dogs.

Mushers take good care of their dogs because finishing a race depends on the health of the team. A musher cannot add a new dog to the team if one gets sick or injured. A musher must also finish the race with at least five dogs pulling the sled.

What does it take to win the Iditarod Trail Sled Dog Race? According to Susan Butcher, it takes long months of hard work. She should know! Susan and her team have passed the cheering race fans many times. For three years in a row, they were the first team to cross the finish line in downtown Nome. They won the race again in 1990.

Think Beyond Why might dog-sleds be less important to people in Alaska today than in the past?

A proud Susan Butcher hugs one of her winning dogs.

Look for these important words:

Key Words
- temperature
- precipitation
- sea level
- growing season

Look for answers to these questions:

1. What is climate?
2. What does temperature depend on?
3. Why is precipitation important?

3 A Land of Many Climates

You probably have heard people ask, "What's the weather like today?" They mean, "Is it hot, rainy, cold, or cloudy?"

People do not ask, "What's the climate like today?" That's because weather and climate are different. Climate is the weather a place has year after year. If a place is usually hot in summer and rainy in winter, that is its climate. Climate has two main parts, **temperature** (TEM•puhr•uh•chuhr) and **precipitation** (prih•sip•uh•TAY•shuhn).

Temperature

Temperature is how warm or cold a place is. Often temperature depends on where a place is. Alaska is near the North Pole. Northern Alaska is the coldest place in our country. Hawaii is near the equator. It is one of the warmest places in our country. The rest of our country lies between these two places. The northern United States is usually colder than the southern part.

Temperature also depends on how high a place is. We measure height from **sea level.** Land level with the surface of the oceans is

LAND AT SEA LEVEL

sea level
ocean   land

46

at sea level. As land gets higher, its temperature gets cooler. Many mountain tops have snow all year. The weather never gets warm enough to melt the snow.

Precipitation

Precipitation is another important part of climate. Precipitation means rain or snow.

Precipitation is very important to plant life. In fact, no plant can live without some precipitation.

When you know the precipitation and temperature of a place, you can begin to understand what grows there. Places with dry climates have few plants. Unless water is brought to them, hot, dry places are poor farmlands. In warmer, wetter climates, grasses can grow. Trees need a lot of rain, though. Only places with very high precipitation have thick forests.

Many parts of our country have warm summers and cold winters. Most plants cannot grow in very cold or freezing weather. The time when the weather is warm enough for plants to grow is the **growing season.** Some places in our country have warmer or wetter growing seasons than others because every place has its own special climate. Your state's climate is different from any other state's.

These juicy oranges will be shipped to different areas of our country. Oranges and other fruits grow all year in sunny places like California and Florida.

Our country's many climates help us grow many kinds of crops. Our different climates also help us grow large amounts of food. Most of the foods we eat are grown in the United States.

Reading Check

1. How is climate different from weather?
2. What are the two main parts of climate?
3. Why is the United States able to grow much of its own food?

Think Beyond How might our diets be different if our country had only one climate?

Look for these important words:

Key Words
- minerals
- fuels
- products
- irrigation

Look for answers to these questions:

1. What are the important natural resources of the United States?
2. How are minerals and fuels used?
3. Why are natural resources important for our country?

4 *A Land of Many Resources*

Among the countries of the world, the United States is a giant. Our people have worked hard to make it strong and wealthy. Our natural resources have also helped to make this country strong. Natural resources are things in nature that people can use.

The land itself is an important resource. Many parts of our country have rich soil. Our climate and soil help us grow huge amounts of food. Our land also has many **minerals** (MIHN•uh•ruhlz) and **fuels** (FYOOLZ). Sand, stone, and iron are minerals. We use these minerals to make machines and buildings. Coal, oil, and natural gas are fuels. We use fuels to make heat and to run many kinds of machines.

Forests are another important natural resource. Our forests are among the world's largest. Forests cover about a third of our country. From them come lumber, paper, and other **products.** A product is something that people make or get from nature.

The United States has good water resources. Our rivers, lakes, and streams provide water for drinking, farming, and manufacturing. They also provide many kinds of fish. Some rivers are used to make electric power.

Some areas in our country have good soil but little rain. People must bring water to them. This is called **irrigation.** Through irrigation we have turned many of our deserts and dry places into valuable farmland.

48

Irrigation sprinklers on a farm in Idaho help make the land productive. Without irrigation, much of this area would be too dry to farm.

From trees we make many things we need, such as writing paper, cardboard boxes, and lumber for building houses.

Stone is one resource needed for building skyscrapers.

Our land, our forests, and our water are resources we need in order to live. They make the United States a strong country and a place of beauty. It is everyone's responsibility to use our resources wisely. If we do not, our country will not have as many. Future Americans will need these resources, too. The way we use them today will shape our country's future.

Reading Check

1. What are the main natural resources of our country?
2. How do we use fuels?
3. Why is irrigation important?

Think Beyond What might happen if we do not use our natural resources wisely?

49

People MAKE HISTORY

John Muir
1838–1914

▶▶▶▶▶▶▶▶▶▶▶▶▶▶▶▶▶

John Muir grew up on a farm in Wisconsin. Every day there was much work to be done. John had to labor from dawn to dusk.

John loved to read, but he could not find the time during the day. So he arose at one o'clock each morning and read until dawn. Afraid he would oversleep, John invented what he called an "early-riser machine." It caused his bed to tilt—and throw him out—at any pre-set hour. John later invented an automatic horse-feeder and a large thermometer.

At the age of 21, Muir entered his inventions in the state fair at Madison. The judges were very impressed with his work. They urged him to attend the University of Wisconsin. Muir agreed.

After he finished his studies, Muir took long hikes to see America firsthand. He fell in love with the beautiful landforms he saw. The land, however, was being settled quickly. Muir grew concerned about protecting wilderness areas for future

generations. He became a popular writer on this subject, which gained him fame.

During his life, John Muir influenced the national government to set aside more than 150 million acres (60 million ha) for parks, such as Yosemite National Park, and for forests and wilderness areas. Muir also founded the Sierra Club, an organization that is still working today to save natural lands and wildlife.

Think Beyond   How might settling a wilderness area threaten its land and wildlife?

Yosemite
National Park

SKILLS IN ACTION

USING SPECIAL-PURPOSE MAPS

Landform Maps

Some maps are called **special-purpose maps**. One such map is the one below, a landform map. Landforms are shapes of the land. The four main landforms are mountains, hills, plateaus, and plains. Landform maps show the different shapes of land. The map key shows what colors they are on the map. Find the brown color in the key. It tells you that mountains are brown on the map. What mountains are in the eastern part of the United States? in the western part? in Alaska?

LANDFORM MAP OF THE UNITED STATES

Mountains Hills
Plateaus Plains

Now look at the center of the landform map. Much of it is green. Look for this color in the key. What kind of land does this area have? Is the land flat or hilly? Where do you find plateaus in our country?

This map also can tell you other things about the land. You know that mountains and plateaus are high. You know that hills and plains are low. So this map also shows the higher and lower parts of the United States. Where are the low parts of our country?

Temperature Maps

Below is a temperature map. It shows the summer and winter temperatures in the United States.

The map key shows the temperatures in summer and winter. For example, it tells you that green areas have warm summers and cold winters. Most of the map is colored green. What kind of temperatures does Chicago have? Now look at Hawaii. It is colored orange. What does the key tell you about Hawaii's temperatures?

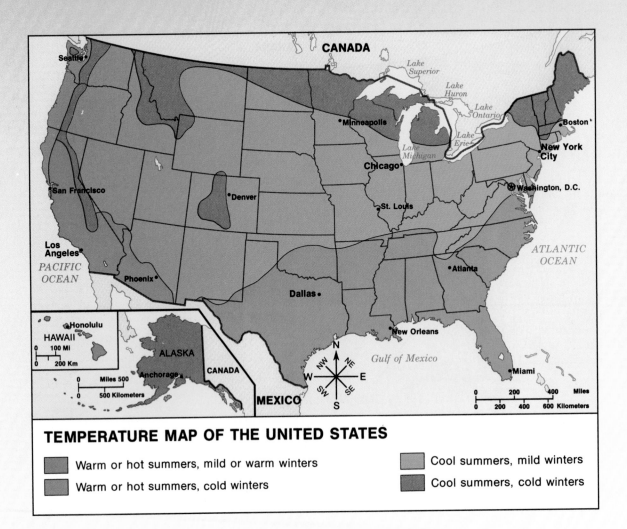

TEMPERATURE MAP OF THE UNITED STATES

- Warm or hot summers, mild or warm winters
- Warm or hot summers, cold winters
- Cool summers, mild winters
- Cool summers, cold winters

52

Precipitation Maps

Another kind of map shows precipitation. The map below shows the usual precipitation in the United States. It tells how much rain or snow falls in an average year.

Find Boston on the precipitation map. Boston is in an area colored light blue. This means Boston receives more than 40 inches (about 100 cm) of precipitation a year. What other cities on this map get the same amount?

Now find Phoenix on this map. How much precipitation does Phoenix have in a year? You can see that Phoenix is in a dry area. Mostly scattered grasses and small bushes grow here. Find St. Louis on this map. How much precipitation does St. Louis have in an average year?

Some areas in the south and the west receive more than 60 inches (150 cm) of precipitation a year. What cities are in those areas?

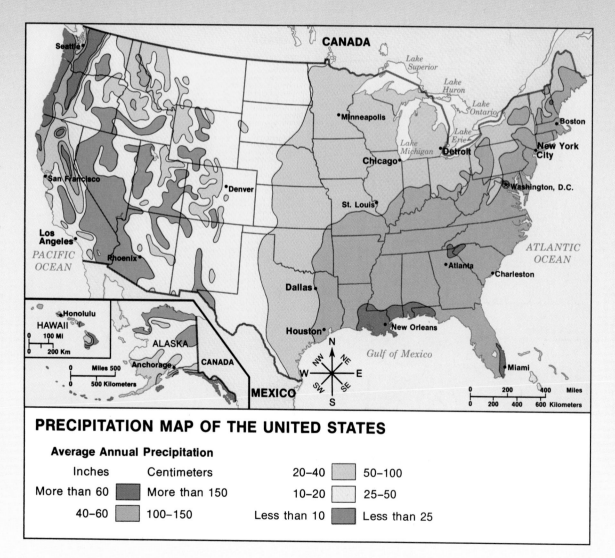

PRECIPITATION MAP OF THE UNITED STATES

Average Annual Precipitation

Inches	Centimeters		
More than 60	More than 150	20–40	50–100
40–60	100–150	10–20	25–50
		Less than 10	Less than 25

53

Resource and Product Maps

The map below is a resource and product map. This map shows the main natural resources and products of our country.

A map like this uses symbols and colors to show different resources and products. The map key explains what the symbols and colors mean. For example, what does ⬟ mean? Now find the symbol for oil in the map key. Near what cities is the symbol for oil? In these places, oil, an important resource, is found.

Now find the color for wheat and other grains. Find the major wheat-growing areas on the map. In these areas growing wheat is important.

Look at the map key. Find the color for little-used land. Little-used land is land that people generally do not use. Now look at the map. Where do you see large areas of little-used land?

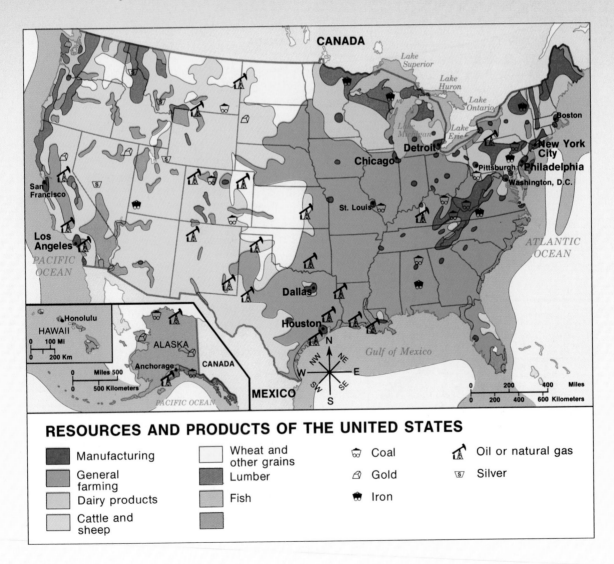

RESOURCES AND PRODUCTS OF THE UNITED STATES

- Manufacturing
- General farming
- Dairy products
- Cattle and sheep
- Wheat and other grains
- Lumber
- Fish
- Coal
- Gold
- Iron
- Oil or natural gas
- Silver

Inset Maps

Look back at Alaska and Hawaii on the maps in this lesson. These states are not shown where they really are. Hundreds of miles separate them from the other 48 states. To show the whole area, all parts of the map would have to be much smaller. Instead, Alaska and Hawaii are each shown in an **inset.** The box around each shows that it is an inset.

An inset often has a distance scale. The scales of an inset and the main map may be different. Below is part of the map on page

51. Look at Alaska. On the Earth, Alaska is more than twice the size of Texas. Here Alaska appears only one-fourth as large as it really should. Notice that the scales of the inset and the main map on page 51 are different.

Look at the inset of Hawaii on this page. All together, the Hawaiian Islands are a little larger than the state of Connecticut. Do the insets for Hawaii and Alaska have the same scale?

CHECKING YOUR SKILLS

Answer these questions. Use the maps in this lesson to help you.

1. Which map shows the high and low parts of our country?

2. Orange trees grow best in warm, sunny weather. They cannot live through cold winters. Which map tells you where oranges can grow?

3. Oil is an important natural resource. Which map tells you where oil comes from?

4. Find the inset of Hawaii on each map.
   a. What kinds of land does Hawaii have?
   b. What is Hawaii's yearly temperature and precipitation?
   c. Which of the maps shows farming and fishing in Hawaii?

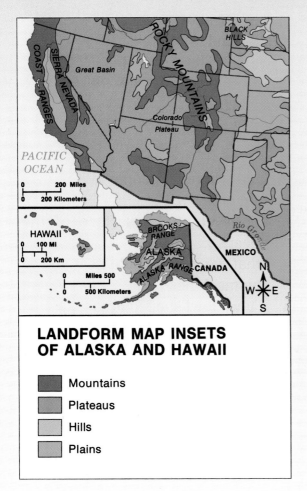

LANDFORM MAP INSETS OF ALASKA AND HAWAII

- Mountains
- Plateaus
- Hills
- Plains

Thinking Back

- The United States is the fourth-largest country in the world. Its borders stretch from the Atlantic Ocean on the east to the Pacific Ocean on the west and from Canada on the north to Mexico on the south.

- The United States has two large plains regions—the Coastal Plain and the Interior Plains. Much of our country's food comes from these plains.

- The Appalachian Mountains stretch through the eastern part of the United States. The Rocky Mountains cover much of the western United States. West of the Rockies are the Sierra Nevada, the Cascade Range, and the Coast Ranges.

- The United States has many different climates and growing seasons. This allows us to grow large amounts of many kinds of food. Most of the foods that we eat are grown in the United States.

- The United States has many important natural resources, including land, minerals, forests, and water. These natural resources have helped to make our country strong.

Check for Understanding

Using Words

Copy the words numbered 1 to 10. Next to each word write its meaning.

1. basin
2. boundary
3. canyon
4. fuels
5. interior
6. plain
7. plateau
8. precipitation
9. sea level
10. wilderness

a. border
b. inside
c. low, flat land
d. land where no people live
e. rain or snow
f. the level of the surface of the oceans
g. what we use to make heat and to run machines
h. a low, bowl-shaped area
i. high, flat land, like a table
j. a narrow valley with steep sides

Reviewing Facts

1. Name four bodies of water that are United States boundaries.
2. What is the largest group of fresh-water lakes in the world?

3. What is the difference between climate and weather?
4. What are two uses of minerals?
5. Why can the United States grow large amounts of food?

Thinking Critically

1. You have read that the United States has many different landforms and climates. Now imagine our country with flat land and a cold climate everywhere. How would flat land and a cold climate change your life?
2. Our country has different kinds of land, climates, and resources. How did these help our country grow?

Writing About It

It is up to you to help protect our nation's resources for future Americans. Write a persuasive paragraph explaining the things you can do to help save resources.

Practicing Geography Skills

Using Special-Purpose Maps
Use the maps on pages 51 to 55 to help you answer these questions.

1. What kinds of land does Alaska have?
2. What kinds of temperatures does Alaska have?
3. About how much precipitation does Anchorage get?

On Your Own

Social Studies at Home

Ask a family member to help you mix about 3/4 cup of laundry powder with 1/4 cup of warm water. Color the left and right edges of a piece of cardboard blue for the oceans. Then use the soap mix to show where mountains and plains are found between America's two oceans. Use toothpicks with small pieces of paper attached to label the mountains and plains.

Read More About It

Anno's U.S.A. by Mitsumasa Anno. Philomel. This wordless story charts a traveler's journey from America's Pacific coast to the Atlantic coast.

Conservation by Richard Gates. Childrens Press. This book describes how people sometimes damage nature and suggests ways to conserve the Earth's resources.

Facts About the 50 States by Sue R. Brandt. Franklin Watts. You will discover many things about our nation's 50 states.

I'm Going to Sing: Black American Spirituals, Volume Two by Ashley Bryan. Atheneum. In this book the words and music of some African-American spirituals are illustrated by woodcuts.

PAUL BUNYAN

IN PUGET SOUND
by
Dell J. McCormick

Many stories and poems have been written about the beauty of our country. People also like to invent stories of how mountains or rivers or deserts were formed. One story about the imaginary folk hero, Paul Bunyan, is popular in the Pacific states.

When he was digging the Sound, Paul hitched Babe, his blue ox, to a giant scoop shovel and started to work. The first load of dirt was so big, people didn't want it dumped on their land. So Paul had to haul it way back in the mountains. He dumped it in two piles. By the time the Sound was completed, the piles of dirt were so high they could be seen for miles. They named these piles Mt. Rainier and Mt. Baker. They are still there to this day.

Paul ran into trouble from the start. Everyone wanted the Sound to run in different directions. The folks from Tacoma wanted it to go their way. Then someone near Everett wanted a harbor there. It kept Paul hopping trying to satisfy them all. That's the reason the Sound has so many twists and turns. When Paul was almost through, he remembered his promise to dig a harbor for some folks to the south. So he scooped out Hood Canal.

Finally the Sound was completed. Everyone was pleased. Paul told his friend, Peter Puget, to arrange for a big celebration. They would name it "Puget Sound" on that day. Of course Peter Puget was very proud that the Sound was to be named after him. He spent a lot of time getting everything ready. But the settlers had a secret meeting. They decided to name it "Whidby Sound." They even had maps printed with the name in big letters.

When Paul heard about it, he was pretty mad. So he just went out with his big shovel and started filling it all up again. In no time at all most of the channel was filled in. He stood there and threw in shovelful after shovelful of dirt. After that, there were almost a thousand islands dotting the Sound.

A group of settlers finally came to him and asked him to stop. They promised to change the name back to Puget Sound. They told him it was the fault of the people living on Whidby Peninsula. They were the ones who had decided to keep the name Whidby Sound. They didn't think Paul could do anything about the matter because the Sound had been completed.

"Let him fill up the Sound!" the people from Whidby Peninsula cried. "It won't matter. We can still haul our vegetables and milk to market along the roads."

Paul hated the way they had tricked his good friend Peter Puget. So he decided to make them pay for it. Well, Paul just took his ax and cut a notch in the land that connected Whidby Peninsula with the mainland. The water from the Sound rushed in and filled up the passage. The force of the water was so great that the tides made it almost impossible to cross, even in a boat. The Whidby people were now on an island cut off from the mainland. Their home has been known as Whidby Island ever since. The channel that Paul cut is filled with raging water to this day. It is known as "Deception Pass."

And that's how Paul Bunyan and his blue ox Babe made Puget Sound.

Here is another version of this story.

One day Paul Bunyan thought his ox
Was going to up and die,
So he picked up a pick and a spade
And a tear drop filled his eye.

And sadly by the sea he dug
A deep hole in the ground,
But Babe got well. The sea surged in.
The hole is Puget Sound.

Harold W. Felton

Unit Review

Words to Remember

Copy the sentences below. Fill in the blanks with the correct words from the list.

customs	immigrants
democracy	irrigation
fuels	minerals
goods	republic
heritage	voting

1. We are a nation of _____ .

2. We manufacture many _____ .

3. Our government is known as a _____ .

4. We choose our leaders by _____ for them.

5. We believe in _____ , or the idea that people are free to make choices about their lives.

6. Americans are proud of their way of life and beliefs, America's special _____ .

7. We use _____ such as coal, oil, and natural gas to make heat and run machines.

8. Special ways of doing things are called _____ .

9. Copper and iron are _____ that help us make machines and buildings.

10. Through _____ we can grow food in dry areas.

Focus on Main Ideas

1. Why is the United States often called a nation of immigrants?

2. Name at least three ways in which people make a living in the United States.

3. In what ways are Americans different from one another? How are they alike?

4. Name a way in which the American people share in their nation's government.

5. What are some responsibilities that Americans have? Give two examples.

6. What are three beliefs that Americans share?

7. Name each of these places.
   a. a group of lakes between Canada and the United States
   b. the mountains in the eastern United States
   c. the large plains inside our country
   d. a state made up of islands

8. Why is the northern United States usually colder than the southern part?

9. What are some natural resources of the United States? Tell what each resource is used for.

10. Why do we need to use natural resources carefully?

Think/Write

Imagine that you are a visitor from another country. Write a travelog describing some of the things you might see in America.

Activities

1. **Research/Oral Report** What part of the world did your family come from? Share some family customs with the class.

2. **Art/Writing** Pick an area of the United States where the land and climate are different from where you live. Draw a picture of it. Then write a paragraph telling why you would or would not like to live there.

Skills Review

1. **Exploring the Library** Use the subject card on page 31 to answer the questions.
   a. What is the book's title?
   b. In what section of the library will you find this book?

c. What information do you need to find this book in the library?

2. **Using Special-Purpose Maps** Use this map to help you answer the questions.

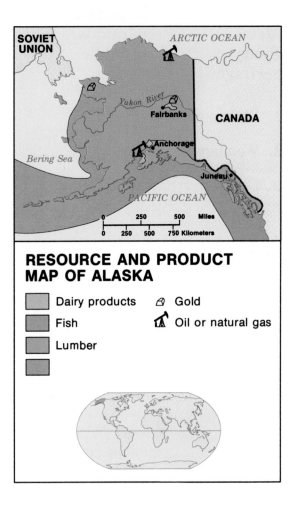

RESOURCE AND PRODUCT MAP OF ALASKA

Dairy products   Gold
Fish   Oil or natural gas
Lumber

a. Near what river has gold been found?
b. In what two parts of Alaska is natural gas found?
c. Near what city in Alaska are dairy products found?

62

You will read about many places in this book. At the same time, you will learn about your own state. You will find a section called Exploring Your State after each unit in this book. Here you will find a number of activities that you can do. These activities will help you learn about your state.

In many activities you will be doing **research,** or finding out facts and information. In doing research you will use this book and library books. Newspapers, television, and other people will also help you.

Learning About Geography

1. Where is your state? Find your state on a United States map and on a globe. On a piece of paper, write the states, the country, or the bodies of water next to your state. In what part of the country is your state located (north, south, east, or west)?

2. Find your state on a map. Measure the longest part of your state. Then measure the widest part. Use the map scale to find out the real distances.

3. What is the climate of your state like? Use the maps on pages 52 and 53 to help you find out. Then draw pictures of winter and summer scenes to show others what this climate is like.

Learning About Government

4. Every state has a state government. A state government makes laws for the people of the state. Your state's leaders make laws in your state's capital city. Draw a simple map of your state. You can use the maps in this book to help you. Find and label the capital city. Use a star to show the capital. Label the large cities and bodies of water in your state.

Learning About Research

5. What books about your state are in your school library? Use the subject cards in the card catalog to find out. Make a list of some of the books. Write down the titles of the books and their authors' names.

UNIT

2

The Shapes of the Land

Some Natural Features of the United States

Mountains		Rivers			
Alaska Range	Cascade Range	Alabama	Delaware	Potomac	San Joaquin
Appalachian Mountains	Great Smoky Mountains	Altamaha	Hudson	Red	Savannah
Black Hills	Ozark Mountains	Arkansas	Mississippi	Rio Grande	Snake
Blue Ridge Mountains	Rocky Mountains	Colorado	Missouri	Sabine	Susquehanna
Brooks Range	Sierra Nevada	Columbia	Ohio	Sacramento	Tennessee
Coast Ranges	Teton Range	Connecticut	Platte	St. Lawrence	Yukon

*T*he land and the ways in which people use it are two important parts of geography. When we study geography, we also look at the climate, landforms, and resources of a place.

This unit explores our country's **natural regions.** A natural region is a large area that has one major kind of natural feature. Mountain regions, for example, have mainly high, rocky land. Desert regions have dry land. Plains regions are low and flat.

Rivers cross all of these regions. Rivers not only connect the regions but also change them.

Think Beyond   What are some of the natural features in the area where you live?

Deserts	Plains	Plateaus	Lakes	
Chihuahuan	Arctic Coastal Plain	Colorado Plateau	Great Salt Lake	Lake Okeechobee
Great American	Central Plains	Columbia Plateau	Lake Champlain	Lake Ontario
Great Basin	Coastal Plain	Ozark Plateau	Lake Erie	Lake Pontchartrain
Mojave	Great Plains		Lake Huron	Lake Superior
Painted	Interior Plains		Lake Michigan	Salton Sea
Sonoran				

CHAPTER 3

Rivers

*"A fleck of gold from Montana, a sliver
of steel from Pittsburgh,
A wheat-grain from Minnesota, an
apple-blossom from Tennessee,
Roiled, mixed with the mud and earth of
the changing bottoms
In the vast, rending floods,
But rolling, rolling from Arkansas, Kansas, Iowa,
Rolling from Ohio, Wisconsin, Illinois,
Rolling and shouting:
Till, at last, it is Mississippi,
The Father of Waters. . . ."*

—from the poem "Ode to Walt Whitman"
by Stephen Vincent Benét

Look for these important words:

Key Words
- source
- riverbed
- banks
- branches
- tributaries
- drains
- river basin
- silt
- sandbars
- mouth

Look for answers to these questions:
1. Why did people live near rivers long ago?
2. Why are rivers important today?
3. How does a small stream become a big river?
4. How do silt and sandbars change a river?

1 *Rivers, Land, and People*

Rivers have always been important to people. Rivers were a good place to find food. Their clean, sparkling water brought deer and other animals to their shores. People could also fish in rivers.

People first learned to grow crops near rivers. The land next to rivers is often good for farming. The soil is rich, and there is plenty of water for plants.

Many of the world's first cities grew up along rivers. Even today most large cities are near rivers. Rivers provide water not only for drinking and for farms, but also for factories. Rivers, like highways, connect towns. Goods are often shipped from place to place by river.

No two rivers are exactly alike. Some are slow, wide, and deep enough for large ships. Other rivers are narrow, fast moving, and full of rocks. Some rivers are sparkling blue. Others are colored red or brown by the tons of earth they carry. Yet all rivers are alike in two ways. They are formed in the same way and they are made up of the same parts.

How Rivers Are Formed

The place where a river begins is called its **source.** Many rivers begin high in the mountains. Water from rain, melted snow, and underground springs collects at the source. This water begins to run downhill as a stream.

As the stream runs downhill, other streams join it. Rain and melting snow feed the stream. It becomes larger and moves faster.

The fast-moving stream carries bits of sand, soil, and rock from the land. These bits grind a deep, wide path into the earth. The bottom of the path is called the **riverbed.** The sides of the stream are its **banks.**

The rushing stream cuts into the earth and becomes lower than the land around it. Rain and melting snow flow into the stream. Soon the stream is large enough to be called a river.

Smaller rivers and streams, called **branches,** join the river. Branches are also known as **tributaries** (TRIB·yuh·tair·eez).

A river **drains,** or carries water away from, the land around it. The area of land drained by a river and its branches is a **river basin.**

Soil washed into the river is called **silt.** On its journey, the river collects tons of silt, small stones, and sand. When the river reaches flat land, it slows down. The river no longer has the force to carry all of its load. Most of the stones and sand settle to the bottom, making the river shallower in these areas.

In some places the sand piles up to form islands. Sometimes the sand forms low mounds called **sandbars.** The islands and sandbars may split the river into smaller parts.

Boats can sometimes be grounded on a sandbar in a river because a sandbar can often be out of sight below the river's surface.

Many rivers begin their journeys to the ocean as shallow streams.

Tributaries are small rivers or streams that flow into a large river.

The water from a river flows out into the ocean.

Sooner or later, most rivers reach the ocean. The place where a river empties into the ocean is called the river's **mouth.** There the river drops its remaining load of silt, and the fresh water of the river mixes with the salt water of the ocean.

Reading Check

1. Why is a river a good place to find food?
2. Why are cities near rivers?
3. How are all rivers alike?

Think Beyond Do you think rivers are as important today as they were long ago? Explain.

69

SKILLS IN ACTION

READING A MAP GRID

Some scientists are digging up an early Indian village. As they work, they make a drawing like the one below. It will help them remember how the village looked.

Notice the lines that cross in the drawing. This pattern of lines is called a **grid.** Around the grid are letters and numbers. In this grid the columns have numbers. Columns run up and down. The rows run from left to right. Each row in this grid has a letter.

The columns and rows form boxes. Find the box with the pots in it. Now find the letter to the left of the box. This box is in the row marked *C*. Next, look above the box. The box is also in column *1*. This is box C–1. The scientists found pots in this part of the village. In what box is the arrowhead? In what box is the ax?

Mapmakers use grids to help people find places on a map. On the next page is a map with a grid.

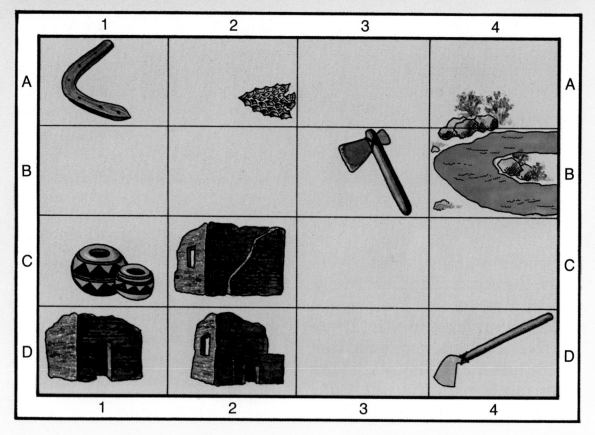

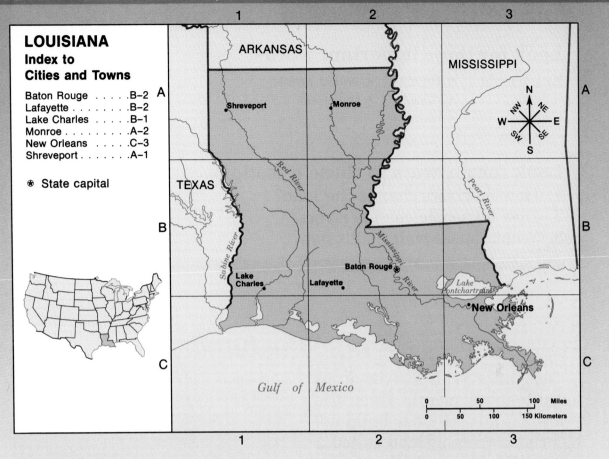

The map shows some cities and towns in the state of Louisiana.

A map with a grid may have an index such as the one you see at the left of this map. The index helps you find the names of places you are looking for. It lists them in alphabetical order. The index also gives the grid letter and number for each place.

This index tells you that New Orleans is in box C–3 on this map. Find row C on the map grid. Place your finger on the letter C. Move it across the map to the column under number 3. This is box C–3. Find New Orleans in box C–3.

Look for Baton Rouge in the index. Baton Rouge is Louisiana's capital. What letter and number do you find for Baton Rouge? Use them to find it on the map.

CHECKING YOUR SKILLS

Answer these questions. Use the map of Louisiana to help you.

1. What lake is in box B–3?

2. What city is in box A–2?

3. In which box is Shreveport?

4. In which box is the mouth of the Mississippi River?

71

Look for these important words:

Key Words
- delta
- erode
- erosion

- floods
- dikes
- dams

- water power
- polluted

Look for answers to these questions:
1. How do rivers change the land?
2. How do people change rivers?
3. What causes water pollution?

2 Rivers Change the Land

Year after year, a river drops its silt at its mouth. Over the years, the silt begins to build up. It forms a piece of land called a **delta.** Find the delta of the Mississippi River on the map on page 71. The land at the mouth of the river spreads out like a fan.

Deltas are good for farming. They are made up of silt, the rich soil that comes from the river's basin. The river is always bringing more silt to the delta. Because of their rich soil, deltas are valuable places to grow crops.

You have seen how rivers build up deltas. However, rivers can also slowly wear away, or **erode,** the Earth's surface. This slow wearing away of large areas of the land is called **erosion** (i•ROH•zhuhn).

Crops grow well in delta areas because of the rich soil.

Water from melting snow and spring rains can cause rivers to flood.
This house, once on the river bank, is in danger of being swept away.

Floods can also change the land. A river that overflows is a flood. Heavy rains and melting snow can cause a flood. A flood can be like a gigantic firehose, tearing away huge pieces of land. It can sweep away houses and trees. The rushing waters knock down everything in their path.

Flooding rivers can also build up the land. When rivers overflow slowly, the water gently spreads out. When the flood waters flow back to the river, they leave silt behind. After many floods, the silt builds up into rich, black soil. This rich soil is very good for farming.

People Change Rivers

People can change rivers in a number of ways. For example, people have learned how to control small floods. The next time you are at a river, look at the banks. Do they look like walls? If they do, people may have built **dikes** there. Dikes are high banks that help stop flooding.

People also build walls, or **dams,** across rivers. A dam holds back a river. People let the water flow through the dam as slowly or as quickly as they want.

Dams have other uses, too. Dams store water for drinking and irrigation. The picture on this

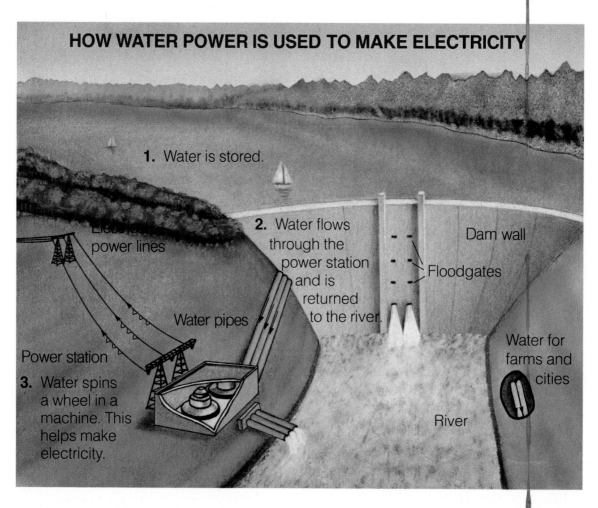

HOW WATER POWER IS USED TO MAKE ELECTRICITY

1. Water is stored.

Electrical power lines

2. Water flows through the power station and is returned to the river.

Water pipes

Power station

3. Water spins a wheel in a machine. This helps make electricity.

Dam wall

Floodgates

Water for farms and cities

River

page shows how dams help make **water power.** The rushing river water spins a wheel very quickly to make electricity.

People change rivers in other ways. They build bridges across them. They make rivers wider and deeper so that ships can travel on them.

People have changed rivers in many useful ways. Yet people have also made some harmful changes. Cities and factories dumped their wastes into rivers. Some rivers became dirty, or **polluted.** Polluted water is a danger to all who

use it. Water pollution is still a problem in American rivers today. However, many cities now clean waste water before returning it to the rivers. By doing this, Americans are working to control pollution.

Reading Check

1. What is a delta?
2. Name two ways in which rivers change the land.
3. How can people control floods?

Think Beyond If we do not control pollution, how will both the rivers and the land change?

IN FOCUS

BRIDGES

Bridges are important to people. Bridges often connect different neighborhoods within a city. Trains and trucks use bridges to carry products to and from markets. Without bridges, rivers would interfere with the movement of people and goods.

Rivers have always challenged travelers. The earliest bridges were probably just logs placed across streams. People later used wooden timbers to build bridges.

The oldest bridges in the United States were built with wooden timbers. Settlers used wood for bridges because trees were plentiful. Some wooden bridges were covered with a roof so that the floors would not rot.

Over time, people learned to use new materials, such as iron and steel, to build bridges. They built bridges that were bigger, stronger, and longer. Today, long bridges are often suspension (suh•SPEHN•shun) bridges. They have a roadway that hangs from steel-wire cables. The cables are attached to tall towers near the ends of the bridge.

One of the world's longest suspension bridges is the Golden Gate Bridge in San Francisco, California. This bridge, shown below, was completed in 1937. The section between the towers is 4,200 feet (about 1,280 m) long. The cables supporting the bridge are more than 36 inches (about 93 cm) thick.

Rivers can divide people, but bridges can bring people together. For example, the Peace Bridge connects the United States and Canada. It crosses the Niagara River from Buffalo, New York, to Fort Erie, Ontario.

Think Beyond   How are bridges important to you and your family?

The Golden Gate Bridge

Reading for a Purpose

Look for these important words:

Key Words
- waterway
- barges
- ports

- industries
- steel mills
- transportation
- current

Places
- St. Lawrence Seaway
- Grand Coulee Dam

Look for answers to these questions:

1. What are six of the largest rivers in our country?
2. Which rivers form part of our country's border?
3. Why are ports useful?
4. How do we use our rivers?

3 Rivers in the United States

The United States has several large rivers. Do you live near one of them? How does this river help you?

The Mississippi River

Mississippi means "Great River" in the language of the Ojibway (oh•JIB•way) Indians. They named this river well because the Mississippi is the longest river in the United States. It begins at Lake Itasca in northern Minnesota. From there it flows 2,348 miles (3,780 km) south to the Gulf of Mexico.

The Mississippi is also called "Old Muddy." When the muddy Missouri River meets it, the Mississippi becomes muddy, too.

The Mississippi is the longest, and in some parts the widest, river in our land.

76

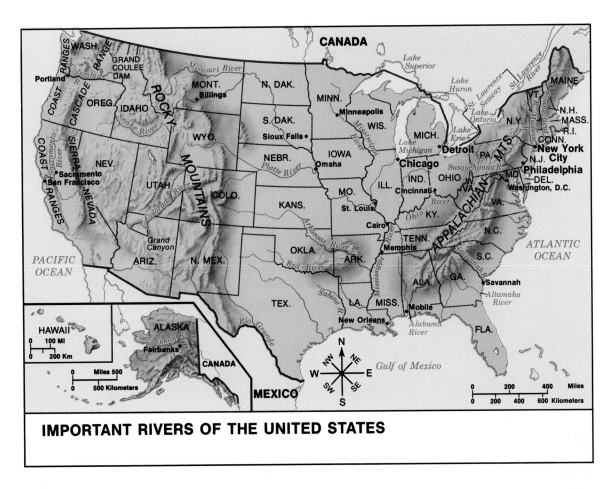

IMPORTANT RIVERS OF THE UNITED STATES

Tugboats push barges carrying grain up the Mississippi.

Besides providing water for farming and manufacturing, the Mississippi provides a route for ships. This great river is the main **waterway** within the United States. A waterway is a body of water that ships can use.

Many of the boats on the Mississippi are **barges.** Barges are large, flat-bottomed boats that are pushed by tugboats. You can often see long strings of barges being pushed up and down the river. Barges carry goods from one part of our country to another. They are the cheapest way to ship heavy goods such as machinery.

At many ports in our country, supply ships unload iron and coal for the manufacture of steel.

Ships load and unload goods at **ports** along the Mississippi. A port is a city with a large, busy harbor. St. Louis, Missouri, and Memphis, Tennessee, are two major Mississippi River ports. From a port, goods are sent by train, plane, or truck to other places.

The Mississippi empties into the Gulf of Mexico near New Orleans, Louisiana. This city is one of our largest ports. Many of our products leave New Orleans for other countries. In turn, many countries bring their products to New Orleans to be sold throughout the United States.

The Ohio River

The Ohio River is an important branch of the Mississippi. Two rivers meet to form the Ohio River in Pittsburgh, Pennsylvania. The Ohio joins the Mississippi at Cairo, Illinois.

Along the Ohio are many important **industries.** Industries are kinds of manufacturing. The steel industry, for example, manufactures steel. Barges use the Ohio to carry coal from places in Kentucky, West Virginia, and Pennsylvania to cities like Pittsburgh. There the coal is burned in **steel mills,** where steel is made.

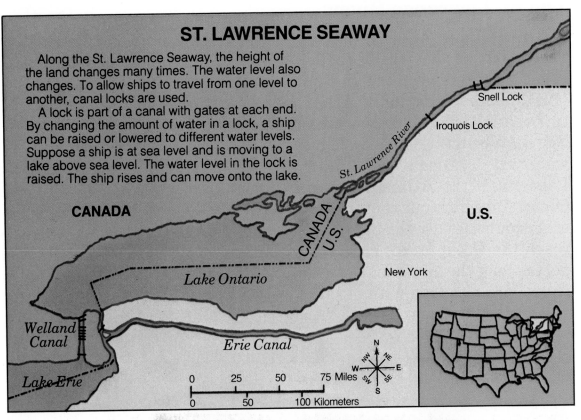

ST. LAWRENCE SEAWAY

Along the St. Lawrence Seaway, the height of the land changes many times. The water level also changes. To allow ships to travel from one level to another, canal locks are used.

A lock is part of a canal with gates at each end. By changing the amount of water in a lock, a ship can be raised or lowered to different water levels. Suppose a ship is at sea level and is moving to a lake above sea level. The water level in the lock is raised. The ship rises and can move onto the lake.

Snell Lock

Iroquois Lock

St. Lawrence River

CANADA

CANADA U.S.

U.S.

New York

Lake Ontario

Welland Canal

Erie Canal

Lake Erie

0   25   50   75 Miles

0   50   100 Kilometers

HOW A SHIP MOVES THROUGH A LOCK

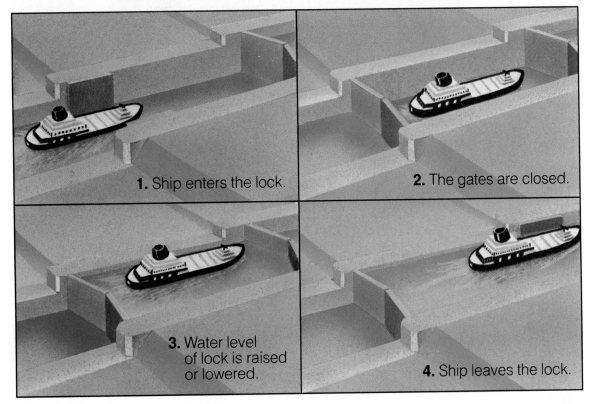

1. Ship enters the lock.

2. The gates are closed.

3. Water level of lock is raised or lowered.

4. Ship leaves the lock.

The St. Lawrence River

The St. Lawrence River forms part of our border with Canada. It begins at Lake Ontario in New York and flows east to the Atlantic Ocean. Part of this river is the **St. Lawrence Seaway.** This waterway connects the Great Lakes with the Atlantic Ocean. Ocean ships from our country and other countries use the Seaway to reach the Great Lakes cities. At ports along the Great Lakes, the ships are loaded with grain, machinery, and car parts. The ships then go east by the St. Lawrence Seaway. From there they carry these products to places around the world.

The Rio Grande

The Rio Grande (REE•oh GRAND) also forms part of the United States border. It separates Texas and Mexico for more than 1,240 miles (about 1,996 km). The Rio Grande begins in the Rocky Mountains and ends at the Gulf of Mexico.

On its journey to empty into the Gulf of Mexico, the Rio Grande carved steep canyons along the Texas border.

80

The powerful Grand Coulee Dam provides irrigation for many farms and controls flooding along the Columbia River.

The river passes through much dry land on its journey south. Like Indians long ago, farmers of today still use the Rio Grande for irrigation. Power plants now also use the river's flow to make electricity. Irrigation and power plants use a lot of water. Parts of the Rio Grande can dry up by late summer. Rain and melting snow later renew the river's water supply.

The Columbia River

The Columbia River begins in the Rocky Mountains of Canada. From Canada the river flows south into the states of Washington and Oregon. Along the way, it passes through the Cascade Range. Its mouth is on the Pacific Ocean.

Much of our country's water power comes from the Columbia. Water power can be used to make electricity. The most important electric power plant on the Columbia is the **Grand Coulee** (GRAND KOO•lee) **Dam.** It makes more electricity than any other American dam. The dams on the Columbia have helped manufacturing to grow in this part of the United States.

The Colorado River widened and deepened its course over millions of years. Cutting through layers of rock, it carved out the Grand Canyon.

The Colorado River

You have seen that rivers have many uses. They are important in **transportation,** or moving people and things from place to place. Rivers provide water power, fishing, and water for irrigation. They also serve as boundaries between states and between countries. The Colorado River is useful in many of these ways.

The Colorado River brings water from the Rocky Mountains to the driest part of our country. Southern California, Arizona, and Nevada depend on the Colorado for water and electricity.

The Colorado River also flows through the Grand Canyon. The river's **current,** or flow, slowly carved out the deep canyon. Today, thousands of people come to admire the Grand Canyon's amazing beauty.

Reading Check

1. Which is the longest river in our country?
2. How is coal transported from Kentucky to Pennsylvania?
3. How was the Grand Canyon formed?

Think Beyond   Why do ports often grow into very large cities?

People
MAKE HISTORY

In 1859 a young Mississippi River pilot was trying to steer his steamboat through shallow water. He listened carefully as a crew member called out the depth of the river. "Mark twain!" shouted a crew member. The pilot knew these words were a warning that the river was getting too shallow. He reversed his engines and headed the steamboat into deeper water.

The pilot was Samuel Clemens. Twenty-four years earlier, he had been born in the town of Florida, Missouri. He and his family later moved to Hannibal, Missouri, a town on the Mississippi River. Every day young Samuel watched steamboats moving up and down the river. He decided to become a steamboat pilot when he grew up.

Clemens spent two exciting years piloting steamboats on the Mississippi River. Then a war broke out, making it dangerous to travel the river. He gave up piloting steamboats.

Clemens headed west and began writing for a newspaper in Nevada. His stories were often funny, but some of them made fun of important people. To keep from getting into trouble, he signed his stories "Mark Twain," after the warning that was used on the Mississippi.

As Mark Twain, Clemens wrote many stories, essays, articles, and books. He went on to become a famous author and speaker. However, Clemens never forgot his days as a steamboat pilot.

Think Beyond How can moving to a new place affect a person's life?

83

SKILLS IN ACTION

USING ELEVATION MAPS

In this chapter you followed the route of many rivers. Some rivers start in the mountains, but others do not. Many empty into oceans, but some do not. All rivers do have one thing in common, though. They all flow from a high land down to a lower land.

The map on this page is called an elevation map. It shows high and low land. Different colors show the **elevation,** or height, of the land. The map key tells what the colors mean.

In this map key the elevation of land colored medium green is from

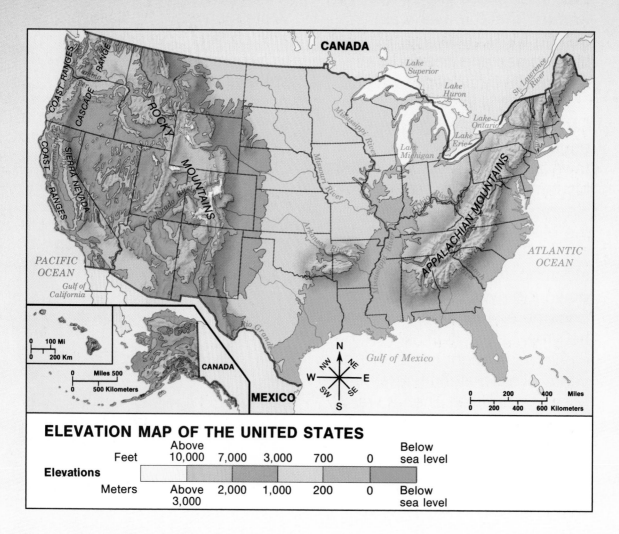

ELEVATION MAP OF THE UNITED STATES

Elevations	Above 10,000	7,000	3,000	700	0	Below sea level
Feet						
Meters	Above 3,000	2,000	1,000	200	0	Below sea level

0 to 700 feet (about 200 m) above sea level. As you have read, land at sea level is the same height as the oceans. The next color shows the elevations of land between 700 to 3,000 feet (about 200 to 1,000 m) above sea level. All places colored light green reach heights between those elevations.

Find the source of the Rio Grande. The source is in the Rocky Mountains. Notice that the land around the source is colored yellow. Find this color in the map key. Yellow stands for land above 10,000 feet (about 3,000 m). The Rio Grande's source is high in the mountains.

Now find the mouth of the Rio Grande. The land around the mouth is colored medium green. What does this color stand for? This is low, flat land. The Rio Grande flows from very high land to low, flat land.

Which Way Do Rivers Flow?

A river always flows in one main direction. You can use an elevation map to find out which way a river flows.

Find the source of the Rio Grande on the map again. Move your finger south down the Rio Grande to the Gulf of Mexico. Your finger is moving **downstream.** Downstream means toward the river's mouth. Now trace the river back up to its source. Your finger is moving **upstream.** Upstream means against the flow of the river.

The word *downstream* tells how a river flows. Water always flows downhill. Rivers can flow from north to south like the Rio Grande. They can flow from east to west like the Columbia. In fact, rivers flow in all directions. Yet their main flow is always downhill from source to mouth. The source is always higher than the mouth.

The source of the Missouri River is in the Rockies. Trace the river to its mouth. What is the elevation of the land there? In which direction does the river flow?

CHECKING YOUR SKILLS

Use the elevation map to help you answer these questions.

1. Which way do rivers flow?

2. What are the elevations of the land around the Missouri River's source and its mouth?

3. The source of the Hudson River is in the Appalachian Mountains. Its mouth is in the Atlantic Ocean.

   a. What are the elevations of the land around the Hudson River's source and its mouth?

   b. In what direction does the Hudson River flow?

CHAPTER 3 REVIEW

Thinking Back

- Rivers are important to people. Rivers provide food and water. The land next to rivers is often good for farming. Most large cities are near rivers. Goods are often shipped on rivers.

- Rivers change the land by forming deltas, eroding the Earth's surface, and flooding the land. People change rivers by building dikes, dams, and bridges. People also widen and deepen rivers and sometimes cause rivers to become polluted.

- The Mississippi, our country's main waterway, is the longest river in the United States. Ships load and unload goods at its ports. The Ohio River is an important tributary of the Mississippi. Many industries are located along its banks.

- The St. Lawrence River forms part of our border with Canada. The Rio Grande, which separates Texas from Mexico, is used to irrigate crops and to make electricity. The Columbia River brings water to the driest part of our country.

Check for Understanding

Using Words

Copy the paragraph below. Fill in the blanks with the correct words from the list.

branches   **silt**
erodes   **source**
mouth

The place where a river begins is its __(1)__. Other rivers and streams, called __(2)__, join it. As the river flows, it wears away, or __(3)__, the land around it. The river carries away soil, or __(4)__. At its __(5)__, a river empties into the ocean.

Reviewing Facts

1. Why were rivers important to people long ago?
2. Why have many cities grown up along rivers? Give at least three reasons.
3. How are deltas formed? Why are deltas good for farming?
4. How do floods change land? Give two examples.
5. How are dams and dikes different?
6. Why are dams useful? Give two reasons.
7. How have people caused rivers to become polluted?
8. What is a port? Name one city that is a port.

9. What river joins the Mississippi River at Cairo, Illinois?

10. What river can carry goods to the Atlantic Ocean? What river empties into the Gulf of Mexico?

Thinking Critically

1. Many people in the United States live in cities located on rivers. What would be good about living in such a city?

2. Why is water pollution dangerous? What might be some ways to protect rivers?

Writing About It

Imagine that you are a drop of water in a river. Write a story telling about how you reached the river. Describe some of the things that might have happened to you along the way.

Practicing Geography Skills

Using Elevation Maps

Answer these questions about the Savannah River. Use the map on page 84 to help you.

1. The Savannah River begins in the Appalachian Mountains. How high is the land there?

2. Does the river flow from northwest to southeast or from southeast to northwest? How can you tell?

On Your Own

Social Studies at Home

Ask a family member to help you make a model of a river that flows into a lake. Use a cardboard tube for the river and a pie pan for the lake. Put a little clean water into the lake. Then pour some very muddy water slowly through the river into the lake. What happens to the water in the lake? Allow the water to sit for a few hours. What has happened to the mud?

Read More About It

The Barge Book by Jerry Bushey. Carolrhoda Books. A journey down the Mississippi River from Minneapolis to New Orleans is described in this book about a barge crew.

The Rio Grande by Raymond Johnson. Wayland/Silver Burdett. In this book you will travel down the river that separates the United States and Mexico.

The St. Lawrence by Trudy J. Hanmer. Franklin Watts. The history and importance of the waterway shared by the United States and Canada is described in this book.

Where the River Begins by Thomas Locker. Dial Books. Two boys and their grandfathers follow a familiar river back to its source.

Mountains

"How glorious a greeting the sun gives the mountains! To behold this alone is worth the pains of any excursion a thousand times over. The highest peaks burned like islands in a sea of liquid shade. Then the lower peaks and spires caught the glow, and long lances of light . . . fell thick on the frozen meadows."

—John Muir on seeing the mountains of California in 1894

Look for these important words:

Key Words
- volcanoes
- lava

- peaks
- altitude
- mountain ranges

Places
- Appalachian Mountains
- Rocky Mountains

Look for answers to these questions:
1. How are mountains formed?
2. How are old mountains different from new mountains?
3. Which are the newer mountains of North America?
4. Which are the older mountains of North America?

1 Mountains Old and New

In a way, mountains have a lifetime. They are formed, they grow older, and they wear down. Some of these changes are so slow that it is hard to see them. Others can be quick and violent.

The Shaping of Mountains

Most mountains are so old that we can only guess how they were formed. One idea is that mountains grew slowly. Little by little, forces deep within the Earth pushed up parts of the Earth's surface. Ripples and ridges formed on the surface, slowly forming mountains.

Mountains can also be formed quickly. **Volcanoes** (vahl•KAY•nohz) form mountains in a quick and sometimes explosive way. A volcano begins as a crack in the Earth's surface. Through the crack comes hot, melted rock. This melted rock is called **lava** (LAH•vuh). The lava flows over the land like oatmeal boiling over in a pot. As the lava cools, it hardens. The land around the crack is built up. Over the years, the volcano explodes again and again. Gradually the volcano's lava forms a mountain shaped like a cone. Volcanoes formed many of the mountains in California, Oregon, Washington, and Hawaii.

Some of them are still active, sending forth lava.

When they are new, many mountains have high, sharp tops, or **peaks.** After many years, mountains start to show their age. Rain, ice, blowing sand, and heat begin breaking up the rock. Water and wind then carry away the bits of broken rock. Through erosion, the shape of a mountain changes. Its peak gets lower and rounder. Erosion is wearing down the mountains you see today.

Mountains of Our Country

The United States has two large areas of mountains. In one, the mountains are old, low, and

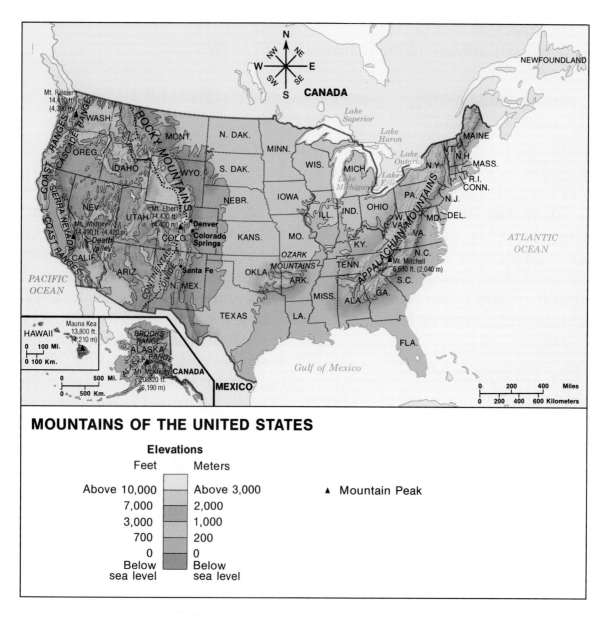

MOUNTAINS OF THE UNITED STATES

Elevations

Feet	Meters
Above 10,000	Above 3,000
7,000	2,000
3,000	1,000
700	200
0	0
Below sea level	Below sea level

▲ Mountain Peak

The gently sloping Appalachian Mountains are 230 million years old.

The Teton Range in the Rocky Mountains has snow-capped peaks.

rounded. In the other, the mountains are new, high, and steep. Look at the pictures on this page. Which mountains are old?

Now look at the map on page 90. Find the **Appalachian Mountains.** These are the older mountains. They cover much of our country's eastern side. The Appalachians begin in Newfoundland (NOO•fuhnd•luhnd), Canada, and end in northern Alabama. They stretch almost 2,000 miles (about 3,220 km).

The newer, taller mountains are in the West. These are the **Rocky Mountains.** The Rocky Mountains begin in Alaska and end in New Mexico. The Rockies are much higher than the Appalachians. Peaks in the Rockies can reach 14,000 feet (4,267 m).

The height of a mountain is called its **altitude.** Altitude is another word for elevation. We measure altitude from sea level, just as we do for elevation.

Mountains are usually in chains or groups, known as **mountain ranges.** The Appalachians and the Rockies have many mountain ranges. What other mountain ranges can you find on the map?

Reading Check

1. How does a volcano form a mountain?
2. How are newer mountains different from older mountains?
3. What is a mountain range?

Think Beyond How might changes in mountains also affect rivers near them?

People MAKE HISTORY

Zebulon Pike
1779–1813

▶▶▶▶▶▶▶▶▶▶▶▶▶▶▶▶▶▶

What was that strange blue cloud up ahead? Zebulon Pike got out his telescope and looked to the west. The cloud was really a large mountain far off in the distance!

Pike was an officer in the United States army. In June 1806, several months before he saw this mountain, Pike had received new orders. He was to explore the Arkansas River region. The United States had recently purchased this land from France, but only a few fur trappers knew anything about the area.

After five months Pike and his troops reached the area of what is now Pueblo, Colorado. In November he saw the mountain that became known as Pikes Peak. He made plans to climb it.

Pike and a small group traveled for three days. They were still far below the mountain-top. Soon they were climbing in snow. They were not dressed for such cold weather. Pike decided that they should give up. They turned around and rejoined the other troops.

In 1810 Pike published a book about his trip, and people all over the world read about his adventure. Unfortunately, Pike only lived for three more years. He was killed in a battle during the War of 1812.

Today, Zebulon Pike is best remembered for the mountain that bears his name. The view from the top is beautiful. It is said that the song "America the Beautiful" was written after the author visited Pikes Peak.

Think Beyond Why do you think Pike at first mistook the mountain for a cloud?

Look for these important words:

Key Words
- moisture
- barriers
- passes

Look for answers to these questions:

1. How do mountains influence climate in the United States?
2. What happens when winds from the Pacific Ocean meet mountains?
3. How are mountains barriers to travel?

2 *Why Mountains Are Important*

You may live hundreds of miles from the nearest mountains. Yet mountains are important to you wherever you live. How wet or dry a place is often depends on mountains. Mountains cause some of the wettest and driest climates in the world.

Mountains and Climate

Look at the drawing on page 94. It shows how important mountains are to climate.

Winds blow from west to east across the Pacific Ocean. Winds are moving air. As the winds blow, the air picks up **moisture,** or water, from the ocean. The winds blow across the Pacific Coast. When they meet mountains, the winds move upward. As they rise, the air grows colder and clouds form. Cold air cannot hold very much moisture. The moisture in the clouds falls as rain. Rain falls mainly on the western side of the mountains. Because of the rain, forests grow thick and green here.

When the air crosses over the mountains, it holds little moisture. The eastern side of the mountains gets little rain. The Cascade Range makes eastern Washington and Oregon dry. The Sierra Nevada in California makes Death Valley, California, one of the hottest, driest places in the United States.

Mountains are important to climate in another way. Like walls, high mountains block

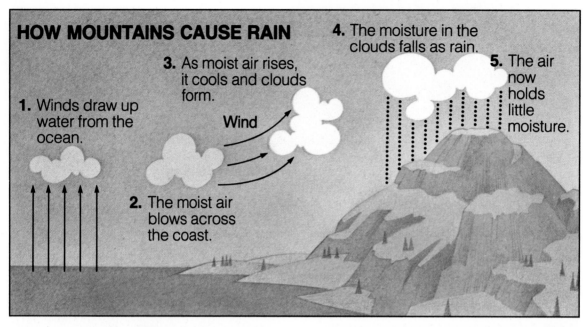

HOW MOUNTAINS CAUSE RAIN

1. Winds draw up water from the ocean.

2. The moist air blows across the coast.

3. As moist air rises, it cools and clouds form.

Wind

4. The moisture in the clouds falls as rain.

5. The air now holds little moisture.

strong winds. Where no mountains block the winds, the weather can get very cold. The centers of Canada and the United States have no mountains. In winter, cold winds from the north sweep south. Many states like North and South Dakota and Montana have cold, snowy winters.

Mountains and Travel

Long ago, mountains were **barriers** to travel. A barrier blocks the way of something. Mountains blocked the movement of people and goods from place to place. People feared the high, rugged slopes. They had no roads to travel. They were not sure what lay beyond. To get across a mountain range, people had to find **passes,** or low areas between mountains.

Even if they did find a pass, mountain travelers had to face the weather. Sudden snow storms and rock and snow slides threatened people's lives. Mountains made it hard for Americans to move west.

Today people cross mountains more often. Airplanes fly over mountains. Roads cross them. These roads are often steep, narrow, and full of curves. Even today, mountain travel is not easy.

Reading Check

1. What kinds of climate do mountains cause?
2. Why do North and South Dakota have cold, snowy winters?
3. What are mountain passes?

Think Beyond What types of things might make travel easier for people in the mountains?

SKILLS IN ACTION

USING LATITUDE AND LONGITUDE

You may recall that the equator is an imaginary line that divides the globe into two halves, called hemispheres. The half from the equator to the North Pole is called the Northern Hemisphere. The other half, from the equator to the South Pole, is the Southern Hemisphere.

Lines of Latitude

Lines of latitude, or **parallels,** help locate places north and south of the equator. The equator itself is a line of latitude that runs east and west around the globe. It is marked 0° (zero degrees). Other lines of latitude also run east and west around the globe. Their numbers get larger as they get farther from the equator.

Lines of latitude in the Northern Hemisphere are marked with an *N*. The *N* tells you that the line is north of the equator. The North Pole is marked 90°N. The South Pole is marked 90°S. The *S* tells you that its location is south of the equator, in the Southern Hemisphere.

Look at the drawing of the globe below. Place your finger on

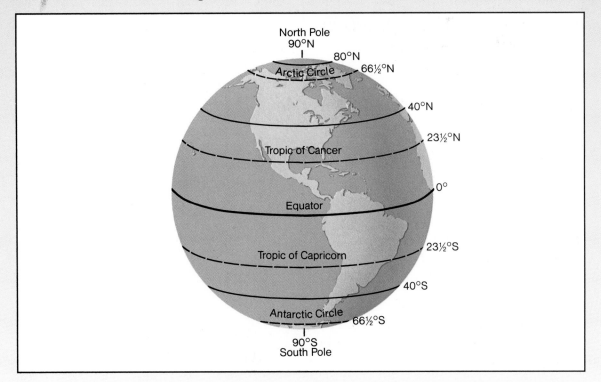

95

the equator. Move your finger toward the North Pole. Your finger will cross two special lines of latitude. These are the **Tropic of Cancer** at 23½°N and the **Arctic Circle** at 66½°N.

Place your finger on the equator again and move it toward the South Pole. Notice that your finger crosses two special lines of latitude. They are the **Tropic of Capricorn** at 23½°S. and the **Antarctic Circle** at 66½°S.

Find the area between the Tropics of Cancer and Capricorn. This area is warm almost all of the time. Now look just north of the Arctic Circle and south of the Antarctic Circle. These areas are usually cold all year.

Lines of Longitude

Lines of longitude, or **meridians,** help locate places east and west, just as lines of latitude help locate places north and south.

Lines of longitude run from the North Pole to the South Pole. One special line of longitude is the **Prime Meridian.** It divides the Earth in half. The half east of the Prime Meridian is the **Eastern Hemisphere.** The western half is the **Western Hemisphere.**

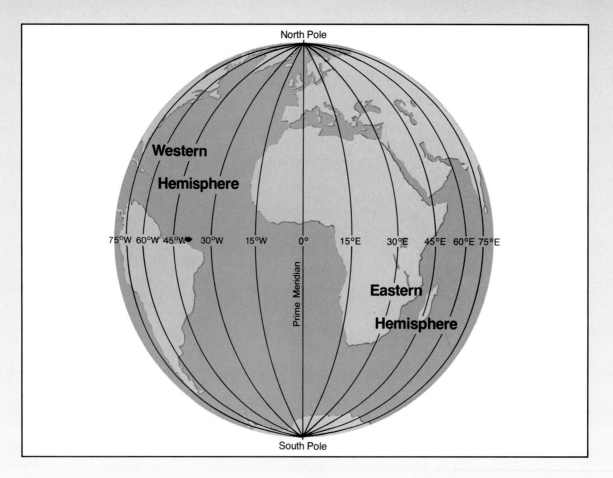

96

The Prime Meridian is the beginning place for locations east and west. It is marked 0° (zero degrees). Lines of longitude in the Eastern Hemisphere are labeled *E* for east. The lines in the Western Hemisphere are labeled *W* for west.

Locating Places with a Grid

Lines of latitude and longitude form a grid on globes and maps. The grid helps locate places on the Earth.

Find Pikes Peak. Which line of latitude is closest to it? Which line of longitude is closest? Pikes Peak is near 39°N, 105°W.

CHECKING YOUR SKILLS

Use the drawings and the map of Colorado to answer these questions.

1. If a city is located at 20°E, is it in the Eastern or Western Hemisphere?

2. Would a city located near 20°N probably have warm or cold weather? Why?

3. What is the nearest line of latitude to Pueblo, Colorado?

4. What line of longitude is at Colorado's eastern border?

5. What lines of latitude and longitude most closely describe the location of Delta?

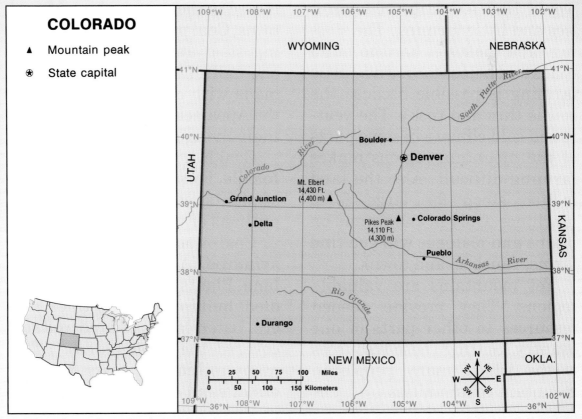

97

Look for these important words:

Key Words	• graze	• recreation
• fossils	• brand	• national parks
• swamps	• fleece	• state parks
• range	• shear	• conservation

Look for answers to these questions:
1. Why are mountains valuable regions?
2. How was coal formed?
3. What are some jobs people have in mountain regions?
4. Why do people like to visit the mountains?

3 *Mountain Regions Today*

If you took a trip through our country's mountain regions, you would find few large communities and little farming. The sloping land makes it hard to build roads and homes for towns. Little farming is possible because the soil is thin and rocky. The year-round cold climate in some parts of the mountain regions makes farming difficult. Also the land is too steep for large farm machines. Only in valleys and on plains and plateaus will you find farms, ranches, and towns.

Yet mountains are valuable regions. They provide needed resources to other parts of our country. Getting these resources is the job of many people in mountain communities.

Mining

Large amounts of coal are mined in the Appalachian Mountains. Coal provides fuel for making steel and electricity. About one-half of all our electricity is made with coal. Many people in the Appalachian Mountains make their living as coal miners.

Coal is a fuel that comes from **fossils.** Fossils are what remains of plants and animals that died millions of years ago.

Coal was formed mainly in **swamps.** A swamp is low, wet land. Plants in swamps lived and died, building up into thick layers. Later, layers of sand and soil covered the dead plants. After many millions of years, the layers of sand and soil turned into

Coal, a valuable fuel, is found deep in the mountains. Miners must wear lighted hats to go underground. Once dug, coal is loaded onto trains and brought to plants to be cleaned.

rock. The layers of rock squeezed the plants into coal. It took a layer of plants about 20 feet (about 6 m) thick to make a layer of coal 1 foot (about 30 cm) thick.

After the coal was formed, some of the earth was pushed up to form mountains. Today the mountains contain the layers of coal formed so long ago.

Though coal is found in the United States today, we must be careful not to waste this important resource. The Earth is not making more coal. We must save some coal for the future.

Like the Appalachians, the Rocky Mountains are rich in coal. Buried within them are other valuable fuels—oil, natural gas, and uranium. The Rocky Mountains are also rich in metals, like copper, silver, and lead.

Forests

When the first European settlers came to eastern America,

forests covered much of the land. As towns grew, some forests were cut down to build houses and stores. Many trees were also cut down to clear the land for farms.

Today, forests cover about a third of our country. Many of our largest forests are in mountain areas and in Alaska.

Trees in forests are cut down for lumber. Most lumber is used for building. Lumber is used to build homes and schools. The wood from trees is also used to make other products, like paper. The United States makes more paper than any other country in the world.

Most forests in our country need at least 20 inches (about 51 cm) of precipitation a year to grow well. The map below shows the main forest areas of our country.

Like coal, trees are an important resource. Unlike coal, however, trees can be replaced. People can plant new trees where others were cut down. By replanting forests, people can make sure they will have enough wood for the future.

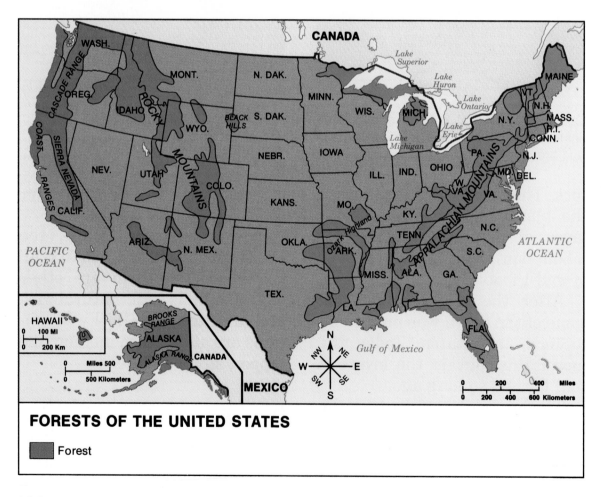

FORESTS OF THE UNITED STATES

Forest

Ranching

Beef cattle and sheep do best in areas that are too dry for forests but rainy enough for grass. For this reason, people in some mountain regions are ranchers. Their cattle and sheep wander over miles of grassland, called the **range.** The animals eat, or **graze** on, the thin grass. It takes many acres of land, and some hay or grain to feed a herd.

Calves are born in the spring. After about two months, the ranchers **brand,** or mark, the calves. The brand shows who owns the calves. During spring and summer the herd grazes on the range. When the cattle can find little grass, ranchers may have to move their herd. Sometimes they must bring water and food out to the herd. Ranchers also raise hay and grain for the herd to eat in the winter.

Sheep ranchers get wool and meat from their animals. The sheep's woolly coat is called **fleece.** In the spring, ranchers **shear,** or cut, the sheep's fleece. Spring is also the time when lambs are born. Soon they are

In spring and summer cattle roam the open range to eat mountain grasses. In late fall ranchers often move their herds into fenced areas, where the cattle can be fed during the winter months.

Skiers skim down a snowy slope in the Rocky Mountains of Wyoming.

following their mothers on the range. Sometimes, though, a lamb wanders off. A rancher may spend hours looking for a lost lamb.

Recreation

Millions of people visit mountain regions each year. The mountains provide **recreation** (rek•ree•AY•shuhn), or things people do for enjoyment. People enjoy the splendid scenery in the mountains. During the summer, people go to the mountains to camp. They hike, fish, boat, and mountain climb. During the winter, people can ski, ice skate, and play in the snow.

National and State Parks

Many places in our country remain wilderness today. Our national and state governments have set aside some of this land for parks. **National parks** and **state parks** are found in mountain regions as well as other parts of the country.

Every visitor to our parks has a responsibility to protect them. Fire safety is especially important. People can start forest fires. Carelessness with matches or campfires easily starts a fire. Each year fires destroy thousands of acres of forests. It can take a hundred years for a burnt-down forest to grow back.

Our national and state parks are a valuable natural resource. Protecting our natural resources is called **conservation** (kahn•suhr•VAY•shuhn). *Conservation* means saving something by using it wisely and carefully. If we protect our parks, we can enjoy them for years to come.

Reading Check

1. What are some resources found in mountains?
2. Why are beef cattle and sheep raised in mountain regions?
3. What kinds of recreation do mountains provide?

Think Beyond What mountain resources do you use each day?

102

IN FOCUS

THE U.S. FOREST SERVICE

In 1950 a brown bear cub was rescued from a forest fire in the Lincoln National Forest near Capitan, New Mexico. A four-year-old girl and her family took care of the injured cub. After the bear recovered, he was moved to the National Zoo in Washington, D.C. Over the years, thousands of people visited him there.

Why did so many people visit this bear? He was none other than Smokey Bear! Americans saw posters about him and heard his message repeated many times: "Remember! Only *you* can prevent forest fires."

Preventing forest fires is just one of the many jobs of the U.S. Forest Service. The Forest Service oversees more than 191 million acres (77 million ha) of land. Forest Service rangers help protect forests from disease and insects. They plant trees on hilly land to prevent soil erosion. They also make sure that not too many trees are cut down in a single year.

Rangers help protect other natural resources such as water

Smokey Bear

and wildlife. They take care of picnic and camping areas in the forests. If people get lost on hiking trails, they rescue them.

Rangers are not the only people who work for the Forest Service. There are also scientists, whose work is to make trees grow better. These scientists study ways to prevent air, water, and soil pollution. The Forest Service works hard to protect our forests for the future.

Think Beyond   Why is it important not to cut down too many trees in a single year?

A U.S. Forest Service ranger

103

SKILLS IN ACTION

USING CROSS-SECTION DIAGRAMS

If you cut an orange in half, this is what you see. This view of the inside is called a **cross section.** Cross sections show the insides of things.

The cross section below shows a view of the inside of a mountain. You can see the layers of stone and soil inside it. Certain places, like the Appalachian Mountains, have layers like these.

The top layer of the mountain below is topsoil. Topsoil is the soil that people walk on. Many mountains are rocky, with little topsoil.

Below the soil on this mountain is sandstone, and below that is shale. Sandstone is made up of sand. Shale is made up of clay.

The next layer in the cross section is limestone. Limestone is rock made up of mud and shells from long, long ago.

Coal lies below the limestone. Coal may also be found just below the topsoil or in large cracks on the sides of the mountains.

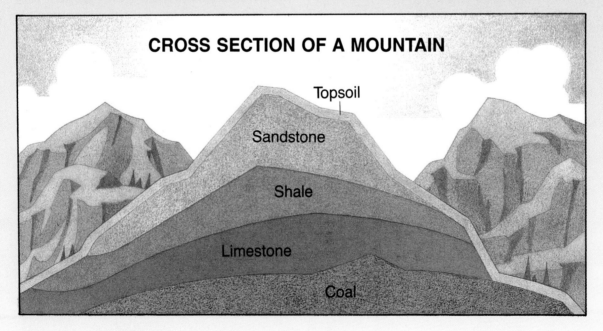

CROSS SECTION OF A MOUNTAIN

Topsoil

Sandstone

Shale

Limestone

Coal

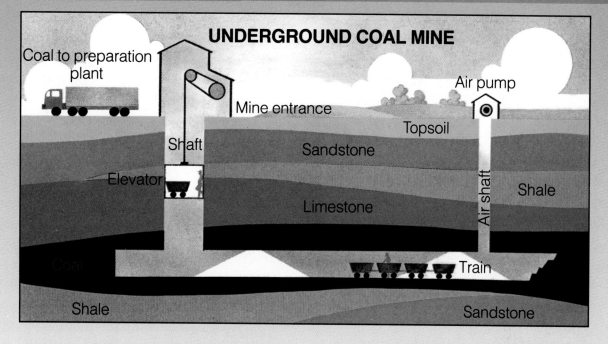

UNDERGROUND COAL MINE

In the Appalachians, coal often lies deep in the earth. Look at the cross section of an underground mine on this page. To get to the coal, people must drill a deep hole called a shaft.

An elevator carries miners to and from the coal. The elevator also brings the coal out of the mine.

The miners sometimes use explosives to dig tunnels. They also use drills to break the coal into chunks.

Small train cars carry the coal to the elevator. Find the train cars in the diagram. Do they move back and forth or up and down?

Harmful gases in the earth sometimes get into a mine. These gases must be pumped out of the mine. Find the air shaft on the cross-section diagram. At the top of the shaft is an air pump. The air pump helps pull these harmful gases out of the mine.

In the mine, coal is mixed in with rock and dirt. The mixture must then go to a preparation plant. There the rock is removed. Now the coal is ready to be shipped.

CHECKING YOUR SKILLS

Answer these questions. Use the cross-section diagram to help you.

1. The mine shaft must go through four layers to reach the coal. What are these layers?

2. How is coal brought to the elevator?

3. What takes harmful gases out of a mine?

4. Where does the coal go when it leaves the elevator?

105

CHAPTER 4 REVIEW

Thinking Back

- Mountains are formed when forces deep inside the Earth push up ridges in its surface. They also form when the action of a volcano deposits lava on the Earth. New mountains have high, sharp peaks, while older mountains have lower, rounder peaks.

- The two largest mountain ranges in the United States are the Rocky Mountains and the Appalachian Mountains. The Appalachians are the older mountains.

- Mountains affect climate. They block winds, which can affect both the rainfall and the temperature in an area. Mountains have also blocked the movement of people from place to place.

- There are few large mountain communities because the sloping land makes it difficult to build roads and towns. Farming is also difficult in mountain regions.

- Mountain regions provide important resources such as coal and lumber. Many people in mountain regions work in mining, lumbering, and ranching.

- Many parks and recreation areas are found in mountain regions.

Check for Understanding

Using Words

Write a sentence for each word. Your sentences should explain the meanings of the words.

1. **volcanoes**
2. **mountain range**
3. **fossils**
4. **recreation**
5. **conservation**

Reviewing Facts

1. What are two ways in which mountains may form?

2. How does erosion change the shape of a mountain?

3. Name some differences between the Appalachian Mountains and the Rocky Mountains.

4. How do mountains make places wet? How do they make places dry?

5. Why are mountains barriers to travel?

6. What are two resources found in mountain regions?

7. How can people make sure that there will be enough wood for the future?

8. Why must ranchers move their herds from place to place?
9. What can people do for recreation in mountain regions?
10. Why has land been set aside for national and state parks?

Thinking Critically

1. Erosion changes mountains. People also change mountains. What are some changes people have made to make mountain travel easier?
2. What are some jobs done in mountain regions only in warm weather? What jobs can be done in good or bad weather?

Writing About It

Imagine that you work for an advertising agency. Your company has been hired by a mountain community that wants to attract tourists. Write a radio advertisement in which you tell people why they should spend their vacations in the mountains.

Practicing Geography Skills

Using Latitude and Longitude

Answer these questions. Use the drawing on page 95 and the map on page 97 to help you.

1. Near what line of latitude is Mount Elbert?
2. Which is closer to Colorado, the Tropic of Cancer or the equator?

On Your Own

Social Studies at Home

Make a poster entitled "A Helping Hand for Trees." Draw a tree trunk and branches. Then trace your hand to make leaves. On each leaf, write a different way that people can help save trees. Ask family members for ideas, too.

Read More About It

Canyon Winter by Walt Morey. E. P. Dutton. When their plane crashes in the Rocky Mountains, the characters in this book must overcome many dangers to reach safety.

A Day in the Life of a Forest Ranger by David Paige. Troll. You will follow a ranger through his day and learn about his duties.

Logging and Lumbering by Kathleen S. Abrams. Julian Messner. Much information about this important mountain industry is given in this book.

Rip Van Winkle adapted by Thomas Locker. Dial Books. Exciting paintings add to this retelling of Washington Irving's classic tale.

When I Was Young in the Mountains by Cynthia Rylant. E. P. Dutton. In this touching story a woman remembers her childhood days when she lived with her grandparents in the mountains.

CHAPTER 5

Deserts

"Although it was not yet nine o'clock, the sun already beat down on us with an intensity that could be felt through our clothes, and the air, which had been cold only thirty minutes before, began to feel warm as the sun beat back, reflected from the sand and gravelly shale of the desert floor."

—A traveler describing the landscape
of the Mojave Desert

Look for these important words:

Key Words
- evaporate
- sand dunes
- flash flood
- cactus

- mesquite

Places
- North American Desert

- Great Basin Desert
- Mojave Desert
- Sonoran Desert
- Chihuahuan Desert

Look for answers to these questions:
1. How are deserts different from each other?
2. How do wind and water change deserts?
3. Why are some plants and animals able to live in a desert?

1 North American Deserts

Deserts can look quite different from one another. Some deserts have mountains and high cliffs. Other deserts are flat. Some deserts have drifting sand and few plants. Other deserts have fairly good soil where flowers and other plants grow and bloom.

Dry Lands

Deserts are alike in one way. They get little rainfall. All deserts receive less than 10 inches (about 25 cm) of rainfall a year.

A very large desert called the **North American Desert** stretches across some of the western part of our country. This desert can be divided into four major areas: the **Great Basin**
Desert, the **Mojave** (moh•HAH•vee) **Desert,** the **Sonoran** (suh•NAWR•uhn) **Desert,** and the **Chihuahuan** (chuh•WAH•wuhn) **Desert.** The map on page 110 shows these desert areas. The Sonoran and the Chihuahuan deserts stretch from the United States into Mexico. The Great Basin Desert is the largest of the four. It lies between the Sierra Nevada and the Rocky Mountains.

Deserts are places of very high and very low temperatures. During the day, temperatures may reach as high as 120°F (about 49°C). When rain falls, it can sometimes **evaporate** (ih•VAP•uh•rayt), or dry up, before it reaches the earth.

109

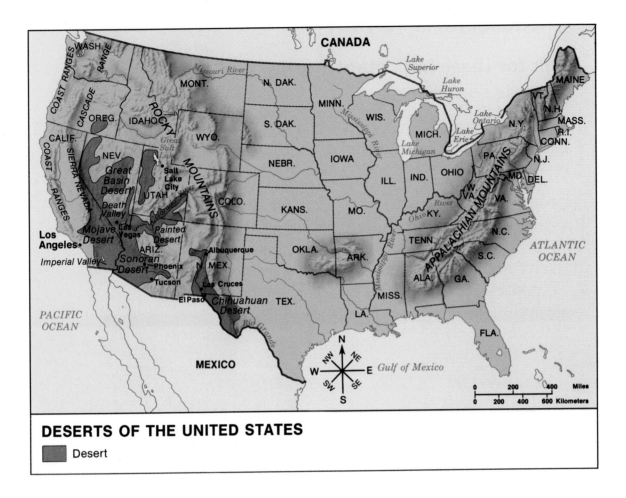

DESERTS OF THE UNITED STATES

☐ Desert

Desert air contains little moisture, so few clouds pass over these dry lands. The sun beats down, baking the ground. The air stays hot all day.

At night temperatures drop quickly. Nights in the desert are often cold.

Wind and Water

Strong winds often blow across deserts. In some deserts the winds blow sand into piles. These rounded piles of sand, or **sand dunes,** take many shapes.

Water changes the desert even more than wind does. A sudden storm may drop several inches of water on the land in just a few minutes. The rain does not sink into the hard, baked ground. Instead, the rain causes a powerful **flash flood.** The racing water streams across the desert, cutting into the land.

Flash floods are often caused by storms that remain in one place for a while. Year after year, such floods change the shape of the land, leaving behind amazing rocks of every size and shape.

110

Monument Valley, above, is a desert area in Utah and Arizona. Red sandstone towers 1,000 feet (about 300 m) above the landscape.

Plants and Animals of the Desert

Though life in a desert may seem impossible, many plants and animals live there. Each kind has developed ways to survive in the dry, hot lands.

One of the well-known American desert plants is the **cactus.** The cactus plant stores water in its thick, fleshy stem. When the earth is dry, the cactus lives on the stored water. Sharp spines keep most animals from eating the plant.

Some American desert plants have long roots. One such plant

Prickly pear cactus grows well in desert areas. Its fruit is good to eat.

A mesquite's roots may grow 60 feet (about 18 m) underground for water.

The tiny kangaroo rat uses its strong back legs to leap across the desert.

is the treelike bush called **mesquite** (muh•SKEET). The long roots of the mesquite help it to reach underground water.

The mesquite grows pods that look like green beans. When the pods open, the seeds drop to the ground. Wind covers the seeds with sand and soil. These seeds may lie buried for a long time. When the rains do come, the seeds grow and blossom. The young plants turn the desert into a carpet of flowers.

Snakes, lizards, rabbits, and mice are some animals that live in the desert. During the day they stay cool in holes or under plants. At night they come out to eat insects, plants, or other animals.

Small desert animals get water from the food they eat. Such small animals are eaten by larger desert animals, like coyotes (ky•OH•teez) and foxes. Coyotes and foxes must get water from springs or waterholes.

Some deer and antelope also make the desert their home. They live mostly on grass. They too must find water to drink at springs or waterholes. There they may also find their enemies. To escape, they run. The pronghorn, a kind of antelope, is the desert's fastest runner. It can run for short periods as fast as 60 miles (about 96 km) per hour.

Reading Check

1. How much rainfall do deserts get?
2. What is the largest desert region in the United States?
3. What is a flash flood?

Think Beyond How might our lives be different if more of our country were a desert?

IN FOCUS

THE PETRIFIED FOREST

A strange forest is found in the desert in northeastern Arizona. The trees in this forest do not stand up straight and tall. They lie flat on the ground and have no branches or needles. In fact, the trees here are **petrified.** This means that the wood has turned into stone!

Welcome to the Petrified Forest National Park. The trees in the park once stood about 200 feet (61 m) tall. They were a kind of pine tree. The trees grew about 150 million years ago. At that time a large river flowed through the area.

What turned these trees into stone? The trees were buried in mud, sand, or volcanic ash millions of years ago. Water seeped through the soil into the buried logs. The water carried certain minerals, which filled the cells of the decaying trees. These minerals then turned the wood into solid stone. The minerals also gave the petrified wood different colors, such as red, yellow, and purple. However, the stone still shows every detail of the original wood, even under a microscope.

Petrified forests can be found in many states, but the one at the Petrified Forest National Park is the largest and most famous. The park has thousands of petrified logs. Some are very large. Others are scattered about in pieces.

At one time people were free to haul away pieces of petrified wood. The stone was cut, polished, and sold. It was used for table tops and other items. Fortunately, other people thought the area should be protected. They told the government that without protection, the petrified forest would soon disappear. In 1962 the petrified forest and surrounding area was made a national park.

Think Beyond   Why is it important to protect areas such as the Petrified Forest National Park?

Petrified wood

SKILLS IN ACTION

USING BAR GRAPHS

Terry is writing a report about climates in four desert cities. First, she gets some information from the library. It looks like this.

Average Annual Precipitation

City/State	Precipitation in Inches
Phoenix, Arizona	7
Winnemucca, Nevada	8
Albuquerque, New Mexico	8
Roswell, New Mexico	10

Terry wants her report to be simple and easy to understand. She decides to put the information in a **graph.** A graph is a drawing that shows numbers. Terry's graph is called a bar graph.

The names of the cities are across the bottom of the bar graph. The numbers on the left are inches of precipitation.

Look at the bar above the name *Albuquerque, New Mexico.* Find the top of the bar. Look across to the number at the left. The bar goes

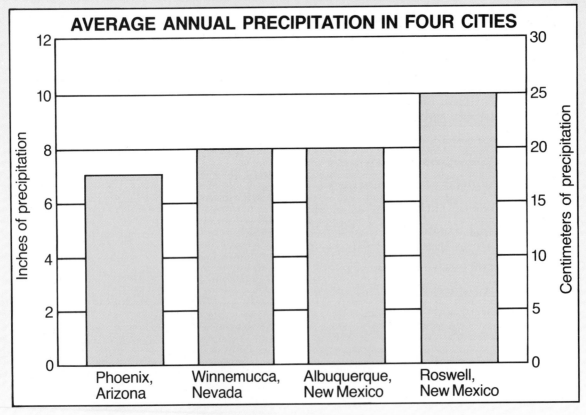

AVERAGE ANNUAL PRECIPITATION IN FOUR CITIES

114

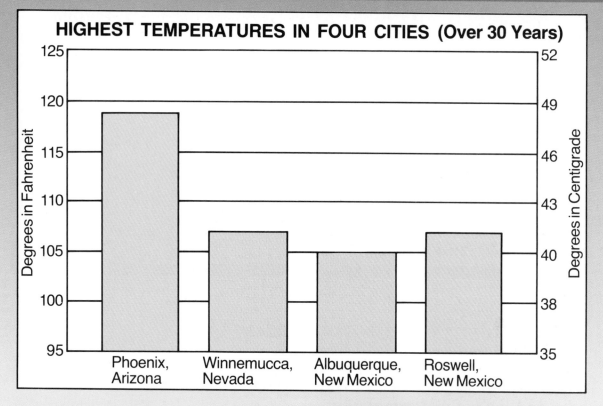

HIGHEST TEMPERATURES IN FOUR CITIES (Over 30 Years)

up to the number 8. This means that Albuquerque has about 8 inches of precipitation a year. Look at the bar for Roswell, New Mexico. Find the top of the bar. Look across to the left. About how many inches of precipitation does Roswell get?

Sometimes the bars stop below or above the lines. Look at the first bar. It shows precipitation in Phoenix, Arizona. The bar goes past the 6 but stops below the 8. This means that Phoenix has more than 6 inches of precipitation.

A bar graph makes it easy to compare numbers. Look at all the bars in the graph. Which city has the highest precipitation? Which city has the lowest precipitation?

CHECKING YOUR SKILLS

Use the graph above to help you answer the questions.

1. What was the highest temperature in Albuquerque?

2. What was the highest temperature in Winnemucca?

3. Which city had the higher temperature, Roswell or Albuquerque?

4. Which city had the highest temperature? Which city had the lowest temperature?

5. Which two cities had high temperatures that were about the same? What was that temperature?

115

Look for these important words:

Key Words
- fertilizer
- canals

Places
- Imperial Valley

Look for answers to these questions:
1. What natural resources do deserts provide?
2. How is water brought to deserts?
3. Why is the Imperial Valley good for farming?
4. How are our deserts changing?

2 Desert Regions Today

In some deserts, you can travel miles without seeing a house. The heat and lack of water make living there hard. In other desert areas, however, towns and cities grow larger every year. Today thousands of people are moving to some desert areas.

Desert regions can be good places to live. Many people enjoy their clear, clean air, hot weather, and sunshine. Air conditioners are machines that cool buildings. They have helped make desert living comfortable.

Deserts are also good places to work. Many people come to desert areas for jobs. Desert regions have valuable minerals. Mining these minerals and manufacturing products from them are two important desert industries that provide jobs for people.

Though surrounded by desert, many people in Arizona live in cities.

Minerals

Some deserts contain important fuels and minerals such as oil, copper, and uranium. The salt on your table may have come from

116

Every place on Earth has its own natural features. These natural features make that place special. The Great Salt Lake, for example, is saltier than any ocean. In fact, it is so salty that no fish can live in its waters. When the lake's water level is low, its islands and the land around it are white with salt. Why is the Great Salt Lake so salty?

All streams and rivers carry tiny amounts of salt in their water. As rivers flow across the land, the water dissolves the salt found in soil and rocks. Most rivers then flow into the ocean, where the salt is deposited.

High mountains surround the Great Basin. Rivers there do not flow into oceans. Instead, they flow into shallow desert lakes. The hot, dry desert air evaporates some or all of the water, leaving the salt behind. Over many years, more and more salt builds up. This causes the water in the lakes to become saltier.

a desert, too. Large patches of salt are found near the Great Salt Lake. The Great Salt Lake is part of the Great Basin Desert. Another valuable mineral in desert areas is potash. Potash is used as a **fertilizer** (FUHR·tuh·ly·zuhr). Fertilizers are materials that help plants grow.

Water

People need water to use the desert's resources. Factories and homes need water. Water is used in mining. With enough water, deserts can be good places for farming. Deserts often have good soil and weather for growing crops.

Irrigation now brings water to many desert areas. Giant pipes and pumps carry water from mountains hundreds of miles away. In some places people dig deep wells to reach underground water.

Irrigation changed a valley in the Sonoran Desert into one of the world's richest farmlands. This valley in southern California is the **Imperial Valley.** It was once a dry and empty land. Irrigation turned it into America's

Canals bring water to the Imperial Valley and turn desert into rich farmland.

"salad bowl." The Imperial Valley grows more lettuce than any other place in the country.

The Imperial Valley gets its water from the Colorado River. Miles of **canals** bring the water to the farmlands of the valley. A canal is a waterway built by people.

The desert soil and the climate of the Imperial Valley are perfect for farming. With irrigation, farmers can grow crops all year long.

The Changing Desert

Some desert areas still look as they did many years ago. Others, however, are quickly growing and changing. Irrigation has helped these places grow. Each year, more people come to live in desert areas.

Growing numbers of people, farms, and industries need more and more water. Most rivers and streams are being tapped for their water. Water is pumped from underground wells faster than rain can replace it. Many people living in desert areas worry about lack of water. Without water, desert cities may not keep growing. Some people, however, believe that more water will be found.

In the past, people thought that deserts were useless. Today, we know that is not true. As we explore our deserts, we find more oil, gas, and minerals. With irrigation, the desert soil can be used for farming.

We must use our desert resources wisely, however. If we do, our desert lands will provide for our needs now and in the future.

Reading Check

1. Why are deserts a good place to live and work?
2. What minerals are found in deserts? Give two examples.
3. Why is the Imperial Valley an important farming area?

Think Beyond Why must people use water wisely in deserts?

People MAKE HISTORY

Maria Martinez
1886–1980

▶▶▶▶▶▶▶▶▶▶▶▶▶▶▶▶

You are visiting a museum in an American city. In one room you notice a glass case. Something round glistens behind the glass. You move closer and see a beautiful black pot.

The person who made this pot was a Pueblo Indian named Maria Martinez. She lived in New Mexico. She learned to make pots when she was a young girl.

In the early 1900s, a scientist visited Martinez's village. He showed her some pieces of shiny pottery. The pieces were from pots Martinez's ancestors may have made. They were about 700 years old. The scientist asked Martinez if she could make a pot with the same shine. After many tries, she learned to make her pots shiny and black.

The materials Martinez used were simple. She dug clay where she lived. To shape the clay, she used her hands as tools.

To make a pot, Martinez started by rolling the soft clay into a long coil. Then she wound the coil into the shape of a pot.

Martinez scraped the pot inside and out. She rubbed it smooth with a stone. Sometimes Martinez painted designs on her pots. She baked the pots in a very hot fire.

Martinez's pots became famous. Museums all over the world collected them. Martinez continued to make her pots in New Mexico for the rest of her long life. She taught her family to make beautiful pots also. Her family now makes the shiny black pots.

Think Beyond What are some special things that an older person has taught you how to make or do?

SKILLS IN ACTION

USING TABLES

The word *table* can be used to talk about different things. A table is a piece of furniture. A book has a table of contents. A table can also be a way to show information.

The table below shows a number of facts about four states. The names of the states are at the left of the table. What are they?

Across from each state name is a row of boxes. All of the first row is about Arizona. What state is the second row about?

The boxes that go down a table are columns. At the top of each column is a title that tells the kinds of information in the table. The first column tells the state names. What do the other columns tell?

Suppose you want to find the nickname of California. Look down the left side to find the row for California. California is the second row, the one colored orange. Now look across the top of the table. Find the column for nicknames. Look

TABLE A

State	Nickname	State Bird	State Flower
Arizona	Grand Canyon State	cactus wren	saguaro cactus blossom
California	Golden State	valley quail	golden poppy
Nevada	Silver State	mountain bluebird	sagebrush
New Mexico	Land of Enchantment	roadrunner	yucca

TABLE B

State	Capital	Population (1988)	Area (in square miles)
Arizona	Phoenix	3,466,000	113,909
California	Sacramento	28,168,000	158,693
Nevada	Carson City	1,060,000	110,540
New Mexico	Santa Fe	1,510,000	121,666

down this column to find the orange row. In the orange row is the name *Golden State*. California's nickname is the "Golden State." What is Arizona's nickname?

A table often shows numbers. Table B gives more information about Arizona, California, Nevada, and New Mexico. Once again, the state names are in the first column. The second column gives the capital of each state. The third column gives the **population** of each state. Population is the number of people who live in a place. What is the population of Nevada?

The last column tells each state's **area.** Area is amount of land. Look at the row for New Mexico. What is its area?

At the back of this book is an Almanac. This section has a long table called "Facts About the States." In this table you will find some information about all 50 states.

CHECKING YOUR SKILLS

Answer these questions. Use the tables in the lesson to help you.

1. What is the state flower of Arizona?

2. What is the nickname of Nevada?

3. What is the population of Arizona?

4. What is the area of California?

121

Thinking Back

- Although deserts can look quite different, they are all alike in that they receive less than 10 inches (about 25 cm) of rainfall a year.

- The four major areas of the North American Desert are the Great Basin Desert, the Mojave Desert, the Sonoran Desert, and the Chihuahuan Desert.

- Like rivers and mountains, deserts are always changing. Wind and rain change the shape of a desert.

- Plants and animals have developed ways to survive in the desert.

- Copper, uranium, salt, and potash are some mineral resources found in deserts.

- Air conditioning and irrigation make it possible for people to live and grow crops in deserts.

- The Imperial Valley in California is an important desert farming area.

- If we use our desert resources wisely, deserts will help provide for our needs in the future.

✔ Check for Understanding

Using Words

Copy the sentences below. Fill in the blanks with the correct words from the list.

cactus   fertilizers
canals   flash flood
evaporates

1. Hot desert air dries up, or _____ , rain water.
2. A _____ cuts into desert land, changing its shape.
3. The _____ stores water in its thick stem.
4. Materials that help plants grow are _____ .
5. Miles of _____ bring water from the Colorado River to the farmlands of the Imperial Valley.

Reviewing Facts

1. Between what mountains is the Great Basin Desert?
2. How does the mesquite plant get water?
3. Why are so many people moving to desert regions? Give at least two reasons.
4. Why are some deserts good for farming?
5. Why are more people today worried about a lack of water in desert areas?

Thinking Critically

1. How do people use the natural resources of deserts? In what ways might we use desert resources in the future?
2. How is living in the desert different from living in other places? How is it the same?

Writing About It

Think about the plants and animals that live in the desert. Choose one and use the library to find out more about it. Then write a poem describing the plant or animal. Share the poem with your class.

 **Practicing Graph Skills**

Using Bar Graphs

Use the bar graph to answer these questions.

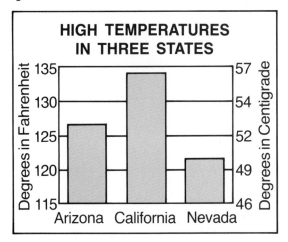

HIGH TEMPERATURES IN THREE STATES

1. Was the temperature higher in Arizona or Nevada?
2. Which of the states had the highest temperature?

 # On Your Own

Social Studies at Home

Write a short play in which two people argue about moving to the desert. One person thinks the desert would be a terrible place to live. The other person tells him or her what the desert is really like. Ask a family member to act out the play with you.

Read More About It

Cactus in the Desert by Phyllis S. Busch. T. Y. Crowell. This book tells about one of nature's most interesting plants.

The Changing Desert by Ada Graham. Sierra Club Books/Charles Scribner's. The many problems now facing America's deserts are described in the book.

Desert Voices by Byrd Baylor. Charles Scribner's. Ten animals tell stories about life in the desert.

Deserts by Clive Catchpole. Dial Books. This book describes the climate and the plant and animal life of a desert.

Eight Words for Thirsty by Ann E. Sigford. Dillon Press. This book describes life in North America's four major desert areas.

One Day in the Desert by Jean Craighead George. T. Y. Crowell. This book explains how animals, plants, and people survive in one desert.

CHAPTER 6

Plains

The land was changing. The smaller hills and red rocks of the South were gone, and day by day, the land got more and more like a blanket—a brown-green, rumpled one. Grandma'd want to pull it neat and flat, but I liked it. Like the sea was supposed to be, and sometimes I felt we were on a boat sailing over an ocean.

—from the book *Grasshopper Summer*
by Ann Turner

Look for these important words:

Key Words	• fertile	Places
• flour mills	• raw materials	• Coastal Plain
• sawmills	• finished products	• Fall Line

Look for answers to these questions:

1. What features of the land make the Coastal Plain important?
2. What old and new industries are found on the Coastal Plain?
3. Why can goods easily be moved in and out of cities on the Coastal Plain?

1 *The Coastal Plain*

A large plain stretches along the Atlantic Coast to the Gulf of Mexico. This low, flat land is the **Coastal Plain.** The Coastal Plain begins as a narrow strip of land in the north. As it stretches south, it gets wider and wider. At Florida the plain swings west.

Some of our largest cities are on the Coastal Plain. New York City, Philadelphia, Boston, Miami, Houston, and Dallas are a few of these large cities. Our nation's capital, Washington, D.C., is also on the Coastal Plain.

The Fall Line

If you look at a map, you will see that many large cities form a line along the Coastal Plain's western edge. These cities are close to what is called the **Fall Line.** The Fall Line comes between the Appalachian Mountains and the Coastal Plain. At the Fall Line, the elevation of the land drops suddenly. Rivers with their sources in the mountains have waterfalls here. Their waters drop to the plain below and from there continue across the Coastal Plain. At their mouths they empty into the Atlantic Ocean.

Early settlers in the east could not travel by water beyond the Fall Line. Instead, they stayed near the Fall Line, building **flour mills** and **sawmills.** Flour mills are factories where wheat is made

125

MILL WHEEL

Mill

Flow of river

Direction wheel turns

Wheel

Post that turns mill machinery

Water empties onto the top of the mill wheel and is caught in bucket-like blades.

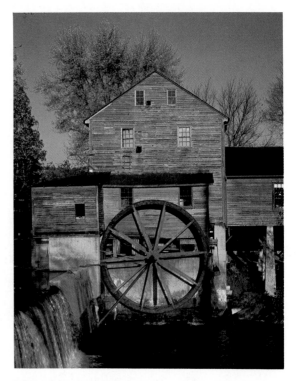

The water's weight moves the mill wheel, which turns wheels in the mill.

into flour. Sawmills are buildings where logs are cut into lumber. The waterfalls provided power for these mills.

In a water-powered mill, the rushing water turned waterwheels. The waterwheels turned other wheels and machines within the mill. Towns grew up rapidly around the mills and factories on the Fall Line. Products from the factories could be shipped on the rivers to cities on the Atlantic Coast.

Today, the waterfalls provide electric power to cities on the Fall Line. Look at the map on the next page. Find the cities on the Fall Line on this map.

Farming on the Coastal Plain

Do you eat peanut butter sandwiches for lunch? Peanuts grow in the southern part of the Coastal Plain. Your jeans and shirts may have been made from the cotton that grows there, too.

Much of the Coastal Plain has rich, **fertile** (FUHR·tuhl) soil. Fertile soil is full of minerals that make plants grow. You may remember that some of the best farmland is near rivers. Many rivers begin in the Appalachian Mountains and flow across the Coastal Plain. On their way to the ocean, the rivers add to the soil

126

the silt carried down from the mountains. The Coastal Plain's climate is good for farming also. Most parts of the plain get plenty of rain. Usually from 30 to 50 inches (about 75 to 125 cm) of rain fall each year.

South of Maryland, the summers are hot and long. In some places, certain crops can be grown all year long. The winters to the south of Maryland are cool and mild.

The climate is different north of Maryland. There the Coastal Plain has colder winters. Summers are warm but shorter. The climate, however, is still somewhat milder than the climate farther west. In the summer, ocean winds help cool the coast. In the winter, ocean winds warm the air over the land.

Coastal Ports

Some of the large cities of the Coastal Plain are ports. One of our busiest ports, New Orleans, Louisiana, lies on the Mississippi River near the Gulf of Mexico. Another large port is New York City, New York. New York City is at the mouth of the Hudson

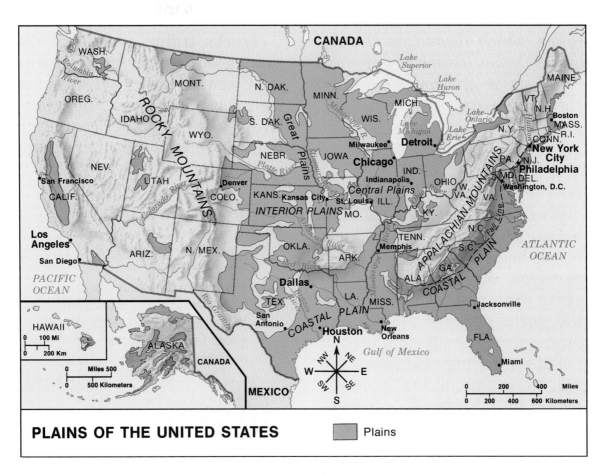

PLAINS OF THE UNITED STATES   Plains

127

New York City is a major world seaport on our country's East Coast. From here, ships carry goods to ports around the world.

River, which flows into the Atlantic Ocean. Hundreds of ships can dock in the harbor around New York City.

Manufacturing and Travel

The cities of the Coastal Plain manufacture many products. Ships bring **raw materials** to ports on the plain. Ships also carry **finished products** from the ports to other places. Raw materials are materials used to make something else. Wool, cotton, wood, and oil are some raw materials. Finished products, such as clothing and furniture, are made from raw materials.

Trucks, trains, and planes also carry goods to and from cities on the Coastal Plain. Highways and railroads criss-cross the plain. Every year, airplanes carry millions of people and many goods into and out of cities.

Reading Check

1. Name three large cities on the Coastal Plain.
2. Name three products grown or made on the Coastal Plain.
3. Why is the Coastal Plain a good farming area? Give two reasons.

Think Beyond How might the United States be different if the Fall Line had not blocked the movement of early settlers?

IN FOCUS

HONEY ISLAND SWAMP

Swamps are an interesting natural feature of the Coastal Plain. Honey Island Swamp is one of the most beautiful and mysterious of these. The swamp is located along the Pearl River in eastern Louisiana and western Mississippi. Narrow waterways in the swamp wind through moss-covered trees and overgrown grasses.

Part of the mystery of Honey Island Swamp lies in its **legends** of pirates, outlaws, and buried treasures. A legend is a story that has come down from earlier times. Parts of the story may or may not be true.

Jean Laffite (lah•FEET) was Louisiana's most famous pirate. He supposedly hid his stolen treasure in Honey Island Swamp. Another pirate, Pierre Rameau (rah•MOH), was known as the King of Honey Island. He also used the swamp as a hiding place for treasures. None of the treasures has been found.

During the 1850s, a gang of outlaws used the swamp as a hideout. They were later captured by police, but the stolen money and goods were never recovered. Some say that they, too, hid their treasures in the swamp.

The real mystery of Honey Island Swamp, however, is in its hidden wilderness. Many unusual animals call the swamp home. Among them are wild pigs, panthers, and nutrias. Nutrias were first brought to the United States from South America in the 1930s. During a flood, they were accidentally released into the wild.

Some people have reported seeing a monster in the swamp. The "monster" is probably an orangutan (uh•RANG•uh•tang), a large ape with long reddish hair. It may have escaped from a circus more than 40 years ago.

Think Beyond Are there any legends about places in or near your community?

Nutrias

129

Look for these important words:

Key Words
- prairie
- feedlots
- drought

Places
- Interior Plains
- Central Plains
- Great Plains

- Corn Belt
- Wheat Belt

Look for answers to these questions:

1. What are the Interior Plains?
2. Why are the Interior Plains good for farming?
3. What is the difference between the Central Plains and the Great Plains?
4. Why are the Central Plains and the Great Plains important to Americans?

2 The Interior Plains

Our largest plains region is "inside" our country. This region, the **Interior Plains,** covers thousands of square miles. The Interior Plains lie between the Appalachian and the Rocky mountains.

There are ten states in the Interior Plains region. Some of our largest and richest farmlands are in these states. They have flat land, fertile soil, and long, sunny summers for growing crops. The Interior Plains provide much of our country's food and meat. Most of the land in this region is used for growing crops and raising animals.

The Interior Plains are two plains really. They are called the **Central Plains** and the **Great Plains.** The Central Plains start in central Ohio. They reach as far west as the middle of Kansas. The Great Plains begin in Kansas, Nebraska, North Dakota, and South Dakota. They end at the Rocky Mountains.

The Central Plains

Long ago, the Central Plains were called the **prairie.** Seas of tall grass and flowers covered the prairie. When the grass died, it rotted and became part of the soil. This made the prairie soil fertile. The fertile soil and the rain of the Central Plains helped new grass and flowers grow.

The tall, waving prairie grass is now almost gone. Settlers came and farmed the rich, fertile soil, planting wide fields of corn. Much of the Central Plains is now called the **Corn Belt.** The map on page 133 shows this area.

Three-fourths of all our corn comes from the Corn Belt. Corn grows better here than anywhere else in the country. Corn, in fact, is a kind of tall grass. Farmers in the Central Plains use more land for corn than for any other crop. They feed most of the corn to the hogs, cattle, and chickens they raise. Only a small part is grown for people to eat.

Today, most prairie land is covered with fields of tall corn.

Early settlers saw the prairie as a "sea of grass," tossing like ocean waves in the wind. Below is some tall prairie grass still found in northern Kansas.

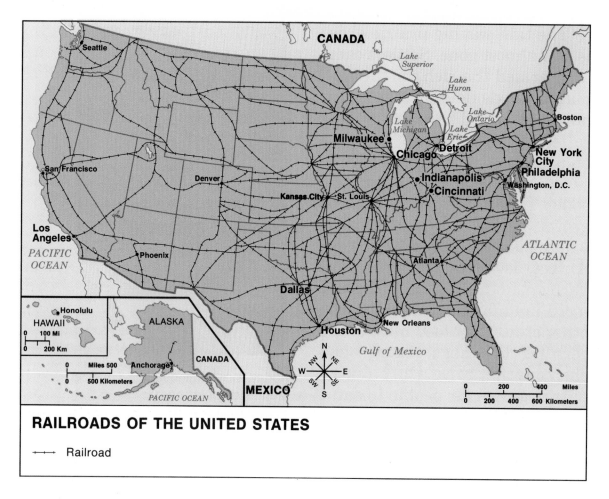

RAILROADS OF THE UNITED STATES

+—+—+ Railroad

Factories and Cities

Not many people live on the farmlands of the Central Plains. Most people live in big cities. Among the largest on these plains are Chicago, Milwaukee, Detroit, Kansas City, St. Louis, Indianapolis, and Cincinnati.

Many kinds of factories are in these cities. Some make tractors and other farm machines. Some manufacture paper, rubber, and steel products.

Your breakfast cornflakes do not come straight from the field either. People in Central Plains cities turn corn into cornflakes and other foods. Factories there also make cereals, cold cuts, and frozen and canned vegetables.

From the factories, trucks, trains, and planes carry products to and from the Central Plains. The broad, flat land of the plains is ideal for highways, airports, and railroads. The map on this page shows the main railroads in the United States. Notice that many railroads meet in the Central Plains region. Chicago, Illinois, is one of the most important transportation centers.

The Great Plains

In contrast to the Central Plains, the Great Plains are a dry, treeless land. In the past, short grass grew on much of the Great Plains. Only short grass could grow because of the lack of rain. Look at the map on page 53. The Great Plains have less than 20 inches (about 50 cm) of precipitation a year. Now look at the Central Plains on the map. These plains have from 20 to 40 inches (about 50 to 100 cm) of precipitation a year. Can you tell why the tall prairie grass grew well?

Short grass still grows in many places on the Great Plains. Herds of cattle on large ranches graze on the grass. Before sending the cattle to market, however, ranchers usually feed their herds grains. The cattle are rounded up and brought to **feedlots.** Feedlots are large pens. In feedlots cattle are fed corn and grain to fatten them for market. When they are ready for market, the cattle are shipped by train or by truck.

Many people in the Great Plains work on ranches and at feedlots. People in Great Plains cities may work at meat-packing plants. Hamburger, steaks, veal, and hot dogs come from beef cattle. Leather, soap, medicines, and fertilizers come from cattle, too.

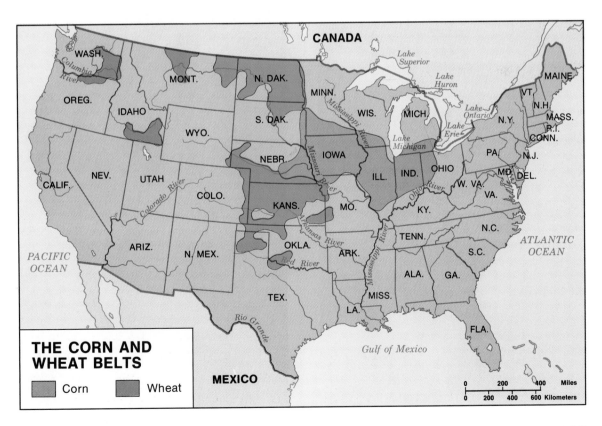

THE CORN AND WHEAT BELTS

Corn   Wheat

Farming on the Great Plains

Wheat is the main crop on most farms in the Great Plains. Wheat grows so well here that the Great Plains are often called "the breadbasket of the world." After corn, wheat is the largest crop in our country. Wheat is in many of the foods we eat each day. Bread, cereal, and noodles are just a few foods made from wheat.

Most of our wheat grows in the area called the **Wheat Belt.** The map on page 133 shows the Wheat Belt of the Great Plains.

The sunny, dry climate of the Great Plains is best for growing wheat. Yet farmers do face problems in this climate. The weather here changes often and suddenly. Huge storms develop quickly on the plains.

One of the farmers' greatest worries is **drought** (DROWT), a time of little or no rainfall. A drought can kill a wheat crop. Droughts are dangerous on the Great Plains for another reason. If the soil gets too dry, it can blow away. These problems make irrigation all the more important.

Cattle weighing up to 900 pounds each (about 400 kg) eat grain in feedlots.

When this wheat is harvested, part of the kernel will be used for animal feed.

134

During a drought, farmers are in danger of losing their farm soil to dust storms. Strong winds can carry the soil for long distances.

Farmers on the Great Plains face other dangers, too. Too much rain can ruin a wheat crop. If winter lasts too long, farmers cannot plant at the right time. If winter comes too soon, it may also kill the wheat. Fire is another danger on the Great Plains.

Farmers on the Great Plains raise much of the food we eat. Their work is difficult, but millions of Americans depend on the crops of the Great Plains. We depend on these crops for jobs as well as for food. Many people besides farmers make a living from food. Some work in the factories that make bread and other food products. Others work at jobs that move food and food products from place to place. Others are butchers, bakers, grocers, and workers in supermarkets and restaurants. What other jobs have to do with food?

Reading Check

1. Where are the Interior Plains?
2. What is the Corn Belt?
3. What are some of the goods manufactured in the Central Plains?

Think Beyond How might a drought in the Great Plains affect people living in other parts of the world?

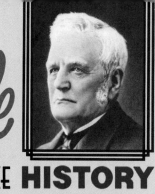

People MAKE HISTORY

John Deere
1804–1886

▶▶▶▶▶▶▶▶▶▶▶▶▶▶▶▶▶▶

John Deere was a **blacksmith** in Grand Detour, Illinois. A blacksmith is a person who works with iron by heating it and hammering it into useful shapes. Deere made shoes for horses and tools for farmers.

One day Deere overheard the farmers saying that they dreaded plowing time. The thick prairie soil in Illinois stuck to the rough surfaces of the iron plows they used. The farmers had to stop plowing every few minutes to clean the dirt from their plows.

Deere wondered if he could make a plow that could clean itself as it worked in the soil. Deere was thinking about this as he walked to the sawmill. When he got there, he noticed something shiny hanging on the wall. It was a steel saw blade. This gave him an idea!

Deere made a steel plow. He believed that the soil would not stick to its shiny surface. He decided to test his plow at a nearby farm.

When Deere arrived at the farm, a noisy crowd of people had already gathered. They wanted to see if the plow would work. The crowd became silent as the steel moved easily through the soil. The plow cleaned and polished itself as it worked!

From then on, Deere spent most of his time making plows. He founded Deere and Company, which manufactured steel plows. Today, the company manufactures all kinds of farming equipment.

Think Beyond   How was the steel plow important to our country's growth?

Deere tests his steel plow.

SKILLS IN ACTION

USING REFERENCE BOOKS

Most of America's grain is grown in the Interior Plains. Suppose you were writing a report about grain. How would you find the information you need?

Your library has different kinds of **reference books** to help you. Reference books are books full of facts. Many reference books are easy to find and use.

Using an Encyclopedia

An **encyclopedia** is a good place to look for information. An encyclopedia has articles on many subjects. The articles are arranged in alphabetical order. For example, an article about *wa*ter comes before an article about *wh*eat.

An encyclopedia can be one large book. More often, though, an encyclopedia has separate books, or volumes.

An encyclopedia may have one volume for each letter of the alphabet. The letters are shown on the books' covers. You would find the article about wheat in volume *W*. What volume would have an article about corn?

Some encyclopedias have guide words instead of letters on

The encyclopedia contains information on nearly every subject.

the covers. For example, a volume might have these guide words: *Virginia–Zurich*. This one volume would have articles that come between *Virginia* and *Zurich* in alphabetical order. You would find an article about wheat in this volume.

Suppose you want to find information about barley. If a volume has the guide words *B-Butter,* would you find information about barley in this volume?

137

main	451	major

main [mān] *adj.* Most important; principal; major.

main·land [mān′land] *n.* The major part of land, not an island or peninsula.

maize [māz] *n.* Corn; the plant or its seeds; also called Indian corn.

maj·es·ty [maj′is·tē] *n.* A title for a king or a queen; a way to address royalty.

Using a Dictionary

Now suppose you are reading about corn. You come across a word you have never seen before. To understand what you are reading, you need to know what the word means.

A **dictionary** can help you learn new words. A dictionary tells you what words mean and how to spell and say them.

Dictionaries list thousands of words in alphabetical order. Above is part of a dictionary page. Find the word *maize* on the page.

The letters in parentheses ( ) tell you how to say the word. The *n.* tells you that *maize* is a noun. A noun is a word that names a person, place, or thing. Next comes the meaning of the word.

You can find words quickly in a dictionary. The top of every page has two guide words. The guide words are the first and last words on the page. The words on a page come between the guide words in alphabetical order. Look at the dictionary page above. What are the guide words on it?

Using an Atlas

Suppose you need to know where grain grows in North America. You can find information about places in an **atlas.** An atlas is a book of maps. Some atlases have road maps. Some atlases have maps of countries around the world. Atlases may include maps showing crops, population, products, and many other things.

Using an atlas as a guide, this student draws a map of the state of Florida.

138

The maps in an atlas are listed in its table of contents. The table of contents also gives the page numbers of the maps.

Here is part of an atlas's table of contents. On what page is a wheat map of the United States?

United States of America
Precipitation 80
Landforms 82
Major Farming Regions 84
Wheat 86
Maize (Corn) 87

Suppose you want to find out where a city or a country is. Many atlases have an index of place names. The index lists the names of places in alphabetical order. It tells on what page of the atlas to find a place. Often, the index will tell where to look on the map grid.

Using an Almanac

Grain grows in certain places year after year. However, the *amount* of grain that grows in a place may change. When you need the latest information, the best reference is an **almanac.** Almanacs are books of facts and figures. They are brought up to date every year.

An almanac often shows information in tables and charts. However, the subjects are not in alphabetical order. The almanac's index will help you find what you are looking for. It lists the subjects in alphabetical order. Look at this index from an almanac:

Wheat —
Amount of 126–127
Prices 112
Seeds 150

Wheat, Amount of tells how much wheat was grown in a year. To find this information, you would look on pages 126 and 127. On what page will you find information about wheat prices?

CHECKING YOUR SKILLS

Answer these questions about reference books.

1. You are using an encyclopedia to find out about sawmills. Would you look in volume *S-Smith* or *Smithsonian-Szechwan?*

2. What are three things a dictionary can tell you about a word?

3. The guide words *Wexford* and *wheedle* appear on a dictionary page. Which words—*well, wheat, world,* or *wharf*—will be found on the page?

4. To find out the price of corn in a recent year, which kind of reference book would you use?

CHAPTER 6 REVIEW

Thinking Back

- The Coastal Plain stretches along the Atlantic Coast to the Gulf of Mexico. This low, flat area has many rivers, fertile soil, a good climate for farming, and large cities and ports.

- Along the Coastal Plain's western edge is the Fall Line. Towns grew rapidly here because waterfalls provided power for mills. Products also could be shipped easily downstream to markets.

- The Interior Plains lie between the Appalachian and Rocky mountains. The Central Plains and the Great Plains make up the Interior Plains. Most people in the Central Plains live in large cities.

- The Central Plains, once called the prairie, now provide most of our corn. The dry, treeless land of the Great Plains is used for raising cattle and growing wheat. This area is often called "the breadbasket of the world."

Check for Understanding

Using Words

Copy the words below. Write the meaning of each word.

1. **fertile**
2. **raw materials**
3. **prairie**
4. **feedlots**
5. **drought**

Reviewing Facts

1. How were waterfalls along the Fall Line important to our country's early settlers?
2. What are two of our country's largest coastal ports?
3. What is the difference between a raw material and a finished product? Give an example of each.
4. Why are plains generally good areas for farming?
5. What two plains areas make up the Interior Plains?
6. What is the corn grown in the Central Plains used for?
7. How are goods shipped to and from our plains regions? Name two ways.
8. What are some products made from beef cattle?
9. Name at least two problems that farmers have on the Great Plains.
10. Name at least three jobs that have to do with food.

Thinking Critically

1. Why are cities on plains important? How do people in cities on the plains depend on ranchers and farmers?
2. What are some of the crops you would choose to grow if you owned farmland on the Coastal Plain? Why?
3. How is the climate of the Coastal Plain different from the climate of the Interior Plains? Why do the Great Plains generally receive less precipitation than the Central Plains?

Writing About It

Imagine that you own a store that sells only items made from products of the Interior Plains. List some items your store would sell. Then write a colorful description about one item. Be sure to tell how the item can be used.

Practicing Study Skills

Using Reference Books

Which kind of reference book would you use to find out each of these?

a. last year's total rainfall in Omaha, Nebraska
b. what *prairie* means
c. how beef cattle are raised
d. where sheep are raised
e. how to say *fertile*
f. how corn was grown long ago

On Your Own

Social Studies at Home

Ask a family member to help you read the labels on packages of food in your home. Look for the ways in which corn or a corn product is used. On a piece of paper, list all foods that contain corn or a corn product. Then discuss with your family why America grows so much corn.

Read More About It

Amigo by Byrd Baylor Schweitzer. Macmillan. In this book a boy tries to tame a prairie dog.

Corn Is Maize: The Gift of the Indians by Aliki. T. Y. Crowell. This book provides interesting information about the important food source Indians called *maize*.

Joel: Growing Up a Farm Man by Patricia Demuth. Dodd, Mead. In this book, 13-year-old Joel Holland tells about his life working on a farm in Illinois.

Owl and the Prairie Dog by Berniece Freschet. Charles Scribner's. This nonfiction story will teach you more about two animals that live on the prairie.

Wheat, the Golden Harvest by Dorothy Hinshaw. Patent, Dodd, Mead. This book tells the complete story of wheat.

Animals in Our Country

Wild turkeys, once found across North America, still live in wilderness areas.

When America was a wilderness, herds of animals roamed free. Many kinds of wildlife filled the forests and rivers.

Some, like the deer, black bear, and beaver, still live in many places. Others, like the buffalo, were almost killed off as people settled in America. Today there are few grizzly bears or condors, our largest bird. These animals live in lonely places far from towns and cities.

Yet each region of our country is still home to many animals. Some of you have seen squirrels, raccoons, deer, and hawks. A lucky few have seen the bighorn sheep of the Rocky Mountains. On these pages are a few of the unusual animals of our country.

The Alligator

How would you like to find an alligator in your backyard? That

At one time large buffalo roamed over the Great Plains.
▼

142

has happened to people in Florida. Alligators live in swamps and rivers in the southern states. Many swamps are being drained to make way for houses and farms. When alligators lose their homes, they sometimes turn up in funny places.

Alligators are related to snakes and lizards. An alligator floating in water looks like a bumpy, greenish-gray or black log. All you can see is the top of the alligator's head.

Alligator babies are black and yellow when they hatch from their eggs. They are only 9 inches (about 23 cm) long. They may be 12 feet (about 4 m) long when they grow up.

Alligators eat fish, frogs, raccoons, snakes, and birds. They only hurt people who get too close to them. Alligators stay away from people when they can.

The Bald Eagle

The fierce-looking bald eagle is a symbol of our country's freedom. Yet the bald eagle is not as free as it used to be.

▲ Alligators sometimes lie on river banks or hide in their dens.

As a symbol of our country, the bald eagle is pictured on United States money. What bills or coins picture the eagle? ▼

Bald eagles live near lakes, rivers, or the sea. They build their nests in the tops of tall trees. In many places the trees have been cut down. Water pollution has killed fish that the eagles eat. Water pollution has made other fish poisonous to the birds. Now the bald eagle is rare in most states.

The bald eagle is not really bald. It has white feathers on its head and tail. The rest of its feathers are brown. The wings of the bald eagle spread seven feet (about 2 m) across. The bald eagle is the second-largest American bird.

Bald eagles choose a partner for life. They come back to the same nest each year to raise a new eagle chick. Every year the parent eagles add more grass and twigs to their nest. The nest can grow very large. One eagle's nest weighed two tons!

The Black Bear

A family is camping in a national park. They see a black bear nearby. The bear sits up on its back legs. It seems to be begging for food.

"Oh, the bear is so cute!" a boy says. "Can I feed it? Can I pet it?"

◀ Black bears are better left alone.

The correct answer is no! Black bears may look cute, but they are not pets. They are wild animals. Most black bears will not look for a fight. Yet they can be quick, strong, and dangerous.

Black bears are the most common bears in the United States. They live in the mountains and large forests of our country. They eat mostly berries, roots, acorns, and grass. They may also eat fish, birds, and insects. For a special treat, a bear sometimes steals honey from a bee's nest.

▶ **Rattlesnakes usually rest during the day and search for food at night.**

The Rattlesnake

The rattlesnake gets information about the world around it in interesting ways. It can smell with its forked tongue. It can sense heat with two pits below its eyes.

A rattlesnake has two long front teeth called fangs. These fangs are hollow. When the snake bites an animal, poison flows through the fangs into the animal's body.

The rattlesnake gets its name from a rattle on its tail. When angry or afraid, the snake shakes this rattle. It makes a dry, hissing kind of sound.

The Caribou

The caribou (KAR•uh•boo), a North American reindeer, lives in Alaska. It is well fitted for its cold home. Its feet have broad, split hooves that help it walk on snow. Its brown coat is thick and warm.

Few animals can live in the plains of northern Alaska. The caribou is one of the animals that can. In the plains of northern Alaska, the ground is frozen all year. In spring the top layer thaws just enough for grasses and small bushes to grow. The caribou feeds on these plants.

As winter gradually approaches, herds of caribou travel hundreds of miles south. They are going to the pine forests. There they use their antlers to dig beneath the snow for food. In spring they will return to the Alaskan plains.

People in Alaska still hunt caribou for food and for hides.

▼

Unit Review

Words to Remember

Copy the sentences below. Fill in the blanks with the correct words from the list.

conservation	prairie
erosion	range
fertilizers	raw materials
industries	transportation
port	water power

1. The wearing away of land is called _____ .

2. Dams help make _____ _____ .

3. New Orleans, Louisiana, is a large _____ .

4. Coal mining and steel manufacturing are important _____ .

5. Ships, trains, and planes are kinds of _____ .

6. Cattle in the mountain regions graze on the _____ .

7. Protecting our natural resources is _____ .

8. _____ are materials that help plants to grow.

9. Wool, cotton, wood, and oil are kinds of _____ _____ .

10. Tall _____ grass and flowers at one time covered the Central Plains.

Focus on Main Ideas

1. Where are most large cities? From the following list, pick two answers. Then explain your choices.
   a. mountain regions
   b. desert regions
   c. plains regions
   d. near rivers

2. Name two ways in which people use the following.
   a. rivers
   b. mountains
   c. deserts
   d. plains

3. Why are port cities generally good places for manufacturing? Give two reasons.

4. How does erosion change mountains and deserts?

5. In what regions are our largest forests?

6. Why is irrigation important to desert regions?

7. How is the climate of desert regions in our country different from the climate of the Coastal Plain?

8. Why are so many cattle raised in the Great Plains?

9. What two large crops are grown in the United States? In which

147

two plains are most of these crops grown?

10. Why is weather important to farmers on the Great Plains?

Think/Write

Imagine that you are the captain of a coal barge that travels on the Ohio River. Write seven entries in your daily log. Be sure to discuss the ports where you load and unload material.

Activities

1. Art/Making a Model Make a model of a desert, mountain, or plains region in a shoebox. Use colored paper, rocks, sand, and clay to show the region's important features.

2. Writing/Making a List Deserts, plains, and mountains have natural resources that make each place special. Make a list of some natural resources that may be found in each region. Then tell why these resources are important.

Skills Review

1. Using Elevation Maps Use the map to answer these questions.

   a. Is this island in the Northern or Southern Hemisphere?

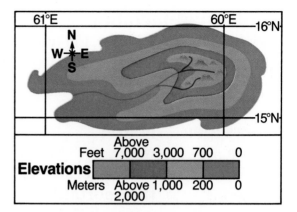

b. Does the river in the map flow from east to west or from west to east? How can you tell?

c. Which line of longitude passes near the mountains?

d. Which line of latitude passes near the island's northern coast?

e. What is the highest elevation in the mountains?

2. Using Cross-Section Diagrams Use the cross section to answer these questions.

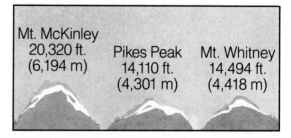

a. What is the elevation of Pikes Peak?

b. What is the name of the highest mountain shown here? What is its elevation?

In this unit you have explored our country's main natural regions—mountains, deserts, and plains. You have learned about rivers, climates, and landforms that are found in these regions. Now learn more about your own state's land.

Learning About Geography

1. Look at a map of your state. Look for mountains, deserts, plains, and large rivers. Next, draw a large outline map of your state. Draw the mountains and rivers you have found and label them. Use different colors to show deserts or plains.

Learning About Using Resources

2. In an atlas or encyclopedia, find a resource and product map that shows your state. Then list the ways people in your state use the land and water. Make up symbols to show how people use resources. For example, a fish can stand for fishing. A tree can stand for logging. Draw these symbols on an outline map of your state.

Learning Facts About Your State

3. Look at "Facts About the States" in the back of your textbook. Find the information about your state. Make a chart or poster showing some of the information. If you wish, draw pictures of your state bird, flower, and flag.

Learning About State and National Parks

4. Use an encyclopedia or an atlas to find out about a park in your state. What kinds of landforms are in the park? What are people doing to keep the park beautiful? If you have visited the park, tell your class about it.

Learning About Recreation

5. Make a poster that shows a popular outdoor activity in your state. Draw pictures or cut out pictures from old magazines to illustrate your poster. Then write a short paragraph about this activity. How does the land in your state make this activity possible?

UNIT

3

Regions of the United States

Some Natural Features of the United States by Region

Northeast		Southeast		Great Lakes States	
Acadia	Mount Marcy	Chimney Rock	Mount Mitchell	Apostle Islands	Mesabi Range
National Park	Mount Snow	Cumberland Gap	Okefenokee	Eagle Mountain	Pictured Rocks
Cape Cod	Mount	Everglades	Swamp	High Falls	Pipestone
Lake Placid	Washington	Florida Keys	Russell Cave	Indiana Dunes	Monument
Long Island	Niagara Falls	Mammoth Cave	Stone Mountain	Kelleys Island	Wisconsin Dells

*E*very state has different kinds of land and natural resources. Where people live and what they do for a living often depends on the land and the natural resources of their state.

In this unit our 50 states are divided into seven regions. They are the Northeast, the Southeast, the Great Lakes states, the Plains states, the Southwest, the Mountain states, and the Pacific states. As you read, you will learn about the people who lived in each of the regions long ago. You will see, too, how people make a living in these regions today.

Think Beyond How do workers in your state depend on land and natural resources?

Plains States	Southwest		Mountain States	Pacific States	
Agate	Big Thicket	Guadalupe	Monument Valley	Mauna Kea	Muir Woods
Fossil Beds	Preserve	Mountains	Old Faithful	Mount Hood	Oregon Caves
Badlands	Carlsbad	Kitt Peak	Pikes Peak	Mount Rainier	Redwood
Jewel Cave	Caverns	Painted Desert	Wind River	Mount	National Park
Writing Rock	Grand Canyon	Petrified Forest	Canyon	St. Helens	Waimea Canyon

The Northeast

"Heaven and earth never agreed better to frame a place for mans habitation. . . . Here are mountaines, hils, plaines, valleyes, rivers and brookes, all running most pleasantly into a faire Bay compassed but for the mouth with fruitfull and delightsome land."

—Captain John Smith describing the landscape of the Northeast during his travels there in 1616

Look for these important words:

Key Words
- glaciers
- river valley
- bays
- humid
- needleleaf
- broadleaf
- ore

Places
- Coastal Plain
- Appalachian Mountains
- Hudson River
- New York City
- New York State Barge Canal System
- Connecticut River

- Delaware River
- Massachusetts Bay
- Delaware Bay
- Chesapeake Bay

Look for answers to these questions:
1. What are major landforms of the Northeast?
2. Why are waterways important here?
3. How is the climate in the Northeast different from the rest of the country?
4. What are the important natural resources of this region?

1 The Land and Its Resources

The Northeast is the smallest region in the United States. Yet it is very crowded. It has many large cities.

Most people in the Northeast live on the **Coastal Plain,** the flat land next to the Atlantic Ocean. The coast there has many large cities with busy harbors. A string of cities runs along the coast from Boston, Massachusetts, to Washington, D.C.

To the west of the Coastal Plain lie the **Appalachian Mountains.** These low mountains cover much of the Northeast region. Among the mountains are rolling hills and green valleys. Large forests cover the mountain slopes in nearly every part of the Northeast.

Land features of the Northeast were formed long ago when the climate turned very cold. **Glaciers** (GLAY•shurz) covered the northern part of this region then. Glaciers are large masses of ice that move slowly. The glaciers scraped away soil and wore down the Appalachian Mountains. They made deep cuts in the land. Later the climate warmed. When the glaciers melted, the cuts filled with water. Today they are rivers and lakes.

Bodies of Water

The **Hudson River** is one of the most important rivers in the Northeast. At its mouth the Hudson flows into the Atlantic Ocean. It forms a large natural harbor. **New York City,** our country's largest city, has grown up around this harbor. The harbor has helped make New York City one of our leading ports.

Starting at the mouth of the Hudson River, a ship can travel

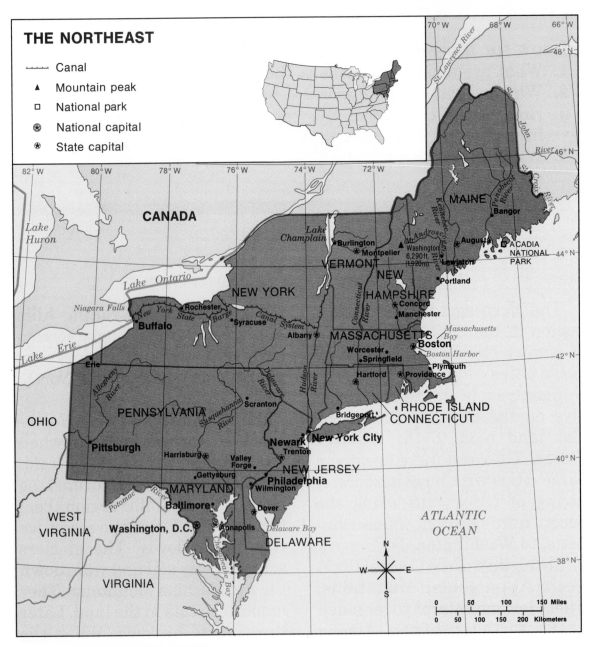

THE NORTHEAST

- ----- Canal
- ▲ Mountain peak
- ▫ National park
- ⊛ National capital
- ✳ State capital

from New York City to the Great Lakes. First the ship moves north up the Hudson River. At Albany, New York, it turns west. There it enters the **New York State Barge Canal System.** The system is made up of four canals built to move freight across New York. At the end of these canals, the ship reaches Lake Erie. From Lake Erie the ship can go through the other Great Lakes. It can go all the way west to Minnesota!

Another important river in the Northeast is the **Connecticut River.** Some of Connecticut's best farmland lies in the Connecticut River Valley. A **river valley** is the low land through which a river flows.

Farther south the **Delaware River** is an important transportation route for goods of all kinds. The city of Philadelphia (fil•uh•DEL•fee•uh), Pennsylvania, is on the Delaware River.

Several large **bays** lie along the coast of the Northeast. A bay is water partly surrounded by land. **Massachusetts Bay, Delaware Bay,** and **Chesapeake Bay** lead to major ports.

HISTORY CONNECTION

In the early 1700s the people of Philadelphia, Pennsylvania, often gathered along the Delaware River waterfront to watch sailing ships arrive. This was an exciting event for them. In addition to needed goods, the ships often brought news from other parts of the world.

Over time, railroads and trucks started bringing goods to the city, and the waterfront became less important. Many buildings stood empty. Others were unsafe or in need of repair.

The city of Philadelphia decided to **restore,** or rebuild, its waterfront. Apartments, a hotel, a marina, and a museum were built. New restaurants

and stores were opened. Once again, the Philadelphia waterfront is an exciting place to visit.

"There's a house *somewhere* under all this snow!" Northeast snowstorms bring a few problems for some people.

Climate

In some parts of our country the climate does not change much all year. In most of the Northeast it really does change! The four seasons are quite different from one another.

Most of the region has cold, snowy winters. Parts of New York State, for example, have heavy snows. Cities like Buffalo and Syracuse (SIR•uh•kyoos) may get more than 100 inches (254 cm) a year.

The land comes to life in spring. Trees bud and flowers bloom. Summers are warm and **humid** (HYOO•mid). Humid air has a lot of moisture in it. Autumn brings cool, crisp days to the region. Leaves turn gold, orange, and red. Everywhere the trees blaze with color.

Natural Resources

Water is one of the most valuable resources of the Northeast. The region's farms, industries, and large cities use great amounts of fresh water. The entire region gets enough rain and snow to meet its needs, however.

The Atlantic Ocean is another valuable water resource. Millions of fish are caught along the

156

coast each year. Much of this catch is sold all over the United States.

Great forests stretched across the Northeast long ago. Some of that great forestland remains today. These forests are made up of **needleleaf** and **broadleaf** trees. All needleleaf trees have long, sharp leaves like needles. The leaves often stay green all year long. Cedar and pine are two kinds of needleleaf trees.

Broadleaf trees have wide, flat leaves. They often shed their leaves in fall. Oak and maple are two kinds of broadleaf trees.

Good soil is a natural resource of the region's southern part. Farmers grow many kinds of crops in its sandy soil.

The forests that cover much of Vermont show off their fall colors—yellow for birches, bright red for maple trees.

Niagara Falls is between Canada and New York. Though most famous for its falls, the Niagara River is also a source of electric power.

The most important fuel resource in the Northeast is coal. Only Pennsylvania has great amounts of it. Most coal is used for making electricity. It also goes to steel mills. Steel is made by heating coal, limestone, and iron **ore** (OHR). Ore is rock that has a mineral in it.

Reading Check

1. Where do most people in the Northeast live?
2. Why is the Atlantic Ocean an important natural resource in the Northeast?
3. Which part of the Northeast has good farmland?

Think Beyond Why is the New York State Barge Canal System important to your family and to all Americans?

? SKILLS IN ACTION

IDENTIFYING CAUSE AND EFFECT

Imagine that you have turned on the water in your bathtub to take a nice warm bath. Just after you have turned on the water, a friend rings your doorbell. You hurry to the door. Soon you and your friend are busy talking. The bathtub is forgotten. You are reminded of it when you see water running from beneath the door.

Something that makes something else happen is a **cause.** What happens as a result is the **effect.** Forgetting to turn off the water before answering the doorbell is the cause of the water

overflowing. The flood in your house is the effect of your forgetting to turn off the water.

We can see cause and effect in nature as well as in daily life. A long period without rain is a cause that can have many effects. Crops might fail. Forest fires may start. Streams and lakes may dry up. People may be forced to move.

When you are reading, word clues may help you recognize causes or effects. Such word clues include *because, as a result of,* and *therefore.*

You have read that glaciers once covered much of the Northeast region. The cause was a change in climate. The effect was the large masses of ice that moved over the land.

Glaciers may be formed when more snow falls during the winter than melts during the summer. Millions of years ago during the Ice Age, summer temperatures in what is now Canada were cooler than they are now. Because of that, some of the snow that fell during the winter remained on the ground throughout the summer.

Year after year the snow piled up. Its great weight caused the

Glacial cirque, or basin

158

snow on the bottom to turn to ice. As a result, the great ice sheets began to move. They moved in every direction, including into the Northeast region.

As the glaciers moved, they carried rocks along their icy bottoms. These rocks cut into the land. The glaciers made valleys wider and deeper. They sliced off the tops of hills and mountains. They plowed away the soil, blocked rivers, and filled in lakes.

Very slowly the climate began to change. Summers became warmer. Winters were shorter and not so bitterly cold. More snow melted than fell during the winter. For these reasons the glaciers began to melt.

Great floods of water, carrying rocks and soil, spread out in front of the melting ice. As a result, some of the water filled valleys that the glaciers had carved, making new lakes and rivers. Low, rocky hills were formed along the edges of the melting glaciers. Large rocks were dropped on the land as the ice slowly retreated.

The landscape of the Northeast region was totally changed by the Ice Age. The rounded mountains and hills show these past events. So do the rocky soil and many lakes. All are the effects of a cause—the changing of temperature—that happened so very long ago.

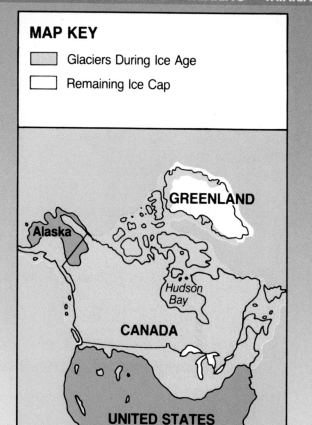

MAP KEY

▭ Glaciers During Ice Age

▭ Remaining Ice Cap

GREENLAND

Alaska

Hudson Bay

CANADA

UNITED STATES

CHECKING YOUR SKILLS

Use the paragraphs about glaciers to answer these questions about *cause* and *effect*.

1. What are some word clues in the paragraphs that signal cause and effect?

2. What caused glaciers to form?

3. How did glaciers affect the land as they moved?

4. What caused the glaciers to retreat?

5. How was the landscape of the Northeast affected by the retreating glaciers?

159

Look for these important words:

Key Words
- *Mayflower*
- history
- colonies
- American Revolution

People
- Squanto
- Benjamin Franklin

Places
- Plymouth
- New England

Look for answers to these questions:
1. What were some of the hardships the Pilgrims faced?
2. Why was Benjamin Franklin important to our country?
3. In what way did America change during Benjamin Franklin's life?

2 The Northeast Long Ago

It is a foggy morning in 1620. The tired travelers find a place to land their boat. They are on the rocky shores of what is now called Massachusetts. The travelers call themselves Pilgrims. Their ship is the **Mayflower.**

The Pilgrims arrived in America in November. Though they built a settlement, which they called **Plymouth** (PLIM•uhth), their first winter was very hard. The Pilgrims had little food. They had never felt such bitter cold. About half of the Pilgrims died within the first year.

Help came in the spring. An Indian named **Squanto** came to Plymouth. Squanto taught the Pilgrims how to live in the new land. He taught them how to grow corn and beans. He showed them how to hunt wild animals. None of the Pilgrims might have lived without Squanto's help.

The Pilgrims are important in America's past, or **history.** They were the first Europeans to settle in the Northeast. The Pilgrims came from England to find religious freedom in America.

Soon other people from Europe came to join them. The nearby town of Boston began to grow. Other towns grew up all over the Northeast. Many of them, like

With Squanto's help, the Pilgrims had their first successful harvest.
They invited the Indians to a feast that became the first Thanksgiving.

Boston, grew into cities. Most of the settlers were from England, as the Pilgrims were. They settled in the present-day states of Connecticut, Massachusetts, Maine, New Hampshire, Vermont, and Rhode Island. The English settlers called this area **New England.** Today we often call these states by this name.

By 1750 many more people lived along the Atlantic coast. New England continued to grow. People started new settlements as far south as Georgia. England ruled these settlements as 13 **colonies** (KAHL•uh•neez). Colonies are places that are ruled by another country.

Ben Franklin's America

In 1723 a 17-year-old boy set out from his home in Boston. Young **Benjamin Franklin** had decided to go to Philadelphia, Pennsylvania. He hoped to make his fortune there. When he arrived in Philadelphia, Ben had one dollar in his pocket.

Ben found a job working for a printer. He worked so hard that he soon had enough money to open his own printing shop. He wrote and printed a popular book called *Poor Richard's Almanac.* An almanac is a book that is printed once a year. People enjoyed the advice, news, and many wise sayings in *Poor Richard's*

Almanac. Here are two sayings from the *Almanac:*

> Don't throw stones at your neighbors, if your own windows are glass.

> When the well's dry, we know the worth of water.

Besides being a printer and an author, Franklin was an inventor. One of his inventions was the Franklin stove. His stove was made of iron and burned wood. It heated homes better than open fireplaces. Another of his inventions was bifocals.

Franklin was always thinking of new ideas and new ways of doing things. He showed that lightning was a form of electricity. He started Philadelphia's first fire department and its first hospital.

America began to change in important ways as Franklin got older. People in the colonies were beginning to draw away from England. Franklin tried to get the 13 colonies to work together more closely.

The English passed laws to make the colonies pay new taxes. Many people refused to pay. They believed the English were ignoring their rights. The two sides were close to war.

The **American Revolution** (rev•uh•LOO•shuhn) began when Ben Franklin was in his seventies. A revolution is a large, sudden change in government and in people's lives. Americans began to fight for freedom from English rule. Franklin was one of the leaders in the American Revolution. He served his country until the day he died. Ben Franklin was then 84.

Ben Franklin served our country both during and after the American Revolution.

Reading Check

1. Who were the Pilgrims? Why did they come to America?
2. How did Squanto help them?
3. What are colonies?

Think Beyond How do you know that freedom has always been important to Americans?

162

IN FOCUS

It is 1770. England rules 13 colonies in America. Few settlers have crossed the Appalachian Mountains. Yet many people from the colonies have already sailed to ports in Europe, South America, and Africa.

These brave sailors crossed the seas in sturdy little ships called brigs. The ships came from New England. The seas of the world were their highways. Brigs took American goods to other countries. They brought back goods people in the colonies needed.

Sugar, tea, clothing, and iron were just some of the goods they carried. Sometimes they even carried cuckoo clocks. One New Englander got rich shipping blocks of ice to the West Indies.

Some New England boys became sailors when they were only 11 years old. Some later became captains of their own ships.

A captain had to be a good sailor, of course, but he also needed many other skills. He was the ship's doctor. He had to be able to **navigate,** or find his way, on the sea. He had to

control his crew. On the seas the captain's word was law.

When a captain returned from a long voyage, he brought treasures for his house. Seashells, precious gems, carved chests, and silk were favorite choices. Some New England families still own these treasures brought back from many distant lands.

Brigs were also used as fighting ships during the American Revolution. The ships remained popular well into the 1800s.

Think Beyond How do you think people in the colonies felt when they saw a brig approaching? Explain why you think they might have felt that way.

The brig *Eliza of Providence*

163

SKILLS IN ACTION

USING A TIMELINE

A **timeline** shows the important events of a certain period of time. The events are marked in order on the timeline. The timeline below shows some important events in Theresa Sastre's life.

This timeline covers ten years in Theresa's life. Notice the marks on the line. The space between two marks is equal to one year. The dates on the left are the earliest. The dates on the right come later. The first year on this timeline is 1980, the year Theresa was born.

A timeline helps you see the order in which events happened. The first event on this timeline is Theresa's birth. Look to the right of that event. It shows the next important thing that happened in Theresa's life. It was the birth of her brother in June 1983. What was the next important event? When did it happen?

You may want to know how many years passed between two events. A timeline can help you figure this out. Let's find out the time between Theresa's birth and her family's move to Delaware. The timeline shows that she was born in 1980. The family moved in 1987. Subtract 1980 from 1987. The difference is seven. Theresa's family moved about seven years after she was born.

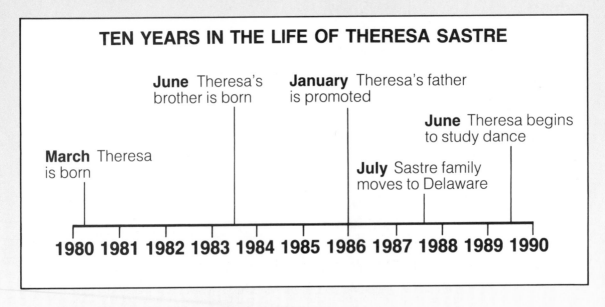

TEN YEARS IN THE LIFE OF THERESA SASTRE

June Theresa's brother is born

January Theresa's father is promoted

June Theresa begins to study dance

March Theresa is born

July Sastre family moves to Delaware

1980 1981 1982 1983 1984 1985 1986 1987 1988 1989 1990

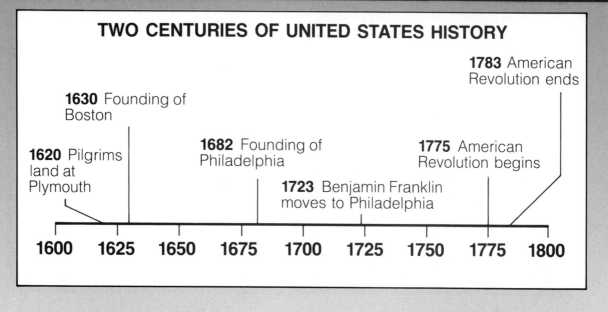

Our Country's History on a Timeline

A timeline can also show a period in history. Of course, many years must be shown on the line. This timeline shows some important events in United States history.

Look to the left of the timeline. The timeline begins with the year 1600. Look to the right of the timeline. What is the last year shown?

This timeline is different from Theresa's timeline. It does not show every year. Instead the marks are 25 years apart. The first year is 1600. The second year is 1625. What is the next year shown?

This timeline shows 200 years. A period of 100 years is called a **century** (SEN•chuh•ree). Thus, this timeline shows two centuries. You might also say that it shows the 1600s and the 1700s. This is just another way in which people talk about centuries. The 1600s are the years from 1600 to 1699. The 1700s are the years from 1700 to 1799.

You read this timeline just as you read Theresa's timeline. The earliest event is the Pilgrims' landing at Plymouth. This event took place in 1620. What is the next event shown?

CHECKING YOUR SKILLS

Use the history timeline to answer these questions.

1. What event took place between 1675 and 1700?

2. Was Philadelphia founded before or after Boston?

3. What event came after Ben Franklin's move to Philadelphia?

4. When did the American Revolution begin? When did it end?

165

Look for these important words:

Key Words
- trawler
- food processing

- poultry
- trade

Places
- United Nations

Look for answers to these questions:
1. What jobs might people have in the Northeast?
2. Why is good transportation important for manufacturing?
3. Why do people in the Northeast have such different backgrounds?

3

The Northeast Today

In some ways the Northeast has not changed all that much since the days of Ben Franklin. Buildings from the 1700s still stand in many places. Many of the newer buildings are made to look like the older colonial ones. People of the Northeast still even work at some of the same jobs.

Fishing

In Ben Franklin's day many people earned their living by fishing. Today many Northeasterners still get food from the sea. Millions of pounds of lobsters, oysters, clams, cod, and other fish are caught in the Atlantic Ocean.

A day aboard a **trawler** (TRAW•luhr), or fishing boat,

Some of the best lobsters in the world come from the waters of the Northeast.

New England supplies much of the nation's cod, flounder, haddock, herring, and scallops. A day's catch is often sold at auction.

starts early in the morning. The boat leaves the harbor. The captain and crew find a good fishing spot. They lower a huge net into the water and tie the net's long ropes to the boat. The boat drags the net along the bottom of the ocean. Fish such as cod or herring swim into the net.

When the net is full, a machine pulls it up. The crew quickly put the fish in refrigerators so the fish stay fresh.

The day's catch is sold to markets near the harbor. Most of the fish is canned or frozen. Factories in Boston and other cities freeze, cook, or can fish, as well as other foods. **Food processing** (PRAHS•uhs•ing) is therefore important, too. After the fish is canned or frozen, markets sell it to stores all over the United States.

Farming

Today most people in the Northeast live in cities. Yet farming is still important to the region. Dairy products, such as milk, cheese, and eggs, come from all the states of the Northeast. Fruits and vegetables grow in New York, New Jersey, Pennsylvania, Maryland, and Delaware.

167

Farmers in these states also raise cattle and **poultry** (POHL•tree). Chickens and turkeys are the main kinds of poultry.

Beyond New York, in the New England states, the stony soil and colder climate make it hard to grow most crops. Unlike the rest of the Northeast, New England has short summers and sudden cold weather. Many farmers raise dairy cows here.

Some Northeastern states grow special crops. New Jersey, the "Garden State," is known for tomatoes. Do you eat cranberries at Thanksgiving? They may come from Massachusetts, the leading cranberry grower. Maple syrup is one of Vermont's main products. Maine is famous for its potatoes. Do you like grape juice? Much of it comes from New York, a leading grower of grapes.

Manufacturing

The Northeast is an important manufacturing area for several reasons. It has coal for making steel and electricity. It has plenty of water. It has excellent

Duck, chicken, and turkey farms in the Northeast supply poultry for many customers in our country.

Workers drive metal spouts into sugar maples and collect the sap in buckets. The sap is boiled into maple syrup.

168

transportation for carrying goods from place to place. The Northeast also has many people there who make or buy these goods.

Look around your classroom and you may see some products made in the Northeast. Your paper may come from Maine, the "Pine Tree State." The steel in your desk may come from Pennsylvania. Some of your books may have been written in Massachusetts. Your clothing may have been made in New York. Perhaps the American flag was made in New Jersey, home of our country's largest flag factory.

Harbors on the Delaware River, like this one in Philadelphia, handle nearly 3,000 ships a year.

Trade and Transportation

The Northeast is an important center of **trade.** Trade is the buying and selling of goods. Each year tons of goods are bought and sold in the Northeast's cities. Goods leave the Northeast's ports for all parts of the world. Goods from other countries also arrive in these cities.

In order to carry on trade, the Northeast must have good transportation. You may already know that the region's rivers are important transportation routes. Boston, New York City, Philadelphia, and Baltimore, Maryland, are a few of the many port cities that make trade easy. Railroads, highways, and airports are also important for trade.

People of the Northeast Today

People from all over the world have settled in our country. The Northeast is a mix of all these people. They come from many different backgrounds. Many people can trace their ancestors to some of the first settlers from England. Many others have ancestors from Ireland, Italy, Poland, and Germany. People with Latin American, African, and Asian backgrounds have also settled in the Northeast region.

169

People from other states and other countries live, work, and play in the cities of the Northeast.

You will find a variety of these people in the northeastern cities, especially a large city like New York City. More people live in New York City than in any other American city. There you can hear people speaking many languages besides English. Newsstands sell newspapers in different languages. Neighborhood grocery stores sell foods people enjoyed in the "old country." Many people in these neighborhoods also celebrate the holidays of other countries as well as such American holidays as the Fourth of July.

New York City has a special building, the **United Nations.** There people meet to talk and settle problems among their nations.

Reading Check

1. Name three foods that come from the Northeast.
2. Name three manufactured goods that come from the Northeast.
3. Why is the Northeast an important manufacturing region? Give three reasons.

Think Beyond What benefits in your life come from having a great mix of people in the United States?

170

People MAKE HISTORY

Eleanor Roosevelt
1884–1962

▶▶▶▶▶▶▶▶▶▶▶▶▶▶▶▶

Eleanor Roosevelt was born into a wealthy New York family. When she was young, her cousins teased her by calling her "ugly duckling." They poked fun at her shyness.

When Eleanor was eight, her mother became ill. Eleanor helped with her care. Later Eleanor remembered that "feeling that I was useful was perhaps the greatest joy I experienced."

Eleanor attended school in England. She did well in her studies and gained confidence. When Eleanor returned home, she went into the poor neighborhoods of New York City and taught children dancing.

Eleanor met and married Franklin Delano Roosevelt, a distant cousin. Franklin began a career in politics. Then a disease called polio paralyzed his legs.

Franklin, however, did not give up politics. He asked Eleanor to travel to places he was unable to visit. With Eleanor's help, Franklin became President of the United States. As First Lady,

Eleanor worked to see that all Americans were treated fairly and equally.

In 1945 Eleanor was asked to represent our country in the United Nations. There she worked to help the people of the world. She was reappointed to the United Nations in 1961. As she entered the meeting hall, a hush fell over the room. One by one the delegates stood to applaud her. Eleanor Roosevelt had become the "First Lady of the World."

Think Beyond Why do you think it is important for people to feel useful?

171

CHAPTER 7 REVIEW

Thinking Back

- The Northeast is a small region with many large cities.

- The Coastal Plain and the Appalachian Mountains are the Northeast's major landforms. Major waterways include the Hudson, Delaware, and Connecticut rivers and the New York State Barge Canal System.

- The Northeast has four distinct seasons. The region's many natural resources include water, forests, good soil, and coal.

- The first Europeans to settle in the Northeast were the Pilgrims.

They came to America to find religious freedom. Indians taught the Pilgrims how to live in the new land.

- Benjamin Franklin was a printer, inventor, and author. He was also an important leader of the American Revolution.

- Many people in the Northeast work in fishing, farming, and manufacturing. The Northeast is also an important center of trade.

- People in the Northeast have different backgrounds because immigrants from many countries settled there.

Check for Understanding

Using Words

Use the following words in sentences. Write a sentence for each word. Make sure that your sentence explains the meaning of the word.

1. bays
2. colonies
3. glaciers
4. humid
5. ore

Reviewing Facts

1. Why did many cities grow up on the Coastal Plain?
2. Name two ways in which glaciers changed the land of the Northeast long ago.
3. Why are rivers and canals important in the Northeast?
4. Why is autumn a beautiful time of year in the Northeast?
5. Why is water an important resource for the Northeast?
6. How are needleleaf trees different from broadleaf trees?

7. Give one reason the Pilgrims are important to the history of the United States.
8. Give three reasons the Northeast is an important manufacturing region.
9. Why is the Northeast a center of trade?
10. Why is Boston an important city in the Northeast?

Thinking Critically

1. Most of the Northeast has a climate that changes a lot during the year. Do you prefer a climate that is much the same all year or one that has changes? Give reasons for your answer.
2. Why is the Northeast important to people all over our country?

Writing About It

Benjamin Franklin included many wise sayings in *Poor Richard's Almanac.* Write your own wise saying. Then write a few sentences to explain its meaning.

Practicing Thinking Skills

Identifying Cause and Effect

Use the paragraphs about glaciers on pages 158 and 159 to answer these questions.

a. What caused the glaciers to move?
b. What was the effect of the moving glaciers?

On Your Own

Social Studies at Home

Ask a family member to help you list some important events in your life or in the life of someone you know. These might include when you first walked and when any brothers or sisters were born. Include the years in which those events happened. Then use these events and dates to make a timeline.

Read More About It

Hannah's Farm: The Seasons on an Early American Homestead by Michael McCurdy. Holiday. Life on a New England farm in the 1800s is described in this book.

Island Boy by Barbara Cooney. Viking. This story about four generations of the Tibbets family also tells the history of New England.

The Pilgrims of Plimoth by Marcia Sewell. Atheneum. This story tells about the Pilgrims.

Sugaring Time by Kathryn Lasky. Macmillan. In this book you can follow a Vermont family as they tap maple trees, collect sap, and make maple syrup.

What's the Big Idea, Ben Franklin? by Jean Fritz. Coward-McCann. Based on careful research, this enjoyable biography describes events in the life of Benjamin Franklin.

CHAPTER 8

The Southeast

"The land on, and adjacent to, this river . . . appears naturally fertile. The peach trees are large, healthy, and fruitful; and Indian corn, rice, cotton, and indigo thrive exceedingly.

—The scientist William Bartram describing the landscape of the Southeast during his travels there in 1791

Look for these important words:

Key Words
- peninsula

Places
- Coastal Plain
- Mississippi River

Look for answers to these questions:
1. What are some of the landforms of the Southeast?
2. Why are waterways important here?
3. What is the climate of the Southeast?
4. What are the important natural resources of this region?

1 *The Land and Its Resources*

The Southeast is a large region. It is almost three times the size of the Northeast. There are 12 states in the Southeast region.

The Coastal Plain

Much of the Southeast is low and level. It is part of the **Coastal Plain.** As it stretches south from Virginia, the plain grows wider. It covers almost all of the Florida **peninsula** (puh•NIN•suh•luh). A peninsula is land with water on three sides of it.

The Coastal Plain in the Southeast has large areas of rich farmland. Other areas of good farmland are found in the valleys of the **Mississippi River** and its branches. River floods have given these valleys some of the Southeast's best soil.

Some parts of the Coastal Plain are large swamps. The largest swamp is the Everglades on the southern tip of Florida.

The Piedmont

To the west of the Coastal Plain is the Piedmont (PEED•mont). The Piedmont is a large area of foothills at the edge of the Appalachian Mountains.

175

The Piedmont is rich in minerals. It has many forests and good farmland. Most of the factories of the Southeast are found in the large cities in the Piedmont, such as Atlanta, Georgia, and Charlotte, North Carolina.

The Blue Ridge Mountains

West of the Piedmont is the part of the Appalachians called the Blue Ridge Mountains. From a distance these forest-covered mountains often look blue. Hickory, maple, oak, and many other kinds of trees abound. The wood from these trees is used to make furniture for the whole country. Small farms lie in the narrow valleys among the mountains.

Bluegrass Country

West of the Appalachians more low land stretches across much of Kentucky and Tennessee. In part of Kentucky many fields are covered with small blue-green flowers. The "Bluegrass" area is known for its racehorse farms. The grass is rich in minerals that make the horses strong.

GEOGRAPHY CONNECTION

People constantly make changes to the places in which they live and work. They build railroads, airports, and highways. They construct dams across rivers and dig canals. These changes often cause other, unplanned changes to take place.

In 1837 the Western and Atlantic Railroad built a new railroad in Georgia. A town grew up at its southern end. Soon other railroads were built, and the town found itself at the center of a whole network of railroads. This town was Atlanta, Georgia.

Today, Atlanta is a large city. It is an important manufacturing and

transportation center. If that first railroad had not been built, however, the city might not even exist.

THE SOUTHEAST

▲ Mountain peak

▢ National park

✵ State capital

Waterways

Waterways are important to the Southeast. The region has several large ports. On the Atlantic is Norfolk, Virginia. Mobile (moh•BEEL), Alabama, and New Orleans, Louisiana, are also large ports in the Southeast.

New Orleans is the largest port in the Southeast. New Orleans lies along the Mississippi River about 100 miles (about 160 km) inland from the Gulf of Mexico. Ships from all over the world bring goods up the Mississippi to New Orleans. They leave with

At the busy port of New Orleans, ships load and unload grain and goods. From here these goods are carried to places around the world.

goods shipped to New Orleans from many parts of the United States.

The Mississippi is by far the Southeast's most important river. With its branches it reaches almost every part of the United States between the Appalachians and the Rockies. Each year these rivers carry millions of tons of freight.

The Tennessee Valley Authority

At one time the valley of the Tennessee River was a dangerous place to live. Floods killed people and destroyed homes. Then the national government formed the Tennessee Valley Authority (TVA). Its job was to help people near the river. The TVA built many dams to control floods. It built power plants to make low-cost electric power. The power from these plants has brought industry and jobs to the valley.

Climate

The climate in much of the Southeast is warm and sunny. Summers in most places are long, hot, and humid. Winters are short and often mild.

The rainy Southeast climate is ideal for growing rice. Arkansas, Louisiana, and Mississippi lead in rice-growing.

Georgia produces more peanuts than any other state. What are some products made from peanuts?

All states in the Southeast receive more than 40 inches (about 102 cm) of precipitation each year. The rain and long summers help farmers grow many different crops. Cotton, rice, peanuts, and almost every kind of fruit grow well here.

The high areas of the region have a cooler climate than the lowland areas. The Appalachians often have snow and cold temperatures in winter.

Natural Resources

Some of the Southeast's most important resources are fuels. West Virginia and Kentucky are leaders in the nation's coal industry. Great amounts of oil and natural gas are found along the Gulf of Mexico in Texas and Lou-isiana. The Southeast also has iron ore and limestone.

The rain and warm weather are also good for growing many kinds of trees. Huge forests of pine as well as oak and hickory trees cover many parts of the Coastal Plain.

The sea is another of the Southeast's important resources. Tons of fish come from the Atlantic and the Gulf of Mexico each year.

Reading Check

1. Which places in the Southeast are best for farming?
2. What is "Bluegrass" country?
3. How has the TVA helped the Tennessee River valley?

Think Beyond Why is the Southeast important to people all over the United States?

179

Look for these important words:

Key Words
- House of Burgesses
- plantations
- Declaration of Independence

People
- Thomas Jefferson
- George Washington

Places
- Jamestown, Virginia
- Yorktown, Virginia

Look for answers to these questions:

1. What did the House of Burgesses change in America?
2. Why did slavery begin in America?
3. Why was the Declaration of Independence written?
4. In what ways was George Washington a leader of our country?

2 *The Southeast Long Ago*

The Pilgrims were not the first settlers in America. In 1607 a group of English came to search for gold. Their ship landed on the coast of what is now the state of Virginia. They called their settlement **Jamestown.**

During the first years at Jamestown the settlers almost starved. One winter they had to eat rats and insects to stay alive. Then the settlers discovered that tobacco grew well there. Tobacco became the main crop they traded for food.

By 1619 the English had formed 11 small towns in the colony of Virginia. In that year something very important happened. England allowed the settlers to help run their government. Before this, the colony was ruled by a governor and lawmakers chosen by the English king. Now each town could vote for two men to help run the Virginia government. This group of lawmakers was called the **House of Burgesses** (BUHR•juhs•uhz).

Plantations and Slavery

As more English settlers came to America, they cleared the land and started farms. They soon realized that the rich soil of the

180

Many large plantations developed in the colonies of the Southeast. Owners became wealthy growing crops such as tobacco and cotton.

Coastal Plain was good for more crops than just tobacco. Many huge farms called **plantations** (plan•TAY•shuhnz) were formed. Tobacco, cotton, and rice became the main crops. Corn and wheat were two other important crops raised on plantations.

Plantation owners needed many workers to grow the crops. Thousands of black people were taken by force from their homes in Africa to work on the plantations. These people were made slaves. They were bought and sold just like goods. They had no rights or freedom.

The American Revolution

As English colonies grew up along the Atlantic coast, troubles with English rule began to grow as well. Lawmakers in England passed new laws and taxes for the colonies. The strict laws and taxes limited freedom and trade in the colonies. The people in the colonies believed these new laws and taxes were unfair. Many refused to obey the English government.

The English government then sent soldiers to make people obey. People in the colonies became

181

even angrier, and fighting broke out. Some people began to talk about breaking away from England. They wanted to fight for their freedom. Some of the people in the colonies wanted to have their own government America.

Thomas Jefferson

The leaders from the colonies met in Philadelphia in 1776. **Thomas Jefferson** was one of the leaders. Jefferson was a young farmer and lawyer from the colony of Virginia. The leaders asked

Benjamin Franklin, seated on the left, worked on the Declaration of Independence with Thomas Jefferson, seen standing.

him to write the **Declaration of Independence** (dehk•luh•RAY•shuhn uhv ihn•duh•PEHN•duhns). *Declaration* comes from the word *declare,* which means "say." *Independence* is another word for freedom.

The Declaration explained why the colonies wanted independence. On July 4, 1776, Independence Day, the leaders of the 13 colonies met and voted to pass the Declaration. The Declaration of Independence said that the colonies were now a free nation with its own government. They called themselves the United States of America.

England did not let the American colonies go without a fight. It ordered soldiers to battle with the Americans. For more than five long years England and the United States fought the Revolutionary War.

George Washington

The Americans chose another Virginian to lead their army. His name was **George Washington.**

Washington's job at first seemed almost impossible. England's army was one of the best in the world. The Americans were poorly armed. They didn't even have warm clothes for winter. Still, they wanted freedom and they had a great leader.

George Washington led the Americans to victory during the American Revolution. He then became our first President.

Thomas Jefferson expressed some of our most basic ideas about freedom in the Declaration of Independence.

The worst time was the winter of 1777. The Americans had lost battle after battle. Washington's army was camped at Valley Forge, Pennsylvania, for the winter. It was bitterly cold. The Americans were in rags. Many of them died. Many others were very sick.

Somehow Washington kept his army together. After terrible defeats, the American army finally beat the English in an important battle at **Yorktown, Virginia.** The English gave in. They sent their army home. The United States was free!

We all know whom Americans chose as their first President. It was George Washington. Do you know who our third President was? It was Thomas Jefferson.

Reading Check

1. Where was the first English settlement in our country?
2. What was a plantation?
3. Who was Thomas Jefferson?

Think Beyond How might your life be different if the American army had lost the Battle of Yorktown?

183

IN FOCUS

SETTLING THE FRONTIER

At the time of the American Revolution, America's **frontier** (fruhn•TIHR) was the edge of the Appalachian Mountains. It was here that the settled areas ended and the wilderness began. West of the frontier were mountains, forests, and wide, open spaces.

Towns, farms, and cities were already crowding the Atlantic coast. Many people wanted to settle the frontier. Few, however, were able to cross the mountains. It was a long, hard trip.

Then a pass through the mountains was discovered. It was called the Cumberland Gap. The famous Daniel Boone and other guides led settlers through the pass.

Many families headed for the frontier. They took very little with them. A family's belongings may have been only a sack of corn and a few tools and pots.

When a family found a place to settle, they built a cabin from logs. They cleared land for fields. After this, it was time to plant.

Frontier families lived far apart, but they helped one another. Neighbors got together to build a new cabin. After the corn was harvested, a family might ask neighbors to a husking bee. Husking is removing the husk, or outer covering, from the corn. Everyone tried to husk the most ears of corn. When the work was done, it was time for a big meal. Someone played a fiddle, and the others danced and sang.

Life on the frontier was hard, yet families kept coming. These people helped our country grow.

Think Beyond People on the frontier helped one another in many ways. What are some ways in which people today help one another?

A husking bee

184

SKILLS IN ACTION

GATHERING INFORMATION FOR A REPORT

Suppose you have to write a short report. The report must tell something about transportation. To write this report, you will need to gather facts. Even before gathering any information, however, you must choose a subject.

Reading for a Purpose

When choosing a subject, you should decide on something that interests you. An interesting subject will be easier to write about.

Perhaps you like airplanes. You might want to report on this subject. However, *airplanes* is too large a subject for a short report. You must pick a smaller part of this subject. Then you will be able to cover your subject in the space you have.

You might decide to write about the first airplanes. You may know that Orville and Wilbur Wright made the first successful airplane flight at a place near Kitty Hawk, North Carolina. Now you need to gather more facts about how they invented the airplane. To do this, you must visit a library and do some reading.

The library card catalog can help you find nonfiction books on a subject. You may also find facts about your subject in an encyclopedia.

When you begin reading about your subject, write a few questions down. They will help you remember the facts you need to find.

Here are some questions about the Wright brothers:

1. How did the Wright brothers learn about flying?
2. When did they start trying to invent an airplane?
3. What did their airplane look like?
4. Where did the Wright brothers build their airplane?
5. Who first flew their airplane?
6. How high did their airplane go on its first flight?

The answers to these questions could be the main parts of your report.

Taking Notes

As you read about your subject, you should take notes. Many students take notes on cards. They write one fact on each card. They also write where the fact came from. This helps them if they must check the fact later on.

Here is an example of a note card:

> The Wright brothers built a small, light engine for the first airplane.
>
> *World Book Encyclopedia*
> vol. 21, p. 421

On this card is a fact about the Wright brothers' early flights. The fact came from an article in *The World Book Encyclopedia*. The article appeared on page 421 of volume 21.

Making an Outline

Once you have found the facts you need, you can **organize** your report. To organize is to put something in order. In this case you are writing about an important event in the past. You should put your notes in the order in which things happened.

Writing an **outline** is the next step. An outline lists the things you want to say in your report. It further organizes your information.

You will probably not use all of your notes in the outline or final report. You should choose the most important facts, ideas, and events to write about.

Here is part of an outline for a report on the Wright brothers:

> TITLE: ORVILLE AND WILBUR WRIGHT
>
> I. The Wright brothers wanted to learn about flying.
>
>   A. Decided to build and test gliders.
>
>   B. Made more than 1,000 test flights.
>
> II. Orville and Wilbur Wright built the world's first successful airplane.
>
>   A. First successful flight at Kitty Hawk, North Carolina, on December 17, 1903.

In this outline the first important idea follows the roman numeral I. It could be the main sentence in a paragraph. The facts marked *A* and *B* tell more about this main idea.

The sentence marked II could be the main sentence in another paragraph. Facts about this main idea would be labeled with capital letters, beginning with *A* again.

CHECKING YOUR SKILLS

Put these steps in order:

1. Choose a subject to write about.

2. Write down questions about the subject.

3. Read and take notes on cards.

4. Write an outline.

5. Use the outline to help you write the report.

6. Put the note cards in order.

186

Look for these important words:

Key Words
- sugarcane
- soybeans
- textiles
- crude oil
- refineries

- pulp
- tourists
- tourism
- slough
- Mardi Gras

Places
- Birmingham, Alabama
- Everglades National Park
- Latin America
- Caribbean Sea

Look for answers to these questions:
1. Why is the Southeast growing so quickly?
2. What kinds of farming and factories are found in the Southeast?
3. Where did the ancestors of many of the people in the Southeast come from?

3 *The Southeast Today*

The Southeast is one of our country's fastest-growing regions. Many businesses move to the Southeast each year. They come because of the region's many resources. Many people move there, too. Some come for jobs. Others come for the mild climate.

Farming

The Southeast has almost anything a farmer might want. Good soil, warm weather, and lots of rain allow almost any warm-weather crop to grow here. Florida leads all other states in growing **sugarcane** and oranges. Sugarcane is a plant from which

Sugar is made from the juice of the sugarcane plant.

187

Fires in "smudge" pots set out among Florida orange tree groves help save the crop from damaging frosts.

sugar is made. Oranges from Florida go to orange juice factories in that state. The frozen juice is sold all over our country.

Soybeans and cotton are main crops of the Southeast. The soybean is a small bean used in many foods. Arkansas grows more rice than any other state. Georgia is our biggest peanut grower. North Carolina and Kentucky grow the most tobacco.

Farmers of the Southeast raise large numbers of beef cattle. They also raise dairy cows, hogs, and poultry. Almost half the chickens we eat come from Arkansas, Georgia, and Alabama. Florida is a leading state for beef cattle.

Manufacturing

At one time most people in the Southeast were farmers. Now more people work in manufacturing. The number of factories has grown fast in the last 20 years.

Two important industries in the Southeast are food processing and **textiles,** or cloth. Many factories process the fruits and vegetables grown in the Southeast. Other factories turn cotton and other materials into wide

Machines pick the cotton and remove its seeds. Workers lay out a pattern to cut the finished textile and turn it into clothing.

Cotton is first made into thread and wound around spools or bobbins. Then a weaving machine blends thread from many bobbins into cloth.

sheets of cloth. This cloth is turned into clothing at still other factories. The Southeast, in fact, leads the nation in the textile industry.

Minerals and Fuels

Though ships bring oil from other countries to the Southeast's ports, some oil comes from the Southeast itself. Factories in the region turn oil into many products. When oil is pumped from the earth, it is called **crude oil.** Factories called **refineries** change crude oil into gasoline and heating oil. Other factories make things such as plastics, paints, and textiles from oil.

Mining is another important industry in the Southeast. Millions of dollars' worth of coal, iron ore, and limestone are mined here each year. The Appalachian Mountains near **Birmingham, Alabama,** contain large amounts of these minerals. For many years these resources made Birmingham a steel-making center.

Lumbering

Large forests cover much of the Southeast. From these forests come lumber for building homes and oils for making paint. In the Southeast an important wood product is **pulp.** This ground-up wood mixed with water is used in making paper. More paper comes from these forests than from anywhere else in America.

The Tourist Industry

Sunny weather and interesting places draw millions of **tourists** (TUHR•uhsts), or visitors, here each year. Favorite ocean resorts are Florida's Miami Beach, South Carolina's Myrtle Beach, and Virginia Beach in Virginia. Florida's Everglades and Kentucky's Mammoth Cave are national parks of special natural beauty. Visitors explore history in places like Jamestown and Williamsburg, in Virginia. Williamsburg looks the way it did in the 1700s. The John F. Kennedy Space Center and Walt Disney World in Florida are also popular for tourists.

Tourism is the selling of goods and services to tourists. Many people in the Southeast work to provide food, shelter, information, and entertainment for visitors. You are going to read about one of these workers.

Places like Miami Beach attract tourists to Florida, the "Sunshine State."

Debby Turner, Everglades Park Guide

Debby Turner welcomes a group of students to **Everglades National Park.** Today she will lead the class on a trip in the park. Ranger Turner is a park guide. She answers questions and tells visitors about things to see and do in the park.

Ranger Turner tells the students about some of these exciting things. If they are lucky, they may see a tiny tree frog. The tree frog has suction cups on its feet. The cups let the frog hang upside down from leaves!

This playful green tree frog is right at home in an Everglades forest.

Willow and bay trees grow on "tree islands" in Everglades swamps.

The ranger leads the group along a trail. The trail is next to a freshwater **slough** (SLOO). In winter the slough is a marshy field of tall, dry grass. After lots of rain the slough becomes a wide river that flows slowly through the grass, moving south. Finally it empties into Florida Bay and the Gulf of Mexico.

Ranger Turner tells how trees fight for space to grow in the Everglades. One tree, the strangler fig, will wrap itself tightly around another tree. In time the fig will strangle the other tree. Another tree, the stopper, smells like a skunk. The unpleasant smell stops rats and mice from chewing it.

When it is time to return, the group walks slowly back along the trail. Ranger Turner stops suddenly. She points to a log by a water hole. The log starts to move. It's a live alligator!

Alligators use their feet and tails to dig water holes in the sloughs, the ranger explains. (Another name for the water holes is gator holes.) In dry times these holes are the only places with water. Fish cannot live out of water, and animals and birds need water to drink. The gator holes help all these animals and birds stay alive. Of course, alligators eat everything they can get in their jaws. Many of the fish become dinner for the alligators.

Ranger Turner enjoys being a guide in the Everglades. She wants people to know how special it is. Even with its mosquitoes, she thinks there is no better place to work!

People of the Southeast Today

Many families have lived in the Southeast for hundreds of years. Their ancestors may have come from Europe, Africa, or **Latin America.** Latin America includes all nations in the Western Hemisphere south of the United States.

Many French-speaking people live in Louisiana. They celebrate a holiday called **Mardi Gras** (MAHR•dee GRAH). Every year at Mardi Gras time the people of New Orleans, Louisiana, hold a giant carnival.

Many African Americans make their homes in the Southeast, too. Their ancestors have added many things to our heritage. Their foods and music and many of their words, such as *yam, banana,* and *banjo,* have made our heritage richer.

Many Spanish-speaking people have settled in the Southeast

As their French-Canadian ancestors did, Cajun families still fish along the Louisiana bayous, slow-moving streams near the river's mouth.

in recent years. Some are from Mexico. Most are from Cuba and other islands in the **Caribbean** (kar•uh•BEE•uhn) **Sea.** This sea is southeast of Florida.

Reading Check

1. What are some of the Southeast's most important crops?
2. What are textiles?
3. How is oil used in the Southeast's industries?

Think Beyond Why do you think the Southeast is growing more quickly than some of the other regions of our country?

People
MAKE HISTORY

George Washington Carver
1864?–1943

▶▶▶▶▶▶▶▶▶▶▶▶▶▶▶▶

For hours George had walked through the Missouri countryside. He was miles from home, and he felt homesick. Suddenly, however, his mood changed for the better. He reminded himself that he was going to school! There was nothing he wanted more, even though it meant leaving home and moving to a new town.

George Washington Carver was born a slave on a Missouri plantation. When George was a baby, he and his mother were kidnapped by slave traders. George's owner, Moses Carver, found him but was not able to find George's mother.

When all slaves were freed in 1865, Moses Carver and his wife decided to raise George. They taught him how to read and write and later sent him to school. At that time, however, African-American children were not allowed to attend school with white children. George had to go to a school in another part of the state.

Carver graduated from college in 1894. He later accepted a teaching job at the Tuskegee Institute in Alabama. This was a new college run by African Americans to train former slaves. Carver taught farmers how to grow better crops.

Carver also ran an experimental farm at the college. There he became famous for his work with peanuts. He learned that growing peanuts actually helps to keep the soil rich. That discovery helped make peanuts a major crop in the Southeast.

Think Beyond Why do you think it is important to get a good education?

Thinking Back

- The Southeast's major landforms are the Coastal Plain, the Piedmont, the Blue Ridge Mountains, and the "Bluegrass" area. The Mississippi and Tennessee rivers are important waterways. The Southeast also has several large ports. New Orleans is the largest.

- Important natural resources include oil, natural gas, coal, iron ore, limestone, forests, and coastal waters.

- Jamestown was the first of several English settlements in the colony of Virginia. Settlers in Virginia chose a group of lawmakers to help run their government. This group of lawmakers was called the House of Burgesses.

- Tobacco, cotton, and rice were crops raised on plantations in the Southeast. Black people were taken from Africa and forced to work as slaves on plantations.

- English colonies joined together and declared their independence. Thomas Jefferson and George Washington were leaders of the American Revolution.

- The Southeast is one of our country's fastest-growing regions. Tourism, mining, lumbering, farming, manufacturing, and oil are all major industries.

Check for Understanding

Using Words

Copy the sentences below. Fill in the blanks with the correct words from the list.

independence   **textiles**
pulp   **tourism**
refineries

1. Americans wanted their _____ from England.
2. Another word for cloth is _____ .
3. Crude oil is changed into gasoline and heating oil in _____ .
4. Paper is made from wood _____ .
5. Selling goods and services to visitors is called _____ .

Reviewing Facts

1. Why is the Mississippi River important to the Southeast?
2. What was the Declaration of Independence?
3. What are some products made from oil?

4. Name three products from the Southeast that use wood.

5. In what ways do people in the Southeast make a living?

Thinking Critically

1. Have you ever been a tourist? What are some of the things you did on your visit? Why was your visit important to the people who lived there?

2. George Washington and Thomas Jefferson were important American leaders. What do you think makes someone a leader? Who do you think are important leaders today?

Writing About it

Imagine that your family has followed Daniel Boone to the frontier. Write a journal entry in which you tell about your new life there.

Practicing Writing Skills

Gathering Information for a Report

Suppose you were asked to write a report on the Everglades National Park.

1. What are some questions you might ask about the Everglades?

2. Where could you look for answers to your questions?

3. What should you do after putting your notes in order?

On Your Own

Social Studies at Home

Check the labels on the clothing in your closet, and list the items you find that are made all or partly of cotton. With permission, you might also check household items such as sheets and towels. Show the list to family members, and discuss why cotton is an important crop.

Read More About It

Cotton by Millicent E. Selsam. William Morrow. This book tells about the cotton industry.

Folk Stories of the South by M. A. Jagendorf. Vanguard. Ninety-five tales from the South are retold in this entertaining book.

Ida Early Comes over the Mountain by Robert Burch. Viking. In this tale set in Georgia during the 1930s you will meet Ida, a character you will never forget.

A Lion to Guard Us by Clyde Robert Bulla. T. Y. Crowell. The adventures of the Freehold children, who leave London to join their father in the Jamestown colony, are described in this tale.

Meet Thomas Jefferson by Marvin Barrett. Random House. This biography describes the life of the man who contributed so much to our nation's early history.

CHAPTER 9

The Great Lakes States

66 *Hog Butcher for the World,*
Tool Maker, Stacker of Wheat,
Player with Railroads and the Nation's
* Freight Handler;*
Stormy, husky, brawling,
City of the Big Shoulders. . . . 99

—from the poem "Chicago"
by Carl Sandburg

Look for these important words:

Key Places
- Ohio River
- Illinois Waterway

Look for answers to these questions:
1. What landforms and bodies of water are found in the Great Lakes region?
2. How do the rivers and lakes here link the Great Lakes states with the rest of our country?
3. What are the important natural resources of this region?

1 | The Land and Its Resources

Thousands of years ago, giant glaciers pushed south over the middle of our country. They flattened hills and filled in valleys with rich soil. They dug five large holes in the soft rock of the region. As the ice melted, water filled the holes, forming the five Great Lakes. These five lakes are the world's largest group of freshwater lakes.

The states lying next to the lakes are called the Great Lakes states. No mountains are in these states. Some hills are found in the north and the south, but most of the land is a plain formed by the glaciers. The flat land and good soil make this a valuable farm region. It is one of the best places

Acres and acres of fertile farmland help make our country a leading producer of corn.

in the world for growing corn, soybeans, and other crops.

Bodies of Water

Few places have the water resources equal to the Great Lakes region. Besides the Great Lakes themselves, many smaller lakes are scattered throughout the region. The northern states in the region—Minnesota, Wisconsin, and Michigan—have hundreds of these small lakes.

Small and large rivers run through all the states. The **Ohio River** forms the boundary of three southern states in the region. They are Ohio, Illinois, and Indiana. Look at the map on page 199. Find the rivers that form the western boundary of the region. Of the five Great Lakes, which ones form the northern boundary?

These rivers and lakes are more than just places on a map. They link the Great Lakes region with the rest of the United States. They also link the region with the world. Using the New York State Barge Canal or the St. Lawrence Seaway, ships can go from Minnesota to the Atlantic Ocean.

Still another group of waterways connects Lake Michigan to

The northern forests of Minnesota are dotted with lakes. "Minnesota" comes from Indian words meaning "sky-reflecting water." Why might this state be called "the land of 10,000 lakes"?

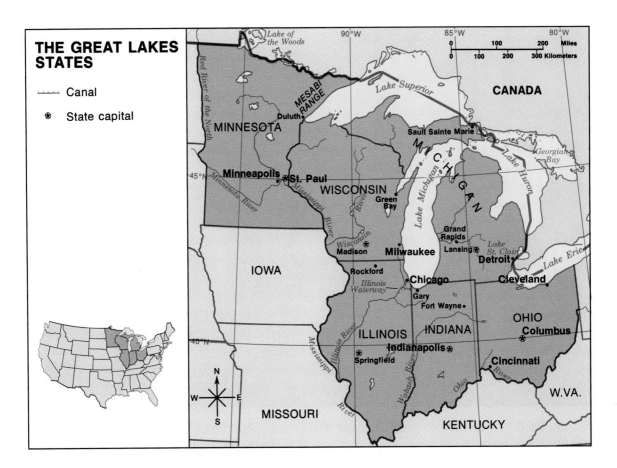

THE GREAT LAKES STATES

—— Canal

⊛ State capital

New Orleans, Louisiana. Beginning at the city of Chicago, Illinois, the **Illinois Waterway** flows along small rivers and canals to the Illinois River. This river runs into the Mississippi. Boats and barges travel the Illinois Waterway. They carry the raw materials and the finished goods of the Great Lakes states.

Climate

Summers in the Great Lakes states are mostly warm, sunny, and humid. These states have fairly high rainfall then. Much of their rain comes from the Gulf of Mexico. This rainfall helps farmers of the Great Lakes states grow many important crops.

Winters in the Great Lakes states are long, cold, and snowy. Harsh winter storms sweep down from the cold north. Cities and towns near the Great Lakes generally get more snow than those farther away. The Great Lakes themselves bring on this weather. The next paragraph explains why this happens.

Bodies of water always change temperature more slowly than land. In winter, the Great Lakes are not chilled as quickly as the surrounding land. The air over

People are drawn to Minnesota's clean air and crystal-clear lakes.
The state has wilderness areas for summer and winter recreation.

The city of Chicago is built up to the edge of Lake Michigan. Parts of
the beautiful lakefront make a playground for the entire city.

the lakes is also warm and holds much moisture. Clouds filled with this moisture blow toward the land from the Great Lakes. As the clouds hit the cooler air of the land, they give up their moisture as snow.

Natural Resources

Some people say that the Great Lakes are the region's most valuable resource. They provide water for homes and factories. They form transportation routes for goods. They also provide recreation for millions of people who enjoy boating, fishing, and swimming.

Rich soil makes the Great Lakes region one of the world's best places to farm. From this fine dark soil, Great Lakes farmers grow record amounts of corn, soybeans, and oats almost every year. Their dairy cattle graze on the thick green grass.

Large forests cover much of northern Minnesota, Wisconsin, and Michigan. They are part of a great pine forest that spreads across Canada. Farther south are scattered woodlands of oak and hickory. In the northern forests are many lakes left by the glaciers.

Many important minerals are found in the Great Lakes states. Wide layers of coal lie beneath the

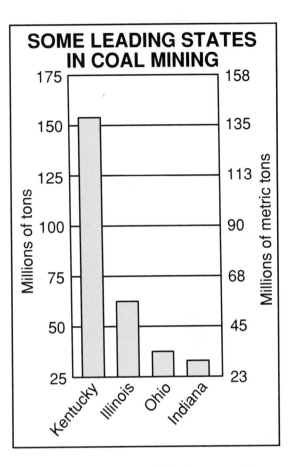

SOME LEADING STATES IN COAL MINING

soil in Illinois and Indiana. Iron ore is mined in Minnesota, Michigan, and Wisconsin, making steel an important industry here.

Reading Check

1. How were the Great Lakes formed?
2. Name two ways a ship can get from the Great Lakes to the Atlantic Ocean.
3. Why do cities near the Great Lakes generally have more snow than those farther away?

Think Beyond Why might many of the goods you use come from the Great Lakes states?

Look for these important words:

Key Words	People	Places
• bartering	• Jean Du Sable	• New Salem, Illinois
• pioneers	• Abraham Lincoln	• Springfield, Illinois
• elected		
• Civil War		

Look for answers to these questions:

1. How did Chicago get its start as a major city on the Great Lakes?
2. What was the early life of Abraham Lincoln like?
3. What was the Civil War?
4. What happened during the Civil War?

2 The Great Lakes States Long Ago

About 200 years ago, only a few brave people went west. They traveled along rivers in canoes, setting traps for beavers. These trappers also brought goods with them for **bartering,** or trading. They traded their goods with the Indians for beaver and other furs the Indians had. Beaver skins were valuable. People in Europe paid high prices for beaver hats.

Jean Du Sable

One of the best traders was an African American named **Jean Du Sable** (ZHAHN doo SAH•bluh). Du Sable was probably born on the island of Haiti (HAY•tee) around 1745. Haiti was then a colony of France. Du Sable later came to New Orleans, Louisiana. From there, he traveled up the Mississippi to work as a fur trader. He married an Indian woman and settled on a farm near what is now Peoria, Illinois.

After settling in Illinois, Du Sable went back and forth from Canada trading furs. On his way he would stop at a certain place on Lake Michigan. It was at the mouth of a small river that ran into the lake. The Indians called it Eschikagon. Here Du Sable built a trading post and a cabin. He brought his family to live there soon after.

To gather the wild rice that grew well in the marshy areas along the Great Lakes, Indian women beat the rice into their canoes with wooden paddles.

Jean Du Sable was Chicago's first permanent citizen. When the American Revolution ended in 1783, he had already started a thriving settlement that would grow into America's third-largest city.

The trading post was in a good place. Du Sable could take his furs along the lake to be sold. He could also take his furs to rivers that ran south into the Mississippi. His fur trade grew quickly.

More trappers and traders came to this place, and a small settlement grew up. Today this place is the city of Chicago. It is now one of our country's most important centers of transportation and trade.

Young Abe Lincoln

Pioneers, or the first settlers, who came to the Great Lakes states came to farm its rich, deep soil. Some came by covered wagon or on foot. Other settlers traveled on river flatboats or rafts. From one such pioneer family came **Abraham Lincoln,** our sixteenth President.

Today New Salem, Illinois, has a state park with the town built to look as it did in the days when Abraham Lincoln studied by firelight.

Abe Lincoln was born in a small cabin in Kentucky. The family moved to Indiana when he was seven. For a time the Lincolns lived in a "half-faced camp." It was a shelter of just three walls facing a campfire.

Since his family was so poor, Abe worked all day in the fields. He often could not go to school, but Abe read all the books he could find. He would walk miles to get a book. At night he stayed up late to read. Sometimes he even plowed the fields with a book on the plow.

Young Abe Lincoln grew up strong and tall. He stood 6 foot 4 inches (193 cm). When Abe was in his twenties, he moved to **New Salem, Illinois.** New Salem was a tiny village near **Springfield,** soon to become the state's capital. Lincoln worked for several years in New Salem.

People liked the friendly, honest Lincoln. While in New Salem, Lincoln was **elected** to the state government. To be elected means to be chosen by vote. Lincoln also became interested in law. He studied on his own. He once walked 30 miles (about 48 km) to hear a court trial.

Abe moved to Springfield to work as a lawyer. Several years later he was elected to the United States Congress in Washington, D.C. Finally, he won the highest honor of all. In 1860 Abe Lincoln was elected President.

The Civil War

Lincoln became President at a dangerous time in our country's history. The country was divided about many things, including slavery. Abe Lincoln hated slavery. He often spoke against it.

Some Southern states voted to break away from the United States. They formed their own government. A terrible war broke out. It was called the **Civil War.**

During the Civil War battles were fought in many parts of our country. Many Americans on both sides were killed. During the war, Lincoln freed the slaves. After four long years, the war finally ended. Lincoln had kept the United States whole. It was now a free country for all.

A book-lover all his life, Abraham Lincoln reads to his youngest son, Tad. Lincoln always remembered a book he had read about another President, George Washington.

Just a few days after the war's end, Lincoln was shot and killed by a man who hated him. Many Americans felt the loss of this tall, quiet, peace-loving President. Today we remember Lincoln as one of our greatest leaders.

Reading Check

1. Why did Jean Du Sable go to the Great Lakes?
2. How did Lincoln learn enough to become a lawyer?
3. What were two causes of the Civil War?

Think Beyond Why do you think Lincoln wanted to keep the United States whole?

People MAKE HISTORY

John Chapman
1774–1845?

▶▶▶▶▶▶▶▶▶▶▶▶▶▶▶▶▶▶

In the early 1800s a young man left his home in Massachusetts. He headed west to Ohio, Illinois, and Indiana. His name was John Chapman.

Chapman traveled alone. He followed Indian trails through the woods. He paddled along rivers in a canoe. At night he slept in the open. When he was hungry, he picked nuts and berries. In his pack Chapman carried apple seeds. When he saw a place he liked, he cleared the brush away and planted some of his seeds.

In a few years the seeds had grown into little apple trees. Sometimes Chapman stayed a while and sold young trees. Often he left his trees for settlers to discover and enjoy. It was not long before people called him Johnny Appleseed.

Sometimes Johnny wore a cooking pot for a hat and a coffee sack for a coat. He often went barefoot, even in the snow! Children loved to hear Johnny tell of his adventures. Their parents also enjoyed his tales.

Johnny enjoyed living in the wilderness. He did not believe in harming any living thing. Johnny once said that he was sorry he had killed a rattlesnake that had bitten him.

Johnny's apple trees are gone now, but he became an American legend. After Johnny died, many stories were told about him. Some of them were tall tales. In fact, no one has ever proved any of the stories were true.

Think Beyond Why do you think settlers made up tall tales about characters like Johnny Appleseed?

Look for these important words:

Key Words
- harvest
- open-pit mines
- coke
- ingots
- assembly plant
- assembly line
- metropolitan area
- location

- construction
- architects
- foundation

Places
- Central Plains

- Mesabi Range
- Detroit, Michigan
- Chicago, Illinois
- O'Hare International Airport

Look for answers to these questions:

1. What farming and manufacturing are done in the Great Lakes states?
2. How are corn and steel used in manufacturing?
3. Why is Chicago an important city?

3 *The Great Lakes States Today*

Even though you may live far from the Great Lakes states, you have probably used something from this region in the past few hours. The farms, mines, and factories of these states provide many things you use each day.

Farming

The Great Lakes region is part of the **Central Plains.** Among the many crops grown in the rich soil here, one in particular stands out. It is corn.

The wide Corn Belt stretches from the Great Lakes states to the Plains region. You will read about this region in the next chapter. The Corn Belt grows more corn than anywhere else in the world. Most of the corn crop is used to feed farm animals. However, there is enough left for each American to eat 85 pounds (about 38 kg) of corn a year!

Corn on the cob, popcorn, and cornflakes all start out as corn kernels, or seeds. Farmers plant corn in spring and **harvest,** or gather, it in late summer or autumn. Corn grows quickly. When it is ready to be picked, the plant may be 10 feet (about 3 m) tall.

Iowa is the leading corn grower, followed by Illinois. Grassy hills make Wisconsin the nation's leading dairy state. Many fruits and vegetables are grown in Wisconsin and Michigan and then sold in cities of the Great Lakes region.

Minerals

The **Mesabi** (muh•SAHB•ee) **Range** has large deposits of iron ore. These low hills are in northern Minnesota. Most of the ore lies close to the surface. Miners there use giant machines to dig the ore from holes in the ground. These deep holes are known as **open-pit mines.**

Railroad cars or ships take the ore to steel mills. Many of the mills are located near coal mines. This is why Illinois, a leading coal state, is also a leader in steel-making. Its neighbors, Indiana and Ohio, are also important in steel-making.

Manufacturing

Thousands of products are made in the Great Lakes states. To list everything would take a whole book! From steel alone come tractors, cars, nails, mattress springs, and refrigerators. The list could go on and on.

The Great Lakes region is one of the world's most important

The Mesabi Range produces all of Minnesota's iron ore. About 95 percent of all iron ore used in the United States comes from Minnesota.

centers of manufacturing. More than one-fourth of all our manufactured products come from these states. Here is how two raw materials—corn and steel—are made into finished products.

Making Cornflakes

To make cornflakes, dry corn kernels are first cut off the cob. Part of the kernel is ground into hominy (HOM•uh•nee). The hominy is cooked over steam for a few hours. Then vitamins are added, and the hominy is dried. A machine turns the hominy into flakes. Now the flakes are toasted in giant ovens. When cool, the cornflakes are packed into boxes and shipped to grocery stores.

Making Cars

Your family car may have begun as minerals from the Great Lakes states. The iron might have been mined in northern Minnesota. Then it might have been shipped by barge on Lake Michigan to a steel mill near Chicago.

At the mill the iron ore goes into a blast furnace with limestone and **coke.** Coke is a fuel made from coal. Limestone helps remove waste materials, and coke helps heat the ore. When these minerals get hot enough, the pure iron melts. It sinks to the bottom.

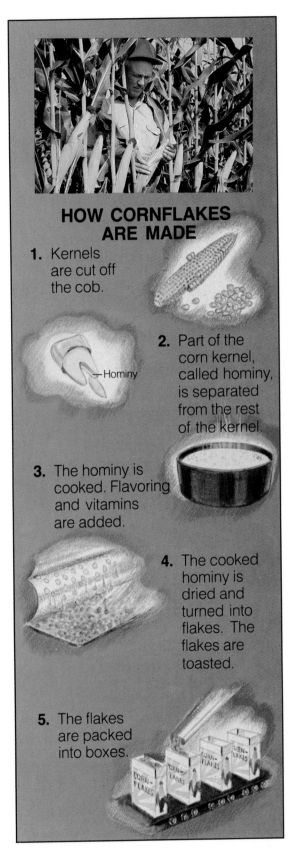

HOW CORNFLAKES ARE MADE

1. Kernels are cut off the cob.

2. Part of the corn kernel, called hominy, is separated from the rest of the kernel.

—Hominy

3. The hominy is cooked. Flavoring and vitamins are added.

4. The cooked hominy is dried and turned into flakes. The flakes are toasted.

5. The flakes are packed into boxes.

The waste materials rise to the top and are poured off.

Next, the melted, or molten, iron goes to another kind of furnace. Here it is mixed with other metals to make steel.

Molten steel is formed into blocks called **ingots.** Some ingots are squeezed through giant rollers to make sheets of steel.

These sheets of steel then go to an automobile factory. Here they are made into an automobile body. Thousands of other car parts are made in different fac-tories. All the parts are put together, or assembled, in an **assembly plant.** Many assembly plants are in and around **Detroit, Michigan.** In fact, Detroit has been called the auto-mobile capital of the world.

Automobiles are built on an **assembly line.** A moving belt carries the unfinished cars past computer-controlled robots. The robots do jobs such as welding and painting. Workers add parts. At the end of the assembly line, other workers test the cars.

Molten steel is made into sheets from which auto parts are cut. Robots next weld and paint the bodies of the cars. Each worker on an assembly line then adds a different auto part to keep the work running smoothly and quickly.

Chicago

More than 45 million Americans live in the Great Lakes states. Most of them live in the cities on or near the Great Lakes. Some of them live in cities on large rivers. Find some of these cities on the map on page 199.

The largest city in the region is **Chicago** (shih•KAHG•oh), **Illinois.** Today about 3 million people live in this busy city. This number of people makes Chicago the third-largest American city. Several smaller cities surround Chicago. A large city with other cities near it is a **metropolitan area.** The metropolitan area of Chicago has more than 8 million people. This is more than twice the number of people in Chicago itself.

Chicago lies near the center of our country at the southern tip of Lake Michigan. Its **location,** where it is, has made Chicago one of our busiest ports. This location has also made Chicago an important center of transportation. It is a perfect meeting place for railroads from the east and the west. Thousands of trucks travel in and out of the city each day. In Chicago **O'Hare International Airport** is one of the world's busiest airports.

When people drive to Chicago they can see the city long before they get there. That's because they see the city's skyscrapers. Chicago was one of the first cities to have skyscrapers. These tall buildings are sometimes 100 stories high. The Sears Tower in Chicago is 110 stories high. It is the tallest building in the world.

Many people are needed to plan and to build skyscrapers. One such person is Jack Kirkland, a construction worker.

The railway systems that meet in Chicago are especially important for transporting goods during the cold winter months, when many of the region's waterways freeze.

On October 8, 1871, a fire broke out on Chicago's southwest side. According to legend, the fire started when a cow kicked over a lighted lantern in a barn owned by Mrs. Patrick O'Leary. Fanned by strong winds, the flames raced through the city's wooden buildings. The fire left 90,000 people homeless.

The people of Chicago decided to rebuild their city. This project attracted some of the nation's finest builders. One builder decided to use new methods and materials to build a new kind of building—a skyscraper. Today, Chicago is one of the

world's great cities. Its skyscrapers tower above the city that was once nearly destroyed by fire.

Jack Kirkland, Construction Worker

Mr. Kirkland is in charge of a **construction** crew. The word *construction* means "building." His daughter, Patty Kirkland, asked him to explain his work to her class. When Mr. Kirkland came to class, the students had many questions to ask him.

Student: Mr. Kirkland, what does your crew do?
Mr. K.: My group welds, or joins together, the building's steel frame.
Student: How many people work on a skyscraper?
Mr. K.: We need hundreds of peo-

ple. First, a group of people make a plan for the building. They are called **architects.**
Student: How long does the planning take?
Mr. K.: It often takes more than a year. The architects must be sure the building will be strong. It has to stand up against the strongest winds. Every part of the building must be just the right size.

The next step is to dig the building's **foundation.** The foundation is the base. For a skyscraper the workers may dig a very deep foundation. It may go down more than ten stories. When the foundation is dug, we can start building up. Workers use cranes to lift the parts into place. Other workers, like my

212

Construction workers follow hundreds of instructions to build a skyscraper.

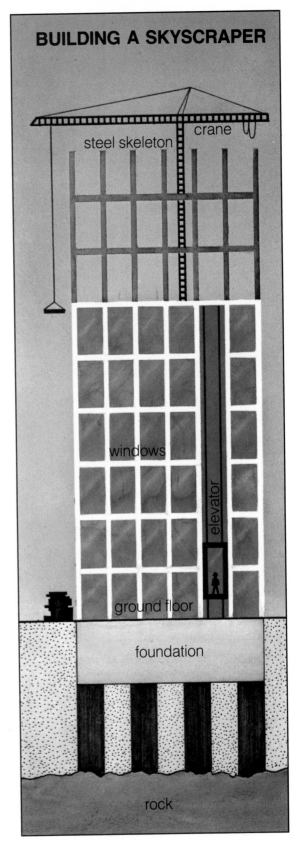

BUILDING A SKYSCRAPER

steel skeleton

crane

windows

elevator

ground floor

foundation

rock

group, weld the steel frame together. Electricians put in wires for electricity. Plumbers put in pipes. Carpenters, painters, and many other workers finish the building.

Student: Is it dangerous to work on a skyscraper?

Mr. K.: Working at a thousand feet above the ground can scare the bravest person. We have ways to protect ourselves. We wear safety belts and shoes with rubber soles. You will always see us with our hard hats on. If a hammer falls from above, it will bounce off the hat.

Student: Mr. Kirkland, what do you like most about your job?

Mr. K.: I like to see the building go up a little higher each day. When it is all done, though, I get a thrill just driving past our building.

Some cheeses in Wisconsin are made from recipes brought from Europe.

A museum in Blue Mound, Wisconsin, displays tools Norwegian immigrants used.

People of the Great Lakes States

As in other regions, the people of the Great Lakes states come from many different backgrounds. They have their family roots in countries all over the world. The ancestors of some families were Scottish and Irish pioneers who came through the Cumberland Gap.

Immigrants from other countries settled in the Great Lakes region a little later. These immigrants named their towns for the countries from which they came. Some even made the towns look like places in Europe. You can still find towns here with names like Germantown, Holland, Poland, and Russiaville. What countries do you think some of the immigrants to this region were from?

Reading Check

1. What is the main crop of the Great Lakes states?
2. Name two minerals that come from the Great Lakes states.
3. What makes Chicago a major transportation center?

Think Beyond It has been said that when the automobile industry does well, other industries do well. Why might this be true?

IN FOCUS

A SPECIAL MUSEUM

"We've got fun down to a science!" That is the slogan of Chicago's most popular museum. The Museum of Science and Industry celebrates discovery and invention. It shows visitors how and why things work.

On a day's visit to the museum, you can walk down into a coal mine, watch live chickens hatch, and stroll along a street from 1910. You can walk through a giant model of a human heart and listen to the thumping, swishing sound effects. You might want to whisper messages to a friend down a long whisper chamber, or watch yourself on television. You will have to make choices. It is not possible to see 2,000 displays in a day!

The Museum of Science and Industry is the oldest science museum in the United States. It opened in 1933 because a father made a promise to his son. The father was Julius Rosenwald, a wealthy man from Chicago.

While on vacation in Europe, the Rosenwald family visited a museum in Munich, Germany. There they saw scientific exhibits and went down into a coal mine. One son was especially fascinated with the coal mine. The hour was getting late, however, and the family had to leave. The boy refused. He did not want to leave the coal mine! Finally, the father made his son a promise. If the boy would leave the museum instantly, the father would build a similar museum in Chicago.

Rosenwald kept his promise. In 1926 he gave the city of Chicago millions of dollars for a science museum. The coal mine was among the original exhibits.

Think Beyond Why do you think museums are important to people?

Museum exhibits

215

SKILLS IN ACTION

READING FLOW CHARTS

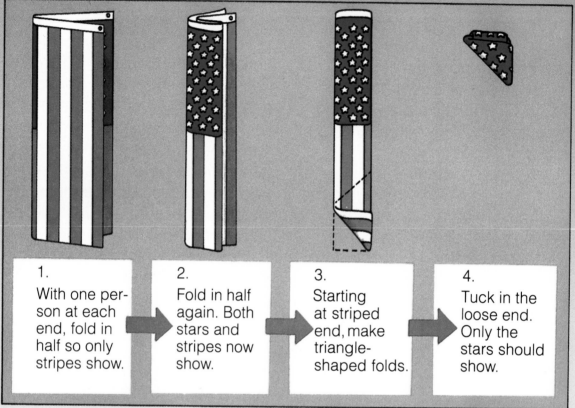

1.
With one person at each end, fold in half so only stripes show.

2.
Fold in half again. Both stars and stripes now show.

3.
Starting at striped end, make triangle-shaped folds.

4.
Tuck in the loose end. Only the stars should show.

Have you ever built a model or baked bread? If you have, you had to do certain steps in the right order. You probably followed directions or a recipe.

Many other tasks also have a number of steps. For example, there is a special way to fold a United States flag. Following the steps in the right order helps you make sure the job is done well. If you complete each step carefully, you will end up with a neat, star-spangled triangle.

One way to show how to fold a flag is by making a **flow chart.** A flow chart is a drawing that shows the order in which a list of steps should be done. Sometimes flow charts include pictures.

Look at the flow chart above. The steps are listed in numbered boxes. Each box explains one step. Each box is illustrated with a picture. The arrows tell you to read the flow chart from left to right. What is the first step? What is the last step?

216

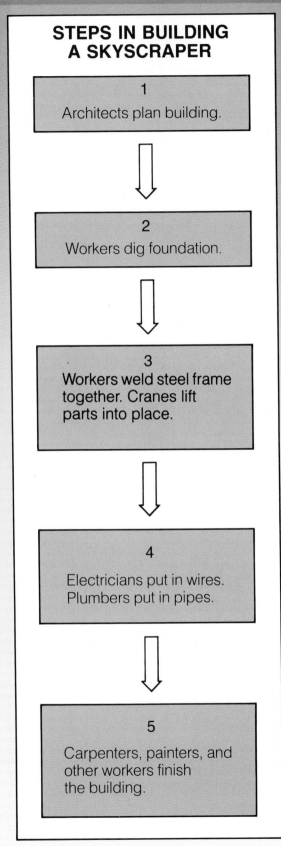

STEPS IN BUILDING A SKYSCRAPER

1
Architects plan building.

2
Workers dig foundation.

3
Workers weld steel frame together. Cranes lift parts into place.

4
Electricians put in wires. Plumbers put in pipes.

5
Carpenters, painters, and other workers finish the building.

Some flow charts have arrows that point down a page. You would then read the chart from top to bottom. Look at the flow chart on this page. It shows how a skyscraper is built. Do you read the chart from left to right or from top to bottom?

Besides following the arrows, you can also sometimes follow the numbers in a flow chart. The chart on this page has five numbered steps. How many steps does the flow chart on page 216 have?

Books often use flow charts to show the order in which things are done. When you read a flow chart, always remember to follow the arrows and the numbered steps.

CHECKING YOUR SKILLS

Use the flow chart on this page to answer these questions.

1. What is the first step in putting up a skyscraper? What is the last step?

2. When is the foundation dug, after step 1 or after step 3?

3. Which step comes first, putting in water pipes or building the outside of the skyscraper?

4. Make your own flow chart showing the steps in which you do some everyday job, such as washing dishes, cleaning your room, or mowing the lawn.

217

Thinking Back

- The Great Lakes are the world's largest group of freshwater lakes. The flat land and good soil near the Great Lakes make this a valuable farming region.

- Water is an important resource of the Great Lakes region. The region's rivers and lakes link it with the rest of the world. Other resources include rich soil, forests, iron ore, and coal.

- Jean Du Sable built a trading post on Lake Michigan that later grew into the city of Chicago.

- President Abraham Lincoln freed the slaves and led our country during the Civil War.

- The Great Lakes states are an important farming and manufacturing region. Major farm products include corn, fruits, vegetables, and dairy products. More than one-fourth of our manufactured products come from the Great Lakes states.

- Chicago is the largest city in the Great Lakes region. Its location has made Chicago a busy port and a center of transportation.

Check for Understanding

Using Words

Write the numbers 1 to 5 on your paper. Use the words from the list to fill in the blanks. Write the words on your paper.

Civil War   pioneers
elected   Springfield
Abraham Lincoln

Our sixteenth President, (1), was born in a log cabin in Kentucky. He and his family later moved to Indiana with some of the first settlers, or (2). Lincoln next moved to a town near (3), the present state capital of Illinois. The people there (4) him to the state government. Lincoln later became a member of the U.S. Congress and then President. During his term as President, Americans fought the (5).

Reviewing Facts

1. Name two ways in which glaciers shaped the Great Lakes states.
2. How do products from the Great Lakes region reach other parts of the world?

3. Why are the Great Lakes states good for farming? What crops grow well there?
4. How did Chicago begin?
5. Why did the Civil War begin?
6. What state leads in growing corn? What state leads in dairy farming?
7. How is most corn used?
8. How do miners get iron ore from the Mesabi Range?
9. Why are many cars made in the Great Lakes states?
10. How does Chicago's location make this city important?

Thinking Critically

The cities of the Great Lakes region have many large factories. What are some good things about having so many factories in one place? What do you think some problems might be?

Writing About It

Write a letter to Abraham Lincoln. In your letter, describe how your schooling is different from the schooling he had as a boy.

Practicing Chart Skills

Reading Flow Charts

Make a flow chart showing how corn-flakes are made. Write at least four steps, and include a drawing for each step. Look back to page 209 for help.

On Your Own

Social Studies at Home

Americans enjoy eating corn in many forms. List all the dishes you can think of that are made from corn. Ask family members to read your list and add other dishes. Then use your list to make a menu for a restaurant that serves only corn dishes. Compare your menu with those of your class-mates, and add new ideas.

Read More About It

Caddie Woodlawn by Carol Ryrie Brink. New ed. Macmillan. A winner of the Newbery Award, this story tells about growing up in Wisconsin a century ago.

The First Book of the Civil War by Dorothy Levenson. Rev. ed. Franklin Watts. The history of America's most troubling conflict is told from a soldier's point of view.

If You Grew Up with Abraham Lincoln by Ann McGovern. Scholastic. In this book you will have a chance to "meet" Abraham Lincoln and "live" his problems.

In Coal Country by Judith Hendershot. Illustrated by Thomas B. Allen. Alfred A. Knopf. This book tells about a coal-mining family.

Skyscrapers by Cass R. Sandak. Franklin Watts. This book describes our tallest buildings.

219

The Plains States

"Vast wheat fields are stitched into the prairie like machine-made carpet. Regiments of sunflowers gaze so uniformly east that I've felt compelled to glance that way too. Along the Red River . . . the state lies flat as a map, with grain elevators and solitary farms penciled on a razor-thin horizon."

—A description of North Dakota's prairie taken from *National Geographic*

Look for these important words:

Key Words
- monument
- gateway
- groundwater
- windmills
- blizzards
- tornadoes
- hailstorms

Places
- St. Louis, Missouri
- Interior Plains
- Central Plains
- Great Plains
- Black Hills

- Badlands
- Mississippi River
- Missouri River

Look for answers to these questions:
1. How does the land change from east to west in the Plains states?
2. What bodies of water are found here?
3. What is the climate of the Plains states?

1 The Land and Its Resources

Let's take a make-believe car trip across the Plains states. Our starting point will be **St. Louis, Missouri.** A huge arch stands along the Mississippi River in St. Louis, Missouri. The arch is the tallest **monument** in the United States. A monument is something that is built to remind people of the past. The arch in St. Louis is in the form of a **gateway,** or entrance. It reminds us that St. Louis was the "Gateway to the West." It was the city many pioneers passed through on their way west. Now as you head west from St. Louis, fields of corn, oats, and soybeans stretch out for as far as you can see.

Trappers, explorers, railroad workers, and settlers passed through St. Louis on their way west. The Gateway Arch is a symbol of their starting point.

221

As you travel farther west, you see a new crop in the flat fields. It is wheat. You see miles and miles of it. There is wheat to the north, south, east, and west.

Now the land begins to become hilly. Not much rain or snow falls here. You see herds of beef cattle and sheep. Your car trip ends as you reach the foothills of the Rocky Mountains. You traveled about 700 miles (about 1,125 km), passing through one of the great farming and ranching areas of the United States.

The Plains states lie within the **Interior Plains.** The Interior Plains can be divided into the **Central Plains** and the **Great Plains.** On the Central Plains corn and tall grasses grow well. On the Great Plains, however, only short grasses and wheat can grow. Missouri and Iowa are two of the Plains states in the Central Plains. The rest of the Plains states—Kansas, Nebraska, South Dakota, and North Dakota—lie mostly on the Great Plains. The land here is quite dry. Much of this land is used for raising beef cattle and sheep.

The Plains states are not perfectly flat. Most of the land has

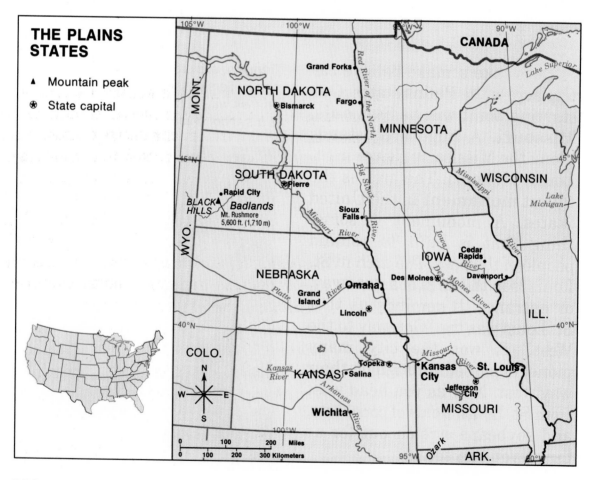

THE PLAINS STATES

▲ Mountain peak

✳ State capital

Forbidding but beautiful, the Badlands got their name by being difficult barriers to travel and impossible lands to farm.

a gentle roll. In South Dakota the **Black Hills** rise to more than 7,000 feet (about 2,130 m). These pine-covered hills are the highest place in the Plains states.

East of the Black Hills is a stretch of dry land called the **Badlands.** The country is rugged and wild here. Few plants grow. Millions of years of erosion and strong winds carved strange shapes in the hills. No pioneers settled here as they moved west. Why might you suppose they would call this the Badlands?

Bodies of Water

Rivers great and small cross the Plains. The **Mississippi** and the **Missouri** rivers are the two largest.

The Mississippi forms the eastern boundary of the Plains states. The Missouri River joins the Mississippi near St. Louis, Missouri. The Missouri begins more than 2,300 miles (about 3,700 km) away in the Rocky Mountains. It crosses the Great Plains on its way to the Mississippi. Look at the map on page 222. Through which states does the Missouri River flow?

Besides using water from their rivers, people of the Plains states use **groundwater** also. Groundwater is the water beneath the Earth's surface. Farmers and ranchers use pumps to bring the water from wells. Some of the pumps are driven by **windmills.** Windmills have wide blades set in the shape of a wheel. When a wind strikes the blades, the wheel turns. The turning wheel makes a pump work. The pump pulls up the groundwater. With windmills farmers make use of the

Early windmills were used to grind grain. In America they are used to pump water.

strong winds that often blow across the Plains.

Climate

Because the Plains states cover such a large area, the northern and southern states of this region have different climates. In the north winters are long and cold. Wild storms sometimes roar down from Canada, bringing snow and freezing temperatures. In the southern states winters are not so cold. The summers are longer and can be very hot.

The farther east you live in the Plains states, the more precipitation there is. In the Central Plains there is enough precipitation for crops and forests. The Great Plains are drier. For most crops except wheat, not enough rain falls in the Great Plains.

The weather in the Plains states can change quickly. In this region cold winds from the North Pole meet warm, moist air from the Gulf of Mexico. When cold and warm air meet, huge storms can develop. During the winter there are **blizzards.** A blizzard is a heavy snowstorm that has strong, freezing winds.

Every spring and summer **tornadoes** (tawr•NAY•dohz), or "twisters," form over the Plains region. A tornado is a tall, dry funnel of whirling wind. This

When a tornado threatens, many people in the Plains states go into their basements or cellars for protection.

funnel travels with the narrowest part near the ground. The bottom of the funnel can be as wide as a house. When the funnel touches the ground, it can blow apart houses and overturn cars and trucks. When a tornado goes through a town, some houses will be ruined while others across the street might remain unharmed.

Hailstorms also threaten the region. These storms drop pieces of ice that can ruin crops. The pieces of ice beat the crops to the ground, breaking the stalks or crushing the grain. Some of these pieces can be as large as marbles or even golf balls. Believe it or not, hailstorms often happen in warm spring weather!

Reading Check

1. What is the highest place in the Plains states?
2. In what ways do the people of the Plains states get water?
3. How do climates in the Central and Great Plains differ?

Think Beyond Imagine that you are a farmer who has just moved to the Great Plains from the Central Plains. How might climate affect your choice about what crops to grow?

$\mathcal{P}eople$
MAKE HISTORY

▶▶▶▶▶▶▶▶▶▶▶▶▶▶▶▶▶

Gutzon Borglum (GUHT•suhn BAWR•gluhm) was a famous American **sculptor.** A sculptor is an artist who shapes figures out of stone, metal, wood, or some other material. Borglum believed the United States needed big art, and that is what he gave it. He carved several large sculptures, including a 6-ton marble head of Abraham Lincoln. Still he dreamed of working on an even larger project.

Borglum's dream came true when he was asked to carve several figures on the side of a mountain in the Black Hills of South Dakota. Borglum suggested carving the faces of four Presidents. He chose George Washington, Abraham Lincoln, Thomas Jefferson, and Theodore Roosevelt. His plan was accepted, and work on the Mt. Rushmore National Memorial, shown here, began. A memorial is something that reminds people of a person or event from the past.

Carving the mountain was no easy task. It involved drilling, dynamiting, and polishing the stone. Borglum had to supervise the work closely because many of his workers simply could not imagine the faces that he saw so clearly in the mountain. "They're in there," he once said. "All I've got to do is bring 'em out."

Borglum worked on the memorial for 14 years but died before it was finished. His son finished the project. Today people from around the world come to South Dakota to view Borglum's "big art."

Think Beyond   Why do you think people are willing to travel so far to see this memorial?

SKILLS IN ACTION

USING ROAD MAPS

A road map shows drivers how to get from one place to another. This road map shows a part of Iowa. The map key helps you read the map. It lists different kinds of highways that are on the map.

Interstate highways go through more than one state. The symbol shows these routes. The number of the highway is inside the symbol. No stop signs or stoplights are on interstate highways.

United States highways also go from state to state. The number of the highway is inside the ⑥ symbol.

State highways connect places inside one state. The highway number is inside the ⑤ symbol.

How do you find your way from one place to another? First, you must find both places on the map. Then run your finger along the highways that connect them. Look for the highway numbers.

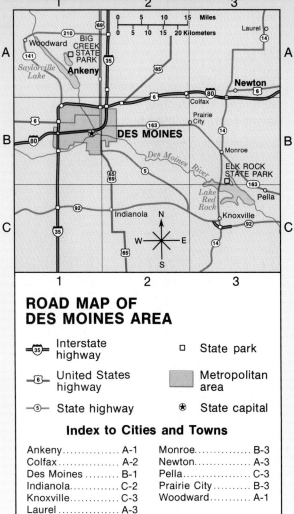

ROAD MAP OF DES MOINES AREA

- ⟨35⟩ Interstate highway
- ⟨6⟩ United States highway
- ⟨5⟩ State highway
- ☐ State park
- ▨ Metropolitan area
- ✶ State capital

Index to Cities and Towns

Ankeny	A-1	Monroe	B-3
Colfax	A-2	Newton	A-3
Des Moines	B-1	Pella	C-3
Indianola	C-2	Prairie City	B-3
Knoxville	C-3	Woodward	A-1
Laurel	A-3		

CHECKING YOUR SKILLS

Use the map to answer these questions.

1. What kind of highway is Highway 35?

2. Use the map grid. What cities are in box C–3?

3. You are traveling from Knoxville to Laurel. Will you go north or south on ⑭ ?

4. What is one way to travel from Indianola to Prairie City?

227

Look for these important words:

Key Words
- bison
- treaties

People
- Buffalo Bill
- Sitting Bull
- George Custer

Look for answers to these questions:
1. What were some of the problems between the Indians and the pioneers?
2. In what ways did the settlers and the railroads change the Plains states?
3. Why did many Indians leave the Great Plains?

2 The Plains States Long Ago

Farms and ranches cover the Great Plains today, but the land was not always this way. About 140 years ago few farms or ranches were here. Roads were just wagon tracks across wide, open grasslands. Millions of **bison** (BYS•uhn), or buffalo, lived on the Great Plains.

In those days most of the people who lived here were American Indians. The Sioux (SOO) were a large group. The Dakota, Kansa, Iowa, and Missouri Indians were part of the Sioux family. The places where they lived are now the states that were named after them.

The Indians of the Great Plains depended on the buffalo. They used almost every part of the

Indians painted picture signs on buffalo skins. The Indian chief in this painting wears such a painted buffalo robe.

animal. They ate buffalo meat. They made bedding and tepees from buffalo hides. They used buffalo bones to make tools.

The buffalo gave the Plains Indians almost everything they needed. What would happen if the buffalo disappeared?

The Railroads and the Hunters

When Lincoln was President, Americans were building a railroad from the Atlantic to the Pacific. One railroad company began building from the Pacific coast. The other started in Omaha, Nebraska.

Thousands of workers helped build the railroad. They all had to be fed. The railroad companies decided to feed them with buffalo meat. The railroads hired hunters to shoot enough buffalo to feed the railroad workers.

The most famous buffalo hunter was a man named William Cody. A railroad company hired him at $500 a month to kill 12 buffalo a day. Few people called Bill Cody by his real name. Everyone called him by his nickname. It was **Buffalo Bill.**

Buffalo were so numerous that trains were often stopped for hours while a herd rumbled across the tracks. Sometimes a million or more would be on the move across the Great Plains.

Sitting Bull

Later many more hunters killed almost all the buffalo. Indians had a hard time finding food. They also became angry at losing their land to the settlers who were coming to the Great Plains. Hundreds of settlers were killed. The U.S. Army moved to stop the Indians. Little by little, many Indians were pushed farther into the Black Hills of South Dakota.

To try to bring peace to the plains, the United States government signed **treaties** with the Indians. A treaty is a written agreement. One of these treaties promised the Black Hills to the Sioux Indians. No settlers were to move onto this land. This treaty was broken when miners discovered gold in the Black Hills. The Indians prepared for war.

One of the Indian leaders was Chief **Sitting Bull.** With him were about 2,500 Indian fighters. They made a camp by the Little Bighorn River in Montana. This river is near the western edge of the Great Plains.

The U.S. government ordered the Indians to move onto reservations. The Indians refused. Several groups of soldiers started to move against the Sioux. The leader of one group of soldiers was General **George Custer.** He and his soldiers marched to the Little Bighorn River to fight the Indians there. The Indians were prepared for the attack. Custer and all of his men were killed. Today this battle is sometimes called "Custer's Last Stand."

The Indians had few victories after Custer's Last Stand. More soldiers were sent to the plains. The Indians were soon defeated. The government moved them to reservations.

As the Indians left the Great Plains, more settlers moved westward. They were not only from the eastern United States. The pioneers also came from Europe. Many came from Russia, Czechoslovakia (chek•uh•sloh•VAH•kee•uh), Norway, Sweden, and Denmark. The pioneers plowed the prairie of the Great Plains. Corn and wheat replaced the grass. Cattle replaced the buffalo. The railroads brought the cattle and the crops of the plains to market.

Reading Check

1. What did the buffalo provide for the Plains Indians?
2. How did building railroads hurt the Plains Indians?
3. Why were treaties with the Plains Indians broken?

Think Beyond Suppose you were a Plains Indian. How would you feel about the new settlers?

IN FOCUS

SETTLERS ON THE PLAINS

Crunch! Clomp! Crunch!

Something was walking on top of the house. The children looked up from their lessons. Pieces of dirt were falling from the ceiling.

"The cow's on the roof again," cried their mother. "Run outside and chase her off!"

This was an everyday event among pioneer families on the plains. When settlers moved to the plains, many had to build **dugouts.** A dugout was a house dug into a hillside. The roof was built of **sod,** a layer of grass-covered earth. Sometimes the family cow wandered from the hillside onto the grassy roof!

The settlers had to face many dangers. During the hot summers fires often swept across the plains. In some years clouds of grasshoppers came. They could eat a whole field of wheat.

The nearest store might be 100 miles (about 160 km) away. Pioneer women and girls had to know how to make soap, candles, and clothing. They learned to **preserve,** or keep, foods in Indian ways, for example, by drying strips of meat in the sun.

The pioneer woman had to take care of both the farm and the family. Without doctors nearby, a woman on the plains learned to treat snakebites, broken bones, and illnesses. If no schools were near, she taught her children.

Life on the Great Plains could be lonely. Neighbors lived miles apart. Everyone in a family worked hard all day long. After dinner they might entertain each other with songs or stories.

Think Beyond What do you think would be the hardest thing about settling on the Great Plains?

Nebraska pioneers
and their family
cow

Look for these important words:

Key Words
- grain elevators
- thresh
- chaff
- combines
- winter wheat
- spring wheat
- meat-packing plants
- county seat
- county

Places
- Goodland, Kansas

Look for answers to these questions:
1. How has farming changed in the Plains states?
2. What kinds of manufacturing have developed in the Plains states?
3. What natural resources are here?
4. Why are there more small towns than large cities in the Plains states?

3 The Plains States Today

Like tall skyscrapers, **grain elevators** tower above the plains. These elevators store the tons of grain harvested in the Plains states. From here the grain is shipped to factories to be turned into cereals and other foods.

Why can the Plains states grow so much food? One reason is that the soil is rich. Another is that the land is level. The fields are big and flat enough to grow large amounts of crops. Still another reason is the climate. In the eastern plains the climate is just right for corn. In the western plains it is right for wheat. Finally, farm machines and new ways of farming have changed farm work.

From grain elevators, grain may be sold to flour mills or to overseas markets.

232

Combined harvester-threshers, or combines, allow today's farmers to do more work in much less time than it took 100 years ago.

Wheat Farming

Wheat farming has changed greatly over the years. Farmers used to plow their fields with horses and mules. They planted seeds by hand. When the plants were ripe, farmers had to cut and **thresh** the wheat. To thresh is to separate the wheat from the **chaff.** The chaff is the outside cover of the grain. Even with horse-drawn machines, it took farmers many hours to plow, plant, cut, and thresh a field of wheat.

Farmers today use machines to prepare the soil and to plant seeds. To harvest the wheat, farmers use huge machines called **combines.** A combine cuts and threshes the wheat all at once.

Today's wheat farmers use better seeds and fertilizers than in the past. They have learned to grow two kinds of wheat also, **winter wheat** and **spring wheat.** Winter wheat grows in the southern Great Plains. It is planted in the fall. The plants grow until winter comes. When spring comes, they start to grow again. In summer, the crop is harvested. Spring wheat grows in the northern Great Plains. It

233

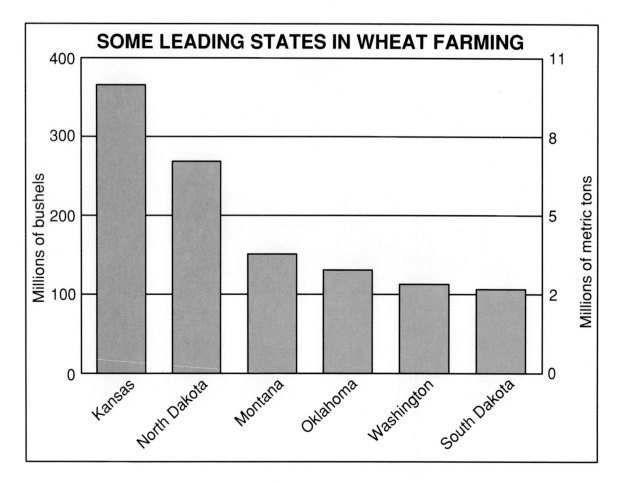

SOME LEADING STATES IN WHEAT FARMING

Millions of bushels — Millions of metric tons

Kansas, North Dakota, Montana, Oklahoma, Washington, South Dakota

cannot live through cold winters. Spring wheat is planted in spring and harvested in summer.

Not only does wheat from the Great Plains feed Americans, but it also feeds many other people around the world. Kansas and North Dakota grow more wheat than any other states.

Beef Cattle and Sheep

Cattle and sheep ranches spread out over Nebraska, Kansas, North Dakota, and South Dakota. In some parts of these states the land is too hilly for growing wheat. Cattle and sheep graze on the short grass there.

One kind of grass that grows on the prairie is buffalo grass. It is one of the best kinds of grasses to feed a herd. In summer the cattle and sheep eat the green grass. In winter they eat the dry brown grass that is left. When snow covers the ground, ranchers put out hay for the animals.

Manufacturing

You have read that wheat, corn, and cattle are important products of the Plains states.

These tractors and farm machinery are for sale in a Plains state.
Why would it be useful to have farm machine factories in this region?

What kind of manufacturing do you think is important here?

Since so much grain and meat come from the Plains states, food processing is an important industry. Factories in these states turn grain into breakfast cereals. Wheat is also ground into flour in large flour mills. Much of the flour is shipped to bakeries where it is made into bread.

Meat-packing plants turn meat into hot dogs and cold cuts. Sides of beef go from the plants to supermarkets. Kansas City, Missouri, and Omaha, Nebraska, are meat-packing centers.

The Plains states make more than food products. They also make farm machines. Such machines as tractors and combines are used on farms all over the Plains states. Factories in Des Moines (dih•MOYN), Iowa, make many of them.

You might not think of this, but small airplanes are also useful in the Plains region. Some doctors and lawyers use planes to cover the many miles between small towns. Wichita (WICH•uh•taw), Kansas, makes more small airplanes than any other city in our country.

235

Minerals and Fuels

The rich soil of the Plains region provides several minerals and fuels. South Dakota has the largest gold mine in the country. North Dakota has large amounts of coal and oil. Many of the Plains states produce cement, sand, and gravel, as well as oil.

People of the Plains States

Most of the land in the Plains states is used for farming or ranching. Yet most of the people in this region are not farmers or ranchers. They live and work in cities and towns.

There are fewer large cities on the Plains than in most regions. Instead there are many small towns. **Goodland, Kansas,** is one of these towns.

Goodland is a small town of about 6,000 people. It is an important center for the people who live around it. It has an airport and a modern hospital. It also has five large parks and a new library.

Goodland is also the **county seat** of Sherman County. A county seat is a town or city that

The school bell of the first schoolhouse in Goodland sits in front of the county seat building.

Did you know that fairs have long been a part of our American culture? The first fair in the English colonies was held in what is now the state of New York. By the early 1700s fairs were popular events in all the English colonies.

Today, all kinds of fairs are held in the United States. However, county fairs are the most common. Many county fairs include a carnival midway with games and rides.

Among the usual rides are Ferris wheels. The largest Ferris wheel was built in 1893 by G. W. Gale Ferris. It was more than 250 feet (about 76 m) high and carried 36 cars. Each car held up to 60 people! This ride was named the Ferris wheel in honor of its builder.

is the center of government for a **county.** A county is part of a state. It includes towns and other communities. Each county has its own government, which builds roads and makes sure laws are obeyed.

Like many towns in the Plains states, Goodland holds a county fair each summer. Large crowds enjoy games, animal shows, and calf-roping matches. Some people come to see new farm machines.

Sometimes when people come to Goodland, they go to the county's historical museum. On display at the museum are costumes worn by the early settlers of the state. Tools, furniture, and all the other things people used long ago are also displayed. Visitors can see pictures of farmers living in sod houses, and the railroad that people rode on their way to Goodland. Many of the early settlers were the ancestors of people still living in Goodland.

Reading Check

1. Where is grain stored?
2. What does a combine do?
3. What do cattle graze on?

Think Beyond Why is Goodland important to the county?

SKILLS IN ACTION

READING NEWSPAPERS

The newspaper's city room is buzzing with activity. As they do every day, people are rushing about. Reporters sit at their desks, writing their stories on computers. The editor calls a reporter over. "I heard about a woman who has started a construction company. Why don't you go see her and get the story?"

In a few hours you can read the story in the newspaper.

Reporters work quickly to gather the latest information for news stories.

ST. LOUIS MOTHER TURNS TO BUILDING HOMES

By Robert Nicholas

ST. LOUIS——For the past five years a St. Louis woman has been running her own construction company. Susan Malcolm has repaired 15 homes in that time. All of the buildings are in the Soulard part of the city. Mrs. Malcolm has also continued to raise her five children during those five years.

First comes the **headline.** Headlines are in large letters to catch your eye. Next is the **byline,** in smaller letters. The byline tells who wrote the story. At the begin-ning of the story is the **dateline.** It tells where the story was written. What is the headline of this story? What name is in the byline? What is the dateline?

Reporters write their stories so people can get the news quickly. The first part of a news story has the most important information. Each paragraph that follows tells more about what happened.

The first paragraph usually tells *who, what, when,* and *where.* In

238

Mrs. Malcolm said she talked to people and did research before going into business. "My family gave me a lot of help, too," she said. "They understood how much I really wanted to do it."

Soulard is one of the oldest parts of St. Louis. Many people from Germany settled there about 150 years ago. They built many large brick houses. Mrs. Malcolm said she has always cared about the neighborhood. She wanted to fix up the charming old buildings.

this story, the *who* is Susan Malcolm. The *what* is that she runs her own construction company and has repaired 15 houses. *When* is during the past five years. *Where* is Soulard, a part of St. Louis.

The second and third paragraphs tell more about Mrs. Malcolm. They help answer the questions *how* and *why*.

Most news stories are written in this way. They have the same parts as the article you just read.

CHECKING YOUR SKILLS

1. Here are the parts of a news story from a school newspaper. The parts are not in the right order. Read the parts carefully. Think about how the story should be set up. Write the letters of the parts in the order you decide is best.

a. Jean Levi and Wally Rogers were elected to the Drew School student council yesterday. The two fourth-grade students are the youngest members of the student council.

b. FOURTH GRADERS WIN ELECTION

c. Drew School

d. The results of the election surprised many of us. Few students expected the fourth graders to win.

e. By Marsha Ferrin

f. Jean said they won "because we worked hard on school projects." They plan to start other projects at Drew School.

2. Now identify the *who, what, when,* and *where* in the first paragraph of the above news story you put in order.

239

CHAPTER 10 REVIEW

Thinking Back

- The Plains states lie within the Interior Plains, which can be divided into the Central and Great Plains. The land in the east is flat. The land in the west is hilly and drier.

- The Mississippi and the Missouri are the region's two largest rivers. The Mississippi River forms the region's eastern boundary.

- The Indians of the Great Plains depended on the buffalo for food, shelter, and tools. Railroad companies hired hunters to shoot the buffalo.

- Indians were angry because settlers were taking away their land. Wars broke out. The Indians were defeated and moved to reservations. More settlers then moved westward.

- Modern machines and new ways of farming help farmers grow much food in the rich, level land of the Plains states. Cattle and sheep graze on buffalo grass.

- Food processing and the manufacturing of farm machinery are important industries in the Plains states.

Check for Understanding

Using Words

Copy the paragraph below. Fill in the blanks with the correct words from the list.

chaff   **thresh**
combines   **windmills**
grain elevators

Plains farmers sometimes use __(1)__ to pump groundwater to their crops. After the wheat is grown, farmers must cut and __(2)__ it. The farmers separate the wheat from the __(3)__. Today wheat farmers use large machines called __(4)__. They store wheat in __(5)__. From there the grain is shipped to factories.

Reviewing Facts

1. Why is corn grown in the Central Plains? Why is wheat grown in the Great Plains?
2. Why was the buffalo important to the Plains Indians?
3. How did the coming of the railroad change life in the Plains states?
4. Why are cattle raised in the western Plains?
5. Why was St. Louis, Missouri, called the "Gateway to the West"?

Thinking Critically

1. Suppose that you and your family had settled in one of the Plains states in 1860. What would your life have been like? In what ways would it have been different from your life today?

2. Which would you expect to find in a Plains city, a meat-packing plant or a steel mill? Give reasons for your answer.

Writing About It

Imagine that you work for an advertising agency. Write a jingle about a breakfast cereal made from corn, oats, or wheat grown on a Plains state farm. Make sure that your jingle tells about the need to eat a good breakfast every morning.

Practicing Geography Skills

Using Road Maps

Use the road map on page 227 to answer the following questions.

a. Which highways will you travel if you want to drive the shortest distance between Des Moines and Elk Rock State Park?

b. On what kind of highway will you travel?

c. What kind of highway connects Indianola with Knoxville?

d. Which interstate highway runs north and south through Iowa?

On Your Own

Social Studies at Home

Find a short newspaper article that interests you and paste it on a sheet of paper. Label the headline, the by-line, and the dateline. Then find and label the *who, what, when, where, why,* and *how* parts. Discuss the article with a family member.

Read More About It

Blind Colt by Glen Rounds. Holiday. A ten-year-old boy adopts and trains a wild colt in this story set in the Badlands of South Dakota.

Children of the Wild West by Russell Freedman. Clarion Books. The daily life of the children who helped settle the Plains is described in this interesting book.

One Day in the Prairie by Jean Craighead George. T. Y. Crowell. In this book prairie animals sense a coming tornado and seek cover before the storm strikes.

An Orphan for Nebraska by Charlene Joy Talbot. Atheneum. In this story based on actual events, a homeless boy leaves New York City for a new home in Nebraska.

Sitting Bull, Great Sioux Chief by Lavere Anderson. Garrard Press. The life of the great Indian warrior who fought to protect his people is described in this book.

CHAPTER 11

The Southwest

My grandmother tells me,

"Small Papago Indian,
girl of the Desert People,
for two summer moons
I will walk with you
across the sand patches,

by the rock ridges
and the cacti,
through the dry washes
and along the sandy trails
that you may know the desert
and hold its beauty
in your heart forever."

—from the story "Along Sandy Trails"
by Ann Nolan Clark

Look for these important words:

Key Words	Places	
• mesas	• Colorado Plateau	• Rio Grande
• saguaro cactus	• Sonoran Desert	• Sun Belt
• yucca	• Chihuahuan Desert	
• cloudburst		

Look for answers to these questions:
1. What landforms are in the Southwest?
2. How did rivers shape the land?
3. Why is the Southwest a good ranching and farming area?
4. What is unusual about the climate in the Southwest?

1 The Land and Its Resources

Some people think that the Southwest is mostly a desert. Though it is true that big deserts are here, the Southwest has many other kinds of land. Under the sunny Southwestern skies lie towering, snow-capped mountains and lush pine forests. There are rainy plains, fertile river valleys, and rocky canyons in brilliant colors. All over the world, people still think of this land as "the wide, open spaces."

The Southwest is a larger region than the Northeast and the Great Lakes states put together. Yet it has only four states. They are Arizona, New Mexico, Oklahoma, and Texas.

The Rocky Mountains and the Colorado Plateau

The highest parts of the region are the Rocky Mountains and the **Colorado Plateau.** The Colorado Plateau begins at the western edge of the Rocky Mountains. This huge plateau covers much of northern New Mexico and Arizona. The Colorado Plateau gets its name from the Colorado River, which runs through it. Very little rain falls on this rough land.

Rivers like the Colorado have cut deep canyons in the plateau. At one time the Colorado River was wider. Over many years it wore away the rock to form the Grand Canyon.

243

The rivers have also helped make flat-topped hills called **mesas** (MAY•suhz). *Mesa* is the Spanish word for table. Spanish explorers were the first people from Europe to see these hills. As they looked across the open land, the mesas must have reminded them of tabletops!

The Great Plains

As the Great Plains stretch west to the Rockies, the land gets higher. The highest part of the plains is in the Southwest. Cattle and sheep graze on the short grass that grows here. In fact, this is some of the world's best cattle country.

The land gets lower south of the Great Plains. This flat land is part of the Coastal Plain that stretches from the Northeast across much of the Southeast. A warm climate and plenty of rain make this part of the Coastal Plain good for farming.

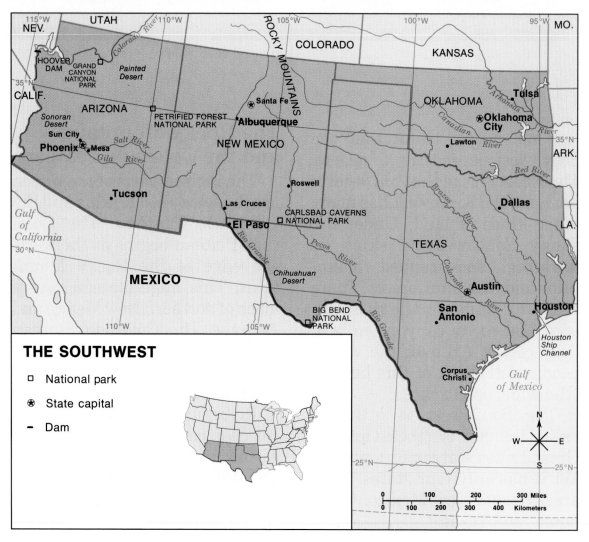

THE SOUTHWEST

□ National park

✷ State capital

– Dam

The Sonoran and Chihuahuan Deserts

The **Sonoran Desert** is one of the world's most beautiful deserts. In no other desert are there so many kinds of cactuses. The largest is the **saguaro** (sah•WAH•roh) **cactus.** The saguaro is a giant plant. It may grow taller than 50 feet (about 15 m) high. Its secret is that it can store almost any rain that falls. About three-quarters of the plant is water.

Miles of white sand dunes cover the northern part of the **Chihuahuan Desert.** One plant that grows in this desert is the **yucca** (YUK•uh). Some sand

Sometimes only the yucca's top shows above a sand dune. Yuccas can grow almost anywhere in the West.

The Sonoran Desert in southwest Arizona has several wilderness preserves that protect its rare animals and plants.

dunes are as high as a five-story building. As the sand dunes get higher, the yucca keeps growing.

Bodies of Water

High in the Rocky Mountains snow melts to form rivers. The Colorado River is the largest one that flows into the Southwest. The second largest is the **Rio Grande.** These two rivers flow in different directions. The Colorado flows southwest to the Gulf of California. The Rio Grande flows southeast and empties into the Gulf of Mexico.

Climate

The Southwest is a land of sun and warm temperatures. It is part of the **Sun Belt,** a wide area of sunny and mild weather. The Sun Belt stretches from Virginia through the Southwest and into southern California.

Not all of the Southwest is dry, however. Eastern Texas gets a lot of rain. Heavy snow falls on New Mexico's mountains in winter.

When it does rain in the dry places, sometimes it really pours! The sky may suddenly get dark. Then a **cloudburst,** or a sudden hard rain, may quickly flood the

Six million years ago the Colorado River's rippling waters began to carve through the colored rock to create the Grand Canyon.

Life would be difficult in some places if people could not change their **environment,** or surroundings. In Arizona, for example, almost one-third of the land is desert. There is not enough rainfall or groundwater to supply all the water that is needed in this fast-growing state.

To help meet their water needs, the people of Arizona decided to get water from a lake on the Colorado River. To do this, they are building a series of canals, tunnels, pumping plants, and pipelines to carry water some 335 miles (about 539 km) across the state. This huge undertaking, called the Central Arizona Project, will provide additional water to people living and working in such desert areas as Phoenix and Tucson.

canyons. Cloudbursts wear away the rock and earth. During a cloudburst half a year's rain may fall in a few minutes.

Natural Resources

Beneath the sandy soil of the Coastal Plain are large pools of oil. Oil is also found underground beneath the Gulf of Mexico.

Other fuels are important in this region. Natural gas is produced in Texas, New Mexico, and Oklahoma. Coal is found in New Mexico and Oklahoma. New Mexico also supplies about half of our country's uranium.

Two valuable minerals, copper and potash, are mined in the desert areas of this region. Potash is used in fertilizers.

Reading Check

1. How is the Sonoran Desert different from other deserts?
2. Why do crops grow well on the Coastal Plain in Texas?
3. Where is the Sun Belt?

Think Beyond What are some ways in which you or someone you know uses the natural resources of the Southwest?

247

SKILLS IN ACTION

USING TRANSIT MAPS

Most cities have **transit systems.** These are buses or trains that people use in their community. Transit maps show where trains or buses travel and stop. Look at this map of downtown Phoenix, Arizona.

The green line shows the route of the Washington-Jefferson bus. Buses on Washington only go west. Buses on Jefferson only go east. What are the other bus routes?

Suppose you are starting at Washington Street and Central Avenue. You want to go to Seventh Avenue and Van Buren Street. You could ride the Washington-Jefferson bus west to Seventh Avenue. Then you would **transfer,** or change, to the Seventh Avenue bus. This bus would take you north to Van Buren Street.

CHECKING YOUR SKILLS

Use the map to answer these questions.

1. You are riding the Central Avenue bus from Van Buren Street to the public library. In which direction are you going?

2. To go from the state capitol to Patriots' Park, what bus would you take?

3. To go from the public library to the state capitol, what two buses would you take?

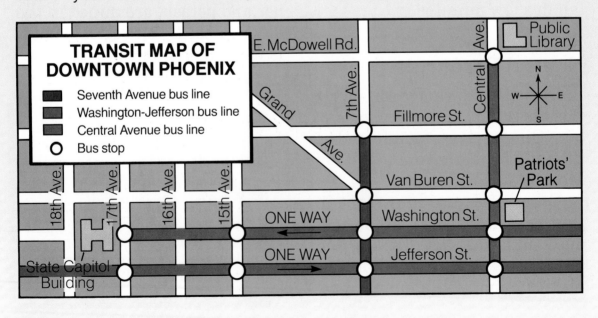

248

Look for these important words:

Key Words	People	Places
• missions	• Sam Houston	• Santa Fe, New Mexico
• plaza		• San Antonio, Texas
• Sooners		• Alamo
		• Indian Territory

Look for answers to these questions:
1. How did Santa Fe, New Mexico, begin?
2. How did Texas become a free country before it became a state?
3. How was Oklahoma settled?

2 *The Southwest Long Ago*

The year was 1610. On the Atlantic coast, Jamestown, Virginia, was three years old. Far away from Jamestown a governor from Spain was building another settlement. It was called **Santa Fe** (SAN•tuh FAY).

Santa Fe

Santa Fe was built between the Pecos River and the Rio Grande. This area is now in the state of New Mexico. The settlement was built as a capital of Spanish New Mexico. It is the oldest capital city in the United States.

Santa Fe also was a center of **missions** (MISH•uhnz). Missions were churches and schools started by priests. The priests came to New Mexico to teach the Catholic religion to the Indians.

Large farms and ranches soon grew up around the town. Mines were dug in the nearby mountains. Gold and silver were brought to Santa Fe. From there they were sent on to Mexico.

Santa Fe was an important town. It had a large **plaza** (PLAH•zuh), or public square, and many beautiful buildings. One was a building for the government. That building still stands.

As Santa Fe grew, Spain built new settlements. In the 1700s many new missions and forts were built in Texas, New Mexico, and Arizona.

Famous heroes such as Davy Crockett and James Bowie were among the 180 Americans and Texans who fought 2,000 Mexican soldiers at the Alamo. The final struggle was within the old mission's walls.

Spain found it could not hold on to its land in North America. In 1821 Mexico fought a war with Spain and won its independence. Mexico took over all the Spanish lands in the Southwest.

New people were coming into the region. In the 1820s farmers from the American frontier started settling in Texas. So many people came to Texas that the Mexican government became worried. It tried to stop Americans from moving into Texas. It made the Americans that were there obey Mexico's laws. When a new leader came to rule Mexico, the laws became harsher.

"Remember the Alamo!"

The Americans in Texas did not like the laws of the Mexican government. They decided to start their own government in Texas and to break away from Mexico. When this happened, a Mexican army marched into Texas. About 180 Americans and Texans went to an old mission in **San Antonio.** It was called the **Alamo.** This name would become well known in our history.

Thousands of Mexican soldiers attacked the Alamo. Both sides fought bravely. Finally, the Mexican soldiers broke into the building. When the battle was over, not one of the Texas fighters remained alive.

Soon other Americans and Texans joined the fight against Mexico. Their leader was **Sam Houston** (HYOO•stuhn). Houston told his army, "Remember the Alamo!" The Texans remembered this message. In 1836 they defeated the Mexican army. Texas became a free country.

Sam Houston became president of Texas soon after. Then in 1845 Texas became a state of the United States.

Sam Houston led the movement to make Texas a state. He then became a United States Senator and was later elected governor of Texas.

The Sooners

It took many years to settle Santa Fe and Texas. One part of Oklahoma, however, was almost settled in a day!

Indians from the Southeast had been forced to move to Oklahoma. For many years the land had been called the **Indian Territory.** Then the government decided to let anyone buy some of the land and settle there. April 22, 1889, was set for the opening. At noon on that day a gun went off. People raced to get the land they wanted. Some people raced away on horses. Some rode in covered wagons. Some even ran. All that day people went off to find good land.

What these people did not know was that others had not waited. The night before, some people had slipped across the line. They wanted to get the best land.

The people who went too soon were known as **Sooners.** Today Oklahoma is known as the Sooner State.

Reading Check

1. What is the oldest capital city in the United States?
2. Why did Mexico fight Texas?
3. What happened at the Alamo?

Think Beyond How do you think the Oklahoma settlers who waited until the opening day to find land felt about the Sooners?

IN FOCUS

COWHANDS

It is nearly dawn. The cowhands are sleeping with their boots on, ready for any trouble, with their horses close by. The cattle are restless. Looking over the herd from his horse, the cowhand on watch notices the gathering storm.

Suddenly lightning flashes. Thunder rumbles. The cattle are wild-eyed. They jump to their feet and run wildly across the range.

"Stampede!" shouts the cowhand on watch.

All the other cowhands quickly saddle their horses. The cowhand on watch rides alone at the side of the racing herd. He looks for the leader and tries to turn it. Soon the other cowhands are riding around the cattle. Working together, they push the cattle into a circle and calm them. Soon the stampede ends.

About 100 years ago stampedes could happen on cattle drives. Cowhands had to drive herds of longhorn cattle from Texas to Kansas and Nebraska. There was no railroad closer for shipping the cattle to market.

On these long drives, cowhands had to work together. It was the only way a few cowhands could control thousands of cattle. Two cowhands rode up front to keep the herd pointed in the right direction. Riders on the sides kept the herd from spreading out. The cowhands at the back kept the slowpokes moving.

A ranch hand may still ride a horse to round up cattle for market, but life on the range is different today. Cattle can be shipped by truck right from the ranch, or by train from a nearby town. The day of the cattle drive is over.

Think Beyond   Would you rather be a cowhand on a ranch today or on a ranch of 100 years ago? Explain your thinking.

A stampede

252

Look for these important words:

Key Words
- reservoirs
- offshore wells
- pueblos
- adobe

Places
- Hoover Dam
- Lake Mead
- Houston, Texas
- Houston Ship Channel

- Carlsbad Caverns
- Painted Desert

Look for answers to these questions:
1. Why do many people come to the Southwest?
2. Why are dams and reservoirs important to the people in the Southwest?
3. What industries are found here?
4. What have various groups of people contributed to the heritage of the Southwest?

3 The Southwest Today

The Southwest is growing fast. Its warm, sunny climate and many new jobs attract more people each year. More people now live here than ever before.

Having more people means that more water is needed. To meet these needs, people here dig wells and build **reservoirs** (REHZ•uhrv•wahrz). A reservoir is a lake that stores water held back by a dam. Wells help people reach groundwater.

The **Hoover Dam** spans the Colorado River on the Nevada-Arizona border. **Lake Mead** is the reservoir formed by the dam. It stores the Colorado's water. This

The Hoover Dam on the Colorado River formed Lake Mead, one of the world's largest reservoirs.

lake is one of the world's largest reservoirs. Communities use the water of the reservoir during dry times of the year.

The Hoover Dam provides water and electricity to many parts of the Southwest. It irrigates a million acres of farmland that used to be desert. It has helped new and old industries grow in the Southwest.

Farming and Ranching

If you have seen cowboy movies, you may know that ranching is important in the Southwest. Texas ranchers raise more cattle and sheep than ranchers in any other state. However, you may not know that wheat is also grown in the Southwest. Farmers grow wheat in Oklahoma, eastern New Mexico, and northern Texas. These areas are at the southern end of the Great Plains.

Cotton is the largest crop of the Southwest. It is grown in every state in the Southwest. Oranges grow in Arizona and near the Rio Grande. Rice grows on the moist Coastal Plain of Texas.

Crops can grow all year long in parts of the Southwest. Many areas do not get too cold for plants to grow. The farming regions have rich, red soil, too. In most places, however, the Southwest's farmland needs irrigation.

Minerals and Fuels

Valuable minerals and fuels lie underground in the Southwest. Metals such as silver and copper are also here. Mines in Arizona produce about half of the copper mined in the United States. The region has fuels such as coal, uranium, natural gas, and oil.

In Oklahoma and Texas are huge amounts of oil and natural gas. Oil is also found off the coast of Texas. **Offshore wells** drill and pump the oil found under the ocean floor.

Valuable "Texas crude" is produced by these offshore oil drilling rigs located in the Gulf of Mexico.

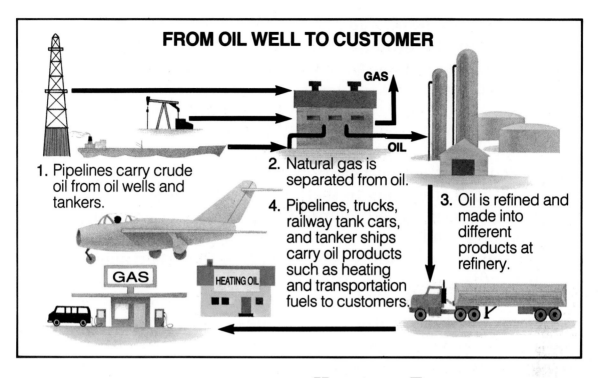

FROM OIL WELL TO CUSTOMER

1. Pipelines carry crude oil from oil wells and tankers.

2. Natural gas is separated from oil.

3. Oil is refined and made into different products at refinery.

4. Pipelines, trucks, railway tank cars, and tanker ships carry oil products such as heating and transportation fuels to customers.

GAS

OIL

GAS

HEATING OIL

Manufacturing

One reason for the Southwest's growth is its modern industries. Computers are made in cities such as Austin and Dallas, Texas, and Albuquerque (AL•buh•kur•kee), New Mexico. Factories in several large Southwest cities build airplanes and rockets.

Products made from oil also come from the Southwest. Some people call oil "black gold." Oil is a very valuable fuel. It's surprising how many things are made from oil. Phonograph records, lipstick, paint, and bug spray are just a few of them. These and thousands of other products make manufacturing important to the Southwest. Tulsa, Oklahoma, and Houston, Texas, are centers where these products are made.

Houston

Like New Orleans, Louisiana, Houston is a port that lies inland, yet it is our country's third-largest port. A wide waterway connects Houston with the Gulf of Mexico. It is called the **Houston Ship Channel.** A channel is a narrow, deep waterway that ships can use.

Houston is an important center of the oil industry. Oil tankers use the channel to bring crude oil to Houston's many oil refineries. Pipelines from Texas oil fields also bring oil to the refineries.

Each refinery has a dock where oil tankers deliver their oil. A large hose brings the oil from the ship right into the refinery. The crude oil is then changed into gasoline and heating oil.

Tourism

The Southwest's great beauty brings millions of visitors to the region each year. The mountains, deserts, and canyons are popular sights to see. Many people visit Indian towns and cities built by the Spanish.

People who like adventure can hike or ride donkeys down trails into the Grand Canyon. Another place adventurers enjoy is **Carlsbad Caverns** in New Mexico. These caverns are the largest caves ever discovered. No one really knows how long they are. The explored part is 23 miles (about 37 km) long. The caverns were discovered in 1901.

The **Painted Desert** in Arizona is another amazing sight in the Southwest. The heat and light of the desert and the minerals in the soil combine to "paint" the landscape in bright blues, reds, and yellows. The Painted Desert is especially beautiful at sunrise and sunset.

The strange, hanging rock "icicles" of Carlsbad Caverns formed when water and minerals dripped from the ceilings of the caves to the cave floor below.

People of the Southwest

One of the most interesting things about the Southwest is its mix of people. Spanish-speaking people, people from other parts of the country, and different groups of American Indians call the Southwest home.

Mexico, our neighbor to the south, has added much to the heritage of the Southwest. All the Southwest states have many Spanish-speaking people. Most cities have radio and television programs in Spanish. Throughout the Southwest are buildings built by settlers from Mexico.

Indian sheepherders learned to raise sheep from the Spanish settlers.

This radio announcer broadcasts music, news, and other programs in Spanish.

People of other backgrounds have come to live here. Some of the earliest farmers and ranchers were from the Southeast. People from Germany settled in east Texas about 140 years ago.

More American Indians live in the Southwest than in any other region. Some Indians live and work in Southwestern cities and towns. This is especially true in Oklahoma, where many Cherokee, Creek, and Choctaw Indians live. Other Indians live on reservations. The Navajo reservation lies in both Arizona and New Mexico. It is the largest reservation in our country.

257

Ancient Southwest peoples such as the Hopi had settled and farmed here centuries before the Spanish named these dwellings *pueblos.*

Many Indians live on the mesas of the Colorado Plateau. More than 800 years ago they built **pueblos** (PWEB•lohz) on the sides of cliffs. *Pueblo* is the Spanish word for village. Pueblo houses were built on top of one another. They were made with sun-dried clay bricks, called **adobe** (uh•DOH•bee). Some Indians still live in the pueblos.

Indians of the Southwest try to keep ancient arts and customs alive. Many still make their own weavings, silver and turquoise jewelry, and pottery. Children learn Indian languages in schools on their reservations.

The mix of people in our country is always changing. In the Southwest it has changed a great deal in the past 25 years. In this region you can meet new people all the time.

Reading Check

1. How do people in the Southwest get their water?
2. What makes the Southwest good for farming?
3. What are some products made from oil?

Think Beyond Why do you think the Indians of the Southwest try to keep their ancient arts and customs alive?

258

People
MAKE HISTORY

Jesse Fewkes
1850–1930

▶▶▶▶▶▶▶▶▶▶▶▶▶▶▶▶

One of the workers stopped digging. He was not sure, but he thought he saw something in the soil. He shouted excitedly to Jesse Fewkes (FYOOKS), the leader of the group. Fewkes got down on his knees and used his hands to scrape away the soil. He very carefully dug out a piece of pottery and wiped away the dirt.

Long before this discovery, Fewkes had decided that he wanted to study ancient people and the places where they had lived. He went to work at the Smithsonian Institution in Washington, D.C. Then in 1895 he was asked to study Hopi pueblo **ruins** in Arizona. Ruins are the remains of destroyed buildings and communities.

That summer Fewkes and a group of Hopi Indians began to explore an ancient pueblo. They discovered spoons, cups, vases, jars, and bowls. Almost every object had a design on it. Some showed birds and animals. Others were simple lines.

Fewkes had no way of knowing what the designs meant. However, many of the designs looked like the ones used on modern Hopi pottery. Fewkes talked with some Hopi Indians. They helped him to understand some of the ancient designs.

Fewkes became well known for his work with the ancient Hopi pottery. He went on to study other Indian ruins in the Southwest and in northern Mexico. As a result of Jesse Fewkes's work, these ruins were preserved, and people learned more about the Hopi Indians.

Think Beyond Why do you think it is important for us to know about people who lived long ago?

259

❓ SKILLS IN ACTION

SEPARATING FACTS AND OPINIONS

A good reader or listener learns to separate **facts** from **opinions.** A fact is a statement that can be checked and proved. An opinion tells what a person thinks or believes. Here is an example of a fact:

The Grand Canyon is in Arizona.

Here is an example of an opinion:

The Grand Canyon is the most beautiful place in the world.

What is the difference between the two sentences?

A newspaper is a good place to find many examples of facts and opinions. Newspapers may even have different pages for facts and opinions.

News Stories

Most newspaper articles are news stories. Their purpose is mostly to tell readers facts. Read the news story below.

The article tells readers about the new rule and what the rule says. The story tells who made the rule,

Teenagers Told to Stay Away from Shopping Center
By Peggy Armstrong

WILMINGTON—The Shady Lane Shopping Center has a new rule, store owners announced today. Teenagers are not allowed at the shopping center at lunchtime. Some adult shoppers thought they were not getting enough attention in the stores. They complained that too many teenagers were shopping at the same time. Store owners said the new rule will begin next week. The shopping center will be closed to teenagers from 11:00 A.M. to 1:00 P.M., Monday through Friday.

when the rule was made, and why. Those are the facts.

Notice that there are also opinions in the story. Adult shoppers *thought* they were not getting enough attention. They thought too many teenagers were there.

Editorials

Newspapers usually have a special section in which newswriters can give their opinions. The editor of a newspaper writes articles called **editorials.** Most editorials give the newspaper's opinions about the news. Read this editorial. As you read, look for opinion words like *think* and *believe.*

New Shopping Center Rule Is Unfair

Shady Lane Shopping Center will not allow teenagers to shop at lunchtime. We think the adults' complaints were unfair. The shopping center is open to the public. Teenagers are members of the public. We believe they have the right to shop there. In our opinion, this rule may be against the law.

This editorial gives facts as well as opinions. It is a fact that the shopping center is open to the public. It is also a fact that teenagers are members of the public. In the newspaper's opinion the new rule is not fair and may be against the law.

The editor uses facts to support the opinion of the newspaper. Using facts and opinions in this way when you write or speak can help you communicate better. Knowing the difference between facts and opinions can help you better understand what you are listening to or reading.

CHECKING YOUR SKILLS

Look at the statements below. Write *fact* if the statement can be proved. Write *opinion* if the statement is what someone thinks or believes.

1. Shady Lane Shopping Center has 25 stores.
2. "I feel funny about the new rule," said Mrs. Thomas.
3. Many teenagers bring their lunches to school.
4. "We believe the new rule is fair."
5. "I think the adults were wrong," said one teenager.
6. The editor used facts and opinions in the editorial.
7. Many teenagers shop at noon.
8. The editorial was better written than the news story.

Now write four sentences of your own that contain either a fact or an opinion. Label each sentence *fact* or *opinion.*

CHAPTER 11 REVIEW

Thinking Back

- Major land areas in the Southwest include the Rocky Mountains, the Colorado Plateau, the Great Plains, and the Sonoran and Chihuahuan deserts. The largest rivers are the Colorado and the Rio Grande.

- Santa Fe, the oldest capital city in the United States, was built as the capital for Spanish New Mexico.

- Texans fought the Mexican army at the Alamo. Sam Houston helped Texans win their independence.

- Oklahoma was once called Indian Territory. Parts of Oklahoma were settled quickly after the government allowed people to buy land.

- The Southwest is a fast-growing region. Wells and reservoirs help the Southwest meet its needs for water and electricity.

- The Southwest is an important farming and ranching region. Factories in the region produce computers, airplanes, rockets, and many products made from oil.

- The Southwest has many Spanish-speaking people and American Indians. More Indians live in the Southwest than in any other region of our country.

Check for Understanding

Using Words

Copy the words numbered 1 to 5. Next to each word, write its meaning from the list that follows.

1. **cloudburst**
2. **mesas**
3. **missions**
4. **pueblos**
5. **reservoirs**

a. flat-topped hills
b. a sudden hard rain
c. settlements run by priests
d. lakes that store water
e. Spanish word for *villages*

Reviewing Facts

1. What is the climate of most of the Southwest?
2. Why are the words "Remember the Alamo!" important in Texas?
3. Name two natural resources of the Southwest. Then name two products of the Southwest that use these resources.
4. Why is Houston an important center of the oil industry?

262

5. In what ways does Mexico add to the heritage of the Southwest?

Thinking Critically

1. The Hoover Dam has brought more people and industries to the Southwest. Why do you think this has happened?

2. What are some good things and some problems a fast-growing region may have?

Writing About It

Study the picture of the pueblo on page 258. Write a paragraph that tells how pueblos were like today's apartment buildings and how they were different.

Practicing Geography Skills

Using Transit Maps

Use the map on page 248 to answer these questions.

1. You are riding the Central Avenue bus from the public library to Jefferson Street. In which direction are you going?

2. You are at the corner of Grand Avenue and Van Buren Street. You want to go to the state capitol. Will you take the Seventh Avenue bus to Washington Street or to Jefferson Street?

3. To go from Fillmore Street to E. McDowell Road, what bus will you take?

On Your Own

Social Studies at Home

Ask permission to use an old newspaper. Find an editorial that interests you. Read each sentence carefully. Underline each sentence that states a fact. Then circle each sentence that states an opinion. Show the editorial to a family member, and share your feelings about the opinions stated in the editorial.

Read More About It

Not Just Any Ring by Danita Ross Haller. Alfred A. Knopf. Jessie is disappointed when she learns that her ring, a gift from her Indian grandfather, is not magic after all.

Spanish Pioneers of the Southwest by Joan Anderson. Photographed by George Ancona. Lodestar Books/E. P. Dutton. Photographs taken at a restored Spanish settlement near Santa Fe, New Mexico, tell the story of life there in the 1700s.

Susanna of the Alamo: A True Story by John Jakes. Illustrated by Paul Bacon. Harcourt Brace Jovanovich/Gulliver. The author vividly describes the famous battle and the woman who survived it.

Thundering Prairie by Mary A. Hancock. Macrae Smith. This lively story takes place at the time of the Oklahoma land rushes in the 1880s.

CHAPTER 12

The Mountain States

"And the Rocky Mountains, with their grand, aromatic forests, their grassy glades, their frequent springs, and dancing streams of the brightest, sweetest water, their pure, elastic atmosphere, and their unequalled game and fish, are destined to be a favorite resort and home of civilized man. "

—from the book *An Overland Journey*
   by Horace Greeley

Look for these important words:

Key Places
- Intermountain area
- Great Basin
- Colorado Plateau
- Continental Divide
- Aspen, Colorado
- Sun Valley, Idaho

Look for answers to these questions:
1. What landforms are in the Mountain states?
2. What is the Continental Divide?
3. What kind of climate is in the Mountain states?
4. What natural resources are found here?

1 The Land and Its Resources

The Mountain states are among the highest states in our country. The mountains in this region are so high that snow covers many of their peaks all year. The highest peaks rise more than 14,000 feet (about 4,270 m).

Mountains are the largest landforms in this region, but the Mountain states have much more than mountains. Three main kinds of land are in these states. In the east are the Great Plains. In the center are the great Rocky Mountains. In the west are the high, dry plateaus known as the **Intermountain area.**

Let's start in the eastern part of the Mountain states. We will look at each of the three parts a little more closely.

The Great Plains

The Great Plains meet the Rocky Mountains in the Mountain states. As the plains stretch toward the mountains, they slope upward. In Colorado, Wyoming, and Montana the plains are almost a mile above sea level. Few trees grow on the plains. Though the land is dry, it is suitable for cattle, sheep, and wheat.

The Rocky Mountains

The Rocky Mountains are not a single mountain range. They are made up of dozens of smaller ranges. They stretch through Colorado, Wyoming, Montana, Idaho, and Utah. Between these ranges are plateaus.

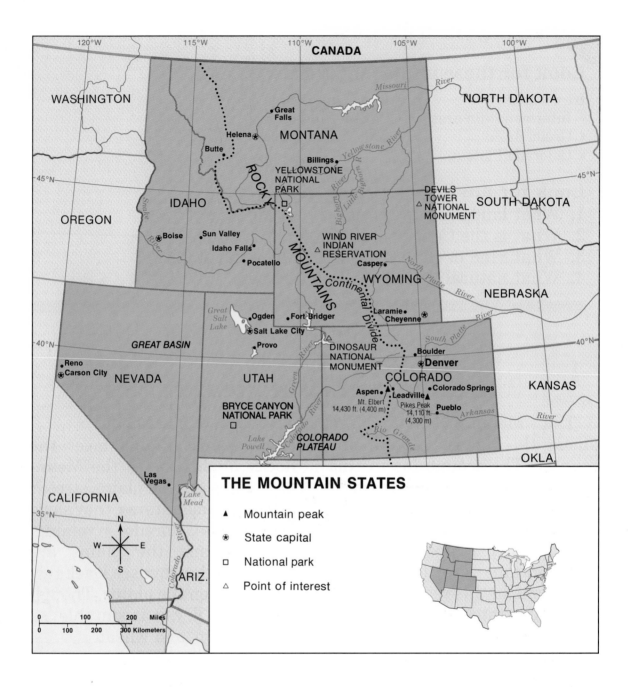

THE MOUNTAIN STATES

▲ Mountain peak

✸ State capital

☐ National park

△ Point of interest

The Intermountain Area

West of the Rocky Mountains is a huge area that is high and dry. Some people call it the Intermountain area. *Inter* means "between." The Intermountain area lies between the Rocky Mountains and the Sierra Nevada of California. This area stretches from Canada to Mexico.

Part of the Intermountain area is made up of basins. You may recall that a basin is low, bowl-shaped land. Rivers inside a basin do not flow out. They either dry up or flow to a lake in the basin.

266

Bryce Canyon National Park shows some of the unusual landforms found on the Colorado Plateau. The many shades of red, pink, copper, and brown on the canyon walls change in the sunlight.

The **Great Basin** is a large desert in this area. Nearly all the lakes in the Great Basin are salty. The Great Salt Lake in Utah is the largest lake in the basin.

High, flat plateaus cover other parts of the Intermountain area. One large plateau is known as the **Colorado Plateau.** Much of this land is high, dry, and hilly. The Colorado River crosses the plateau. It and other rivers have cut deep canyons and valleys into the land. With irrigation the valleys are useful for growing many kinds of crops. They also provide good grazing land for beef cattle and sheep.

Throughout the Intermountain area are small mountain ranges. Someone once wrote that these ranges look like caterpillars wriggling northward!

The Continental Divide

Many great rivers begin in the Rocky Mountains. Some, like the Snake, Columbia, and Colorado, flow west into the Pacific Ocean. Others, like the Arkansas, Missouri, and Platte, flow east. They join the Mississippi or flow into the Gulf of Mexico.

Look back at the map on page 266. A line runs down the Rocky Mountains. On one side are the rivers that flow east. On the other side are the rivers that flow west. This imaginary line is called the **Continental Divide.**

Climate

The Mountain states are the driest part of the United States. They get only about 15 inches (about 38 cm) of precipitation a year. Some areas are drier than others. Nevada gets only about 7 inches (about 18 cm) a year. It is the driest state in our country. About 30 inches (about 76 cm) fall in eastern Idaho in a year.

Most of the region's precipitation is snow. Melting snow from the mountains feeds the streams and rivers. Without these streams the Mountain states would not have enough water.

Temperatures change a lot from season to season in the Mountain states. In the northern states, such as Idaho and Montana, winters are mostly long and cold. Freezing blizzards howl down from Canada. Yet summers are warm and mild in these states. In the southern Mountain states the climate is quite different. Summers in Utah and Nevada can be very hot. Winters can be cold, but they are mostly mild.

Natural Resources

The Rocky Mountains themselves are the greatest natural resource of the Mountain states. The beauty of these mountains draws millions of visitors each year. National parks such as the

The deep winter snows that blanket some mountain areas make snowshoes, skis, or snowmobiles necessities.

This melting snow will soon be part of the valuable water supply of a Mountain state.

Mountain lions keep well hidden as they stalk the canyons and valleys.

Aspen trees grow among the pines in moister areas of the Rockies.

Grand Teton National Park in Wyoming and the Rocky Mountain National Park in Colorado preserve this wilderness for camping and hiking. Two popular places for skiing are **Aspen, Colorado,** and **Sun Valley, Idaho.** Besides recreation, the mountains provide minerals, fuels, and lumber.

The Rocky Mountains are rich in minerals. Early miners came to the mountains to find copper, silver, and gold. Today these metals are still mined in the Rocky Mountains. Other metals important to manufacturing, such as lead and zinc, are also mined here.

Oil, natural gas, and coal are three fuels that come from the Mountain states. Covering the Rocky Mountains' lower slopes are forests of pine trees.

Reading Check

1. What are the three main parts of the Mountain region?
2. Where is the Intermountain area? What kinds of landforms are in this area?
3. What separates rivers flowing east from rivers flowing west?

Think Beyond Why do you think it is important to preserve the land in the national parks in the Rocky Mountains?

269

SKILLS IN ACTION

USING INTERVIEWING SKILLS

Sara Fox is a student in Leadville, Colorado. She wants to learn what this old mining town was like long ago. She decides to **interview,** or talk with, someone to find out.

Preparing for the Interview

Sara makes a list of people to interview. Then she calls one of them, Mr. Harry Abnet, to ask if he will see her. When she speaks to Mr. Abnet, Sara tells him what she wants to talk about. They make an **appointment,** deciding on a time and place to meet.

Sara takes a few notes when she interviews Mr. Abnet. She has a list of questions ready to ask.

Sara calls Mr. Abnet to make an appointment to interview him.

The Interview

Sara's interview with Mr. Abnet begins like this:

> **Sara:** How did Leadville get its start, Mr. Abnet?
> **Mr. Abnet:** Well, some gold was discovered near here and then silver. The silver was found in lead, so that's how Leadville got its name. The town grew fast after the railroad was built.

Sara started with a question she had thought up before the interview. She has a list of questions to ask. Mr. Abnet's answers make her think of other questions, too.

270

As they talk, Sara does not argue or interrupt. She is there to get information. Mr. Abnet is happy to talk to someone who is interested in his story.

When the interview is over, Sara thanks Mr. Abnet. This thank-you makes Mr. Abnet feel that his time has been well spent.

After the Interview

Sara has taken a few short notes during the interview. She knows that she could not write every word. Later she will use her notes to help her write everything she can remember from the interview.

Using a Tape Recorder

Next week Sara will interview someone else. She wants to use a tape recorder during that interview. However, Sara knows that some people do not like to use a tape recorder. She will ask the person she is interviewing if it is all right to bring the machine.

CHECKING YOUR SKILLS

Look at the pairs of sentences below. They are rules to follow during an interview. Write down the sentence in each pair that is a good rule.

1. a. Start interviewing the person when you call on the telephone.
   b. Make an appointment to interview the person.

2. a. Make a list of questions to ask.
   b. Do not bring a list of questions.

3. a. Write down every word the person you are interviewing says.
   b. Take a few short notes during the interview.

4. a. Never use a tape recorder.
   b. Ask the person you are interviewing if you may use a tape recorder.

Pick a classmate or family member who has visited an interesting place. Interview that person according to the rules you have learned in this lesson.

After the interview, Sara fills in her notes with everything she remembers.

271

Reading for a Purpose

Look for these important words:

Key Words
- Shoshone
- Mormons
- Meriwether Lewis
- William Clark

People
- Sacajawea

Places
- Pikes Peak

Look for answers to these questions:
1. How did Lewis and Clark help to open up the West to American pioneers?
2. What did Sacajawea do to help our country grow?
3. Why was crossing the Rocky Mountains so difficult long ago?
4. What attracted pioneers to the Mountain states?

2 The Mountain States Long Ago

She was only 16 years old at the time of her greatest adventure. She was a **Shoshone** (shuh•SHOH•nee) Indian. At the time of her adventure, only a few people knew her name. Today we know **Sacajawea** (sa•kuh•juh•WEE•uh) as an American hero who helped our country grow from coast to coast.

Why was Sacajawea important? Let's go back hundreds of years before she was born. People from Europe were exploring America then. They could travel only as far as the Rocky Mountains. The high, rugged mountains were a huge wall blocking the way. It would take many years before the region could be settled.

The Spanish came first. Spanish settlers pushed north from Mexico in the 1700s. Next came French fur traders from Canada. They found many Indian tribes living here. Yet Americans in the East knew very little about the Rocky Mountains in the early 1800s. Was it possible to take a wagon through the mountains?

272

Could a person go by river from the Atlantic to the Pacific? No one could say for sure.

Lewis and Clark

President Thomas Jefferson sent two men to find out. Their names were **Meriwether Lewis** and **William Clark.**

Lewis and Clark with a small group of men left St. Louis, Missouri, in May 1804. They spent the summer and fall going up the Missouri River. In November they stopped at an Indian village to spend the winter. The village lay at the edge of the Rocky Mountains. The hardest part of their journey was just ahead.

Sacajawea now enters our story. She was the wife of a trapper staying at the village. Lewis and Clark hired the trapper to help them find a way through the mountains. Sacajawea joined them because she could speak to the Indians.

Across the Rockies

In the spring the party started up the Missouri again. One day one of their boats tipped over. All

Sacajawea guided Lewis and Clark and a small group of men in six canoes up the Missouri. She courageously faced many dangers and stayed with the explorers throughout their journey to the Pacific.

their goods fell into the icy water. Sacajawea did not waste a moment. She jumped in and saved almost everything.

Now the party was in the mountains near Shoshone country. Lewis and Clark set up a meeting with the Shoshones to buy horses from the Indians. The Shoshones did not want to sell their horses. Sacajawea stepped forward. The Shoshone chief gasped in surprise. Sacajawea was his sister! He had not seen her in five years.

Sacajawea persuaded her brother to sell the horses. The Shoshones also helped guide the group through the mountains.

Lewis and Clark reached the Pacific after much suffering. Then they turned around and made the same trip back. They traveled 8,000 miles (about 12,900 km). The trip took them nearly three years! They had gone from the Mississippi River to the Pacific Ocean, opening up the land to Americans. Sacajawea had helped them do it.

Wagon Trains West

Wagon trains began crossing the mountains years later. The pioneers traveled some of the paths that Lewis and Clark had discovered.

When these pioneers were crossing the Rocky Mountains, they had no roads to travel. Their wagons broke down. Their oxen

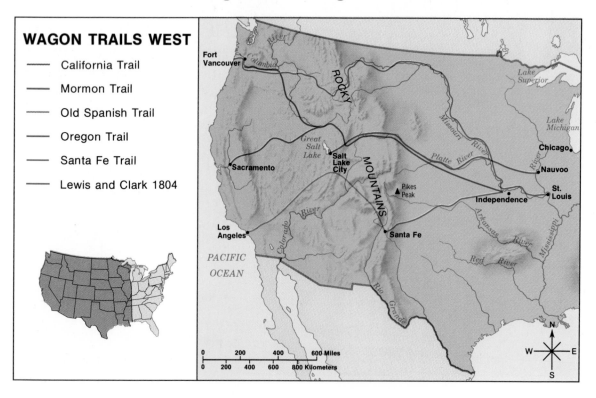

WAGON TRAILS WEST
— California Trail
— Mormon Trail
— Old Spanish Trail
— Oregon Trail
— Santa Fe Trail
— Lewis and Clark 1804

274

Though the land was dry, the soil was fertile near the Great Salt Lake. The Mormons built their city there and irrigated the land for their farms.

died. There was little water. The Rocky Mountains are steep and wide. Many settlers died before they finished crossing them.

The **Mormons** were the first large group to settle in the Mountain states. They came in search of religious freedom. The Mormons built Salt Lake City near the Great Salt Lake in Utah. Using irrigation, they turned the desert there into farmland.

Many pioneers came to the Rocky Mountains to search for gold and silver. Gold was discovered near **Pikes Peak,** Colorado, in 1858. Wagon trains set out for Colorado. The words "Pikes Peak or Bust!" were painted on their wagons. All too many people did not find the riches they were looking for. Even so, people kept coming west.

Finally the railroad reached the Rocky Mountains, bringing more people west. Towns, farms, and ranches began to spring up.

Reading Check

1. Why did it take so long for people to explore and settle the Rocky Mountains?
2. How did Sacajawea help Lewis and Clark?
3. Why did the Mormons settle in Utah?

Think Beyond What kind of person do you think an explorer or early settler of the Rocky Mountains must have been?

People MAKE HISTORY

Jim Beckwourth
1798–1867?

▶▶▶▶▶▶▶▶▶▶▶▶▶▶▶▶

More than anything else, young Jim Beckwourth wanted to get away from St. Louis, Missouri, and see the unexplored land of the West. One day this African American would do more than see the West. He would become one of the legendary Mountain Men.

Mountain Men were fur trappers who explored the wilderness. As they explored the land, Mountain Men sometimes found paths through canyons and passes over mountains. They often lived among the Indians. From the Indians they learned how to live off the land by gathering plants and hunting.

Mountain Men faced great danger. Many had exciting adventures. Beckwourth's greatest adventure happened one day when he was attacked by unfriendly Indians. Beckwourth was hurt in the attack but managed to get away. Four days later he was rescued by Crow Indians. Beckwourth was made a member of their tribe. After a few years he was made a chief!

Beckwourth eventually left the Crow Indians and traveled to California. To reach California, he had to cross the Sierra Nevada. This was the most dangerous part of the trip.

After traveling through the rugged land for several days, Beckwourth came upon a valley he had never seen before. It turned out to be a pass through the mountains! Wagon trains carrying settlers West would no longer have to struggle over the mountaintops.

Think Beyond Why do you think Mountain Men were willing to risk their lives exploring the West?

A wagon train

Look for these important words:

Key Words	• Douglas fir	Places
• geysers	• volunteers	• Yellowstone National Park
• sugar beets		• Ouray, Colorado
• U.S. Mint		

Look for answers to these questions:
1. What kinds of farming and ranching are found in the Mountain states?
2. Why might the Mountain states be called a "treasure chest"?
3. What kinds of jobs might people have in the Mountain states?

3 *The Mountain States Today*

Fewer people live in the Mountain states than in other regions of our country. Yet some of America's most beautiful places are in the Mountain states. Millions of visitors come here each year for vacations. They make tourism an important industry in this region. You can visit "dude" ranches, ski lodges, and almost a dozen national parks here.

Yellowstone National Park in Wyoming is our country's oldest national park. Here visitors can see bubbling mud volcanoes and **geysers.** Geysers are springs of water that shoot jets of steam and hot water into the air. The most famous geyser here is Old Faithful.

Old Faithful erupts faithfully every 33 to 93 minutes. None of the other geysers at Yellowstone erupt as regularly.

Farming and Ranching

Many people in the Mountain states are farmers. Even more people are ranchers. Raising beef cattle, sheep, and dairy cows is important in the Mountain states. The cattle graze on land that is too dry or too steep for crops. The sheep graze on land that is too steep for cattle.

Wheat is the most important crop in the Mountain states. It grows well on the dry lands of the Great Plains. Most of the wheat grown in the Mountain states comes from Montana, Wyoming, and Colorado.

Farmers grow other crops by irrigating the land, but irrigation costs a lot of money. Therefore, farmers must often grow crops that sell for high prices. Some of these crops are peas, beans, and **sugar beets.** A sugar beet is a white beet from which sugar is made.

Irrigation has made a particularly dry part of southern Idaho bloom. The Snake River runs through this part of the state. Irrigation canals from the Snake bring water to the many large farms in this area. Potatoes are grown on many of them. In fact,

More than a few sweaters will come from the fleecy coats of these wool sheep. Western ranchers raise mostly wool sheep, either in fenced pastures or on large enclosed areas of the range.

These Idaho potatoes are well on their way to becoming hash browns or powdered mashed potatoes.

Idaho grows more potatoes than any other state.

Minerals and Fuels

The Mountain states could be called the "treasure chest" of our country. Almost 200 minerals and fuels are found here.

All the Mountain states except Wyoming have huge amounts of copper. Gold and silver are mined here, too. The Sunshine Mine in Idaho produces the most silver in the United States. In Denver, Colorado, a large **U.S. Mint** turns these metals into pennies, dimes, and other coins.

Just as valuable as these metals are the region's fuels. Wyoming has a lot of oil and natural gas. Large amounts of coal come from Colorado, Wyoming, Montana, and Utah.

Manufacturing

Food processing is one of the important industries in the Mountain states. Workers in Idaho turn their state's biggest crop into french fries, hash browns, and potato chips. Because of the surrounding ranches, Denver, Colorado, has become a major meat-packing center.

279

Most of the Mountain states' industries make products from minerals. Iron and steel are processed in Pueblo, Colorado, and other cities. Copper is refined in Salt Lake City, Utah. Wyoming has many oil refineries. Factories in Cheyenne (SHY•an), Wyoming, turn out fertilizers and other things made from oil.

The Mountain states do less manufacturing than some other regions for two reasons. First, fewer people live here. Second, it costs more money to move goods through the mountains.

Lumbering

The huge forests of the Rocky Mountains provide lumber and wood pulp for making paper. The most valuable tree here is the **Douglas fir.** This tree grows in many parts of the West. The Douglas fir provides much of our lumber. Small Douglas firs make great Christmas trees!

People of the Mountain States

Settlers from all over Europe helped build the Mountain states.

HISTORY CONNECTION

Bull riding, calf roping, barrel racing: these are just a few of the many exciting events in a rodeo. Rodeos are held in all the Mountain states and in other regions of the United States as well. These colorful shows combine cowhand skills with the spirit of the Old West. They attract large crowds.

Rodeo is a Spanish word meaning "a gathering place or marketplace for cattle." No one knows when or where the first organized rodeo was held, but it probably occurred sometime during the 1800s. Rodeos grew out of the contests that cowhands sometimes held among

themselves after work. Over time, these contests developed into the organized event that we know today. Contestants in today's rodeos can win sizeable cash prizes.

People from Canada and Mexico settled here, too. Some became ranchers or miners. Others became loggers or store owners. People from China came to help build railroads through the mountains.

Many Indians still live in the Mountain states. The huge Wind River Reservation is in west central Wyoming. It is home to thousands of Shoshone and Arapaho (uh•RAP•uh•hoh) Indians.

You can still get the feel of frontier times in the Mountain states today. Cowboy clothes are very popular. Many old buildings look as they did long ago.

Small towns like Ouray, Colorado, are spread out miles apart across the Rocky Mountains.

The feeling of frontier times is shown in another way, too. It is shown in the way people lend a hand to a neighbor. The people in mountain towns depend on one another for help just as settlers in the Mountain states did years ago. **Ouray** (YOO•ray), a small town in Colorado, will show you how people help out.

Fire Fighters of Ouray

Most cities and towns have fire departments. Ouray is no different. However, Ouray, just like many small towns in our country, has no paid fire fighters. They

Volunteer fire fighters learn to use all the equipment on a fire engine. They also practice working together.

With an oxygen mask, a fire fighter can enter a burning building to save a life.

At a moment's notice, this volunteer fire fighter can answer an alarm.

are **volunteers.** They get no money. Their only pay is the good feeling they get from helping out.

As volunteers, these fire fighters must know how to handle the fire hoses. They must also know how to run the pump that forces water through the hoses. They must learn how to use the air masks. The masks keep them from breathing deadly smoke.

When the volunteers are not practicing or putting out fires, they have other jobs. One owns a store. Another, Roy Franz, works for Ouray Public Works. The Fire Chief, David Ficco, also works for the town of Ouray.

All the volunteers keep fire jackets, hats, and boots in their cars. If the alarm sounds, they stop what they are doing and answer it. Fire fighting has a special meaning to the volunteers of Ouray. The building they save may be the home or the store of a friend.

Reading Check

1. What is our country's oldest national park? Where is it?
2. What minerals and fuels are found in the Mountain states?
3. What kind of manufacturing is done in this region?

Think Beyond Why is it important for people to volunteer their time to their communities?

IN FOCUS

LUMBERJACKS

People who cut down trees are called **lumberjacks.** In the early days lumberjacks used long saws with a wooden handle on each end to cut down big trees. It often took two men all day to cut down a large tree.

Lumberjacks lived at camps far from town. They got up before dawn and worked until dark. At night, after a big meal, they sat up and talked.

Lumberjacks loved telling tall tales. Sometimes they held bragging matches. One man might say he could chop down a tree in a day. Another might say he could do it in half a day. Some of the tales were about a made-up hero named Paul Bunyan.

As the lumberjacks made up stories about Paul Bunyan, he began to sound almost real. Soon Paul was a hero. He was supposed to be bigger, braver, and stronger than anyone else.

Each lumberjack tried to tell a better story about Paul Bunyan than the next person. One logger might say that Paul Bunyan was so big that he pulled up pine trees by the roots to comb his beard. Another might tell how Paul mowed down a forest with his three-mile-long saw. Another might tell how Paul dug a harbor in just one day. That was nothing special for Paul Bunyan, still another logger would say. He could remember when Paul had to get some logs out of the forest and float them to the harbor. With just a sweep of his mighty hand, he scooped out a river!

Think Beyond Why do you think lumberjacks enjoyed telling tall tales about Paul Bunyan?

Lumberjacks at work

SKILLS IN ACTION

USING YOUR TELEPHONE BOOK

People do not often think of the telephone book as a reference book. However, there is a lot of useful information in your community's telephone book.

The White Pages

The white pages list the names and telephone numbers of people. The list is alphabetical, by last name. Businesses are also listed in alphabetical order. The first word in a business's name is used. If a name begins with *the* or *a,* the second word is used. This means that "The Record King" appears in the *R* list. It is listed as *Record King, The.* Look at the white page below. What is the telephone number of The Reader's Corner Bookstore?

The Yellow Pages

You will find the telephone numbers of most businesses in the yellow pages. They are listed by what they sell or do. A store called The Record King would be listed under *Records—Phonograph.* In the yellow pages types of businesses appear in alphabetical order. *Banks* comes after *Airlines* and before *Carpenters.*

Rainbow Records
    157 Montgomery 498-2768
Raintree Bakery
    693 Stevens St 234-0965
Rainwater, Michael 17 Davis Dr . . 234-9875
Ralston, Jeffrey 518 Jones St 987-5487
Ramirez, Robert
    1215 Washington Av 769-5439
Randolph, Peter 212 Bay Dr 654-7904
RAPID TRANSIT DISTRICT
    Transit Information 564-0965
    Main Office 645 Market 564-0943
Ray, Mark 105 West Civic Dr 769-3045
Reader's Corner Bookstore, The
    1302 Lake Av 563-0982
Record King, The 111 Grant Av . . . 987-2456
Recreation & Park Dept
    2396 Civic Dr 743-9872
Recycling Center, The
    212 Parkridge 987-6537
Red Hen Cafe, The 1720 Post . . . 987-0532
Redding Hospital 850 Baker 489-6523

REAL ESTATE

A & A Realty Co
    2497 Broadway 525-9843
Abbott Real Estate, Inc
    1515 Grant Av 987-2887
Action Real Estate
    698 South Portal Dr 587-6543

RECORDS—PHONOGRAPH

A-1 Records 354 Westgate Av 474-8756
All About Music 2135 Lincoln Av . 226-8767
American Music 5678 Jackson . . 987-4537
Arnold's Used Records
    2435 Garden Dr 234-0985

RESTAURANTS

Abbie's Coffee Shop
    56 Parker St 862-9854
Alberto's Pizza 564 Glenn Dr 987-0465
Anchor Seafood Restaurant
    1517 Creekside Dr 286-7908

Fire

Fire _____

Areas	Police and Sheriff	Fire
Adams County Sheriff		
all emergencies	911 or 544-9898	
non-emergency	327-8655	
Boulder —		
all emergencies	911	911
non-emergency	763-9654	763-9654
Coal Creek Canyon	875-0965	875-0965
Denver — (within city limits)		
all emergencies	911	911
non-emergency	652-2265	623-7648

Police

Police _____
Sheriff _____

Other Emergency Numbers

Ambulance & Hospital

Denver Emergency Ambulance	324-9865
Denver Emergency Hospital	567-0987
(For private Ambulance, see "Ambulance Service" in the Yellow Pages)	
(For private Hospitals, see "Hospitals" in the Yellow Pages)	
Rocky Mountain Poison Control Center	234-9863
Colorado State Patrol	658-7634

The Front of the Telephone Book

Have you ever looked at the front pages of your telephone book? These pages tell you what to do in an **emergency.** An emergency is something bad that happens all of a sudden. In an emergency, you often need to get help fast. The front pages of the telephone book have a list of emergency telephone numbers. You can find numbers for reporting fires, for calling the police, or for calling an ambulance. An ambulance is used to quickly transport people to a hospital. Use these telephone numbers only in emergencies!

Look above at the page of emergency numbers for areas around Denver, Colorado. Some places use the emergency number 911. What places use 911?

CHECKING YOUR SKILLS

Answer these questions. Use the telephone-book pages in this section to help you.

1. What is the telephone number of The Red Hen Cafe?

2. What is the telephone number of Robert Ramirez?

3. What is the telephone number of a pizza restaurant?

4. What is the emergency telephone number for reporting fires?

285

Thinking Back

- The three major land areas in the Mountain states are the Great Plains, the Rocky Mountains, and the Intermountain area. The Continental Divide separates rivers that flow east from rivers that flow west.

- Lewis and Clark, with help from Sacajawea, found a route from the Mississippi River to the Pacific Ocean.

- Wagon trains brought early settlers to the Mountain region. The Mormons were the first large group to settle there. The Mormons came in search of religious freedom.

- Ranchers in the Mountain states raise beef cattle, sheep, and dairy cows. Farmers grow many crops, including wheat, potatoes, and sugar beets.

- Food processing, meat packing, lumbering, and mining are important industries. Almost 200 minerals and fuels are found in the Mountain states.

Check for Understanding

Using Words

Copy the sentences below. Fill in the blanks with the correct words from the list.

Intermountain area
Mormons
sugar beets
U.S. Mint
volunteers

1. Pioneers called _____ settled near the Great Salt Lake.
2. The land between the Rocky Mountains and the Sierra Nevada is called the _____
3. Many of our coins are made at the _____ in Denver, Colorado.
4. Sugar is made from sugarcane or from _____ .
5. The fire fighters of Ouray, Colorado, are _____ .

Reviewing Facts

1. What are the three main areas of the Mountain states? Tell whether each is in the east, west, or center.
2. What is the Continental Divide? Name two rivers that flow east or west from there.
3. Name two ways in which Sacajawea helped Lewis and Clark.

4. What brings tourists to the Mountain states?

5. Why would a factory in Idaho be more likely to make french fries than cornflakes?

Thinking Critically

The Mountain states have fewer people than other regions of our country. What are some good things about having fewer people living in a place? How might having fewer people cause some problems? How might these problems differ from the problems that more crowded places have?

Writing About It

Think about Lewis and Clark's trip to the Pacific Ocean and the help that Sacajawea gave them. Choose one event that happened along the way. Then write a short play about that event. The play should tell about the event and the characters' feelings.

Practicing Reading Skills

Using Your Telephone Book

Find and write down the telephone numbers of the following people and businesses. Use the telephone-book pages on page 284.

1. Michael Rainwater
2. Redding Hospital
3. Recreation and Park Department
4. Rapid Transit Information
5. Abbott Real Estate
6. Robert Ramirez

On Your Own

Social Studies at Home

Write riddles about some of the key words, people, or places in this chapter. Think of at least two clues for each riddle. Then ask friends or family members to solve your riddles.

Read More About It

Buck Wild by Glenn Balch. T. Y. Crowell. This book tells about a horse's struggle to remain free.

Cassie's Journey: Going West in the 1860s by Brett Harvey. Holiday. This easy-to-read story describes the fears and hardships faced by a real family who moved to the West.

Cowboy by Bernard Wolf. William Morrow. This book offers you a chance to meet working cowboys on a modern Montana cattle ranch.

The Incredible Journey of Lewis and Clark by Rhonda Blumberg. Lothrop, Lee & Shepard. The adventures of the two explorers on their journey from St. Louis to the Pacific Ocean are told in this book.

Melinda Takes a Hand by Patricia Beatty. William Morrow. In 1893 a 13-year-old girl's mix-ups turn a Colorado town upside down!

Stone Fox by John Reynolds Gardiner. T. Y. Crowell. Willy challenges a champion Indian dog-sled racer to save his grandfather's Idaho farm.

CHAPTER 13

The Pacific States

"Great joy in camp   we are in view of the Ocian, this great Pacific Octean which we been so long anxious to See. and the roreing or noise made by the waves brakeing on the rockey Shores may be heard distinctly. . . ."

—The explorer William Clark on seeing
the Pacific Ocean in 1805

Look for these important words:

Key Words
- fjords
- salmon
- tundra
- Japan Current
- Lower 48

- Inuit

Places
- Alaska Range
- Yukon River
- Brooks Range

- Arctic Coastal Plain
- Anchorage
- Juneau
- Fairbanks

Look for answers to these questions:
1. What is unusual about Alaska's land and climate?
2. Why can Alaska no longer be called a "wasteland"?
3. How do people make a living in Alaska?

1 *Alaska*

Our forty-ninth state, Alaska, is our biggest state. Alaska has more land than any other state. It is more than twice as large as Texas. Alaska is also our northernmost state. It is a peninsula bordered on the east by Canada.

The Land

Because Alaska is so far north, many people think it is covered with ice and snow. This is true of many parts of Alaska. Thousands of glaciers can be found in mountain valleys and canyons in the state. It is also true that Alaska has vast forests, rich farmland, and modern cities.

To understand Alaska's land, think of it as four parts. In the south mountains come right down to the coast. These mountains are called the **Alaska Range.** The high cliffs jut out into the Pacific Ocean, forming long, narrow channels. These channels are called **fjords** (fee•YORDZ).

Two of Alaska's most important resources are found in the south. Thick pine forests cover the mountains. Billions of fish live in the coastal waters. **Salmon** (SAM•uhn) are the most important.

In the center of Alaska the land flattens out into low, rolling hills. Large rivers such as the **Yukon River** flow through this land.

289

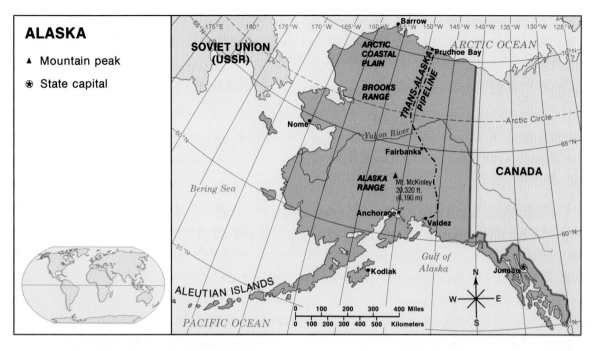

ALASKA

▲ Mountain peak

✳ State capital

North of the hill country is the **Brooks Range.** This huge range is part of the Rocky Mountains.

The northernmost part of Alaska is the **Arctic Coastal Plain.** This plain lies next to the Arctic Ocean. Much of the Arctic Coastal Plain is **tundra.** Tundra is flat, treeless land that stays frozen most of the year. In summer the top inches of soil thaw and turn into a grassy swamp. Beneath the tundra lies oil, the state's most valuable resource.

Like its land, Alaska's climate changes from south to north. On the southern coast, winter temperatures can be fairly mild. These mild temperatures are caused by the **Japan Current.** The Japan Current is a river of warmer water within the ocean. Winds that pass over the Japan Current warm up and then blow in over the coast. They bring mild temperatures and rain to southern Alaska.

Farther north the winters are long and bitterly cold. Northern Alaska is thousands of miles from the equator. It gets little of the sun's heat.

Alaska Long Ago and Today

Alaska was once a part of Russia. The United States bought Alaska in 1867. At that time many people thought it was foolish to own this frozen "wasteland." They changed their minds when gold was discovered in 1899. Since then even more valuable resources have been discovered. Alaska became a state in 1959.

The people of Alaska are not spread evenly over the state. Nearly half live in the city of **Anchorage** (ANG•kuhr•ij). This city is on the warm southern coast. Anchorage is a large, up-to-date city with tall buildings and new highways. It is also Alaska's main seaport. Near Anchorage farmers grow vegetables and raise dairy and beef cattle. Other major cities are **Juneau** (JOO•noh), Alaska's capital, and **Fairbanks.**

Life in Alaska's cities is much like that in any other American city. The big difference is that many goods cost a lot more money in Alaska. They must be shipped from the **Lower 48.** This is what Alaskans call the 48 states of our country that touch one another.

Life is very different outside of Alaska's large cities. People live in small villages. Many Alaskans hunt and fish for food.

Today Native Americans are the only people living in some parts of Alaska. One large group is the **Inuit** (IN•yuh•wuht), or Eskimos. The ancestors of the Inuit were among the first people in Alaska. They learned how to live in Alaska's difficult climate.

The modern city of Anchorage is surrounded by Alaska's famed wilderness beauty.

Many of Alaska's people live in small seaside towns all along the coast. Fishing is one of Alaska's important industries.

291

Some of Alaska's oldest Inuit families live in Kotzebue, an Arctic Circle town.

Walruses and other Alaskan wildlife live happily in the icy Arctic waters.

Alaska's daring bush pilots fly people and goods to outlying areas too rugged for land travel. Canned foods and fresh oranges are some of the foods flown in.

The Inuit live along the coasts of Alaska. In the past they spent their winters in houses made of sod. Their summer houses were tents of skins. The Inuit hunted whales, walruses, seals, and other animals for food, clothing, shelters, weapons, and tools. For example, the blubber, or fat, of whales was used as a fuel for lamps. These lamps provided both light and heat.

Though some of Alaska's Native Americans still follow the old ways, most now live in modern houses. Their lives have changed in other ways as well.

Crossing three mountain ranges and hundreds of rivers, the Trans-Alaska Pipeline carries about 1.5 million barrels of oil daily.

Airplanes now bring supplies to the villages. Snowmobiles allow people to travel more easily.

Important changes have also come since oil was discovered in northern Alaska. Many people of the villages as well as many people from other places now work for oil companies on the Alaska pipeline. This long pipe threads its way from the northern coast south through the wilderness. The Trans-Alaska Pipeline brings oil 800 miles (about 1,290 km) to the southern coast.

Many visitors now come to see the beauty of Alaska's great wilderness. Long ago the people of the Aleutian Islands called Alaska "The Great Land." Today we often call Alaska the "Last Frontier."

Reading Check

1. What is the tundra? Where in Alaska is it?
2. What country once owned Alaska?
3. How is life now changing in Alaska's villages?

Think Beyond Alaska has been called the "Last Frontier." Do you agree with this description? Why or why not?

Look for these important words:

Key Words
- Polynesians
- paniolos

Places
- Honolulu
- Oahu

Look for answers to these questions:
1. What landforms are in Hawaii?
2. Why does Hawaii have a warm, rainy climate?
3. What kinds of jobs might Hawaiians have?

2 Hawaii

Thousands of miles south of Alaska, a chain of beautiful islands rises out of the Pacific. This is Hawaii, our fiftieth state. It is made up of more than 130 islands.

The Land

The islands of Hawaii are really the tops of mountains rising from the ocean floor. Volcanoes formed these mountains millions of years ago. Though most of these volcanoes are inactive, a few, such as Mauna Loa (MOW•nuh•LOH•uh) and Kilauea (kee•low•AY•uh), still erupt from time to time.

The islands of Hawaii have high peaks as well as deep canyons. Lining the island coasts are miles of sandy beaches. In some places steep cliffs rise right out of the sea. Palm trees and bright flowers grow all over Hawaii.

Pali is the Hawaiian word for the steep cliffs, mostly of volcanic rock, that line the shores of the Hawaiian Islands.

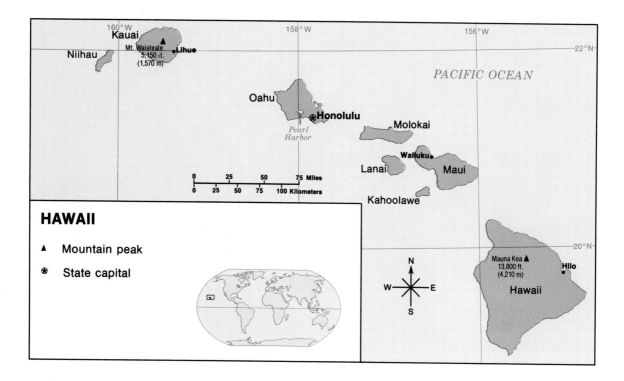

HAWAII

▲ Mountain peak

✦ State capital

The state of Hawaii has eight main islands. People live on seven of them. The other islands are small and do not have fresh water. The largest island is called Hawaii, the same as the state's name. The name means "big island."

Most of the time Hawaii's temperatures are warm, but not too hot. Winter and summer are much the same. In both seasons the temperatures are usually in the upper 70s F (20s C). Winds cool off the islands. They also bring heavy rains to parts of the islands. Mount Waialeale (wy•ahl•ee•AHL•ee), on the island of Kauai (KOW•eye), is the wettest spot in the world. This mountain gets at least 460 inches (about 1,170 cm) of rain every year.

Hawaii Long Ago and Today

Hawaii has a mix of people from different backgrounds. The first Hawaiians came to the islands about 2,000 years ago. These people are known today as **Polynesians** (pah•luh•NEE•zhuhnz). They came from other islands in the Pacific. Many different groups later came to Hawaii from Asia. Among them were people from China, Japan, and the Philippine Islands. Americans have been coming to Hawaii for more than a hundred years. The first of these American visitors came to build schools and churches. American planters came later to start sugarcane and pineapple plantations.

295

A harvester-conveyor speeds up the pineapple harvest. Workers
pick the fruit by hand, and a moving belt carries it to a truck.

Cannery workers trim the pineapples
before the fruit is sliced by machine.

Waikiki Beach attracts tourists to Honolulu. Diamond Head faces this beach.

"Hold on to your hat!" A junior cowboy gets a few tips and a riding lesson from his father, a paniolo on the Parker Ranch on the "Big Island" of Hawaii.

Hawaii's warm climate allows farmers to grow special crops. Among Hawaii's biggest crops are sugarcane, pineapples, and coffee. Some of these crops, such as coffee and pineapples, cannot grow in other parts of our country. Orchids (AWR•kihdz) and macadamia (mak•uh•DAY•mee•uh) nuts are other major crops. Trees that produce hardwoods are also important.

Many Hawaiians work in the fields where these crops grow. Other Hawaiians work in factories that make sugar and other food products. Hawaiians also raise beef cattle. **Paniolos** (pan•ee•OH•lohz) are the cowboys of Hawaii. They are some of the best riders and ropers in the world.

Honolulu (hon•uh•LOO•loo) is the largest city and capital of Hawaii. It is on the island of **Oahu** (oh•WAH•hoo). Four out of five Hawaiians live on this island. Honolulu began as a place where ships could get supplies. Today it is the center of trade and banking in Hawaii.

Honolulu is also the center of tourism, Hawaii's biggest industry. Waikiki (wy•kih•KEE) Beach is the most famous tourist spot. Facing this beach is Diamond Head, once an active volcano. Millions of visitors come each year to enjoy Hawaii's great beauty.

Reading Check

1. How were the islands of Hawaii formed?
2. What kind of climate does Hawaii have?
3. What groups of people live in Hawaii?

Think Beyond How is Hawaii different from Alaska?

The most famous song in Hawaii is "Aloha Oe." This beautiful and gentle farewell song was written by Queen Liliuokalani (lih•lee•uh•woh•kuh•LAHN•ee), Hawaii's last ruler and only queen. Hawaiians still sing this song to honor her memory and Hawaii's past.

When Kamekeha Liliuokalani was just a few days old, she was adopted by the king. He called her Lydia. Lydia had a happy childhood. She lived in a palace and was given a good education.

Princess Liliuokalani's life seemed perfect at first, but it did not stay that way. Many American sugar planters lived in Hawaii. They were very powerful.

In 1891 Princess Liliuokalani became the queen of Hawaii. She loved her people and wanted to do great things for them. She promised to take away some of the power held by the planters.

The planters were upset by the queen's promise. They wanted to do away with her and make Hawaii part of the United States. Fighting broke out between supporters of the queen and of the planters.

The planters were successful. They set up their own government and arrested Queen Liliuokalani. To protect her followers, she agreed to give up her throne. Queen Liliuokalani was allowed to live in her palace the rest of her life. As time passed, she even forgave the planters for what they had done.

Think Beyond Do you think Queen Liliuokalani made the right decision when she agreed to give up her throne to stop the fighting?

Look for these important words:

Key Words
- spawn
- Chinook Indians
- aluminum

Places
- Pacific Northwest
- Coast Ranges
- Cascade Range

- Columbia Plateau
- Seattle, Washington
- Puget Sound
- Portland, Oregon

Look for answers to these questions:
1. How are Washington and Oregon alike?
2. What landforms are in the Pacific Northwest?
3. What kinds of industries are important here?

3 — The Pacific Northwest

Washington and Oregon are sometimes called the **Pacific Northwest.** These two states are alike in many ways. They both have rocky coasts, high mountains, and heavy rainfall. Both have thick pine forests. A total of 23 national forests are here.

The Land
Like two long fingers on the land, a pair of mountain ranges run from north to south through Washington and Oregon. In the west are the **Coast Ranges.** Farther east is the **Cascade Range,** the higher of the two ranges.

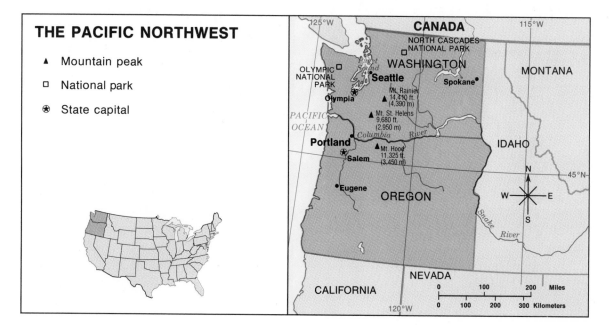

THE PACIFIC NORTHWEST

▲ Mountain peak

◻ National park

✹ State capital

CANADA

NORTH CASCADES NATIONAL PARK

OLYMPIC NATIONAL PARK

Puget Sound

WASHINGTON

Seattle

MONTANA

Spokane

Olympia

Mt. Rainier ▲ 14,410 ft. (4,390 m)

PACIFIC OCEAN

Mt. St. Helens ▲ 9,680 ft. (2,950 m)

Columbia River

Portland

Salem

Mt. Hood ▲ 11,325 ft. (3,450 m)

IDAHO

N
W—E
S

45°N

Eugene

OREGON

Snake River

NEVADA

CALIFORNIA

0   100   200   Miles
0   100   200   300   Kilometers

125°W   115°W   120°W

299

Fertile farm valleys lie in the areas between both of these mountain ranges.

Winds from the Pacific Ocean bring heavy rains to the Coast Ranges. Some parts get as much as 140 inches (about 355 cm) of rain a year. These winds also drop rain on the Cascades, but by the time they cross the Cascades, the winds are dry. The land east of the Cascades gets little rain. This high, dry land east of the mountains is called the **Columbia Plateau.** This plateau gets only from 10 to 20 inches (about 25 to 50 cm) of rain a year.

Where it is rainy in the Pacific Northwest, the trees grow very tall. The mountain slopes are covered with towering Douglas firs and other kinds of pine trees. The forests of the Pacific Northwest give us much of our country's lumber. Most of it is used for building. However, as trees are cut down, new trees are planted to grow in their place.

The mountains of the Pacific Northwest have many rivers flowing toward the ocean. Many kinds of fish live in these streams. The salmon is the most valuable as well as the most unusual fish.

The Coast Ranges are near the Pacific Ocean. Why do they receive such heavy rainfalls?

We plant new forests so we will have lumber in the future. What are some of the ways people use wood?

Near the foot of Mount Rainier and along Puget Sound, Seattle developed in an area rich in water and timber resources.

Salmon are born in mountain streams. After a time they swim down to the Pacific. They live in the ocean from six months to five years. Then they swim back to lay their eggs in the streams where they were born. On the trip back, the salmon must leap over waterfalls and rapids. Some are caught in fishing nets. Those salmon that reach their goal **spawn,** or lay their eggs, in quiet pools of water. Then, weary from their trip, the salmon die. Soon their eggs hatch, though, and life begins again.

The Pacific Northwest Long Ago and Today

The **Chinook** (shih•NUHK) **Indians** live on the Northwest coast. Many Chinooks today work as farmers or ranchers. In the past these Indians fished and gathered food from the forest.

Farther north other Indian groups built villages along the rugged coast. They made large boats from logs to carry them in search of food. They caught fish and hunted seals and sea otters.

When American settlers came to the Northwest, they started farms. Today many crops grow in the mild climate and heavy rains of this region. Farmers grow fruits, nuts, berries, and vegetables. Washington is well known for its apples. Oregon grows many kinds of berries, which are frozen or eaten fresh. Some are made into jams or jellies.

Most people of the Northwest live in big cities. **Seattle** is the largest city in Washington. It lies on **Puget** (PYOO•jit) **Sound.** Puget Sound is a body of water somewhat like a bay. It is almost 100 miles (about 160 km) long. From Seattle people can see Mount

Washington state is the nation's top manufacturer of the giant aircraft used by the world's large airlines.

Rainier, one of the highest mountains in North America.

Seattle began as a port for shipping lumber. Today Seattle still ships large amounts of wood products. Factories in Seattle build ships and airplanes. **Aluminum** (uh•LOO•muh•nuhm) is also manufactured in Washington. Aluminum is a lightweight metal used to make airplane parts.

Along the Columbia River lies **Portland,** Oregon's biggest city. Ocean ships go up the Columbia to Portland. There they load lumber from Oregon's forests. Some factories in Portland process foods and make paper. Other factories make machines such as chain saws for the lumber industry.

Reading Check

1. What two groups of mountains are in the Pacific Northwest?
2. Why is the Pacific Northwest rainy in the west and dry in the east?
3. Why is Seattle important?

Think Beyond Why must people be careful not to catch too many of the salmon swimming upstream?

Look for these important words:

Key Words
- redwoods
- sequoias
- Gold Rush
- forty-niners
- balsa

People
- Junipero Serra

Places
- Sierra Nevada
- Central Valley
- Sacramento River

- San Joaquin River
- San Diego
- San Jose
- San Francisco
- Los Angeles
- Hollywood

Look for answers to these questions:
1. What different kinds of climate are in California?
2. Who were the first settlers in California?
3. What was the Gold Rush?
4. How do people make a living in California?

4 California

California is the third-largest state in size, with more people than any other state. It has a treasure chest of natural resources on the land, under the ground, and in the nearby sea. Its mountains, ocean beaches, rich farmland, and large cities make it a land of variety and contrast.

The Land and the Climate

From Washington and Oregon the Coast Ranges stretch all along the coast of California. Higher mountains lie east of the Coast Ranges in California. They are the **Sierra Nevada.** Between the Coast Ranges and the Sierra Nevada is the huge **Central Valley.**

The Central Valley gets very little rain. Nevertheless, it is one of the best farmlands in the world. Hundreds of crops grow in the Central Valley. Among the main ones are lettuce, tomatoes, grapes, sugar beets, rice, and cotton.

Miles of irrigation canals provide water for this rich farmland. These canals connect the Central Valley to California's largest rivers, the **Sacramento** and the **San**

Joaquin (SAN wah•KEEN). Snow in northern California's mountains melts to feed these rivers.

Another important farming area, the Imperial Valley, is in southeast California in the Sonoran Desert. The Colorado River supplies water to this fertile but dry farming valley.

Different parts of California have different climates. The deserts in southeast California get fewer than 10 inches (about 25 cm) of rain a year. As many as 80 inches (about 200 cm) fall along the northern coast. In the damp, foggy northern region grow the **redwoods,** some of the world's tallest trees. Redwoods may grow to a height of 300 feet (about 91 m) or more.

Redwoods live to be hundreds of years old. They live so long because they are not bothered by insects or even fires.

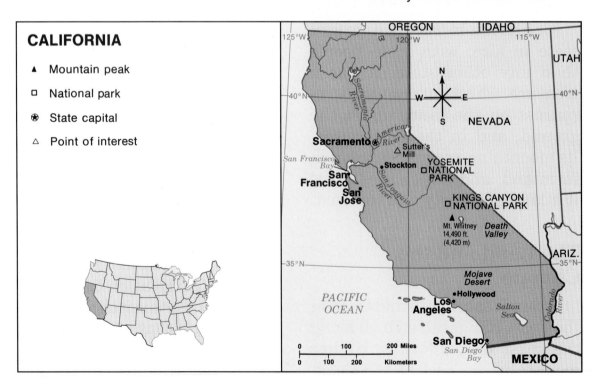

CALIFORNIA

▲ Mountain peak

▫ National park

✪ State capital

△ Point of interest

Along the coast and in the valleys of California, the climate is usually mild all year. Since the temperature rarely drops below freezing, farmers there plant year round.

Although some parts are wetter than others, most of California has two seasons. The wet season comes in the winter. The dry season runs from about April to November.

California has many beautiful places. High cliffs and rocks line much of its northern coast. In the north, the mountains are covered with forests. During the winter, much snow falls in the mountains.

At King's Canyon, in the southern Sierra Nevada, are the giant **sequoias** (si•KWOY•uhz). These huge trees are among the oldest living things in the world. Nearby is Mount Whitney, the second-highest peak in the United States. Farther south and east, in the Mojave Desert, is Death Valley. Death Valley is one of the hottest and driest places in the United States. At 282 feet (86 m) below sea level, this valley is the lowest point in the Western Hemisphere.

Death Valley is a 130-mile-long (209 km) desert of drifting sand in southern California. About 125 years ago borax was discovered here, and 20-mule teams were used to haul it out of the valley.

California Long Ago

Junipero Serra (hoo•NEE•puh•roh SER•uh), a Spanish priest, led the first settlers to California from Mexico. Father Serra built a chain of missions in California in order to teach the Indians here. Over the years large cities grew up around some of the missions. These cities include **San Diego** (SAN dee•YAY•goh), **San Jose** (hoh•ZAY), and **San Francisco.**

California became part of the United States after a war with Mexico in 1848. By that time, wagon trains of pioneers were pushing west. Then a discovery suddenly brought many more people west. The discovery was gold.

The Gold Rush

A man named John A. Sutter decided to build a sawmill on the American River in northern California. To build the mill, workers had to dig into the riverbed. As they dug, some shiny flakes of yellow metal appeared in the water. The yellow flakes turned out to be gold.

The word spread that gold had been discovered at Sutter's Mill. The **Gold Rush** was on! Many

Forty-niners could pan for gold or use a cradle. The heavy gold sinks to the bottom of the container as water washes out the dirt.

thousands of people crossed the Rocky Mountains to California. Others sailed from the Atlantic coast all the way around South America to California. The ocean trip often took six months.

The miners came to be called the **forty-niners** because they arrived in California in 1849. A few forty-niners became rich. Many more never found the gold they were seeking.

Along with the miners came other people who started hotels and stores. Suddenly towns were springing up all over. In 1850 California became a state.

California Today

Nine out of ten Californians now live in cities and towns. In the north San Francisco is the largest city. It is a city built on hills overlooking San Francisco Bay. Besides drawing thousands of visitors each year, San Francisco is also an important business center in the West. Many large companies have offices in San Francisco.

Farther south is California's largest city, **Los Angeles** (LOSS AN·juh·luhs). More than 12 million people live in the Los Angeles metropolitan area. The area

HISTORY CONNECTION

In the 1880s most borax came from Death Valley. Borax is a mineral used to make many products, including detergents, paper, and glass.

Huge wagons were built to carry the borax out of Death Valley. The wagons were pulled by teams of mules. Although the actual number of mules used varied from 12 to 20, these teams became known as 20-mule teams.

Today, trucks and railroads are used to haul the borax. Although it still comes from deserts in southern California, most of it is mined outside of Death Valley, where it is easier for people to live and work.

Many of California's Spanish-speaking people are of Mexican-American heritage.

includes the city of Long Beach as well as many smaller communities. So many towns surround Los Angeles that it is hard to tell where one town ends and another begins!

Like San Francisco—and all of California—Los Angeles has a large mix of people. A great many Spanish-speaking people make their home in Los Angeles.

Why have so many people come to live in the Los Angeles area? Many have come for its pleasant, sunny climate. Others have come for jobs. Factories in the city process food, build airplanes, and make clothing. Oil from southern California wells goes to refineries near Los Angeles.

Los Angeles is famous for one industry in particular—moviemaking. The part of Los Angeles called **Hollywood** is known as the movie capital of the world.

Mary Chung, Special-Effects Artist

The lights in the movie theater dim, and a movie begins. On the screen a huge spaceship is speeding toward Earth. When it lands, a giant red space monster steps out. It is bigger than a two-story house! Everyone in the audience screams except Mary Chung. She smiles. She knows that the spaceship, the monster, and the house are not real. They are tiny models she made as a special-effects artist. A special-effects artist makes what is not real seem real.

Mary works for a movie company near Hollywood. In her job she uses everything from computers and cameras to toothpicks and **balsa** wood. Balsa is a soft wood that is easy to carve.

For the space movie, Mary spent many hours molding the clay model of the spaceship. Then she spent many more hours painting it. Later she worked

In the movies a whole village or even outer space may fit on top of the worktable of a special-effects artist.

A camera will capture on film every carefully crafted detail of this tiny model village.

with other special-effects artists to photograph the model.

To make the spaceship look as if it were traveling through space, Mary and the other artists did several things. First they mounted the spaceship model on a computer-controlled mechanical arm. Then they photographed the spaceship as the arm moved it in front of a blue screen. Later they replaced the blue background on the film with a filmed background of real space.

To photograph the giant space monster walking toward the house, they used a method called stop motion photography. In this method, Mary changed the position of the monster's arms and legs many times. Each time she did this, she stepped away from the model. Then the monster was filmed for one moment. When the film of all the changes was run at once, the monster looked as if it were walking. The background was added later, using film of a model city.

The real test of Mary's special effects is the movie audience. Mary is pleased that the audience thinks her special effects look real. For just a moment, so does Mary!

Reading Check

1. What are California's two main areas of mountains?
2. Name two dry places in California that have been turned into rich farmland.
3. Why did many settlers come to California in 1849?

Think Beyond How did the Gold Rush change both California and the United States?

IN FOCUS

THE CHINESE NEW YEAR

Each winter a giant dragon winds its way through the streets of San Francisco's Chinese community. Although the dragon has a big head and sharp teeth, no one is afraid of it. In fact, people line the streets, cheering the dragon. "Gung hay fat choy!" the people call out. *Gung hay fat choy* means "Happy New Year" in Chinese.

San Francisco has a large Asian-American population. The Chinese community formed during the California Gold Rush, when Chinese workers came to help mine gold. Today, the community continues to celebrate the traditional Chinese New Year. This spectacular celebration is the biggest event of the year.

A Chinese New Year parade

The Chinese New Year celebration begins in late January or February. It lasts four days. Colorful flags, paper lanterns, and strings of firecrackers are hung from buildings. Singers and dancers in colorful costumes perform Chinese operas and folk dances. People wear masks and go to parties.

The highlight of the Chinese New Year, however, is the parade led by the Chinese dragon. The block-long dragon is really many people wearing one large costume. Parade watchers see dozens of pairs of feet moving beneath the dragon. The feet belong to the young people under the costume.

Unlike the dragons in many fairy tales, the Chinese dragon is a friendly one. It has long been believed to chase away evil spirits. Seeing the Chinese dragon is supposed to bring good luck in the new year.

Think Beyond How is the Chinese New Year celebration similar to and different from other New Year's celebrations?

310

SKILLS IN ACTION

USING POPULATION MAPS

A population map is a map that shows where people live. It also tells how many people live in different areas.

The map on the next page shows where people live in California. The map key tells what the colors stand for. The red areas show the centers of large cities. Many people live close together in these areas.

The red areas take up less space than all the other colors. Yet about half of California's people live in these places.

Yellow shows places that have fewer people than the red parts. Yet they still have many people. These places may be small cities or suburbs of large cities. Many people who live in suburbs work in nearby large cities.

In cities many people live in hotels or apartment houses. These buildings are usually close to other large buildings.

People who live in suburbs outside of large cities may live in houses for one or two families.

311

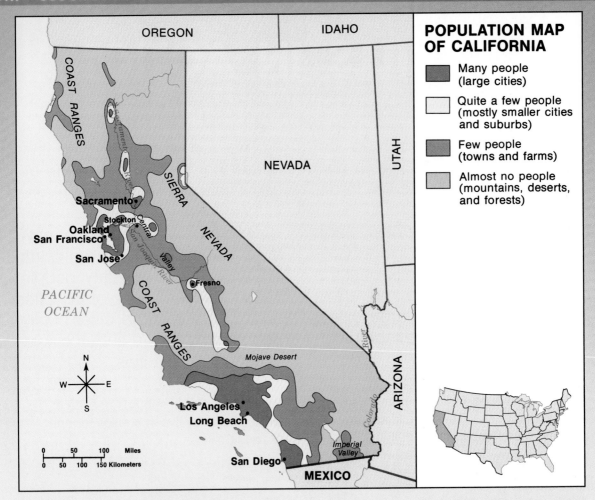

The purple color shows places that do not have many people. On this map of California you can see two large purple strips. One runs through the center of the state. The other is in the southern part of the state. The purple strip in the center of the state is the Central Valley. This valley has small cities and towns as well as mile after mile of farmland.

The green parts on the map stand for places that have very few people. This land is mostly forest, mountain, or desert.

CHECKING YOUR SKILLS

Use the map in this section to answer the questions.

1. Do more people live in eastern or western California? Are more large cities located along California's coast or inland?

2. Do more people live in the green or the red parts?

3. Is Stockton a small or large city?

4. Which is shown in purple on this map, the Mojave Desert or the Central Valley?

312

CHAPTER 13 REVIEW

Thinking Back

- Alaska is our largest state. Oil is found under the tundra. The Trans-Alaska Pipeline brings the oil to Alaska's southern coast.

- Anchorage is Alaska's main seaport. Farmers nearby grow vegetables and raise dairy and beef cattle. Inuit live along the coasts.

- Hawaii is made up of eight main islands. The first Hawaiians were Polynesians. Major crops include sugarcane, pineapples, and coffee.

- Washington and Oregon have rocky coasts, high mountains, and heavy rainfall. Forests provide much lumber. Farmers grow fruits, nuts, berries, and vegetables. Factories produce wood products, ships, airplanes, aluminum, and food products.

- California has more people than any other state. Lettuce, tomatoes, grapes, sugar beets, rice, and cotton grow in the Central and Imperial valleys.

- Junipero Serra led the first settlers to California. The Gold Rush brought more people to California. San Francisco and Los Angeles are important business centers.

Check for Understanding

Using Words

Copy the words numbered 1 to 5. Next to each word, write the meaning from the list below.

1. fjords   4. spawn
2. Inuit   5. tundra
3. paniolos

a. long, narrow channels
b. flat, frozen land
c. Eskimos of Alaska
d. Hawaiian cowboys
e. lay eggs

Reviewing Facts

1. Why do most Alaskans live along the southern coast?
2. How has Alaska changed?
3. Why do many people go on winter vacations to Hawaii?
4. Why is farming in Hawaii important to people all over the United States?
5. Name two ways in which Alaska and Hawaii are alike.
6. Why does the Pacific Northwest have a large lumber industry?
7. Name two ways in which Washington and Oregon are alike.

313

8. The Central Valley and the Imperial Valley have dry climates. Why is so much food grown there?

9. Why did people move to California long ago?

10. In what ways is the Pacific Ocean important to the people of the Pacific states?

Thinking Critically

Which part of the Pacific region would you most like to visit? What are you most interested in seeing? How is this place different from where you live? How is it like where you live?

Writing About It

Choose one landform found in a Pacific state. Then write a short descriptive paragraph about it. Be sure to include good descriptive adjectives in your paragraph.

Practicing Geography Skills

Using Population Maps

Use the population map on page 312 to answer these questions.

1. Does most of the Central Valley have "quite a few people" or "few people"?

2. A metropolitan area is a large city with smaller cities around it. What metropolitan areas are there in California?

On Your Own

Social Studies at Home

Make a flow chart about the life of a salmon. Include a sentence about each stage in the salmon's life, and draw pictures to illustrate what you describe. Then use the flow chart to explain the salmon's life story to a family member or a classmate.

Read More About It

Backbone of the King: The Story of Paka'a and His Son, Ku by Marcia Brown. University of Hawaii Press. This folktale is from a time when kings ruled the Hawaiian Islands.

Berry Woman's Children by Dale De Armond. Greenwillow. In this collection of Eskimo legends a grandfather tells about Berry Woman and the many animals in her care.

By the Great Horn Spoon by Sid Fleischman. Little, Brown. Jack and his aunt get caught up in the California Gold Rush.

The Hawaiians: An Island People by Helen Gay Pratt. C. E. Tuttle. This book tells about Hawaii in the years before Western settlement.

Pacific Coast Indians of North America by Grant Lyons. Julian Messner. This nonfiction book contains much information about the Indians of the Pacific Northwest.

UNITED STATES TERRITORIES AND PUERTO RICO

American Samoa

Puerto Rico

Guam

U.S. Virgin Islands

Did you know that you can go nearly halfway around the world and still be in the United States? Besides our 50 states, the United States has 2,300 islands. These islands are **territories** of the United States. They are governed by our country. You can use the Atlas in the back of your textbook to find these places. Some Pacific territories are **American Samoa** (suh•MOH•uh), **Guam** (GWAHM), **Wake Island**, and the **Midway Islands**. In the Caribbean are the **U.S. Virgin Islands** and **Puerto Rico** (PWAIR•toh REE•koh). Puerto Rico is a kind of territory called a **commonwealth**. As a commonwealth, Puerto Rico governs itself.

Puerto Rico

Puerto Rico is an island about 1,000 miles (about 1,610 km) southeast of Florida. It has more than two-thirds of all the land in the territories. It also has about nine-tenths of all the people in the territories. All Puerto Ricans are American citizens. They can vote in American presidential elections.

The Land and Climate

Puerto Rico is a beautiful, warm, and sunny island. Along the shore are miles of smooth sandy beaches. All around the island's coast is a plain that measures from 5 to 12 miles (about 8 to 19 km) wide. A mountain range runs through the center of the island.

From time to time the mild weather of Puerto Rico gives way to fierce, driving storms called **hurricanes**. These storms bring strong winds and heavy rains. A hurricane can destroy trees, houses, and bridges. Long ago, Indians living in Puerto Rico named these storms Huracan (hoor•uh•KAHN). Huracan was one of their gods, the evil god of storms. Our English word *hurricane* comes from this Indian name.

Long Ago in Puerto Rico

Christopher Columbus landed on Puerto Rico in 1493. Spanish settlers soon followed him. The island became the last stop for ships returning to Spain with gold from other colonies.

During its 400-year rule, Spain brought many changes to Puerto Rico. The Spanish

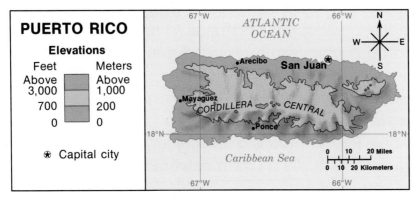

PUERTO RICO

Elevations

Feet		Meters
Above 3,000		Above 1,000
700		200
0		0

⊛ Capital city

ATLANTIC OCEAN

67°W   66°W

N
W—E
S

•Arecibo   San Juan ⊛

•Mayagüez
CORDILLERA   CENTRAL

•Ponce

18°N   18°N

Caribbean Sea

0 10 20 Miles
0 10 20 Kilometers

67°W   66°W

built large sugar-cane plantations. They brought the language, religion, and laws of Spain to the island. The Spanish laid out each new town around a plaza, or public square, in the center of the city. Cities in Spain are often built around a plaza.

Spain gave up Puerto Rico to the United States after a war in 1898. Puerto Rico kept much of its Spanish heritage, but it became more like the United States as well. Today Puerto Rico has a mix of Spanish and American customs.

Puerto Rico Today

What is it like to live in Puerto Rico today? In some ways it is like living in one of the 50 states. In other ways it is like being in a different country. Like the people in the 50 states, most Puerto Ricans live in or near cities. The largest city is the capital, **San Juan** (SAN WAHN). It is on Puerto Rico's northern coast. In San Juan you will find modern apartment buildings, large stores, factories, and rush-hour traffic jams. These are things you would find in any other city in our country.

In the heart of the city is "Old San Juan." Here the buildings have been fixed up to

► **An early Spanish settlement on Puerto Rico.**

An ancient Spanish fort looks out over modern San Juan.

◄ A plaza scene in old San Juan

look as they did when the Spanish built them long ago. The houses and shops have tiled roofs and floors, balconies, and shutters on the windows. Palm trees and flowers line the streets.

All over the island are signs of the new and old Puerto Rico. **Ponce** (PON•say) is a city on the southern coast. Ponce has the feeling of the old Spanish days. Yet Ponce also has some of Puerto Rico's newest and

most important industries, including oil refineries and chemical plants.

More than a million people visit Puerto Rico each year. Tourism is one of the most important ways that people make a living on the island. Visitors come to Puerto Rico for its warm climate, sunny beaches, and clear, blue water.

Arecibo (ah•ray•SEE•boh) is one of the most unusual places to visit. It is the home of a large telescope. Scientists use this telescope to learn the secrets of faraway stars and planets.

For early explorers, Puerto Rico was a far frontier of the Earth. Today people in Puerto Rico are exploring the vast frontier of space.

Unit Review

Words to Remember

Copy the sentences below. Fill in the blanks with the correct words from the list.

food-processing   refineries
glaciers   reservoir
humid   textiles
metropolitan area   trade
needleleaf trees   valley

1. The Appalachian Mountains and the Great Lakes were formed by _____ , which pushed south over the middle of our country thousands of years ago.

2. Floods used to destroy buildings and crops in the Tennessee River _____ .

3. The Northeast and Southeast have moist, or _____ , summers.

4. Large forests of pine and other _____ _____ grow along the Pacific coast.

5. New York City is a center of _____ . Many goods are shipped to and from this city.

6. Meat-packing plants and bakeries are part of the _____ industry.

7. The Southeast leads in making cloth, or _____ .

8. In _____ , crude oil is changed into gasoline and heating oil.

9. The Los Angeles _____ _____ includes the many towns and suburbs surrounding the city.

10. Lake Mead, the _____ of the Hoover Dam, stores water from the Colorado River.

Focus on Main Ideas

1. Name at least two reasons why the Northeast is an important place for manufacturing.

2. Why was the Declaration of Independence important to the people of the 13 colonies?

3. Why are the Great Lakes the most important resource of the Great Lakes states?

4. Name two regions in which tourism is very important. Explain why people visit these regions.

5. What foods come from the Interior Plains? From what part of the plains does each of these products come?

6. What are some ways in which people can make the land better for farming?

7. How are both the Atlantic Ocean and the Pacific Ocean important to the lives of the American people?

319

8. A good place for manufacturing needs several things. Name three of them.

9. For each product below, name a region in which it is important.
   a. corn
   b. wheat
   c. beef cattle
   d. oil

10. In what regions are these?
   a. Coastal Plain
   b. Central Plains
   c. Coast Ranges
   d. Great Basin

Think/Write

Imagine that a group of students from another country is planning to visit the region of the United States in which you live. Write a letter to the group describing your region. Tell about its climate, landforms, and industries.

Activities

1. **Research/Timeline**   You have read about many important people in the Long Ago sections in this unit. Choose one of them and read more about him or her in an encyclopedia. Make a timeline of the important events in that person's life.

2. **Making Lists/Mapmaking**   On a piece of paper, list some of the foods that are grown in each of the seven regions of the United States. Next draw outline maps of the Lower 48, Alaska, and Hawaii on a large piece of cardboard. Then cut out pictures from old magazines, or draw pictures, of the foods you listed. Paste these pictures in the right places on your maps.

Skills Review

1. **Using Road Maps**   Use the road map on page 227 to answer these questions.
   a. What kind of highway is Highway 65?
   b. You are going from Newton to Woodward. On what highways will you travel? In what directions will you travel?

2. **Separating Facts and Opinions** Which of the statements below are facts? Which are opinions? Explain your answers.
   a. In 1980 Alaska had about 400,500 people.
   b. He is the best pitcher in the United States.
   c. California grows more food than any other state.
   d. One of Hawaii's biggest crops is pineapples.

EXPLORING
YOUR STATE

In this unit you have seen that your state and others make up a region of our country. The states of your region grow or manufacture things that are needed in other parts of the United States.

A number of activities are explained below. As you do them, you will find out how people all over our country depend on your state. You will also see how your state depends on other states.

Learning About Geography

1. Pick one plant or animal that is raised in your state for food or for use in other products. Make a list of the things that are made from this plant or animal.

2. Use an almanac to find out at least four important products made in your state. Use the names of these products to make a word-search puzzle. First, list the products. Then, on a piece of graph paper, make a large square. Next, write the product names on the graph paper, one letter to a square, within the large square. Write some of the names from left to right. Write some from top to bottom. Fill in the empty spaces with other letters. Have your classmates find the words.

3. Make a table that shows how your state is important to the rest of our country. Use an encyclopedia or a book about your state to help you find the important resources and products.

Learning About People

4. At the library, find out about the people of your state. Who were the first people to live in your state? Who came after them? What people live there now?

5. Make a population map of your state. Use one color to show the largest cities. Use another color to show less-crowded areas. Label the large cities.

Making a Timeline

6. Make a timeline of your state's history. Have each mark cover 100 years of history. Be sure to show when your state joined the United States.

UNIT 4
America:
A United Country

Some Historical Landmarks and Monuments of the United States by Region

Northeast		Southeast		Great Lakes States	
Fort McHenry	Saugus	Appomattox	Fort Sumter	Dickson Mounds	Mackinaw
Gettysburg	Iron Works	Court	Old Mint	Fort Snelling	Island
Independence	Statue of Liberty	House	Williamsburg	Grand Portage	New Salem
Hall	U.S. Capitol	Castillo de	Wright Brothers	Monument	Perry's Victory
Lexington Green	Valley Forge	San Marcos	Memorial	Lincoln Boyhood	Memorial
Old North Church	West Point	De Soto Falls		Memorial	

Our country is made up of different regions, each with its own resources and kinds of land. Our country is also made up of different people. Yet the people and places of our country are united.

People in the United States share many things. We share our government. We are united by trade and transportation, too. Newspapers, radio, and television let us know what people in our country are doing. In America we work together to meet our needs. We depend on one another to help solve the problems we share.

Think Beyond Why is it important to work together to solve problems?

Plains States		Southwest		Mountain States	Pacific States
Amana Village	Knife River	Alamo	Fort Union	Custer	Fort Ross
Effigy Mounds	Villages	Canyon de	Montezuma's	Battlefield	John Day
Fort Larned	Mount	Chelly	Castle	Golden Spike	Fossil Beds
Homestead	Rushmore	El Morro	Taos Pueblo	Nez Perce	Pearl Harbor
Monument	Wounded Knee	Fort Davis	Tombstone	Virginia City	Sutter's Mill
	Battlefield				

Americans Depend on One Another

"This land is your land,
This land is my land
From California
To the New York island.
From the redwood forest
To the Gulf Stream waters,
This land was made for you and me."

—from the song "This Land Is Your Land"
by Woody Guthrie

Look for these important words:

Key Words
- self-sufficient
- society
- specialization
- labor
- producers
- consumers
- wage
- cost
- profit
- interdependence

Look for answers to these questions:
1. Why must people buy what they need or want from other people?
2. What is the difference between producers and consumers?
3. What does interdependence mean?

1 *People Depend on One Another*

Do you know the story of Robinson Crusoe? Long ago, Robinson Crusoe was stranded alone on an island. He had to build his own house and get his own food and water. As his clothes wore out, he had to make new ones. Robinson Crusoe was **self-sufficient.** That means he did everything for himself.

People in our **society** live very differently from Robinson Crusoe. A society is a group of people who share many things in common. People in our society, for example, have the same needs for food, clothing, and shelter. However, we do not make everything ourselves. We usually buy the things we need. We depend on others to help us meet our needs.

Specialization

Many people do many different jobs to provide you with food, clothing, and shelter. For example, it takes many people to build a house. Some people use machines to cut down trees in the forest. Other people work at sawmills where the trees are cut into lumber. Other people use the lumber to build the house. These are just a few of the jobs people do before a house can be built.

325

Often a person does only one special kind of job. This is called **specialization** (spehsh•uh•luh•ZAY•shuhn). With specialization, people do not have to spend all their time making food, clothing, and shelter. They do certain jobs and are paid money for their **labor,** or work. Then they use this money to buy some of the things they need and want from other people.

Producers and Consumers

When people make goods or provide services, they are **producers.** (Remember, a service is an activity a person does for another.) When people spend money to buy things that they need or want, they are **consumers.** People can be both producers and consumers.

Most of you have bought things, but have you ever been a producer? If you deliver newspapers or walk the neighbor's dog, you are a producer. You are providing a service. In return, you may receive a **wage.** A wage is money paid for the work you have done.

If you make a product like lemonade and sell it, you are a producer, too. You are making a good. You must buy lemons, sugar,

Producers provide services that help our society run smoothly.

Producers stay in business by supplying goods that fill consumer needs.

Producers offer a variety of products and services to meet different consumer needs.

and paper cups to make the lemonade. The money you spend to make a product is your **cost** of doing business. The money you make after you have bought these things is your **profit.** Profit is the money left over after you sell your product and pay your costs.

As a producer, you earn money. When you spend that money, you become a consumer. As a producer, you depend on other people to pay you for your goods or services. As a consumer, you also depend on other people. You depend on them to have stores and other businesses where you can buy things you need and want. You depend on other people and they depend on you. This is called **interdependence** (in•ter•dee•PEN•dens).

Reading Check

1. What is specialization?
2. What is a producer? What is a consumer?
3. What are three costs in making lemonade to sell?

Think Beyond How do you depend on other people to meet your needs?

SKILLS IN ACTION

BEING A CAREFUL CONSUMER

Anyone who buys goods or services is a **consumer.** A careful consumer is someone who spends money wisely. Careful consumers get what they want without spending more than they need to.

Here are some ways you can be a careful consumer.

Compare Before You Buy

When you **compare** things, you see how they are alike and different. When you are shopping, you need to compare prices. You also need to compare **quality,** how good the products are. Comparing quality and prices is always a good idea. This kind of shopping is called **comparison shopping.**

Suppose you want to buy an electronic space game. What would you do first? The first step in comparison shopping is to find out what products are available. You can find this out by looking in stores and by reading advertisements. You might find that three space games are available— Cosmic Conflict, Galactic Clash, and Star Smash.

Next you must find out more about each product. Advertisements may tell you some impor-

How might comparison shopping help you stretch your money further?

tant things. For example, an ad for Cosmic Conflict might tell you that this game has four steps, or stages. The ads for the other games show that they have only three stages.

However, advertisements almost never tell you what is bad about a product. To find out about quality, you have to look further. One way to check on a product is to look at it and touch it. Some products that look large and strong in advertisements turn out to be small and breakable.

Another way to check the quality of a product is to talk to someone who has the product. For example, a friend of yours might have Star Smash. Ask your friend how he or she likes the game. If your friend says that Star Smash is too hard or too easy, you might not want to buy it.

Once you have compared quality, it is time to compare prices. Perhaps Cosmic Conflict and Galactic Clash seem about equal in quality. You must now find out which game costs less, and where you can buy it.

You can check prices by visiting or telephoning stores. You can check newspaper ads, too. As you find out prices, you might make a list. Look at the list below. It is in the form of a table.

As you can see from the table, different stores sell the same game for different prices. Cosmic Conflict is more than four dollars cheaper at Big Toy Village ($16.88) than at Northeast Variety ($20.99). What is the lowest price in the table? Which game is offered for this price? Which store offers this price?

Now that you have compared quality and prices, you can decide which game to buy. Which would you choose? Where would you buy it?

Watch for Sales

Wise shoppers learn to wait for sales. Some items go on sale at a certain time of year. Usually this is after the time when they are most popular. Stores have these sales

Stores	Cosmic Conflict	Galactic Clash
Big Toy Village	$16.88	$15.77
Johnson's Toys	$17.97	$17.97
Northeast Variety	$20.99	$18.99

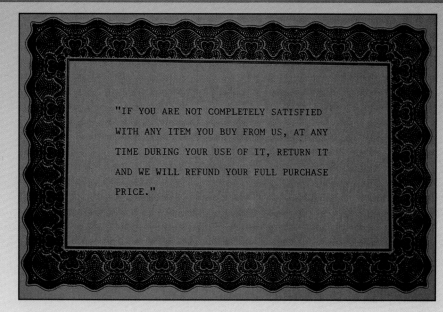

"IF YOU ARE NOT COMPLETELY SATISFIED WITH ANY ITEM YOU BUY FROM US, AT ANY TIME DURING YOUR USE OF IT, RETURN IT AND WE WILL REFUND YOUR FULL PURCHASE PRICE."

A product guarantee tells you that a manufacturer stands behind its product. For some products you may have to fill out a special form and send it to the manufacturer.

to clear their shelves. For example, ice skates often go on sale in spring. Store owners know that many people will not want ice skates until winter. To get people to buy ice skates, store owners sell them at a lower price.

Pay Attention to Guarantees

When you buy something, it should work the way it is supposed to. Many products come with a written **guarantee** (gair•uhn•TEE), a promise that the product will work. You have the right to return any product that does not work. National and state laws protect this right.

To make sure you can return a product, ask the person who sells it to you. Usually you will need to keep the sales slip. The store may limit the time in which you can bring back the product.

CHECKING YOUR SKILLS

Now answer the following questions.

1. What do advertisements tell you about a product? What *don't* they tell you?

2. Which cost less, 3 muffins for 90 cents, or the same muffins for 35 cents each?

3. How would you use comparison shopping to help you buy a bicycle pump?

4. You want to buy swim fins. You know that many people buy swim fins during the summer. You also know that few people buy them in September. Why might you buy swim fins at the end of summer?

5. Why is it better to buy a radio that has a guarantee?

330

Look for these important words:

Key Words
- communication
- technology
- industrialized

Look for answers to these questions:
1. Why do people in different regions of our country depend on one another?
2. How do transportation and communication link regions of our country?
3. How has technology helped the United States?

2 *Regions Depend on One Another*

Just as people specialize in jobs, regions of our country specialize in different goods and services. Just as people have different talents and skills, regions have different natural resources.

No one region has everything it needs. Like people, regions trade what they have for what they need. People in one region depend on people in other regions for things they need and want.

Here are some examples. People of the Pacific states catch much more fish than they can eat. They freeze or can the extra fish. To do so, they use machines built in other parts of the country. They sell their fish to people all over the United States.

Canning is one way to preserve products for shipment to other regions.

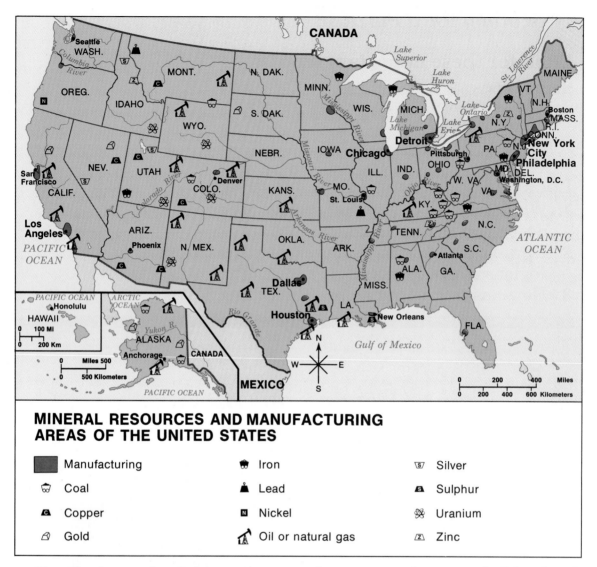

MINERAL RESOURCES AND MANUFACTURING AREAS OF THE UNITED STATES

- Manufacturing
- Coal
- Copper
- Gold
- Iron
- Lead
- Nickel
- Oil or natural gas
- Silver
- Sulphur
- Uranium
- Zinc

People in coal-mining mountain regions sell their coal to people in manufacturing regions. The coal is used in factories. People in manufacturing regions make clothing and equipment to sell to people in mining regions.

Farmers in the Interior Plains grow wheat and corn. They sell their grain to factories that make flour for bread and enough breakfast cereal for the whole country. The farmers and the factory workers probably drink orange juice from Florida, Texas, or California.

Even a small business like a lemonade stand depends on several regions of the United States. The lemons might come from Florida, Texas, or California. The sugar might come from Hawaii. The paper cups are made from wood pulp that might come from the forests of Maine, Washington, Oregon, or Georgia.

Links Between Regions

You could not sell lemonade if you could not buy lemons, sugar, and paper cups. Some of these goods have to come from other regions. You depend on people from other regions to send you goods.

Interdependence is possible because the United States has an excellent system of transportation. In America, people can send goods by truck, train, ship, and airplane. Raw materials travel to factories from many different places. Factories send their finished products all over the country.

Before people send raw materials or products anywhere, however, they must know what to send and where to send it. People come to know these things through **communication** between the

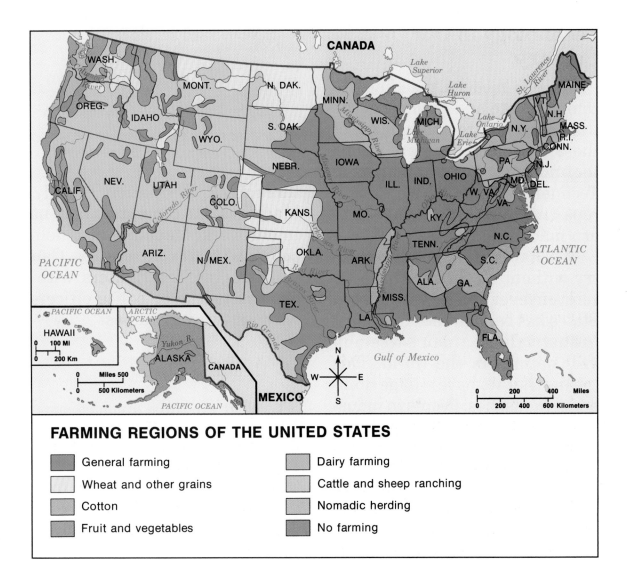

FARMING REGIONS OF THE UNITED STATES

- General farming
- Wheat and other grains
- Cotton
- Fruit and vegetables
- Dairy farming
- Cattle and sheep ranching
- Nomadic herding
- No farming

regions. Communication is the way we send and receive messages. Through communication, people know how much to charge for what they are sending also. Farmers, factory owners, shippers, storekeepers, and consumers need to communicate all the time. Telephones, telegrams, letters, and computers are some of the ways we communicate over long distances.

Technology in Our Country

We use modern machines to communicate and to move goods from one place to another. All of these machines are part of our **technology** (tek•NAHL•uh•gee). Technology is building, using, repairing, and improving modern machines.

It is hard to imagine our country without all the machines we rely on every day. The United States has become one of the most **industrialized** (in•DUS•tree•uhl•yzd) nations in the world. This means that we have a huge number of industries. People in industries use many kinds of machines to manufacture large amounts of goods.

Machines allow us to make more jeans, television sets, and toys faster than ever. Machines help us package and move goods

Today a message can be sent to the other side of the world in just seconds.

throughout the nation quickly. Machines like computers help us in our work. Machines also help people who provide services. Can you imagine fire fighters without fire trucks or police officers without two-way radios?

Reading Check

1. What are three kinds of communication that people use?
2. How do people depend on transportation systems?
3. What is technology?

Think Beyond How do you or members of your family rely on technology in your daily life?

334

IN FOCUS

MONEY

Nickels, dimes, quarters, and paper bills are all money. Money is what we use to pay for goods and services.

Using coins and paper bills is not the only way to pay for things, however. People often write checks. If you keep your money in a bank, you can write checks to the people to whom you owe money. The check gives your bank permission to give these people a certain amount of your money.

People can also pay for things with credit cards. A credit card is a piece of plastic with your name and account number on it. Stores use the card to fill out a form when you buy something. Each month you receive a bill that shows your purchases. You can then send a check to the credit card company to pay this bill.

Money is not always coins, bills, checks, or cards. Money is whatever people decide to use to pay for goods and services. Long ago, American Indians in the Northwest used sea-otter pelts, shells, and decorated copper as money. The Plains Indians used buffalo skins, corn, and horses.

Early settlers in North America used coins from Europe. When our country became a nation, the government began to make its own coins. Later it began to print paper money. What people have used for money has changed a lot in the last 200 years.

Think Beyond   Do you think that money in the future will be different from what it is today?

Paper bills of the United States

335

SKILLS IN ACTION

USING TIME ZONES

The sun does not shine on all the Earth at once. For this reason, people in different parts of the world set their clocks to different times. An area in which people use the same clock time is called a **time zone.** A time zone map is a map that helps you figure out what time it is in different time zones.

This map shows the time zones in the United States. The time zone farthest to the east is the Eastern Time Zone. Just to the west of the Eastern Time Zone is the Central

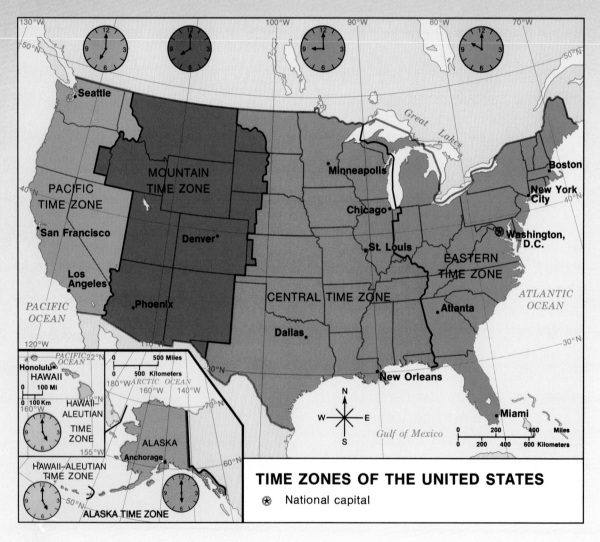

TIME ZONES OF THE UNITED STATES

⊛ National capital

Because different regions are in different time zones, it may still be broad daylight in Hawaii while the streetlights are lit in New York.

Time Zone. The time zone west of the Central Time Zone is the Mountain Time Zone. To the west of that is the Pacific Time Zone. Alaska and Hawaii have their own time zones. What are their time zones called?

Look at the clock face that shows 10:00. It is above the Eastern Time Zone. Now find the clock face that shows 9:00. It is above the Central Time Zone. When it is 10:00 in the Eastern Time Zone, it is 9:00 in the Central Time Zone. Find the clock face that shows 8:00. In which time zone is it 8:00? When it is 10:00 in New York City, what time is it in Denver?

If you know the time in one time zone, you can figure out the time in another zone. For each time zone to the west, subtract one hour. For each time zone to the east, add one hour. For example, when it is 6:00 in the Pacific Time Zone, it is 9:00 in the Eastern Time Zone. Since the Eastern Time Zone is three zones to the east, you add three hours.

CHECKING YOUR SKILLS

Use the time zone map to answer these questions.

1. In what time zone is Chicago?

2. Is Mountain Time one hour earlier or one hour later than Pacific Time?

3. If it is 8:00 in Chicago, what time is it in San Francisco?

4. If it is 2:00 in Phoenix, what time is it in Dallas?

337

Look for these important words:

Key Words
- economy
- free enterprise
- competition
- standard of living

Look for answers to these questions:
1. What has free enterprise done for Americans?
2. How does competition help consumers?
3. Why might Americans have more choices than people in some other countries?

3 *Free Enterprise in America*

We Americans have plentiful natural resources and up-to-date technology. We produce the greatest variety of goods and services in the world.

The way a country provides and uses goods and services is called its **economy.** Not all economies are alike. In America, we have a **free enterprise** economy. Free enterprise means that people are free to own and run businesses and industries.

In a free enterprise economy, people have many choices about what they make, buy, and sell. The government does not make these choices for people. Free enterprise has helped the United States become one of the wealthiest nations in the world.

To understand how many choices our economy allows us to make, imagine you are shopping for a bicycle. In one store you find ten different kinds of bicycles. Why, you ask yourself, are there so many kinds of bicycles?

In our country, producers try to make bicycles that most people will want to buy. One producer may make the fastest bicycles. One may make the cheapest bicycles. Each producer wants the consumer to buy his or her product. Out of this **competition** (kahm•puh•TISH•uhn), or contest to get customers, comes a great variety of bicycles. Consumers in our country are then free to choose the bicycle they want and have enough money to buy.

Americans Have the Freedom to Make Choices

In the free enterprise economy, producers try to make and sell what consumers want. The government does not tell them what to make. The government does, however, set rules for health and safety that producers must follow.

In countries that do not have a free enterprise economy, people have less freedom of choice. In some countries, the government tells producers what they must make. The government may decide that factories must make tractors instead of bicycles. A few factories would be allowed to make bicycles, but people would have fewer kinds of bicycles to choose from.

Under free enterprise, producers of good products or services have more customers and make a good living. Free enterprise has helped many Americans have a high **standard of living.** *Standard of living* means how well people live in a country. It includes how much money a person has to spend on food, clothing, and shelter. It also includes the medical care and the education people can get in a country.

In a free enterprise economy, consumers are provided with a wide choice of products that differ in price and quality.

The United States has been called "a nation of immigrants." More immigrants have come to the United States than to any other nation. Between 1860 and 1930, for example, more than 32 million people came to the United States. Most of them came from Europe. Many entered the United States through Ellis Island, in New York Harbor. Ellis Island was once a reception center for immigrants to our country.

In recent years most immigrants have come from countries outside of Europe. About eight out of every ten now come from Latin America and Asia. Many of these newcomers have settled in Pacific coast cities, such as Los Angeles, and in cities in the Southwest.

A Land of Opportunity

The United States has been called "the land of opportunity." For more than 200 years, people have been coming to our country to start new lives. They want to be able to meet their needs. They also want to be able to make their lives and their children's lives more pleasant.

Americans have the opportunities and the freedom to make their lives better. In our country, people can decide for themselves what jobs they want to do and where they want to work. With hard work, many people in our country are able to improve their standard of living.

Because so many people would like to live good lives here, we need to take care of our country. To keep America "the land of opportunity," we must use resources and technology wisely.

Reading Check

1. What is the meaning of the term *free enterprise*?
2. What is competition? Why is competition among producers good for consumers?
3. What things make up a standard of living?

Think Beyond America has been called "the land of opportunity." What does this mean to you?

340

Ninfa Laurenzo
1925–

▶▶▶▶▶▶▶▶▶▶▶▶▶▶▶▶

Some people like Mexican food. Others like Italian food. Ninfa Laurenzo used her skill at making both kinds of food to build a successful chain of restaurants called Ninfa's.

Ninfa and her husband, Domenic, moved to Houston, Texas, in 1948. They started a company called Rio Grande Food Products in the city's **barrio.** A barrio is a Spanish-speaking neighborhood. In addition to traditional foods of the Southwest, such as barbecue sauce, the Laurenzos' business made and sold tortillas, tamales, pizza dough, and spaghetti sauce.

Then, in 1969, Domenic died. Ninfa had to work hard to keep the company going. To improve business, she opened a restaurant inside the company building. She was the cook, and her five children were the servers. Soon people were waiting in line to eat in her restaurant.

Despite her success, Laurenzo had to overcome problems. A fire in the restaurant almost destroyed the whole business. Laurenzo, however, refused to give up. She and her children rebuilt the restaurant.

Today, Laurenzo is known all over Texas as "Mama Ninfa." She owns restaurants in Texas and Louisiana. New restaurants are planned for other states as well. Laurenzo knows she may have more problems as her restaurant business grows, but she will take that chance. Ninfa Laurenzo does not give up just because she has problems!

Think Beyond Why is it important to work hard at whatever you decide to do?

341

CHAPTER 14 REVIEW

Thinking Back

- We depend on other people to help us meet our needs. Workers are paid for their labor.

- Producers make goods or provide services. Consumers buy goods and services. A person may be both a producer and a consumer.

- Regions of our country specialize in different goods and services. People in one region depend on people in other regions for the things they need and want. This interdependence is possible because our country has excellent transportation and communication systems.

- Industries rely on modern technology to help them manufacture goods. Machines help workers produce both goods and services.

- Americans enjoy a free enterprise economy. Americans are free to make choices about what they make, buy, and sell.

- Americans have the opportunity and the freedom to make their lives better. With hard work, many in our country are able to improve their standard of living.

Check for Understanding

Using Words

Copy the words numbered 1 to 5. Next to each word, write its meaning from the list that follows.

1. **communication**
2. **competition**
3. **labor**
4. **producers**
5. **standard of living**

a. work
b. people who make goods
c. sending and receiving messages
d. contest to get customers
e. how well people live in a country

Reviewing Facts

1. How was Robinson Crusoe self-sufficient?
2. How do people specialize?
3. How are people both producers and consumers?
4. What is interdependence?
5. How does specialization work in regions?
6. Why do we need a good communication system in the United States?

7. Give three examples of how regions are interdependent.
8. How do machines help people?
9. What does it mean to live in a free enterprise economy?
10. Why is America called "the land of opportunity"?

Thinking Critically

1. Suppose that we did not have a free enterprise economy. How would your life be different?
2. If you look in the yellow pages of the telephone book, you will see that different businesses often sell the same things. How might this competition give you better products and services? What might happen if a product were sold by only one business?

Writing About It

There is a saying that money cannot buy happiness. Do you agree or disagree with this saying? Write a paragraph telling why you think as you do.

Practicing Time Skills

Using Time Zones

Use the time zone map on page 336 to answer these questions.

1. In what time zone is Washington, D. C.?
2. What time is it in Los Angeles, California, when it is 4:00 in Anchorage, Alaska?

On Your Own

Social Studies at Home

On a piece of paper, list at least ten products that you use every day. Then suppose that you are completely self-sufficient. Circle those items on your list that you could not produce by yourself. Beside each circled item, write something that you might use in its place. Share your list with a family member, and discuss the importance of interdependence.

Read More About It

How Does It Get There? by George Sullivan. Westminster. This book discusses the importance of trucks, trains, boats, and planes to America's economy.

Kid Power by Susan Beth Pfeffer. Franklin Watts. This entertaining book tells the tale of Janie's money-making business.

Louisville Slugger: The Making of a Baseball Bat by Jan Arnow. Pantheon Books. This book describes how baseball bats are made.

Prices Go Up, Prices Go Down by David A. Adler. Franklin Watts. A lemonade stand in action shows how free enterprise works.

This Book Is About Time by Marilyn Burns. Little, Brown. This book gives information about time and time zones.

Americans Make Decisions Together

"We the people of the United States, in order to form a more perfect Union, establish justice, insure domestic tranquility, provide for the common defense, promote the general welfare, and secure the blessings of liberty to ourselves and our posterity, do ordain and establish this Constitution for the United States of America."

—The Preamble to the Constitution

Reading for a Purpose

Look for these important words:

Key Words
- majority rule
- represent
- republic
- local government
- state government
- federal government

Look for answers to these questions:
1. What do people in a democracy do to make choices?
2. Why do Americans elect leaders?
3. What kinds of problems do local, state, and the federal governments handle?

1 *Americans Make Choices*

What do you do when you and your friends cannot decide what game to play? You might take a vote. You and your friends agree to play the game that gets the most votes. This way of deciding is called **majority rule.**

Majority rule is a way to make choices that are fair to the most people. Majority rule is the basis of democracy. In a democracy, people are free to make choices about their lives. They often make these choices by voting.

The United States has more than 200 million people. With so many people, countless choices must be made every day. Some choices have to do with only a few people. Only you and your friends must pick a game to play. Some

choices have to do with many more people. All the people of your community, state, or country must choose what to do about shared problems. Should a new bridge be built in your community, or a new school? Should more money in America be spent on medicine or on transportation? These are examples of some of the choices that citizens must make.

Certainly, 200 million people cannot get together in one place to talk over every problem. Everyone cannot take part in every choice, and every choice does not concern every person. Instead, the leaders of our country work together to solve problems. Leaders make up our government. A government is the group of people who make and carry out laws for a community, state, or country.

In the United States we elect leaders who must speak for, or **represent,** us. When people elect their leaders, the government is called a **republic.**

Kinds of Government

In the United States there are three kinds of government. The first kind is the **local,** or community, **government.** Then there is the **state government.** Finally, there is the **federal,** or national, **government.**

These three kinds of government help people solve problems that they could not solve alone. Each kind of government handles problems of a different size.

Some problems belong only to the people of your community. These are problems like fixing streets and deciding whether to buy a fire truck. The people of your community are the best people to decide what to do. For this reason, local government takes care of problems like these.

Other choices belong to all the people in your state. Statewide problems include building highways, paying for schools and state parks, and setting rules for drivers. State governments take care of problems like these.

Local governments repair streets. State governments build highways.

Some problems concern everyone in our country. We must have an army, navy, and air force to protect us. We must make choices about trading with other countries. We must have fair rules that apply to all. These problems concern everyone, so the federal government deals with them.

Reading Check

1. How does majority rule work?
2. What is a government?
3. What problems might the federal government deal with?

Think Beyond What are some things that the government does for you that you could not do by yourself?

SKILLS IN ACTION

MAKING CHOICES

Personal Choices

Suppose you have five dollars to spend. You are trying to decide how you will spend it. Here are some steps to help you make up your mind.

First you need to think of the choices you have. You could spend the five dollars to see a movie and buy some popcorn. You could put the money in the bank and save it. Then, when you have more money, you could buy something like a special T-shirt or a bicycle.

Next you should think carefully about the **results** of each choice. Think of the good and bad things that could happen. For example, if you go to the movie, you will have fun. On the other hand, you will have spent all your money. If you put the money in the bank, you will miss some entertainment now. Later, however, if you add to that money in the bank, you might buy something that you could enjoy for a long time.

After you have thought about the results, you can make your choice wisely. You can then spend your money to get something that is most important to you.

Choices a Government Makes

Government leaders have choices to make, too. Suppose a state has $50 million to spend. This money could be used to build a new highway or a new state park.

People in government follow the same steps as you would to make a decision. They think about the possible results of each choice. For example, they might draw up a table like this one.

Choices	Good Points	Bad Points
highway	quick travel brings in business and jobs	very expensive divides a neighborhood
park	recreation for people conservation, adds beauty to the state	less room for houses and businesses will not create many new jobs

347

People running for government often tell what they would do if elected. By listening to views of possible future government leaders, citizens can be sure to elect the person they want to represent them.

The government leaders must compare the two plans. Which is needed more, a park or a highway? Which would cause fewer problems for people? If you were a government leader, which would you choose? Why?

Voters Help Make Choices

The citizens of a state help to make choices. Suppose two people, Mr. Antolini and Mrs. Harrold, want to be elected to the state government. The state government must decide whether to build the highway or the park. Mr. Antolini thinks the park should be built. Mrs. Harrold thinks the highway should be.

The voters will choose the person they want to represent them. If they want the park, they may decide to vote for Mr. Antolini. If they want the highway, they may vote for Mrs. Harrold. The leader they choose will help the government make the choice most people want.

CHECKING YOUR SKILLS

Now answer the following questions.

1. Imagine you have ten dollars to spend. What choices will you have? How could you spend the money? Explain the reasons for the choice you make.

2. How do citizens help to make choices in government?

3. Your community has enough money to build a new library or a community swimming pool. What might be the good points and bad points of each choice? What choice would you make?

348

Look for these important words:

Key Words
- self-government
- Constitution
- branches

- Congress
- Senate
- House of Representatives
- executive branch

- President
- courts
- Supreme Court

Look for answers to these questions:
1. How did early leaders set up our government?
2. What are the three branches of the federal government?
3. What are the duties of each branch of the federal government?

2 *How Government Works*

In a small group of people, each person can help solve a problem. In a large group, people need to tell representatives how they would like things done. Voters in our towns, states, and country elect representatives to speak for them in government.

Our nation's early leaders believed in **self-government.** They wanted the people of America to govern themselves. They did not want to be ruled by a queen or king in England.

After our country won its freedom from England, our leaders wrote the **Constitution** of the United States. The Constitution contains the most important laws of our country. It gives citizens

the freedom to elect people to represent them. It gives the plan for our federal government.

Local and state governments used this plan as a model. They are set up in much the same way as our federal government. Each government has three parts, or **branches.** Each branch has a separate job to do. Each branch is just as important as the other two. Here is what each branch of our federal government does and how each works with the others.

Congress

One branch of government makes the laws. In the federal government, the lawmaking

The Senate and the House of Representatives usually meet in separate groups. Sometimes, however, they come together in what is called a joint session of Congress.

branch is called **Congress.** Voters in each of the 50 states elect people to Congress.

Two groups of people make up our Congress. One group is called the **Senate.** Each of the 50 states elects two senators to the Senate.

The other group that makes up our Congress is the **House of Representatives.** Members of this group are also elected from each state. However, different states have different numbers of representatives. The number of representatives elected depends on the population of a state. States with larger populations have more representatives in the House.

Members of Congress meet together in Washington, D.C., to make laws for the whole country. They give their opinions about each suggested law. Then they vote for the laws they think will be good for the most people.

Congress makes different kinds of laws. Some laws deal with spending money to protect our country, to build highways, and to help schools. Other kinds of laws protect our health and safety. Some laws make sure that all people are treated equally in schools, jobs, and housing. The Congress also makes laws that protect our country's natural resources.

BRANCHES OF OUR FEDERAL GOVERNMENT

Congress   President   Courts

The Executive Branch

To see that all of these laws are carried out, there is another branch of government. This branch is called the **executive** (ihg•ZEHK•yuht•ihv) **branch.** Besides seeing that laws are carried out, the executive branch often suggests laws to Congress.

In the federal government, the head of the executive branch is the **President.** The President and the Vice President are elected by all the voters of the country.

The President of the United States has one of the most important and difficult jobs in the world. The President is in charge of dealing with other countries for the United States. In addition, the President is the leader of the army, navy, and air force.

To help the President see that our nation's laws are carried out, many departments have been set up under the executive branch. The executive branch has more people than either of the other branches of our government.

The Courts

The third branch of government is the **courts.** Judges in courts make sure that laws are applied fairly. They decide how people who break laws should be punished.

The most important court in the federal government is the **Supreme Court.** The Supreme Court has nine judges. Their main job is to make sure that the Constitution of the United States is followed. Supreme Court judges, or justices, decide whether laws passed by Congress agree with the Constitution. They make sure that state laws and court decisions follow the Constitution.

Reading Check

1. Why did our nation's early leaders want self-government?
2. What is the Constitution?
3. What is the Supreme Court?

Think Beyond Why is Congress divided into two groups?

351

People MAKE HISTORY

James Madison
1751–1836

▶▶▶▶▶▶▶▶▶▶▶▶▶▶▶▶

James Madison was not strong when he was a child. He could not take part in many physical activities, but he loved to read. By the time he was 11 years old, he had read every book in his house.

In the summer of 1787, representatives from most of the 13 states gathered in Philadelphia, Pennsylvania, for an important meeting. Their job was to plan a new government for the United States. James Madison had been chosen to represent his home state, Virginia.

Madison helped write a plan that divided the federal government into three equal branches. He worked hard to convince the other representatives that the plan was good. By the end of the summer, the new Constitution was approved.

Madison's work, however, was far from over. At least 9 of the 13 states had to approve the Constitution. When Madison received word that Virginia might not support the Constitution, he raced home. He convinced the people there that they should approve the Constitution.

Several years later, James Madison became the fourth President of the United States. Two years before he died, Madison said, "The advice nearest to my heart and deepest in my convictions is that the Union of the states be cherished and perpetuated." For his important work James Madison is remembered as the Father of the Constitution.

Think Beyond   How is James Madison's work important to you today?

Representatives sign the Constitution.

? SKILLS IN ACTION

SOLVING PROBLEMS

The Flint family has just received its March gas and electric bill. It is much higher than the Flints expected. The family cannot pay such high bills every month.

The Flints have a problem that they must work to solve. The first step in solving a problem is to say exactly what the problem is. The problem for the Flints is that they are spending too much money on **energy.** Energy is the power that makes things work. Gas and electricity are two kinds of energy.

The second step in solving a problem is to break it into smaller parts. The Flints decide to look at the parts of their gas and electric bill.

Look at this bill. It tells the *TOTAL DUE*, or the amount the Flints owe. It shows how much of the total is the cost of gas and how much is the cost of electricity. The high costs are the two parts of the Flints' problem. Which cost is higher?

The third step in problem solving is to work on one part of

Statewide Power Company		
1758 N. Albatross Memphis, Tennessee 38101 (901) 555-8600	Thomas Flint 63 Weather Road Memphis, Tennessee 38106	Account Number NVT 18 23002-3 March 31, 1990
From March 1 to March 31:	This month last year:	
Gas $ 23.86 Electricity $ 89.72	Gas $14.86 Electricity $50.24	
TOTAL DUE $113.58	TOTAL $65.10	

353

the problem at a time. The Flints, for example, need to save money on their gas and electric bill. They must first decide whether to lower their gas or their electric costs.

The Flints want to know which kind of energy use became greater in the past year. Find the part of the bill that says "This month last year." Notice that the costs are lower. In March 1989, the amount of electricity the Flints used cost almost $40 less than it did in March 1990. How much less did the gas they used cost?

During the next month, the Flints are careful about using electricity. They turn off lights when they leave a room. They open the

What are some ways to solve the problem of rising energy costs?

refrigerator as little as possible. They turn off the television and radio when no one is watching or listening. When the bill for April comes, the Flints compare it with the bill for March. It is lower!

The fourth step in solving a problem is to check whether you have really solved the problem. Each month, the Flints check their bill. It remains lower! They see that their electricity costs less.

The Flints have solved the problem of their electric bill. They are happy about the amount of money they have saved. Now they decide to lower their gas costs. They keep the heat lower in their house and wear sweaters when it is cold. On sunny days, they open the shades to let warmth into the house. They are glad to see that they have saved energy and lowered their bill.

CHECKING YOUR SKILLS

Now answer the following questions.

1. What are the four steps in solving a problem?

2. What problem did the Flints have to solve?

3. How did the Flints use less electricity?

4. How did the Flints know their efforts worked?

354

Look for these important words:

Key Words
- legislature
- governor
- council
- mayor
- city manager
- municipal court
- taxes

Look for answers to these questions:
1. What are the differences between state and local governments?
2. Why must people pay taxes?
3. What responsibilities do Americans owe to the American government?

3 *State and Local Governments*

Like the federal government, state governments have three branches. The lawmaking branch of state government is the state **legislature** (LEJ•uh•slay•chuhr). The voters in a state elect their representatives to the state legislature.

Representatives in the legislature meet in the state capital. There, they make laws for all the people of the state. These laws govern highways, colleges and schools, state parks, and many other things.

State government has an executive branch to see that all laws are carried out. The head of the state executive branch is given the title of **governor.**

Laws made by state legislatures may differ from state to state.

Some state court cases require a jury, a group of ordinary citizens who listen to two points of view and make a decision about the case.

The third branch of state government is the courts. State courts judge people accused of breaking state laws. Many state laws have to do with crime. The laws about crime are usually a bit different in every state. Judges in state courts make sure state laws are obeyed. If they are not obeyed, judges and courts decide how the lawbreaker must be punished.

Local Government

As you might expect, many local governments also have three parts. The lawmakers of a community are members of the town or city **council.** The council passes laws for police and fire protection. It makes laws about schools and libraries, parks and playgrounds.

The head of the local executive branch of government is the **mayor** or **city manager.** Sometimes a community has both a mayor and a city manager. These people make sure the laws passed are carried out. They make sure that community departments, such as the fire department, are running smoothly.

If your community is big enough, it will have a **municipal court.** This kind of court judges people accused of breaking laws in the city. These laws often have to do with traffic, parking, and other things important to the smooth working of a community.

Paying for Government

Our local, state, and federal governments provide many services that people could not provide for themselves. All of these government services, from bridges to libraries, cost money. Police, fire fighters, teachers, and other public workers must be paid.

People pay for government services with **taxes.** Taxes are the money that government collects from people who work or own property. When you buy certain things, you pay a sales tax. That money also goes to the government.

A city's police department makes sure that all laws are obeyed.

Protecting Our Rights and Freedom

One of the most important jobs of our government is to protect the rights and freedom of Americans. The Constitution tells about our many rights and freedoms. For example, Americans are free to express their opinions about their government. Americans have the right to vote for their leaders. All Americans have the right to a fair trial. These are rights that people in some other countries do not have. These rights make the United States the "land of the free."

Our government provides many services and protects our rights and freedoms. In return, we Americans have certain responsibilities that we owe to our government. We should be loyal to our country. We must obey local, state, and federal laws. As adults, we must pay our fair share of taxes. We must vote for the people we think will work hardest to keep our country strong and free.

Reading Check

1. What is the lawmaking branch of state government?
2. Who is the head of the state executive branch?
3. What is a city council?

Think Beyond   What taxes do you pay?

357

IN FOCUS

THE BILL OF RIGHTS

The Constitution that was approved by the states in 1789 said almost nothing about individual rights. Many Americans were upset by this. They remembered that the United States had fought the American Revolution to win freedom from English rule. They wanted to make sure that their hard-won freedoms were protected by the Constitution.

Leaders promised to add a **Bill of Rights** to the Constitution. The Bill of Rights is the first ten **amendments,** or changes, to the Constitution. These amendments list the basic rights and freedoms of American citizenship. They also say that government cannot take away these rights and freedoms. Among the freedoms protected by the Bill of Rights are freedom of religion, freedom of speech, and freedom of the press.

Freedom of the press allows broadcasters to report the news to Americans.

American citizenship is protected by the Bill of Rights.

Although the Bill of Rights guarantees our rights and freedoms as citizens of the United States, there are limits to those freedoms. For example, freedom of speech does not protect a person who causes harm by yelling "Fire!" in a crowded place when there is no fire. Freedom of speech does not protect a person who hurts another person by telling lies. Our courts have said that citizens have a responsibility to use their freedoms wisely.

The Bill of Rights first went into effect on December 15, 1791. Today, December fifteenth is celebrated as a national Bill of Rights Day. This day is set aside to remind all Americans of their rights and responsibilities as citizens.

The Bill of Rights is important to all Americans. The pictures here show some of the ways in which the Bill of Rights protects your rights and the rights of your family and neighbors.

Think Beyond How does the Bill of Rights affect your daily life?

Americans can assemble, or gather together, peacefully to express their opinions.

The Bill of Rights guarantees freedom of religion to all Americans.

Americans have the right to a speedy and public trial by jury.

CHAPTER 15 REVIEW

Thinking Back

- People in a democracy make choices by voting. Majority rule makes sure that choices are fair to the most people.

- Citizens elect government leaders. In the United States there are three kinds of government—local, state, and federal.

- The Constitution gives the plan for our federal government. The federal government has three equal branches. Congress makes the laws. The executive branch makes sure that laws are carried out. The courts make sure that laws are applied fairly.

- State and local governments also have three branches. The lawmaking branch of a state government is the legislature. The head of the state executive branch is the governor. The lawmaking branch of a community government is the council. The head of the local executive branch is the mayor or city manager.

- Governments provide many services and protect our rights and freedoms. People pay for services with taxes.

Check for Understanding

Using Words

Copy the sentences. Use the words that follow the sentences to fill in the blanks.

1. The _____ contains the most important laws of our country. (President, Constitution)
2. Congress is a branch of the _____ government. (federal, state)
3. The _____ is one group in Congress. (court, Senate)
4. Judges work in _____ . (courts, councils)

5. A _____ is the leader of a state. (governor, mayor)

Reviewing Facts

1. What are the three kinds of government in our country?
2. Why is it useful to have three kinds of government?
3. Name three problems state governments take care of.
4. What is the lawmaking branch of our federal government?
5. What jobs does the President of the United States do?
6. What jobs do judges in the Supreme Court do?

360

7. What jobs does the mayor of a community do?
8. How do people pay for government services?
9. Name three rights that all Americans have.
10. How can we as Americans be responsible citizens?

Thinking Critically

1. How are local, state, and federal governments alike? How are they different from one another?
2. How can citizens express their opinions?

Writing About It

In many elections almost half of our citizens do not bother to vote. Write a paragraph telling why it is important for all citizens to vote.

Practicing Citizenship Skills

Making Choices

Your community has some money to spend on schools. The money can be used to buy computers for classrooms or instruments for music classes.

1. What steps should be taken to make the choice?
2. What are some good and bad points for each choice?
3. What choice would you make? Why would you make it?

On Your Own

Social Studies at Home

Our local, state, and federal governments provide many services. Think about all the government services you use each day. Write down as many as you can on a piece of paper. Then show your list to a family member. Explain how your lives would be different without these services.

Read More About It

Congress by Harold Coy. Rev. ed. Franklin Watts. This book takes a close look at the lawmaking branch of the federal government.

Local Government by James A. Eichner. Revised and updated. Franklin Watts. This book explains how city, county, and state governments make decisions that affect us all.

Molly's Pilgrim by Barbara Cohen. Lothrop, Lee & Shepard. This is a story of an immigrant family learning the American way of life.

A More Perfect Union: The Story of Our Constitution by Betsy Maestro. Lothrop, Lee & Shepard. The story of the Constitution is told in this nonfiction book.

The Supreme Court by Harold Coy. Rev. ed. Franklin Watts. The author describes how the Supreme Court works with Congress and the executive branch.

Shh!
We're Writing the Constitution

by Jean Fritz   **pictures by Tomie dePaolo**

The job of creating a government for our country was not an easy task. Even getting people to meet and discuss a plan was difficult. However, delegates from the new states did meet in 1787 to begin the long debate. Their discussions resulted in a national government that has been successful for more than 200 years.

After the Revolutionary War most people in America were glad that they were no longer British. Still, they were not ready to call themselves Americans. The last thing they wanted was to become a nation. They were citizens of their own separate states, just as they had always been: each state different, each state proud of its own character, each state quick to poke fun at other states. To Southerners, New Englanders might be "no-account Yankees." To New Englanders, Pennsylvanians might be "lousy Buckskins." But to everyone the states themselves were all important. "Sovereign states," they called them. They loved the sound of "sovereign" because it meant that they were their own bosses.

George Washington, however, scoffed at the idea of "sovereign states." He knew that the states could not be truly independent for long and survive. Ever since the Declaration of Independence had been signed, people had referred to the country as the United States of America. It was about time, he thought, for them to act and feel united.

Once during the war Washington had decided it would be a good idea if his troops swore allegiance to the United States. As a start, he lined up some troops from New Jersey and asked them to take such an oath. They looked at Washington as if he'd taken leave of his senses. How could they do that? they cried. New Jersey was their country!

So Washington dropped the idea. In time, he hoped, the states would see that they needed to become one nation, united under a strong central government.

But that time would be long in coming. For now, as they started out on their independence, the thirteen states were satisfied to be what they called a federation, a kind of voluntary league of states. In other words, each state legislature sent delegates to a Continental Congress which was supposed to act on matters of common concern.

By 1786, it was becoming obvious that changes were needed. People were in debt, a few states were printing paper money that was all but worthless, and in the midst of this disorder some people could see that America would fall apart if it didn't have a sound central government with power to act for all the states. George Washington, of course, was one who had felt strongly about this for a long time. Alexander Hamilton was another. Born and brought up in the Caribbean Islands, he had no patience with the idea of state loyalty. America was nothing but a monster with thirteen heads, he said. James Madison from Virginia wanted a strong America too. He was a little man, described as being "no bigger than half a piece of soap," but he had big ideas for his country.

In 1786 these men, among others, suggested to the Congress that all the states send delegates to a Grand Convention in Philadelphia to improve the existing form of government. It sounded innocent. Just a matter of revising the old Articles of Confederation to make the government work better. No one would quarrel with that.

But they did.

Rhode Island refused to have anything to do with the convention. Patrick Henry, when asked to be a delegate from Virginia, said he "smelt a rat" and wouldn't go. Willie Jones of North Carolina didn't say what he smelled, but he wouldn't go either.

But in the end the convention was scheduled to meet in the State House in Philadelphia on May 14, 1787.

James (or "Jemmy") Madison was so worked up about it that he arrived from Virginia eleven days early. George Washington left his home, Mount Vernon, on May 9 with a headache and an upset stomach, but he arrived in Philadelphia on the night of May 13th. The next morning a few delegates from Pennsylvania and a few from Virginia came to the meeting but there needed to be seven states present to conduct business. Since there were only two, the meeting was adjourned.

It was May 25th before delegates from enough states showed up. They blamed their delays on the weather, muddy roads, personal business, lack of money. Delegates from New Hampshire couldn't scrape up enough money to come until late July, but even so, they beat John Francis Mercer of Maryland. He sauntered into the State House on August 6th.

The most colorful arrival was that of Benjamin Franklin who at eighty-one was the oldest of the delegates. Because he experienced so much pain when he was bounced about in a carriage, Franklin came to the convention in a Chinese sedan chair carried by four prisoners from the Philadelphia jail. (He lived in the city so they didn't have far to carry him.)

In all, there would be fifty-five delegates, although coming and going as they did, there were seldom more than thirty there at the same time. The first thing the delegates did was to elect George Washington president of the convention. They escorted him to his official chair on a raised platform. Then the other members of the convention took their seats at tables draped with green woolen cloth. James Madison sat in the front of the room and as soon as the talking began, he began writing. Never absent for a single day, he kept a record of all that was said during the next four months, stopping only when he, himself, wanted to speak.

They knew that there would be many arguments in this room, but they agreed that they didn't want the whole country listening in and taking sides. They would keep the proceedings a secret. So before every meeting the door was locked. Sentries were stationed in the hall. And even though it turned out to be a hot summer, the windows were kept closed. Why should they risk eavesdroppers? Members were not supposed to write gossipy letters home. Nor to answer nosy questions. Nor to discuss their business with outsiders. Benjamin Franklin was the one who had to be watched. He meant no harm but he did love to talk, especially at parties, so if he seemed about to spill the beans, another delegate was ready to leap into the conversation and change the subject.

For fifty-five men to keep a secret for four months was an accomplishment in itself. But they did.

More interesting details about our Constitution can be found in Jean Fritz's award-winning book, *Shh! We're Writing the Constitution.* (G.P. Putnam's Sons, copyright 1987)

Unit Review

Words to Remember

Copy the sentences below. Fill in the blanks with the correct words from the list.

executive
free enterprise
industrialized
interdependence
legislature
local government
represent
specialization
taxes
technology

1. Doing just one kind of job is called _____ .

2. People and regions depending on one another is called _____ .

3. The United States is one of the most _____ nations in the world.

4. Building, using, repairing, and improving modern machines is _____ .

5. In a _____ _____ economy people are free to own and run their own businesses.

6. We elect leaders to _____ us.

7. A city council is a branch of a _____ _____ .

8. Our President is the head of the _____ branch.

9. The lawmaking branch of a state government is the _____ .

10. People pay for government services with _____ .

Focus on Main Ideas

1. Why do people specialize in their jobs?

2. Give three examples of people acting as producers. Then give three examples of people acting as consumers.

3. Why are regions of the United States interdependent?

4. How do transportation and communication systems bring our country together?

5. How does technology make our country strong?

6. Name two advantages of our free enterprise economy.

7. What does each of the three branches of government do?

8. What are some of the problems that the federal government must take care of?

9. What are some of the kinds of laws that Congress makes?

10. Why is America called "the land of the free"?

Think/Write

Imagine that a new state highway is being planned near your home. Do you think it will be good for your community? Write a letter to the governor of your state explaining your feelings about the highway.

Activities

1. **Research/Art** Imagine that you want to run for mayor of your community. What jobs would you do as mayor? What things would you change? Make a poster that tells people why you should be mayor.

2. **Time Zone Maps** Find out which time zone you are in by looking at the time zone map on page 336. When it is 5:00 in your time zone, what time is it in these places?
   a. New York City
   b. Denver
   c. Los Angeles
   d. Anchorage
   e. Minneapolis

Skills Review

1. **Being a Careful Consumer** Use the table to answer the following questions.
   a. What are the three kinds of bikes for sale?

Stores	Bikes and Prices		
	Speedy 1	Super Ride	Deluxe
Mike's Bikes	$70	$75	$90
Deals on Wheels	$75	$85	$95
Bike Mania	$65	$70	$85

   b. Which is the least expensive? Which is the most expensive?
   c. You decide to buy a Super Ride. Which store would be the cheapest place to buy your bike?
   d. How much would your bike cost at that store?

2. **Solving Problems** The Hosleys' phone bill is too high. Here is their bill:

   Long distance: $75.00
   Local calls: $4.50

   a. What steps should the Hosleys take to solve their problem?
   b. What part of the bill do they need to cut back? How can they do that?
   c. How will the Hosleys know if they have solved the problem?

368

In Unit 4 you read how people and regions in the United States depend on one another to meet their needs and wants. You also read how Americans solve problems together through a representative form of government. The following activities will help you understand interdependence and government in your state.

Learning About Government

1. Find out the name of the governor of your state. Find out the names of the senators who represent you in the federal government. Look in some newspapers or news magazines to find out what people in government are doing. Share with the class the newspaper articles you find.

Learning About History

2. Find out when your state became part of the United States. Try to find a picture of your state capital. What special landmarks are there? What government groups meet there? If you can, take a trip to visit your state capital with a parent, a guardian, or your class.

Learning About Interdependence

3. As explained in Unit 4, interdependence means that people in different regions depend on one another for the things they need and want. Use an encyclopedia to find out about three resources or products your state is famous for.

   Can you think of three things your family uses that come from another region? Where do they come from? How did they get to your region?

Learning About Specialization

4. What special jobs do people in your state have? For example, many people in your state might specialize in coal mining or in making computers. Tell about a few of these jobs. Then draw a picture of yourself doing a job you would like to specialize in. Write two sentences telling why you would like that job.

U N I T

5

Other Lands, Other People

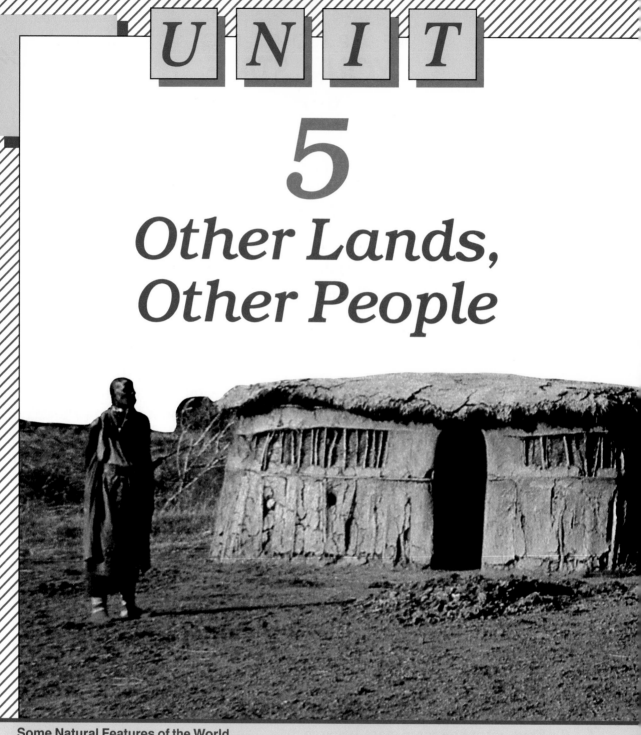

Some Natural Features of the World

North America		**South America**		**Europe**	
Death Valley	Mount Elbert	Amazon River	Chimborazo	Black Forest	Rhine River
Diamond Head	Mount McKinley	Andes	Volcano	Matterhorn	Rock of
Grand Canyon	Popocatépetl	Mountains	Mount	Mount Blanc	Gibraltar
Horseshoe Falls	Sierra Madre	Angel Falls	Aconcagua	Mount Elbrus	White Cliffs
Hudson Bay	Yoho Valley	Atacama Desert	Pico de	Pyrenees	of Dover
		Cape Horn	Bandeira		

About 3,000 different languages are spoken in the world today. There are more than 160 nations. Each of these nations has its own special customs and its own government.

Life in some parts of the world is much the same as it is in the United States. People eat foods, wear clothes, and live in houses that are very similar to ours. In other places, however, life is very different.

In this unit you will read about many regions of the world. You will see how other people's lives are like—or different from—your own.

Think Beyond Why is it important to learn about people in other parts of the world?

Asia		Africa		Australia	
Chang Jiang	Mount Everest	Atlas Mountains	Nile River	Ayers Rock	Great Dividing
Dead Sea	Mount Fuji	Cape of	Olduvai Gorge	Great Australian	Range
Ganges River	Pamir Knot	Good Hope	Sahara	Desert	Mount
Gobi	Persian Gulf	Kalahari Desert	Victoria Falls	Great Barrier	Kosciusko
Khyber Pass	Victoria Peak	Mount		Reef	
		Kilimanjaro			

CHAPTER 16

Rivers Around the World

"*The sun rose over the Eastern Desert. The valley below was shrouded in mist, but I could make out the thin line, gleaming in the sunrise, that stretched far off to the north and south where the tawny desert met the bright green patchwork of the fields along the river.*"

—A description of the Nile River
taken from *National Geographic*

Look for these important words:

Key Words	Places	
• rain forest	• Lake Victoria	• Alps
	• Mediterranean Sea	• Rotterdam, the Netherlands
	• Sahara	• North Sea
	• Aswan High Dam	• Andes Mountains

Look for answers to these questions:

1. Why is farming in the Nile valley easier today than long ago?
2. Why is the Rhine River important to the people of six countries?
3. How is the Amazon River different from the Nile and the Rhine?

1 *Major Rivers of the World*

Some of the world's great rivers flow through Africa, Europe, South America, and Asia. Many of the world's people live along these rivers. As you read about each river, find it on the map on pages 374 and 375.

The Nile River

The Nile, the longest river in the world, is in Africa. It is about 4,145 miles (about 6,670 km) long. The Nile gets its water from a number of different lakes and rivers. Much of the water comes from **Lake Victoria** in the center of Africa. From Lake Victoria the Nile cuts through the middle of the Sudan and Egypt. It ends its long run north at the **Mediterranean** (med•ih•tuh•RAY•nee•uhn) **Sea.**

In Egypt the Nile crosses the world's largest desert, the **Sahara** (suh•HAIR•uh). Yet the valley of the Nile is rich and fertile. Almost all of Egypt's people live on this strip of farmland. The most fertile part is the Nile delta, formed by the river at its mouth.

People have been living in cities on the Nile for thousands of years. Each summer, heavy rains made the river flow over its banks. The floods left tons of silt that made the land rich. Farmers in Egypt planted their crops after the water level dropped. Since the rains came once a year, Egyptian farmers planted once a year.

Today farmers can plant crops twice a year in the Nile valley of Egypt. Sometimes they can plant three crops. Dams built across the Nile have made this possible. The largest of these is the **Aswan** (a•SWAHN) **High Dam.** Now the Nile does not flood in Egypt. The dams hold back much of the water from the fall floods. During the dry season, the water is slowly let out into the Nile. Egyptian farmers can use it to water their crops. Water power from the dam provides electricity to the people of the Nile valley.

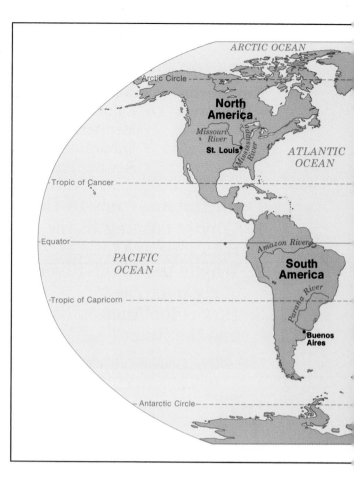

Some of the world's richest farmland is found along the banks of the Nile River.

Irrigation from the Aswan Dam has doubled crop production along the Nile.

374

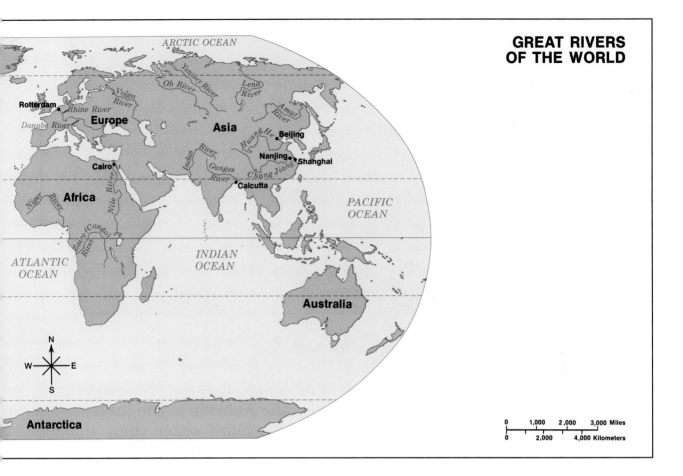

ARCTIC OCEAN

Ob River

Yenisey River

Lena River

Volga River

Amur River

Rotterdam

Rhine River

Europe

Danube River

Asia

Huang He

Beijing

Indus River

Nanjing • Shanghai

Cairo

Ganges River

Chang Jiang

Calcutta

Niger River

Africa

Nile River

Zaire (Congo) River

PACIFIC OCEAN

ATLANTIC OCEAN

INDIAN OCEAN

Australia

N W E S

Antarctica

| 0 | 1,000 | 2,000 | 3,000 Miles |
| 0 | 2,000 | | 4,000 Kilometers |

The Rhine River

The Rhine (RYN) River touches six countries in Europe. Three of these countries lie far from the sea. The Rhine links these countries to ocean ports. Along much of the river are some of Europe's largest factory areas. This makes the Rhine River the most important waterway in all of Europe.

The Rhine begins in Switzerland, high in the **Alps,** the large area of mountains that cross central Europe. From there it flows north to the tiny country of Liechtenstein (LIK•tuhn•styn) and crosses Austria. It passes by many large cities in West Germany and France. These cities have many factories. The Rhine then winds west through the Netherlands. More large factories are found here. The river ends its journey in **Rotterdam,** the world's busiest port. Here the Rhine empties into the **North Sea,** a part of the Atlantic Ocean.

The Rhine is filled with ships. Long lines of barges travel the river. These barge trains carry coal and iron ore to the factories.

375

A waterway deep enough for the world's large oceangoing ships links the Rhine River port city of Rotterdam to the North Sea.

They also carry to Rotterdam goods made in the factories of the many countries along the river. Large oceangoing ships arrive at and leave from Rotterdam. The ships carry their cargoes to places around the world.

The Amazon River

The Amazon (AM•uh•zahn) is a giant river, much larger than the Rhine. It is also the second-longest river in the world. Only the Nile River is longer.

The Amazon is on the continent of South America. Most of it lies in the country of Brazil. The Amazon begins high in the **Andes** (AN•deez) **Mountains** of Peru. Hundreds of branch rivers feed it along its route.

Although it is not the longest river, the Amazon *is* the largest. It carries more water than any other river. In fact, it carries more water than the Nile, the Rhine, and the Mississippi put together.

Because the Amazon is near the equator, its basin is hot all year. It is also very humid. Heavy rains fall almost every day. The rains water the **rain forest** covering most of the land along the river. A rain forest is a place where trees, vines, and other plants grow close together.

It is so hot and humid in the Amazon forest that few people live in it. It is very difficult to clear the rain forest for farms, roads, or cities. Soon after the plants are cut down, they grow back again.

The Amazon rain forest has more kinds of trees than any other place on Earth. It also has many different kinds of animals. In recent years, however, people have cleared millions of acres of the rain forest for crops and livestock. Lakes and highways have been built, and mineral resources are being mined. Many people fear that development will destroy the rain forest. Scientists fear that not only would this threaten the wildlife of the region, it also could cause harmful changes in the world's climates.

Although few people live in the Amazon Basin, it is home to many animals. High in the trees live noisy monkeys and parrots. Down below on the river's banks are snakes and alligators. The ruler of the rain forest is the jaguar (JAG•wahr), the largest wild cat in the Americas.

For most of its route the Amazon flows east through Brazil. It travels about 4,000 miles (about 6,430 km) and empties into the Atlantic Ocean. Large ships can travel up the Amazon for 2,300 miles (about 3,700 km). That is almost as far as from New York City to San Francisco! These ships carry raw materials out of the Amazon rain forest. The most important raw materials are rubber and valuable woods, like mahogany and ebony.

Rubber comes from the bark of trees in the rain forest. It is used to make many things, from boots to machine parts.

Today the river is the only way to travel through most of the Amazon Basin. As a result, little of the region has been explored. This may change in the years to come because the government of Brazil is now building highways there.

Reading Check

1. Why is the Nile River important to Egypt's people?
2. What is the world's busiest port?
3. Why do few people live near the Amazon River?

Think Beyond Do you think people in other lands depend on rivers more than Americans do? Why or why not?

SKILLS IN ACTION

STUDYING THE EARTH AND THE SUN

At this moment you may think you are sitting still. Actually you are moving through space at thousands of miles an hour. The Earth is always moving. As the Earth moves it causes daylight and darkness. It also causes summer and winter. The movement of Earth helps explain why some places are warm and some are cold.

Night and Day

The Earth **rotates** (ROH•tayts), or spins, like a top. It takes 24 hours, or one day, for the Earth to make one whole turn. Look at the picture on this page. See how the Earth turns around an imaginary line. The line runs from the North Pole to the South Pole. This line is called the Earth's **axis** (AK•suhs).

Here is a simple way to show why we have day and night. The flashlight stands for the sun. It shines on the part of the globe that faces it. On this part of the globe it is day. The dark part of the globe is turned away from the light. On this part of the globe it is night. As it rotates, part of the Earth is always moving into light. Part of it is always moving into darkness.

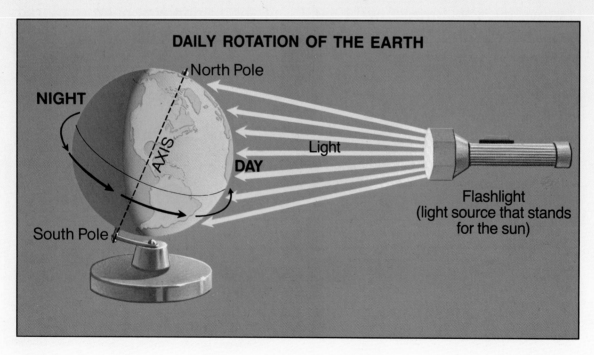

DAILY ROTATION OF THE EARTH

North Pole

NIGHT

AXIS

Light

DAY

South Pole

Flashlight
(light source that stands
for the sun)

The Changing Seasons

The Earth rotates all the time. It also **revolves** (rih•VAHLVZ) around, or circles, the sun. One trip all the way around the sun is called a **revolution** (rev•uh•LOO•shuhn). Each revolution of the Earth takes 365 days, or one year.

As the Earth revolves, our seasons change. This happens because the Earth's axis is not straight up and down. It is always tilted toward the North Star. Because of the tilt, a place gets different amounts of sunlight as the Earth revolves. A place gets more sun in summer and less in winter.

Look at the Earth on June 21. See how the Northern Hemisphere is tilted toward the sun. The Southern Hemisphere is tilted away from the sun. The tilt allows sunlight to shine more directly on the Northern Hemisphere. The sun's rays give more light and heat. It makes lands in the Northern Hemisphere warmer in June, July, and August. During these months there are more hours of light than darkness.

Now look at the Earth on December 21. It shows the Northern Hemisphere tilted away from the sun. The sunlight is less direct there. The days are shorter.

Seasons in the Southern Hemisphere are just the opposite. When the North has summer, the South has winter. When the North Pole tilts toward the sun, the South Pole tilts away. Then the Southern Hemisphere gets less direct sunlight.

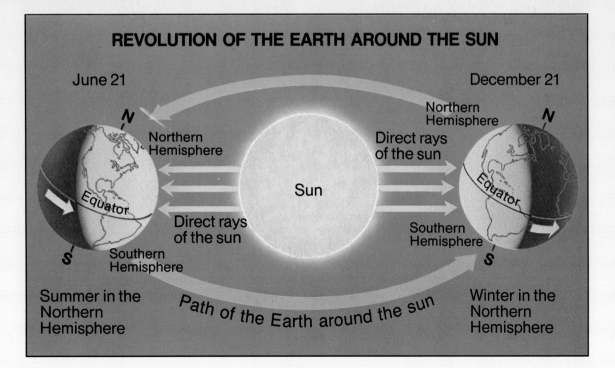

REVOLUTION OF THE EARTH AROUND THE SUN

June 21

N

Northern Hemisphere

Equator

S

Southern Hemisphere

Direct rays of the sun

Sun

Summer in the Northern Hemisphere

Path of the Earth around the sun

December 21

Northern Hemisphere

N

Direct rays of the sun

Equator

Southern Hemisphere

S

Winter in the Northern Hemisphere

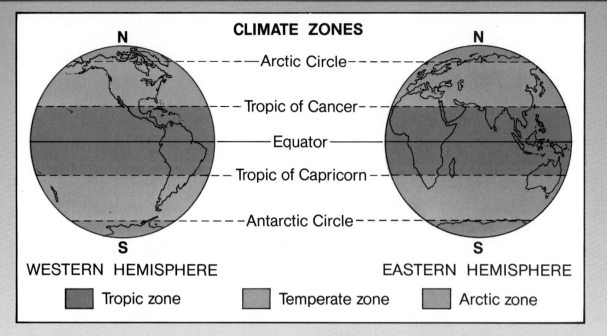

CLIMATE ZONES

Arctic Circle

Tropic of Cancer

Equator

Tropic of Capricorn

Antarctic Circle

WESTERN HEMISPHERE   EASTERN HEMISPHERE

Tropic zone   Temperate zone   Arctic zone

Climate Zones

The tilt of the Earth as it moves around the sun causes **climate zones** also. Climate zones are wide bands that circle the Earth. All the places in a climate zone have about the same climate.

The drawing above shows the Eastern and Western hemispheres. Find the equator, the Tropic of Cancer, and the Tropic of Capricorn. Look at the zones between the equator and the tropic lines. These zones are called the **tropics.** Places in the tropics have a warm climate. On Earth, these zones are the closest to the sun and receive the most heat and light. It is mostly hot all year. However, even near the equator, high mountains can be cool.

Now find the Arctic Circle and the Antarctic Circle. The zones between these circles and the tropic lines have a **temperate,** or mild, climate. It is usually warm in summer and cold in winter here.

Look now at the zones north of the Arctic Circle and south of the Antarctic Circle. Most areas in these zones have **arctic** climates. They are cold all year because they are the farthest from the sun.

CHECKING YOUR SKILLS

Use the pictures in this section to answer the questions.

1. Why do we have night and day?

2. Why do the seasons change?

3. Why is it colder at the Arctic Circle than at the equator?

4. What climate zone covers most of the United States?

Reading for a Purpose

Look for these important words:

Key Words
- paddies
- flood plain
- bamboo
- shoots

- silkworm
- junks
- sampan

Places
- Chang Jiang
- East China Sea
- Grand Canal
- Huang He
- Shanghai

Look for answers to these questions:

1. Why is the Chang Jiang an important link to China's interior?
2. How do the Chang Jiang's floods help people?
3. How do people make a living along the Chang Jiang?
4. Why is the Grand Canal important?

2 *The Chang Jiang*

More people live in China than in any other country. Most of them are farmers. Yet the land in much of China is either too dry or too mountainous for farming. Because of this, the Chinese live mostly along rivers or on the coast.

The **Chang Jiang** (CHAHNG jee•AHNG) in China is the world's third-longest river. Half of China's people live near its banks. In fact, more people live along the Chang Jiang than live in the whole United States!

The name *Chang Jiang* means "The Long River." The Chinese used to call the river by another name. It was once called the Yangtze (YANG•see). *Yangtze* means "Child of the Ocean."

The Chang Jiang flows through China's history. One legend tells of an emperor who shot a dragon in these waters. Mao Zedong (MOW dze•DONG), a former leader of China, once swam across the river to encourage his people to keep fit. Many other Chinese writers and leaders, as well as the families who live near its banks, have been touched by the great river.

The Chang Jiang is very long. It flows more than 3,900 miles (about 6,276 km) through the

381

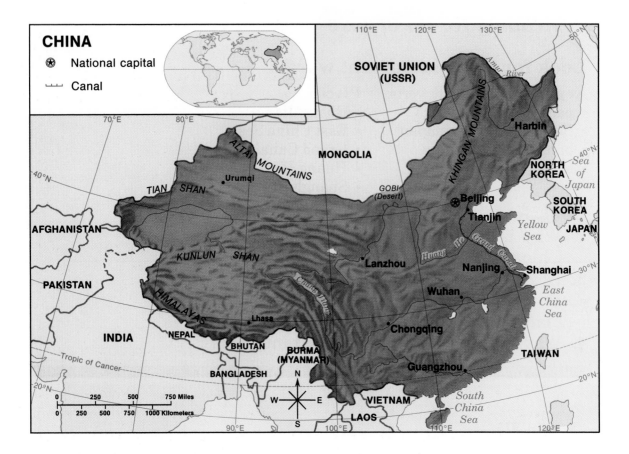

CHINA

⊛ National capital

⊔⊔ Canal

110°E 120°E 130°E 50°N

SOVIET UNION
(USSR)

Amur River

KHINGAN MOUNTAINS

Harbin

40°N

Sea
of
Japan

NORTH
KOREA

MONGOLIA

Urumqi

GOBI
(Desert)

Beijing

SOUTH
KOREA

JAPAN

ALTAI MOUNTAINS

TIAN SHAN

Tianjin

Yellow
Sea

AFGHANISTAN

KUNLUN SHAN

Huang He

Grand Canal

Lanzhou

Nanjing

Shanghai 30°N

PAKISTAN

Chang Jiang

Wuhan

East
China
Sea

HIMALAYAS

Lhasa

Chongqing

INDIA

NEPAL

BHUTAN

BURMA
(MYANMAR)

TAIWAN 20°N

Tropic of Cancer

20°N

BANGLADESH

N

Guangzhou

0 250 500 750 Miles

0 250 500 750 1000 Kilometers

W   E

S

VIETNAM

LAOS

South
China
Sea

90°E 100°E 110°E 120°E

Some parts of the Chang Jiang
flow through steep, misty mountain
canyons.

center of China. The center is also China's busiest region. To the south of the river are China's richest farmlands. To the north are China's biggest factories.

Many cities and factories lie along the Chang Jiang because it is the only river in China that is wide enough and deep enough for large ships. In addition, it links China's interior to the sea. Its mouth is on the **East China Sea,** a part of the Pacific Ocean.

The Chang Jiang starts high in the mountains of southern China. From there the river flows east. Much of the river's water is from melting snow in the mountains.

382

At first the Chang Jiang tumbles through miles of steep canyons. Some of these canyons are more than a mile (1.6 km) high. As it leaves this steep land, the river grows calmer and wider. It flows through a plateau of rich farmland. This is China's "rice bowl." Miles and miles of rice fields, or **paddies,** stretch out from the banks of the river.

Rice is an important food in this country of more than 1 billion people. In fact, the Chinese grow more rice than any other people in the world. The rice paddies along the Chang Jiang help feed China's people.

East of the plateau the river enters more canyons. Here the river drops to a **flood plain.** A flood plain is formed by river floods. The river carries silt with it as it floods the land. When the river drops back down into its bed, the silt remains on the land. After years of flooding, the silt builds up into a fertile plain.

Chinese farmers have grown crops on the Chang Jiang flood plain year after year. Yet the soil is still good for farming. Heavy rains flood the river every summer. Each time the river leaves behind a new layer of silt which keeps the soil rich. The plain also has mild winters and a long growing season. It is ideal for growing cotton, wheat, and many other crops. Cotton is one of China's most important crops. Most Chinese clothing is cotton.

To grow rice, people flood the land. When the rice begins to ripen, the water is drained off so that the soil can dry by harvesttime.

Plant Life Along the Chang Jiang

A tall plant grows all along the Chang Jiang. It looks like a tree, but it is really a giant grass. It is **bamboo.** Bamboo may grow as high as 100 feet (about 30 m). It is the world's fastest-growing plant. Some bamboo grows more than 3 feet (about 91 cm) a day!

Bamboo has many uses in China. It is as stiff and strong as wood. The Chinese make bowls and fences from bamboo. They also use it to make baskets, rope, and roofs. Bamboo pipes carry water from the river. The tender new **shoots** of bamboo are used in many Chinese meals. Shoots are the young branches of a plant.

What are some of the ways in which the Chinese use the sturdy bamboo plant?

From the cocoons of these silkworms will come some of China's prized silk.

China kept a great secret from the rest of the world for hundreds of years. Only the Chinese knew how to make silk. The mulberry tree, another plant of the Chang Jiang, was part of that secret.

Today we know that silk is made from the small cocoons of **silkworm** caterpillars. Silkworms are young moths. The Chinese collect the eggs from the adult insect. Silkworm caterpillars hatch from the eggs. The caterpillars love to munch on tasty mulberry leaves! When it is old enough, the silkworm spins a cocoon. Each cocoon provides a thousand threads of silk.

Living on the Chang Jiang

Millions of Chinese live in cities near the mouth of the Chang Jiang. Other Chinese live in small towns or settlements along the river. Some of these people are farmers or factory workers. Others make their living by fishing.

Two kinds of fishing boats are used on the Chang Jiang. **Junks** are light boats with tall square sails. These sails catch the slightest breeze moving over the river.

The other type of boat is a **sampan.** At one time sampans were homes for many fishing families. Some people who lived on sampans never set foot on land. The Chinese government does not want people to live on these boats anymore. The government says that this way of living is making the river unhealthful for others. Also, it is difficult for the government to keep track of people living on sampans.

Some 500 kinds of fish are caught in the Chang Jiang. Many settlements along the river also have fish ponds. People use the ponds to raise fish for food. Fish is an important food in China. Some of the fish are

Wooden Chinese junks are used for fishing in harbors and on the open seas.

Today sampans are used mostly as cargo barges along rivers and canals.

385

Shanghai is a major Chinese port and industrial center. Everything from ocean-going ships and heavy machinery to textiles and carpets is made here.

familiar to us. One such fish is the catfish. Then there is the giant paddlefish. This fish has a smaller cousin that lives in the Mississippi River. The Chang Jiang paddlefish is a strange-looking animal. It has a long nose. The giant paddlefish is truly a giant. It can grow as long as 20 feet (about 6 m).

The **Grand Canal** joins the Chang Jiang near the East China Sea. The Grand Canal is one of the world's great wonders built more than 2,000 years ago. It connects the Chang Jiang with the **Huang He** (HWANG HEE). The Huang He is China's second-largest river. Even today the Grand Canal is used for travel and trade. It is the oldest canal in the world still in use.

At the end of its long journey the Chang Jiang empties into the East China Sea. Near the river's mouth lies the port of **Shanghai.** Shanghai has the largest population of any city in China. A city of skyscrapers and factories, it is China's business capital.

Reading Check

1. Why is the Chang Jiang flood plain good for farming?
2. Name two crops that grow along the Chang Jiang.
3. What is the Grand Canal?

Think Beyond How would a lack of rainfall affect life along the Chang Jiang?

People MAKE HISTORY

Ru Chih Chow Huang
1932–

▶▶▶▶▶▶▶▶▶▶▶▶▶▶▶▶

Ru Chih Chow Huang (ROO CHEE CHOW HWAHNG) was born in Nanjing, China. As a child, Ru Chih looked forward to the days when she and her mother traveled to the outdoor market at the edge of the city. If there was any money left after the groceries were purchased, Ru Chih's mother sometimes bought her a book.

Books were a special treat. Ru Chih loved to read, and she visited the library often. One day Ru Chih read a book about Dr. Marie Curie, the scientist who discovered radium, a material used in X rays. Ru Chih decided that she, too, would become a scientist.

Ru Chih studied hard and made good grades. She was accepted into a college in the United States. After completing college, she continued her education at other schools.

Today, Huang is a professor at The Johns Hopkins University in Baltimore, Maryland. She was the first woman professor in the university's science department. In addition to teaching classes,

Huang is trying to find out what causes cancer. She is also studying how cells age. Huang hopes that this will help her to find out more about how people age.

"Don't wait for someone else to tell you that you can succeed. Believe in yourself. And make your own plans." This is the advice that Huang gives her students. Believing in herself and making her own plans are things that Ru Chih Chow Huang has done all her life.

Think Beyond   Why is it important to make plans and to believe in yourself?

387

Look for these important words:

Key Words
- luxuries
- responsibility system
- wharves

Places
- Nanjing
- Chang Jiang Bridge
- Beijing

Look for answers to these questions:
1. What is daily life like in a city on the Chang Jiang?
2. What do students in China learn during their school years?
3. How do people live in farming and factory communities?
4. Why is Nanjing a busy city?

3 | *Nanjing, a City on the Chang Jiang*

About 200 miles (almost 320 km) from the mouth of the Chang Jiang is the city of **Nanjing.** Nanjing is a lovely old city with many parks and beautiful buildings. Graceful sycamore trees line its streets.

Most people in Nanjing live in small apartments. When they leave for work in the morning, some people walk. Others may take a bus or ride a bicycle. Very few Chinese own cars. Cars are still **luxuries** (LUHKSH•uh•reez) in China. A luxury is something expensive that only a few people can afford.

The great port city of Nanjing is also a center of Chinese learning and culture.

Rush hour in a Chinese city may bring fender-to-fender bicycle traffic. Farmers even use bicycles to bring their crops to market.

Almost everyone in Nanjing has a bicycle. Chinese shoppers park their bicycles in front of stores. They do not lock them. They know that the bicycles will not be stolen.

School in Nanjing starts at 7:30 A.M. It may still be dark when many young Chinese go to school. Both girls and boys wear long padded pants in winter. They also wear layers of padded cotton jackets. In China people sometimes measure cold weather by how many jackets they wear. Cold days are "one-jacket days." Colder days are "two-jacket days." Finally, there are very cold "three-jacket days." When the weather is hot, young people wear T-shirts and pants.

Chinese girls and boys like to play volleyball or table tennis at recess. Classes often exercise together. Everyone learns to sing in school. Many young people play musical instruments. Chinese children study reading, writing, and arithmetic. They study about their country's history and government.

There are not enough universities in China for all students to attend. The best students go to special schools that prepare them to enter the universities. Other students go to schools where they learn to do certain jobs that do not require a college education.

Older students who attend school in farming areas may spend some of their school time working on nearby farms. Students who go to school near factories may help out in the factories when they are needed.

Farm and Factory Communities

Farmers in farming communities outside Nanjing grow rice, wheat, cotton, vegetables, and fruit. Pigs and ducks are raised in almost every farm community.

Not all communities outside large cities are made up of farms. There are also large communities centered around factories. The workers live near the factories with their families. Often all the workers share doctors, libraries, shops, and other services.

Residents of China's farm and factory communities work very hard. On their days off they may fish, swim, or visit nearby parks. Workers often use free days to work in small gardens. The food grown in these gardens may be used to feed the family or may be sold to other families.

The government owns all the farms and factories in China. The Chinese are not allowed to choose which job they want or which community they want to live in. These decisions are made by the Chinese government.

People who live in farming communities do make some decisions. They decide what crops to plant, how to sell them, and what tools to buy. Each farmer rents land from the

Factories in Nanjing manufacture trucks and other heavy farm machinery important for China's agriculture.

government. This is called the **responsibility system.** Each farmer is responsible for producing a certain amount of crops for the government. Any extra crops the farmer produces may be sold. Farmers may keep any money they earn in this way. The farmers often work together and share farm equipment.

Factories also are expected to produce a certain amount of goods for the government. They are then allowed to sell any extra goods they produce to other people in China or to people in foreign countries.

A Busy Port

The Chang Jiang connects Nanjing with the rest of the world. Huge ships travel up and down the Chang Jiang from Nanjing to Shanghai. These ships stop at the **wharves** that line the Chang Jiang at Nanjing. A wharf is a platform built along the shore. Ships can load and unload their cargo here.

The ships carry many of the goods made in Nanjing's factories. Some of these goods are fertilizer, cotton clothing, and steel. Mines near Nanjing provide iron for the city's steel mills.

Ships loaded at the wharves of Nanjing carry their cargoes along the Chang Jiang. With all of its branches and canals, the Chang Jiang is a giant water transportation system of more than 18,000 miles (about 30,000 km).

The Chang Jiang Bridge at Nanjing completed the important railroad link between the cities of Shanghai and Beijing.

Nanjing is one of the few places where a bridge crosses the Chang Jiang. It is called the **Chang Jiang Bridge.** This new bridge stretches 3 miles (about 5 km) across the water. It is a double-decker bridge. The bridge has two levels. One level is above the other. On the upper level is a road for bicycles, cars, and people on foot. On the lower level a railroad crosses the river. This railroad connects Nanjing with China's capital, **Beijing** (BAY•JING), farther north. It also connects Nanjing to the port city of Shanghai.

The people of Nanjing are proud of the Chang Jiang Bridge. Now many more people can come to Nanjing from other parts of China. They, too, can now enjoy the beauty of this city.

Reading Check

1. How do many people travel about the city of Nanjing?
2. Who owns the farms and factories in China?
3. What are some factory goods shipped from Nanjing's port?

Think Beyond How are Chinese schools similar to and different from your school?

IN FOCUS

ALONG THE CHANG JIANG

It is Saturday afternoon. Mei Li thinks, "When will this school day end?" There is one more class to go, but this class is Mei Li's favorite. She is learning **calligraphy** (kuh•LIHG•ruh•fee), a beautiful way of writing.

Mei Li hopes she can become an artist when she grows up. She does not tell anyone, though. When she grows up, the Chinese government will tell her what work she will do.

When school is over, Mei Li walks home. As she walks, she looks over the green fields that stretch out on all sides of her community. In the distance she can see the Chang Jiang.

People are still working in the fields. They use heavy hoes to break up the soil. Some communities have tractors, but Mei Li's does not.

Mei Li visits the ducks. Some ducks swim up for the few grains of rice Mei Li tosses to them. These ducks are being raised for food in a stream that flows into the Chang Jiang.

When Mei Li arrives home, she goes to work in her family's garden. Most families have gardens rented to them by the government. Families can use or sell what they grow.

After supper, Mei Li is ready for the evening movie. A movie screen is stretched across the street at one end of the row of village buildings. The story is about the history of China. Mei Li enjoys the movie, but she is thinking about tomorrow. It is her day off.

Think Beyond   How would you feel if our government decided what kind of work you would have to do when you grow up?

The community at work

393

Thinking Back

- Many of the world's people live along rivers. The longest river in the world is the Nile River in Africa. For thousands of years, people have farmed the rich land along this river.

- The Rhine River touches six European countries. The river links these countries to ocean ports. The Rhine River also provides water for some of Europe's largest factory areas.

- The Amazon River is located in South America. Few people live along the Amazon.

- The Chang Jiang links the interior of China to the sea. Many cities and factories lie along the Chang Jiang. Farmers grow rice, cotton, and wheat on the river's flood plain.

- People living in China enjoy few luxuries. The government owns all farms and factories. The Chinese people cannot choose their jobs or the community in which they want to live.

- Under the responsibility system, each farmer is responsible for producing a certain amount of crops. Factories also are expected to produce a certain amount of goods.

Check for Understanding

Using Words

Copy the sentences below. Fill in the blanks with the correct words from the list.

flood plain   **sampan**
luxury   **wharves**
rain forest

1. A rainy place where trees and vines grow close together is a _____ _____ .

2. A _____ _____ is a flat place formed by silt left after floods.

3. A Chinese fishing boat is called a _____ .

4. Something that many people cannot afford is a _____ .

5. Platforms where ships can load or unload cargo are _____ .

Reviewing Facts

1. Why did the government of Egypt build dams across the Nile River?

2. Name two reasons why the Rhine is an important river.

3. Name two ways in which the Nile and the Chang Jiang are alike.

How are they different from the Amazon River?

4. How is the Chang Jiang important to the people of China?

5. What is life in a Chinese farm community like?

Thinking Critically

1. Name three ways Nanjing is like a city in our country. Name three ways it is different.

2. Name the things people need and some of the luxuries people want. Why do people want luxuries?

Writing About It

Take an imaginary boat trip down one of the four rivers that you read about in this chapter. Then write a travelog about your trip. Be sure to include a description of the river and the things you might see along its banks.

Practicing Time Skills

Studying the Earth and the Sun
Answer these questions about the rotation of the Earth and its revolution around the sun.

1. How long does one rotation of the Earth take? How long does one revolution take?

2. It is summer in the Northern Hemisphere. Is the North Pole tilted toward the sun or away from it?

3. In what climate zone does most of Brazil lie?

On Your Own

Social Studies at Home

Use the information in your textbook to write several trivia questions about the rivers, cities, and people described in this chapter. Challenge a family member to answer your trivia questions correctly.

Read More About It

The Amazon by Glenn Alan Cheney. Franklin Watts. In this book you will learn more about the Amazon region and the many problems it faces.

Chinese Writing: An Introduction by Diane Wolff. Holt, Rinehart and Winston. This is a "how to" book that tells about the art of Chinese handwriting.

Holding Up the Sky, Young People in China by Margaret Rau. Lodestar Books. An accurate picture of daily life among children in China is given in this book.

The Nile by E. Barton Worthington. Silver Burdett. Photos and maps help the author describe the world's longest river and the people who live along its banks.

The Rhine by C.A.R. Hills. Silver Burdett. The people, cities, and industries that crowd the banks of the Rhine River are described in this book.

Mountains Around the World

"On a projecting cliff, stood the old uncle's hut, exposed to every wind, but also open to every ray of sunlight and with a wide view of the valley below. . . . Farther back, the mountain with its old gray rocks rose higher still, now displaying lovely, fertile pastures, now a tangle of great stones and bushes, and finally, above them all, bare, steep cliffs."

—from the story *Heidi*
by Johanna Spyri

Look for these important words:

Key Words	• Sherpas	Places
• imports	• yak	• Mount Everest
• export		

Look for answers to these questions:
1. What do the Alps provide for the people living in Switzerland?
2. How do the Atlas Mountains change the climate in northern Africa?
3. How do people make a living in the Himalayas?

1 *Mountain Regions of the World*

Wide bands of mountains cross all of the continents. Snow and glaciers cover their highest peaks, and powerful winds rush between them. The land is steep and rocky. Yet people have lived on mountains for thousands of years. They probably first moved to mountains for protection from warlike peoples. The mountains were land that no one else wanted.

In some mountain regions of the world, people live higher than 10,000 feet (about 3,050 m) above sea level. They must depend on themselves for food and for shelter. Almost everything they use comes from the natural resources around them.

In the following pages you will take a look at some of the world's mountain regions. As you read about each region, find it on the map on the next page.

The Alps

The Alps are the largest group of mountains in Europe. They cover most of the countries of Switzerland, Austria, and Liechtenstein (LIK•tuhn•styn). The Alps also reach into the nearby countries of France, Italy, Germany, and Yugoslavia.

For most of its history Switzerland was protected by the high, rugged Alps. Armies could not easily enter the country through the snowy mountain passes. The people in Switzerland lived in peace for hundreds of years.

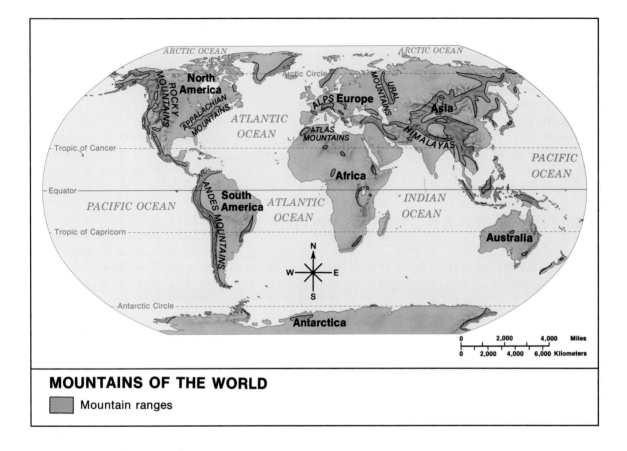

MOUNTAINS OF THE WORLD

☐ Mountain ranges

Glaciers long ago carved out the beautiful valleys that lie among the Alps.

The Alps protect Switzerland but provide few mineral resources. Farming is difficult on the steep sides of the mountains. In the valleys of the Alps, however, dairy cows graze on thick, green grass. From the milk of their herds, the Swiss make cheese. The United States **imports** much of their cheese. To *import* something is to bring it into a country for sale. What do you suppose we call one well-known cheese that comes from Switzerland?

Although Switzerland has little farmland and few mineral resources, it has several large

398

cities. These cities have many factories. The Swiss manufacture watches, machines, chemicals, and textiles. They **export** these products to other countries. To *export* something is to send it to another country to be sold.

The beauty of the Swiss Alps attracts tourists. Many people climb the Alps or ski the snow-covered slopes. Rivers that begin in the Alps make electricity. The electricity provides power for a railway that passes through the mountains.

The Atlas Mountains

The Atlas Mountains stretch across northwestern Africa. North of the Atlas Mountains is a plain that gets plenty of water.

In which areas of the Atlas Mountains might you find fertile land?

To the south of the mountains is the Sahara, the world's largest desert.

Why is land north of the mountains so different from land to the south? The Atlas Mountains prevent rain-carrying winds from reaching the desert. Most of the rain falls north of the mountains. The remaining moisture falls as snow on the mountain peaks. Small rivers begin in the mountains and flow to the plain in the north. The other side of the mountains gets little or no moisture. The slopes are dry and rocky. Very little can grow there.

A few people live in the Atlas Mountains. Some of them have small farms in the valleys. Others graze animals in places where plants can grow.

On which side of the Atlas Mountains are deserts found?

The yak helps the Sherpas survive the bitter Himalayan climate.
People even saddle and ride these animals through the mountains.

The Himalayas

The Himalayas (him•uh•LAY•uhz) are the highest mountains in the world. **Mount Everest,** the world's highest mountain, is in the Himalayas. It is more than 29,000 feet (about 8,840 m) high. The Himalayas separate the countries of China and India. They are like a wall 5 miles (about 8 km) high. Many of these mountains are covered with ice and snow all year.

From three to five million people live in the high peaks of the Himalayas. Among them are the **Sherpas,** who grow crops such as potatoes, rice, and soybeans. They herd animals also. The animal the Sherpas depend on for just about everything is the **yak.** The yak is a cousin of the American bison. It has a long, thick coat that helps it live in the cold mountains. The yak provides meat, milk, butter, wool, and leather. It also carries goods.

Reading Check

1. In what countries are the Alps located?
2. What kind of land is south of the Atlas Mountains? What kind of land is north of the mountains?
3. Why is the yak important to the people of the Himalayas?

Think Beyond   What might happen if a country always imports more than it exports?

IN FOCUS

VOLCANOES

About a hundred years ago, a mountain exploded on the island of Krakatoa in the Indian Ocean. A dark cloud of ash covered the sky. Huge **tidal** (TYD•uhl) **waves** 100 feet (about 30 m) high swept over nearby islands. More than 30,000 people drowned. The mountain was a volcano.

A volcano begins as a crack in the Earth's surface. Lava flows out of the crack. Over the years and after many lava flows, the lava builds up around the crack to form a mountain.

Some volcanoes are quiet for many thousands of years. Others erupt, or throw out lava, every few years. These are called **active volcanoes.**

When Krakatoa erupted, the whole side of the mountain blew open. Mount St. Helens in the state of Washington erupted in the same way in 1980. Some volcanoes erupt from the top. Then the melted rock flows evenly over the mountain. This gives the mountain a shape like a cone. Japan's Fujiyama is a cone-shaped volcano. At the top is a **crater,** the opening.

About 500 active volcanoes are on land. There are thousands more in the sea. Underwater volcanoes often form islands. Volcanoes made many of the islands in the Pacific Ocean.

Hot lava and ash from volcanoes can do great damage. A river of lava can move as fast as 35 miles (about 56 km) an hour. It destroys everything in its path before it finally cools and becomes rock. Volcanoes can be helpful, though, as well as harmful. Lava and ash mix with the soil and make it rich in minerals.

Think Beyond   Why do you think there are more volcanoes in the sea than on land?

An active volcano

401

Look for these important words:

Key Words
- Incas
- Quechua Indians
- *chuña*

- terraces
- ponchos
- llama

People
- Francisco Pizarro

Places
- Cuzco, Peru

Look for answers to these questions:

1. How do the Andes Mountains compare to other mountains of the world?
2. In what ways did Francisco Pizarro change the Inca kingdom?
3. How are the Quechuas able to live in the Andes Mountains?
4. How do llamas help the Quechuas?

2 | *The Andes Mountains of South America*

Near the Pacific coast of South America are the Andes (AN•deez) Mountains. The Andes stretch the whole length of South America, more than 4,000 miles (about 6,440 km). They are the longest group of mountains in the world.

The Andes are also some of the world's youngest mountains. They are high, rugged, and steep. Wind and water have not yet worn down the peaks of the Andes. Some of the Andes Mountains are over 20,000 feet (about 6,100 m) high. Glaciers and snow cover their peaks all year. Only the Himalayas are higher than the Andes.

Among the high peaks and deep canyons of the Andes are many high plateaus. People have made these high lands their home for thousands of years. Between 15 and 20 million people now live in the Andes.

The Andes Long Ago

More than 400 years ago, an explorer from Spain landed on the western coast of South America. **Francisco Pizarro** (puh•ZAHR•oh) was searching for gold and silver. Pizarro and his soldiers climbed the Andes Mountains.

Irrigation water from mountain rivers has helped turn some of the dry lands among the Andes into farmland.

Incas made beautiful objects of gold, the metal sought by the Spanish.

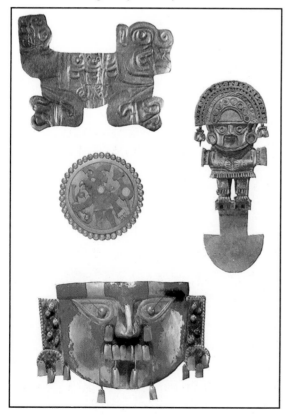

There they found the huge, rich kingdom of the **Incas** (ING•kuhz). The Incas were a number of Indian groups ruled by a king. They lived in the region stretching from Ecuador to Argentina. The king of the Incas lived in the city of **Cuzco** (KOOS•koh). Today Cuzco is a city in the country of Peru.

The Incas had built beautiful cities, roads, and bridges high in the mountains. They farmed the mountain slopes. They mined gold, silver, and copper.

Pizarro wanted the gold and silver of the Incas. He and his soldiers killed the Inca king. Soon the Inca kingdom fell apart. The Indians of South America then came under the rule of Spain.

The Quechua Indians

The Incas were the ancestors of today's **Quechua** (KECH·uh·wuh) **Indians.** Most Quechuas live in the Andes Mountains of Peru and Bolivia.

The Quechuas live far from modern cities. It is cold high in the Andes where they live. The temperature is near or below freezing almost every day.

Farming is difficult in the Andes. Few crops can grow at the mountains' high altitudes. The potato is one crop that can grow here. The Indians of the Andes were the first people in the world to grow potatoes. It is still their most important food.

The Quechuas have learned how to keep potatoes from spoiling. They leave the potatoes on the ground to freeze at night. The potatoes dry in the sun the following day. After several days and nights, the dried potatoes are ground into a meal. The meal is called **chuña** (CHOON·ya). The *chuña* will keep for many months.

With few flat places to farm in the Andes, Quechua farmers must plant crops on the sides of the mountains. To do this, the Quechuas build **terraces** on the mountain slopes. A terrace is a flat shelf dug out of the mountainside. From far away these terraces look like steps.

Following Inca methods, the Quechuas build rock walls, sometimes 15 feet (about 5 m) high, to prevent erosion of terraced farmlands.

Thin and Cold Air

If you are like most people, you are not used to the high altitudes of mountains. The higher you go in the mountains, the thinner the air will be. You do not have as much oxygen to breathe at these heights. You will get tired easily and feel dizzy. Yet the thin air of the mountains does not bother the Quechua Indians.

The people of the Andes have very large lungs. They can take in a lot of air with each breath. This helps them get enough oxygen. Because their arms and legs are shorter than ours, their blood does not have as far to travel. The people are strong from walking up and down mountains.

The thin air of the mountains cannot hold the sun's heat. The Quechuas wear many layers of clothing to protect them from the cold mountain temperatures. Men wear wool **ponchos** over shirts and pants. A poncho is a blanket with a hole in the middle. The wearer's head slips through the hole. Women wear several layers of warm skirts. The skirts are made of brightly colored wool.

The Llama

The Quechuas make their own clothing from wool. Children help gather the wool and make thread.

The Quechuas' wool comes from the **llama** (LAH•muh). The

Quechuas often weave warm, colorful ponchos with ancient designs.

Llamas are dependable pack animals along the old Inca trails still in use.

405

The Andes produce much of the world's copper. *Andes* is thought to come from a Quechuan word meaning "copper."

llama has a woolly coat and looks a little like a camel without a hump. It is the most important animal to the people of the Andes. From its wool a fine yarn is spun for clothing and blankets. The llama also carries loads up the steep mountain paths. The llama is very valuable to the Quechuas. They rarely kill the llama for meat.

Mining in the Andes

Many Quechuas work in mines. Some mines in the Andes have gold and silver. However, the Andes's tin and copper mines are more important today. Tin is used in making cans. The mines of the Andes meet much of the world's needs for these metals.

Long ago, llamas carried minerals from the mines to cities on the coast. Train tracks were later built over the mountains. One of the trains in Peru passes through a tunnel more than 15,000 feet (about 4,570 m) above sea level. It is the highest train ride in the world.

Reading Check

1. What is one crop that grows well at high altitudes?
2. Why are the Quechua Indians not bothered by the high altitude of the mountains?
3. What are llamas? How do the Quechuas depend on them?

Think Beyond Why do you think Pizarro killed the Inca king?

People MAKE HISTORY

Atahualpa
1500?–1533

▶▶▶▶▶▶▶▶▶▶▶▶▶▶▶

Atahualpa (aht•uh•WAHL•puh) was the last ruler of the Incas. It must have been quite a sight as he entered the city plaza to meet with Francisco Pizarro, the Spanish explorer. Servants carried Atahualpa on a bed with a feather canopy. He wore gold sandals, a gold-and-silver headdress, and colorful robes.

The Spaniards demanded that Atahualpa accept Christianity and the rule of their king. When Atahualpa refused, Pizarro's soldiers surrounded him and then attacked the other Incas gathered in the plaza. More than 4,000 Incas died that day.

Atahualpa was taken prisoner. Pizarro promised to release Atahualpa if he could fill his prison room with gold and silver. Atahualpa called on his people for help. They quickly filled the room with gold and silver, but Pizarro did not keep his word. He saw how easily the Incas obeyed their king's commands. He was afraid that if he let Atahualpa go, the Inca ruler would organize a revolt against him. Pizarro had Atahualpa put to death.

Pizarro, however, did not get all the gold that had been on its way to free Atahualpa. When the Incas heard that Atahualpa had been killed, they hid the gold in the nearby mountains. It was never found!

Think Beyond   The Incas greatly outnumbered the Spaniards. How do you think the Spaniards were able to defeat the Incas?

Look for these important words:

Key Words | Places
- ruins
- Lima
- Machu Picchu

Look for answers to these questions:

1. What sights might someone see in Cuzco?
2. How do people make a living in Cuzco?
3. Why do people from all over the world visit Cuzco and Machu Picchu?

3 | *Cuzco, a City in the Andes*

Cuzco is a city high in the Andes of Peru. Once it was the capital of the Inca kingdom. Today Cuzco is still the center of Quechua Indian life.

Many people fly to Cuzco from all over the world to see the Inca **ruins.** Ruins are the remains of buildings, towns, and cities that have been destroyed. Several planes leave for Cuzco every day from **Lima** (LEE•muh). Lima is the capital of Peru.

Lima is a large and modern city. Signs everywhere are in Spanish. They remind people that Pizarro, the Spanish explorer, founded this city.

Imagine that you are flying from Lima to Cuzco. You will see many differences between living in the city and in the mountains. You leave Lima, which is at sea level. You reach Cuzco, more than 2 miles (about 3 km) above sea

PERU

⊛ National capital

△ Inca ruins

Modern buildings, as well as traditional Spanish architecture, are found in Lima.

How is Cuzco (above) different from and similar to Lima?

The people of Cuzco still use these well-made stone streets built by Incas.

level. As you step from the plane, you begin to feel dizzy. The altitude makes it hard to breathe.

Some of Cuzco's streets do not look like streets at all. They are steep stairways. Cars and buses cannot drive up the stairs. Llamas, on the other hand, have no trouble with them. They travel in herds up and down the streets.

The Incas built Cuzco's stone streets almost a thousand years ago. Much of the Inca past remains in Cuzco today. Stone walls that once were large Inca buildings still stand. The Incas built the walls with huge stones. No cement holds the stones together. Still, they fit together so tightly that it is often impossible to push a knife between two of the stones.

The Marketplace

Near the Inca ruins in Cuzco are new hotels and restaurants that serve tourists. Tourism brings money into Cuzco. The people of Cuzco gather each day along the narrow streets to sell tourists handmade wool blankets, ponchos, sweaters, rugs, and caps.

The women spread blankets on the street to show their goods. Each one wears a different kind of hat. The shape, color, and decoration of a hat tells where the person wearing it was born.

On market day the people of Cuzco sell goods to one another. Most of them do not use money. They barter for goods. Someone might trade baskets for brightly woven cloth. Another person might trade a llama for food.

Children help their families at home. They also help them at the market. There are few schools for children. They and their families have no radios, televisions, or newspapers, either. The boys often watch over the family's small herd of llamas. The girls spin thread and weave the heavy, warm cloth.

At the market in Cuzco, people trade and sell crafts made according to traditions that go back at least 3,000 years.

Machu Picchu was an ancient Inca city only discovered in 1911. Why would its high mountain location keep it well hidden?

Machu Picchu

There is much to see in Cuzco. However, there is even more to see about two hours by train from the city. There, high up in the Andes, are the ruins of **Machu Picchu** (MACH•oo PEEK•choo). The Incas built this city on the top of a mountain. Machu Picchu is even higher than Cuzco. From Machu Picchu you can see the peaks of the Andes for miles around. People who visit Machu Picchu never forget the sight.

Many people come to Cuzco and Machu Picchu each year. Yet even with all these visitors, life in the Andes has changed little over the years. The Quechuas must work hard. They are poor. They live in tiny mud or stone houses that have no heat or electricity. The Quechuas manage to live on these cold, steep mountains for a reason. They want to follow the customs of their ancestors, the Incas. In this way the Inca heritage remains alive today. It is a heritage of which the Quechuas are proud.

Reading Check

1. What is the capital of Peru?
2. How do the Quechuas sell goods to one another?
3. What reminders of the Incas might a visitor to Cuzco see?

Think Beyond How is Cuzco similar to and different from Machu Picchu?

SKILLS IN ACTION

USING DIFFERENT KINDS OF GRAPHS

A graph is a drawing that helps you compare facts or numbers. Different kinds of graphs show different kinds of information. Each kind of graph looks different from the others. Each kind of graph has a special purpose.

Reading Picture Graphs

Picture graphs are an interesting way to show numbers. This kind of graph uses pictures that stand for numbers. The key shows what each picture stands for.

The graph below shows how many very high mountains are in some South American countries. Each symbol (△) stands for one mountain. The graph tells you that there are 14 mountains over 20,000 feet (about 6,100 m) high in Chile. Now count the mountains in the box

HIGH MOUNTAINS IN THREE COUNTRIES	
Chile	△ △ △ △ △ △ △ △ △ △ △ △ △ △
Peru	△ △ △ △ △ △ △ △ △ △ △ △ △ △
Bolivia	△ △ △ △ △
△ = Mountain higher than 20,000 feet (about 6,100 m)	

for Peru. How many mountains over 20,000 feet high are in this country?

Sometimes picture graphs are used to compare large amounts. Look at the graph below. It shows how many people live in three large cities in South America.

POPULATION OF THREE CITIES IN SOUTH AMERICA	
City and Country	
Buenos Aires, Argentina	𝕏 𝕏 𝕏
Santiago, Chile	𝕏 𝕏 𝕏 𝕏 ⟩
Bogotá, Colombia	𝕏 𝕏 𝕏 𝕏 𝕏
= 1,000,000 people	

In this graph each 𝕏 stands for 1 million people. Count the 𝕏 in the box for Bogotá (boh•guh•TAH). Four whole 𝕏 and more than half of another are in this box. This means that Bogotá has more than 4½ million people. Now look at the box for Buenos Aires (BWAY•nuhs AHR•eez). About how many people live there?

Reading Line Graphs

Line graphs show changes over time. The line graph below shows how much gold was mined in Colombia from 1980 to 1984.

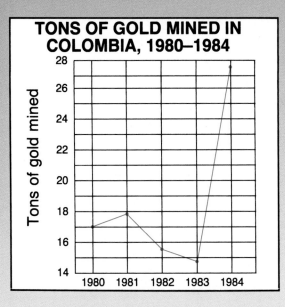

TONS OF GOLD MINED IN COLOMBIA, 1980–1984

Along the bottom of the graph are the years. Along the left side of the graph are numbers. These numbers stand for the tons of gold that were mined.

Find the year 1980 at the bottom of the graph. Now go up to the first dot. The line starts at this dot. It tells you that Colombia mined 17 tons of gold in 1980.

The next year listed is 1981. The dot for this year is just below the 18. In 1981 Colombia mined almost 18 tons of gold. Look at the line that goes from the 1981 dot to the 1982 dot. It slopes down. This lets you see quickly that gold mining went down in 1982. Did gold mining go up or down in 1983?

Reading Circle Graphs

A circle graph shows how a whole is divided into parts. This circle graph shows how many Peruvians are in different age groups.

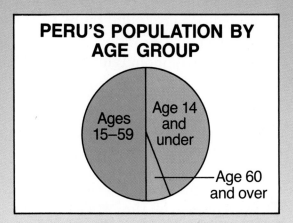

PERU'S POPULATION BY AGE GROUP

The green part of the circle graph stands for people between ages 15 and 59. This part is half of the circle. This means that half of the people in Peru are between the ages of 15 and 59. Does the blue part show more or fewer people than the green?

CHECKING YOUR SKILLS

Use the graphs on these pages to answer these questions.

1. Which country has more very tall mountains, Bolivia or Peru?

2. Which city has more people, Santiago or Bogotá?

3. Did Colombia mine more or less gold in 1984 than it did in 1983?

4. In Peru are more people age 14 and under or age 15 to 59?

413

CHAPTER 17 REVIEW

Thinking Back

- Mountains are found on all of the continents. The Alps are the largest group of mountains in Europe.

- Few people live in the Atlas Mountains, which stretch across northwestern Africa. The Sahara lies south of these mountains.

- The Himalayas are the highest mountains in the world. Among the people who live in the Himalayas are the Sherpas. They depend on the yak for most of their needs.

- The Andes Mountains of South America are the longest group of mountains in the world. Long ago, the Incas lived in the Andes. The Quechua Indians live there today. The Quechuas grow potatoes and use wool from the llama to make clothes.

- Cuzco is a city in the Andes of Peru. It was once the capital of the Inca kingdom. Machu Picchu was an ancient Inca city high in the Andes in Peru. Today, tourists from around the world visit the ruins of this famous city.

Check for Understanding

Using Words

Copy the sentences below. Fill in the blanks with the correct words from the list.

exports   terraces
imports   yak
ponchos

1. The United States ____ cheese from Switzerland.
2. Switzerland ____ watches to other countries.
3. The ____ is the most valuable animal for the people of the Himalayas.
4. The Quechuas grow potatoes on ____ dug on the sides of the mountains.
5. To keep warm, Quechua men wear wool ____ over their clothes.

Reviewing Facts

1. Name two ways the Alps are a valuable resource to people.
2. Why is the land south of the Atlas Mountains drier than the land north of the mountains?
3. Why is the potato the main food of the Quechuas?
4. What is the highest mountain in the world? In what group of mountains is it?

414

5. Why might a llama be as valuable to a Quechua Indian as a car is to an American?

Thinking Critically

1. Because most Quechuas live far from modern cities, they must depend on themselves to meet their needs. How is their life in the Andes different from life in a big city?

2. How is your way of life different from that of the Quechua children who live in the Andes?

Writing About It

Look at the pictures of mountains shown in this chapter of your textbook. Choose one picture, and then write a descriptive paragraph about the view it shows. Try to use words that will help your reader to "see" the picture.

Practicing Graph Skills

Using Different Kinds of Graphs
Copy the items below. Decide which kind of graph would best show the information. Write *picture graph*, *line graph*, or *circle graph* for each item.

1. how much you have grown in each of the last three years

2. what part of your class knows how to swim

3. numbers of students in each of five schools

On Your Own

Social Studies at Home
Fold a piece of paper to make two columns. In one column, write the ways in which mountains can be helpful to an area. In the other column, tell how they can create problems. Use these notes to help you explain to a family member or friend how mountains can affect the lives of people in mountain regions.

Read More About It
Children of the Incas by David Mangurian. Four Winds Press. In this book you will meet Modesta, a 13-year-old Quechua Indian.

Disastrous Volcanoes by Melvin Berger. Franklin Watts. This interesting nonfiction book describes Krakatoa, Mount St. Helens, and other destructive volcanoes.

Heidi by Johanna Spyri. Alfred A. Knopf. This classic is set in the Swiss Alps.

Llama and the Great Flood: A Folktale from Peru by Ellen Alexander. T. Y. Crowell. This Quechua folktale tells the story of the llama that saved the people from the great flood.

Secret of the Andes by Ann Nolan Clark. Viking. In this book, which won a Newbery Award, a South American Indian boy, Cusi, searches for his past and future.

CHAPTER 18

Deserts Around the World

"It was like casting off from a small port, leaving the land behind; indeed, a desert crossing is often like a voyage across open seas. We knew that . . . there would be little but sand. "

—A desert adventurer describing
the beginning of a long
journey across the
Sahara

Look for these important words:

Key Words
- oasis
- nomads
- nonrenewable resource
- stations
- Mongols

Places
- Arabian Peninsula
- Rub' al Khali

Look for answers to these questions:
1. What kinds of work do people do in the Sahara?
2. Why has life changed for the people of Saudi Arabia?
3. How do people make use of the Australian Desert?
4. What kind of life do people live on the Gobi?

1 Desert Regions of the World

You read about deserts of the United States in other parts of this book. You found out that a desert gets less than 10 inches (about 25 cm) of precipitation a year. When you look at the map on the next page, you will see that large deserts stretch across almost every continent. As you read about the deserts in this chapter, find them on the map.

The Sahara

The word *sahara* means "desert" in Arabic. It is also the name of the world's largest desert. The Sahara lies across the northern third of the continent of Africa. The Sahara would cover almost all of the United States, including Alaska and Hawaii.

The Sahara is very hot and very dry. The Sahara desert town of Azizia, Libya, once had the hottest day ever measured—136°F (about 58°C). Most of the Sahara gets less than 1 inch (about 2.5 cm) of rain a year, and parts of this desert have gone more than ten years without a single drop!

417

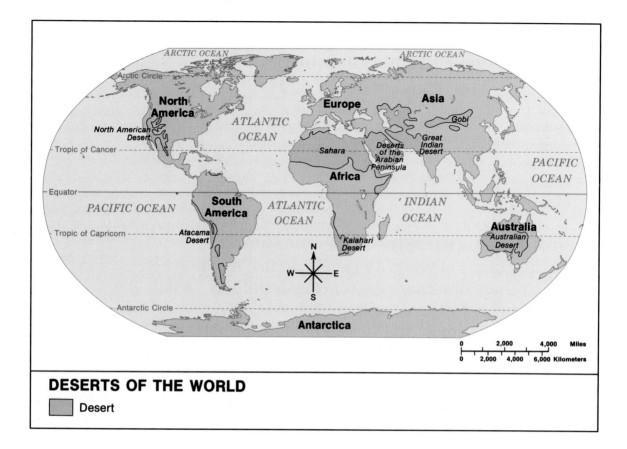

DESERTS OF THE WORLD

Desert

The Sahara has mountains, gravel-covered plains, and sand dunes.

418

Though some nomads own land on oases, other people farm the land for them. Most nomads move from one oasis to another, searching for grazing land for their animals.

Although the Sahara is hot by day, it can get very cold at night. The temperature may drop below freezing. In a single day the temperature can change as much as 80°F (about 27°C).

You may be surprised to learn that most of the Sahara is gravel. Sand dunes cover only about one-tenth of the desert.

About 2 million people live in the Sahara. Most of them live near an **oasis** (oh•AY•suhs). An oasis is a desert place with water. Most of it comes from springs that run under the ground. The people on oases (oh•AY•seez) grow grains such as wheat and barley. They may also grow olives, nuts, dates, and figs. Oranges are grown with the help of irrigation.

About 90 oases dot the Sahara. Groups of people wander from one oasis to another. They look for pasture for their sheep, goats, and camels. These people are **nomads.** They do not have one home. Instead they move from place to place.

The Deserts of the Arabian Peninsula

East of the Sahara is the Red Sea. If you crossed the Red Sea, you would come to the **Arabian Peninsula.** On this peninsula is the country of Saudi (SAWD•ee) Arabia.

Most of the land of Saudi Arabia is desert. In the desert in the center of the country, oases

419

provide water for small farms and herding animals. One desert, however, supports no life. This desert is called the **Rub' al Khali.** Its name means "empty quarter." It covers most of the southern part of the Arabian Peninsula.

In the past, people could not have crossed this desert were it not for the camel. The camel is often called the ship of the desert. It carries people and supplies across the Rub' al Khali. The camel can travel several days on only a little water. The humps of a camel store fat that is used when food and water are scarce.

For many years people thought most of Saudi Arabia's deserts were useless. Since they are so hot and dry, it is almost impossible to grow anything there. The people in some areas were either poor farmers or nomads. In the 1930s the old way of life began to change. Oil was discovered beneath the sands of the Eastern Lowlands. This part of Saudi Arabia is on the Persian Gulf. These oil fields became some of the world's most valuable land!

Today our world depends on oil. Without oil our lives would be very different. Oil supplies nearly half of our needs for fuel in the United States. The supply of oil is limited, however. Oil is a **nonrenewable resource.** A nonrenewable resource cannot be remade by nature or by people.

For this reason, oil is expensive. It has made some nations on the Arabian Peninsula very

Some of the world's largest oil deposits are found in eastern Saudi Arabia.

Oil wealth has helped the rapid growth of Kuwait's cities.

wealthy. Besides Saudi Arabia, one of the wealthiest is Kuwait (kuh•WAYT). Both of these nations have used some of their new wealth to build homes and hospitals. They have also built many schools and roads and even whole cities.

Life is changing quickly for the people of these nations. People who had been nomads now live in houses. People who used to herd goats and sheep now work in oil fields. They use trucks instead of camels for transportation. Today oil is helping people find new ways to live in the desert.

The Australian Desert

Large deserts cover nearly half of Australia. Together they are called the Australian Desert. The Australian Desert is not as dry as the Sahara. Much of it gets about 5 inches (about 13 cm) of rain a year. The edges of the desert get enough rain for grass to grow. This is rangeland used for raising cattle and sheep.

Brahman cattle, such as the one in the lower left corner of the picture, can stand the heat and the insects of northern Australia.

Many Mongols live in lightweight tents that are easily carried by pack animals.

Mongol nomads ride strong, small horses to herd their sheep and goats.

The people who live on the Australian Desert are not nomads. Australians raise sheep and cattle on large ranches that they call **stations.** More wool comes from Australia than from any other nation.

The Gobi

The Gobi (GOH•bee) is a desert north of China in central Asia. It lies mostly in the country of Mongolia (mahn•GOH•lee•uh). Winters are very cold in this desert. Summers are very hot.

A people called the **Mongols** (MAHN•guhlz) live in the Gobi. Many Mongols are nomads. They raise herds of sheep, cattle, goats, horses, and yaks. They move from one place to another in search of water and pasture.

In recent years the Mongolian people have begun to leave the nomadic way of life. Some are going to work in new industries in Mongolia's cities. Others have settled on farms to grow grain.

Reading Check

1. Which is the largest desert?
2. What is an oasis?
3. Who are the Mongols?

Think Beyond What are some ways in which you and your family use oil?

People MAKE HISTORY

Robyn Davidson
1950–

▶▶▶▶▶▶▶▶▶▶▶▶▶▶▶▶

Robyn Davidson crossed the Australian Desert in 1977. For seven months she hiked the harsh, empty land that Australians call the **outback.** Most of the time she was alone, except for four camels and a dog.

Together they were a **caravan,** travelers on a desert journey. Dookie was the lead camel. He was dependable and strong. The second camel was Bub, who sometimes refused to obey commands. After Bub came Zeleika and her baby, Goliath. Alongside ran Diggity, Davidson's dog.

Davidson faced many hardships. Water and food were usually in short supply. When water was low, Davidson forced her camels on to the next well.

On the 195th day, Davidson knew she was nearing her journey's end. "Oh, how my spirits soared! Two hours later I saw it, glinting on the far side of the dunes—the Indian Ocean. . . .

The camels simply couldn't comprehend so much water. They would stare at it, walk a few paces, then turn and stare again. Dookie pretended he wasn't scared, but his eyes were popping out. . . . I was riding Bub, and when the surf sent globs of foam tumbling over his feet, he danced and bucked and shied and nearly sent me flying."

Davidson left her camels in the care of friends and flew home. There she wrote a book about her adventures.

Think Beyond Why do you think a person might want to make such a long, hard journey?

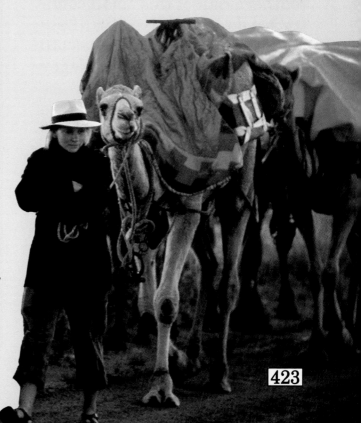

423

Look for these important words:

Key Words
- Nabataeans
- Bedouins
- reclaim

Places
- Israel
- Negev

Look for answers to these questions:
1. Why did the Israelis believe the Negev could be used for farming?
2. How have the Israelis changed the Negev from desert to farmland?
3. What natural resources are found in the Negev Desert?

2 *The Negev of Israel*

Northwest of the Arabian Peninsula is the small country of **Israel** (IHZ•ree•uhl). The entire southern half of this small country is a desert, the **Negev** (NEHG•ehv). No more than 4 inches (10 cm) of rain falls on the Negev each year. Yet the Israelis are slowly making the Negev a place where people can live. They have built farms, towns, and factories. They have turned dry desert into fertile farmland.

How have the Israelis done this? We must go back in history to understand it. We must look at the Negev as it was 2,000 years ago.

In those days almost 300 farming towns were strung across

In the middle of a desert in Israel sprouts green, fertile farmland.

424

the Negev. The people who built these towns were known as the **Nabataeans** (nab•uh•TEE•uhnz). They learned to collect the little rain that fell in the desert. They built canals and tanks to save the rain. With this water they irrigated small pieces of land. They grew figs, dates, and grapes. They even raised cattle.

About 1,200 years ago, desert nomads attacked the Nabataeans. These nomads were **Bedouins** (BED•uh•wuhnz). The Bedouins were herders, not farmers. Like all nomads, they moved from place to place in search of grass and water for their animals. They had no need for farming.

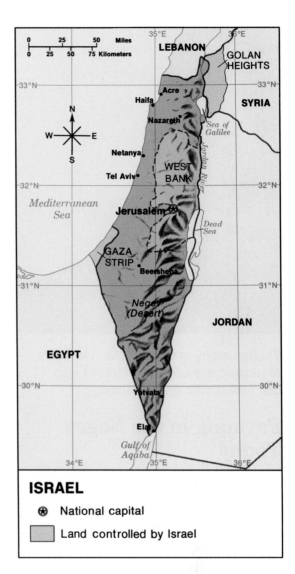

ISRAEL

⊛ National capital

☐ Land controlled by Israel

Bedouins still herd their animals through unsettled areas of the Negev.

As the Nabataean towns died out, their ways of farming were forgotten. Until about 40 years ago, only nomads lived in the Negev.

The nation of Israel was formed in 1948. Its new citizens, needing more land for farming, looked to the Negev. They knew that this desert was farmland long ago. They decided to try to make it farmland once again.

425

Though many of the Nabataeans' ways of farming are used, the Israelis also use new plastic greenhouses.

Tender strawberry plants need lots of moisture. Sheets of plastic help keep that moisture from evaporating.

Farming in the Negev Today

Today Israelis are finding that many of the old Nabataean ways of farming still work. They have built tanks under the ground to collect and store water. They have built miles of irrigation canals also. The canals carry water from the Sea of Galilee in northern Israel.

Like the Nabataeans, the Israelis make use of the moisture, or dew, that forms at night. In the desert, temperatures drop at night. During the night, dew forms on cooled surfaces. By putting stones next to plants, the Israelis collect the night dew. The small amount of water that col-

lects on the stones drips down into the soil to the roots of plants. In the Negev every drop counts!

The Israelis also have ways of farming that the Nabataeans never even dreamed of. They are using plastic to change the Negev. They have built huge plastic greenhouses that hold in moisture. Sheets of plastic also cover the soil. They keep water in the ground. Water drips right to the roots of plants through thin plastic pipes buried underground. If the plants were sprinkled from above, much of the water would evaporate in the dry desert air.

These ways of farming save water. New ways and old ways are making the Negev green again.

Low plastic tunnels cover crops in the Negev. Water from the Sea of Galilee is pumped south through canals and pipelines for irrigation.

Other Natural Resources of the Negev

The people of Israel have found other natural resources in the Negev besides farmland. They discovered some oil as well as minerals for fertilizers. The Israelis also found a 3,000-year-old copper mine and are now using it. The Israelis use clay from the Negev for pottery and some of the desert's sand for glass. The Negev is much more useful than it once seemed!

Israelis hope that many people will settle in the Negev in the next 20 years. These people will **reclaim,** or take back, more land from the desert. They will turn it into settlements. Today, there is just sand and stone in these places. In 20 years farms may bloom everywhere.

Reading Check

1. What did the Israelis learn from the Nabataeans?
2. Name three ways in which desert farmers use plastic.
3. In a desert, why is it better to water underground?

Think Beyond Why do you think it is important to reclaim land from the desert?

427

SKILLS IN ACTION

COMPARING AND CONTRASTING

Read these two groups of ideas:

a. Like the Sahara, the Negev is a desert.

b. The Nabataeans settled villages and farmed the land. The Bedouins moved from place to place and did not farm.

Sentence *a* tells how two things are alike. The Negev is like the Sahara because they are both deserts. When you **compare** things or people, you look for ways in which they are alike. You want to find out what these things or people have in common.

The sentences in *b* explain differences. The Nabataeans were different from the Bedouins. The Nabataeans stayed in one place and farmed the land. The Bedouins were nomads. They raised goats and camels instead of crops. When you look for ways in which people, places, or things are different, you **contrast** them.

The Sahara in northern Africa is the world's largest desert.

The Negev is a desert that covers the entire southern half of Israel.

	Ginny	Tom
Age	10	10
Height	54 inches (about 85 cm)	56 inches (about 90 cm)
Weight	67 pounds (about 30 kg)	75 pounds (about 34 kg)
Eye/Hair Color	brown eyes, brown hair	blue eyes, blond hair
School	Fox Park	Fox Park
Favorite Food	strawberry yogurt	apples

Comparing and contrasting things is nothing new for you. For example, it is easy for you to tell when two things are alike in shape. It is easy to tell when two things are different in color. Comparing or contrasting things can be more difficult, however. There may be many parts to the things you are comparing or contrasting.

Meet Ginny and Tom. You can learn some things about them from the table above.

In some ways Ginny and Tom are alike. They are both 10 years old. They both go to the Fox Park School. In some ways they are different. For example, Ginny has brown hair, but Tom has blond hair. How many other differences can you name?

Now you know some of the ways Tom and Ginny are alike and different. What else do the facts in the table tell you about them?

CHECKING YOUR SKILLS

Copy each sentence. Next to each sentence write *compare* if the sentence shows how deserts are alike. Write *contrast* if the sentence shows how they are different from each other.

1. All deserts get less than 10 inches (about 25 cm) of precipitation a year.

2. The Sahara has about 90 oases, but the Rub'al Khali in Saudi Arabia has none.

3. Sheep and cattle are raised on the Australian Desert and the Gobi.

4. Australians raise sheep on stations, but the Mongols move their sheep from place to place.

5. Kuwait and Saudi Arabia are both wealthy nations because of the oil found in their deserts.

429

Reading for a Purpose

Look for these important words:

Key Words
- kibbutz
- moshav

Look for answers to these questions:
1. What is the difference between a kibbutz and a moshav?
2. What did the early settlers of Yotvata do to change the desert?
3. What do kibbutz members raise on their desert lands?

3 Yotvata, a Kibbutz in the Negev

In Israel people farm the land on two different kinds of settlements. One kind of settlement is called a **kibbutz** (kihb•UHTS). *Kibbutz* means "group" in Hebrew, the language of Israel. Almost everything is shared on a kibbutz. The members own the land together. They live and work together. They build houses and grow food for one another. Some kibbutz members teach school or are doctors or nurses.

The other type of settlement in Israel is the **moshav** (moh•SHAHV). Unlike a kibbutz, each family on a moshav owns part of the land. The government provides supplies and helps farmers sell their crops.

A Difficult Beginning

Yotvata (yot•VOT•uh) is a kibbutz in the Negev. When it began in 1951, Yotvata was only a few tents in one of the hottest, driest parts of the Negev. Eighty men and women started Yotvata. They put in a pump to draw water from under the ground. Then they built houses and cleared spaces in the sand and rock for fields.

The Negev was a challenge to the early settlers at Yotvata. They tried all sorts of crops. Only dates and tomatoes did well at first. Then the settlers built fences to protect their crops from wind and sand. They covered their fields with sheets of plastic. The plastic kept water from escaping into the

430

Yotvata is a modern kibbutz that provides schools, food, and medical care for all its members.

hot desert air. They put pipes in the ground to water the roots of their plants. Little by little the people of Yotvata brought their part of the Negev to life.

Yotvata Today

Today Yotvata is an example of what people can do to change the desert. If you were to visit the kibbutz, you would see many surprising things. Fields of flowers blooming on this dry land are the first surprise. To grow flowers the kibbutz members must remove the salt from their well water. Desert soil is very salty, so the water below it is salty, too. The kibbutz members filter the water to remove the salt. They use the water in their gardens. They also use it for their cattle.

Yotvata is very proud of its herd of dairy cows. Raising cows in the desert is not easy. Since the cows have no place to graze, they live in sheds. The kibbutz members bring food to the cows every day. During the summer they give the cows three showers a day. The showers keep the animals cool.

Kibbutz members also raise winter fruits and vegetables. They sell the food they raise to nearby towns. The money they earn belongs to everyone at Yotvata. They use this money for food, clothing, medical care, and

Kibbutz members eat meals together.

Dates are one of the kibbutz's products.

Milking machines speed up milking.

Kibbutz trucks bring food to towns.

education. Some of the money is used for air conditioning to make life in the desert more pleasant.

Daily life at Yotvata begins at four o'clock in the morning. People have to start work early, before it gets too hot. By afternoon the sun beats down on the desert. The kibbutz members take naps during the early afternoon. It is too hot then to do anything else.

Life at Yotvata is not easy. Still, the people of Yotvata are happy there. They like the challenge of making the desert green. The kibbutz members are always trying out new ways of living in the desert. What they learn may help people in other dry places all over the world.

Reading Check

1. What is a kibbutz?
2. From where do the kibbutz members get much of their water?
3. How do the people of Yotvata raise dairy cows in the desert?

Think Beyond Why do you think it is so important for people on a kibbutz to work together?

IN FOCUS

Have you ever left a garden hose out in the sun? After a while, the water lying in the hose can get very hot. Sunlight made that heat. When sunlight is used for power, it is called **solar** (SOH•luhr) **energy.**

People have used the sun's heat for thousands of years. Today we have discovered new ways to use the sun's energy for heat. One way is to have sunlight heat water in pipes built into the roofs or sides of buildings. The hot water is then stored in a tank for later use.

Deserts get many hours of full sunlight, so they are good places to use solar energy. Some desert communities now use solar energy to power machines. For example, communities in Saudi Arabia use solar-powered pumps to bring water to the desert.

Solar cells are batteries that turn sunlight directly into electricity. Solar cells can be used to power radios and calculators or to cook food. They are also used to power **space probes.** Space probes are spacecraft that explore our solar system. Solar cells can power a space probe for years.

Collecting and storing the sun's energy is expensive. Scientists are working to find inexpensive ways to use solar energy. As other fuels become more expensive, light from the sun may help us meet our energy needs.

Think Beyond Why might solar energy become more important in the future?

Solar panals are used to heat water.

Thinking Back

- The Sahara, in northern Africa, is the world's largest desert. Most of the people in the Sahara live near oases. The rest are nomads who move from place to place.

- Saudi Arabia and Kuwait are desert nations on the Arabian Peninsula. Oil has made these countries wealthy.

- The Australian Desert covers nearly half of Australia. Cattle and sheep are raised on rangeland along the edges of the desert.

- The Gobi is a desert in central Asia. People called Mongols live there. Many Mongols are nomads.

- The Negev is a desert in Israel. The people of Israel combine new ways of farming with old Nabataean ways to make farmland out of the desert.

- The kibbutz and the moshav are two kinds of farming settlements in Israel. Members of a kibbutz own land together and share housing and food. Each family on a moshav, however, owns part of the land.

Check for Understanding

Using Words

Copy the words numbered 1 to 5. Next to each word, write its meaning from the list that follows.

1. **kibbutz**   4. **reclaim**
2. **nomads**   5. **station**
3. **oasis**

a. a place in the desert with water, which comes from springs
b. people who move from place to place
c. an Australian ranch
d. a kind of community in Israel
e. take back

Reviewing Facts

1. How much rainfall do deserts receive?
2. Why do desert nomads move from place to place?
3. How is life changing in the deserts of Saudi Arabia?
4. Name one way in which people of the Sahara are different from people of the Negev.
5. Name two ways in which farming in the Negev is the same today as in the past. Name a way in which it is different today.
6. Why have the Israelis settled in the Negev?
7. How is a moshav different from a kibbutz?

8. How did the people of Yotvata change the Negev?

9. Why do the people of Yotvata filter their water?

10. How can Yotvata help other people who live in deserts?

Thinking Critically

How does life on American deserts differ from life on the Sahara, the Gobi, or the Negev?

Writing About It

Imagine that you and your family are visiting a kibbutz. Write a postcard to someone you know. Tell about the things you are doing on the kibbutz.

 ## Practicing Thinking Skills

Comparing and Contrasting
Copy each sentence. Next to each sentence, write *compare* or *contrast*.

1. Like the Gobi, the Australian Desert is very dry.

2. The people of the Gobi are nomads, but the ranchers of the Australian Desert are not.

3. On a kibbutz almost everything is shared, but on a moshav each family owns its land and provides for itself.

4. Life for the early settlers of Yotvata was not easy, and life continues to be difficult for the people who live there today.

 # On Your Own

Social Studies at Home

Use a glass to stand for a rock in the desert. Fill the glass with ice, and set it on a kitchen counter. After a few minutes, observe the glass. What has happened on the outside of the glass? Use this demonstration to explain to a family member how desert farmers collect dew from rocks to water plants.

Read More About It

The Boy from Over There by Tamar Bergman. Houghton Mifflin. This award-winning novel describes a child's life on a kibbutz in 1947.

Camels: Ships of the Desert by John F. Waters. T. Y. Crowell. This book provides a close look at these strange but useful animals.

Gavriel and Jemal: Two Boys of Jerusalem by Brent Ashabranner. Photographs by Paul Conklin. Dodd, Mead. This book is about a Jewish boy and a Palestinian boy, both of whom live in Jerusalem.

Nadia the Willful by Sue Alexander. Pantheon Books. In this exciting story, Nadia's brother is missing from their desert camp.

Red Earth, Blue Sky: The Australian Outback by Margaret Rau. T. Y. Crowell. Life in the outback is described in this book.

CHAPTER 19

Plains Around the World

We were over the flat grainlands of the Ukraine. . . .
The endless fields lay below us, yellow with wheat and
rye, some of it already harvested, and some of it being
harvested. There was no hill, no eminence of any kind.
The flat stretched away to a round unbroken horizon. And
streams and rivers snaked and twisted across the plain.

—from the book *A Russian Journal*
by John Steinbeck

Look for these important words:

Key Words
- Calgary Stampede
- Masai
- steppe

Places
- Calgary, Alberta
- Nairobi, Kenya
- European Plain
- Ukraine
- Moscow

Look for answers to these questions:

1. How are the Canadian Plains like our Great Plains?
2. What is unusual about the plains in the country of Kenya?
3. What are the land and the climate like on the plains of the Soviet Union?
4. How do people make a living on the European Plain?

1 *Plains Regions of the World*

The United States has two large areas of plains, the Interior Plains and the Coastal Plain. The farmlands of the Interior Plains produce much of the food our country needs. Some of our largest cities lie on the Coastal Plain and on the Interior Plains.

Plains in other parts of the world are also places for cities, farms, and ranches. Most plains produce food for many people. As you read about each large plain, find it on the world map on the next page.

The Canadian Plains

The Interior Plains of the United States stretch into Canada, our neighbor to the north. These Canadian Plains reach across most of Canada's eastern half.

The Canadian Plains are much like our Great Plains. They have rich soil, enough rainfall, and a growing season just right for raising wheat. Each year farms on these plains grow thousands of bushels of wheat. Like American farmers, Canadian farmers

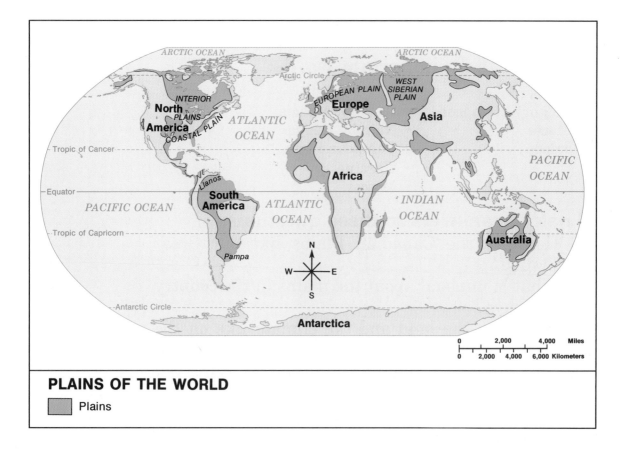

PLAINS OF THE WORLD

Plains

Fields of wheat and other grains spread out in a patchwork pattern across the fertile Canadian Plains.

The chuck wagon races are only part of the fun at the Calgary Stampede.

Herds of elephants and many other animals roam the plains of Kenya.

watch the weather carefully. Canada's interior has very cold winters. Farmers worry that early snows will ruin their wheat.

The western part of the Canadian Plains is not flat enough for growing wheat. This land, near the Canadian Rockies, is cattle country. **Calgary, Alberta,** is a city in the heart of cattle country. Every year it holds a rodeo called the **Calgary Stampede.** Many people come to Calgary's rodeo to see cattle shows and wagon races.

Beneath the rich soil of the Canadian Plains lies another valuable resource, large fields of oil. Oil from these plains has become one of Canada's most important products.

The Plains of Kenya

Plains cover three-fourths of Kenya. Kenya is a nation on the east coast of Africa. Look at the world map on page 438. First, find Africa. Then find where the equator crosses Africa's east coast. The plains of Kenya lie near this point. The climate of the plains of Kenya is different from the climate of our Interior Plains. In Kenya it is warm all year long.

Kenya's plains are often dry. Except for the rainy seasons in spring and fall, little rain falls during the year. Only bushes and short grasses grow on this land.

The grasslands of Kenya are the home of elephants, lions,

zebras, and other wildlife. The government in Kenya's capital city, **Nairobi** (ny•ROH•bee), has set up huge parks to protect its wildlife. The parks are one of the few places where these animals can live in their natural home. Visitors from around the world come to Kenya to see them.

The **Masai** (mah•SY) are nomads of Kenya's plains. Herding cattle is the main way these people make a living. Yet few of the cattle are killed for meat. They are valued for their milk and used in trading. The Masai make their living mostly from their herds.

The Masai move with their herds of cattle across the land.

For thousands of years the Masai have lived on some of Kenya's driest lands.

When the cattle have eaten all the grass in one place, the Masai move to another. The Masai keep the cattle from running away by herding them into corrals. The fences are made from thorn bushes that grow on the land.

The Plains of the Soviet Union

In size the Soviet Union is the world's largest country. It is so large that it reaches across parts of two continents, Europe and Asia. The Soviet Union is divided by the Ural Mountains. The Urals are very old, low mountains like the Appalachian Mountains. East of the Ural Mountains is Soviet Asia. This covers all of the northern part of Asia. West of the Urals is the European part of the Soviet Union. It covers the eastern half of Europe.

A vast plain covers more than half of the Soviet Union. It lies mostly in Europe. This large plain, called the **European Plain,** is made up of rolling hills and flat land.

The southern part of this plain stretches into Asia and includes the **steppe** (STEHP), or grassy plain. This treeless grassland of the Soviet Union has dark, rich soil good for growing wheat. Where the steppe is very dry, it is used as grazing land.

Beef and dairy cattle graze on parts of the steppe too dry or too cold to farm.

The wheat crop of the Ukraine helps feed many of the Soviet Union's people.

Summers on the steppe are hot, with little rain. They can be too dry for growing wheat. This causes poor harvests. The steppe is far from the Atlantic Ocean. Winds from the Atlantic reach the steppe, but by then they have lost almost all their rain. Parts of the steppe may get as little as 8 inches (about 20 cm) of rain a year. The hot, dry winds can kill the wheat crop. Cold can be a problem, too. In some years winter comes early and kills the crop before it can be harvested.

Bordering the steppe in the southwestern part of the Soviet Union is the **Ukraine.** The Ukraine region of the Soviet Union has the best farmland of the country. This part of the plain is often called the "breadbasket" of the Soviet Union.

North of the Ukraine and the steppe are more humid regions. At one time the land was covered by maples, oaks, and other broadleaf trees. Much of this land is cleared today. The Soviet Union's largest cities and largest factories are here.

More than 275 million people live in the Soviet Union. Three of every four live on the European Plain. One reason they live here is the climate. Although much of the plain is hot in summer and very cold in winter, the climate is better here than in most other parts of the Soviet Union.

Located in the heart of the European Plain, Moscow is the political, industrial, and cultural center of the Soviet Union.

Another reason so many people live here is the area's natural resources. This area has minerals and fuels for industry. Large amounts of iron, coal, oil, and natural gas mean jobs for people in factories and refineries. The area also has good soil for growing grain, potatoes, sugar beets, and sunflowers. The oil from sunflower seeds is used for cooking and making soap.

Among the cities in this region **Moscow** is the largest. Moscow is the capital of the Soviet Union. The area around Moscow is the nation's leading factory center. Cars, trucks, and buses are made in factories here. Moscow is also an important center of transportation. Highways and railroads connect Moscow to other parts of the nation. A canal and the Volga River connect Moscow to some of Europe's seas.

Reading Check

1. What plain is much like the Great Plains of the United States?
2. Why is the steppe of the Soviet Union very dry?
3. Why do most people in the Soviet Union live on the European Plain?

Think Beyond How do you know that most people in Kenya value their country's wildlife?

442

IN FOCUS

RETURN OF THE HORSE

For thousands of years people used horses for sport, hunting, and war. Long before the car and the tractor were invented, the horse was one of the most useful animals.

The draft horse was one important kind of horse. Long ago, the draft horse carried a knight wearing heavy armor. Later, farmers in Europe and America used draft horses to pull their wagons and plows.

Draft horses are the giants of the horse world. The tallest are the Shires of England. These horses measure 6 feet (about 183 cm) from shoulder to ground. They weigh about as much as a small car.

Draft horses have thick legs and strong muscles. They can pull very large loads. Though they are huge, these horses are gentle and easy to handle.

Many farmers stopped using draft horses when the tractor was invented. They thought tractors were better and cheaper. A tractor did not have to be fed. Horses needed oats and hay every day, whether they worked or not.

Today tractors are expensive. So is gasoline. Some farmers in Europe and the United States have decided to use horses again. On small farms a horse may be more practical than a tractor. Horses do not get stuck in the mud, as tractors sometimes do. Horses can work on steeper hills. Horses can eat food that is grown on the farm. A horse can do something else that tractors cannot do. Horses can make new horses.

Think Beyond   Why might horses be more practical on a small farm than on a large one?

Draft horses at work

SKILLS IN ACTION

CONSERVING ENERGY

More than 5 billion people live in the world today. These people use huge amounts of the Earth's natural resources. More natural resources will be needed in the future. What can we do to make our resources last longer?

One thing we can all do is to **conserve,** or save, energy. Coal, gas, and oil are used to make energy. How can you help save energy? It all begins at home!

- In cold winters, you can try using less heat. Wear warm clothes instead of turning up the heat. At night close window curtains to keep the heat inside the house.

- In summer, try not to use an air conditioner. Instead, keep window curtains closed. That way the house will stay cool during the day.

- It's easy to save electricity. Turn on only the lights you need. Turn off lights when you leave a room. Turn off the television or radio when no one is using it. After you take something from the refrigerator, close the door.

- Using the car too much is a waste of gas. Instead of going by car, see if you can walk or ride a bike. If you are going on a trip, perhaps you can use a bus or train. Share rides with friends when you are going to the same place.

Taking public transportation often saves time and energy.

444

Newspapers are one of the easiest, most inexpensive materials to recycle.

Recycling cans prevents waste from building up in the environment.

- **Recycling** saves both energy and natural resources. *To recycle* means "to use materials again." Many American towns and cities now have recycling centers. People can bring cans, bottles, and newspapers to them. Recycling saves the raw materials that go into making these things. Recycling also saves energy. It takes less energy to turn used cans, bottles, and newspapers into new products than it does to start with raw materials.

- Being a careful consumer is another good way to save resources. When you buy something you don't really need, you waste resources. Buy only the things you actually need. Use what you have for as long as it lasts.

CHECKING YOUR SKILLS

Write answers to these questions.

1. What are two ways you can save energy in winter?

2. What are two ways you can use less electricity in your house?

3. How can you save energy when you go on a trip?

4. What are some other ways you can save energy?

445

Look for these important words:

Key Words | Places
- pampa
- alfalfa
- *estancias*

- Patagonia
- Buenos Aires
- Salado River

Look for answers to these questions.
1. What kind of rainfall and climate does the pampa have?
2. What are some of the important products that come from the pampa?
3. Why is meat packing an important industry in Argentina?
4. What are *estancias*?

2 ⫸ *The Pampa of Argentina*

Argentina is South America's second-largest country. Along the western edge of the country are the Andes Mountains. As you have read, these mountains are steep and cold.

To the east of the Andes is a large, dry plateau. This plateau is called **Patagonia** (pat•uh•GOH•nyuh). Though mostly desert, Patagonia does support a few people as well as some unusual wildlife.

One unusual animal that lives along the coast is a type of penguin. These penguins actually only live on land for a short time, when they are raising their

Though awkward-looking on land, penguins are graceful swimmers.

Buenos Aires, Argentina's capital, is the center of its government and trade.

LANDFORM MAP OF ARGENTINA

- Mountains
- Plateaus
- Hills
- Plains

chicks. The rest of the year they spend swimming in the Atlantic Ocean.

Northeast of Patagonia, in the middle of Argentina, is a large grassland called the **pampa.** *Pampa* is the Spanish word for plain. Argentina's pampa is one of the world's largest plains.

Most of Argentina's products come from the pampa. More than half of Argentina's people live there, too. Most of them live in Argentina's capital city, **Buenos Aires** (BWAY•nuh SAR•eez).

Buenos Aires is a large, modern city with skyscrapers and wide highways. It lies on the eastern edge of the pampa, near the Atlantic Ocean. Buenos Aires is also a busy port. Ships from around the world dock in its harbor.

The Pampa

Spreading out from Buenos Aires for hundreds of miles is the pampa. Endless fields of wheat and grass stretch out in all directions.

447

Each rainy season produces a thick growth of grass that makes the pampa Argentina's most valuable grazing land.

The pampa has a mild climate and good rainfall. The western part of the pampa receives about 20 inches (about 51 cm) of rain each year. The eastern half receives close to 40 inches (about 102 cm) of rain a year. Yet you can travel for miles across the pampa and not see a stream. The **Salado River** is the only large river that flows across the pampa. You will, however, see windmills rising above the flat land. They pump water from under the ground.

Argentina is in the Southern Hemisphere. Therefore the seasons are just the opposite of those in our Northern Hemisphere. January is the hottest month on the pampa. June through August are the winter months. However, the winters are mild. They are much like winters in our southern states.

Farmlands and Cattle Ranches

The rich soil of the pampa makes it one of the world's best farmlands. Wheat, corn, and **alfalfa** are three of the important crops of the pampa. Alfalfa is a leafy plant grown as cattle feed. Much of the wheat and corn crops is exported to other countries.

By far the most valuable product of the pampa is beef cattle. The grasslands and alfalfa crop feed many large herds of cattle.

Spanish settlers of the *estancias* built beautiful houses like those of Europe. Today, this *estancia* mansion houses a university.

After about two years the cattle are ready for market. They are shipped to meat-packing plants in Buenos Aires. Meat packing is Argentina's most important industry. Much of Argentina's beef is exported to other countries.

Cattle were first brought to Argentina by Spanish settlers. Like most South American countries, Argentina was settled by the Spanish. Many Italian, German, and English people settled there later. However, Argentina is still a Spanish-speaking country.

Some of the settlers from Europe started **estancias** (es•TAHN•see•uhs), or large ranches, on the pampa. The *estancias* covered thousands of acres. The owner of each *estancia* built a large, beautiful house filled with costly furniture from Europe. Near the house the owner planted trees and gardens.

Estancia owners divided the land among family members over the years. Today most of the old *estancias* are much smaller. Yet some *estancias* still stretch for thousands of acres.

Reading Check

1. What is the most important product of the pampa?
2. Why is alfalfa important in Argentina?
3. Why have *estancias* become smaller over the years?

Think Beyond What American city might be compared to Buenos Aires? Explain.

Look for these important words:

Key Words
- gauchos
- *facón*
- lasso

- round up
- *asado*

Look for answers to these questions:
1. What was the life of a gaucho like 150 years ago?
2. What tools does a gaucho need?
3. In what ways has gaucho life changed?

3 *Life on an Estancia*

Most of the people who own *estancias* live a comfortable life. During the year they might invite guests to their ranches to enjoy their swimming pools, tennis courts, and gardens. Some *estancia* owners live on their ranches all year. Others live in Buenos Aires most of the year. Some even live in other countries.

The first *estancias* were built when the pampa was a wild, unsettled land. Modern conveniences are part of life today.

Gauchos of the pampa have rich traditions in music and poetry.

A gaucho sips *maté* from a gourd through a metal straw.

The *estancia* owners hire **gauchos** (GOW•chohs) to take care of their cattle. Today's gauchos are ranch hands. About 150 years ago, however, they were the cowboys of Argentina.

Many people in Argentina remember the gauchos of the past and consider them heroes. Poems and songs praise their brave deeds. They tell of the free life on the pampa in days gone by.

Gauchos Long Ago

Before the *estancias* were built, gauchos lived on the pampa in small groups. They chased the wild cattle there. These animals had been born to cattle that had escaped from Spanish settlers. The gauchos hunted the cattle for food and for hides.

Gauchos later herded cattle for the owners of large *estancias*. The gauchos followed the herds for hundreds of miles across the pampa. There were no fences or roads, just miles and miles of flat grassy lands. The gauchos led a hard life. They spent many days in the saddle. They slept on the ground and lived mostly on beef and a bitter tea called *maté* (mah•TAY).

Few things were more important to the gaucho than his horse. Without his horse he could not

451

chase the cattle. Without his horse he was not free to go anywhere he wished. Gauchos took good care of their horses. They were known for their skills on horseback.

In the early days the gauchos drove cattle herds to Buenos Aires. There the cattle were sold for meat. Then refrigerated railroad cars came to the pampa. The long drives were no longer needed. Meat could now be shipped long distances without spoiling.

Other countries began to buy more beef from Argentina. Cattle ranching soon became more important on the pampa. Many people moved to the pampa to start cattle ranches. They brought new kinds of cattle to improve their herds. The herds of cattle grew much larger. The ranchers planted fields of alfalfa to feed

the cattle. Immigrants from Europe came to work in the fields. The ranchers built fences. Now the gauchos were no longer free to wander anywhere they chose.

Gauchos Today

Today fences, highways, and railroads cross the pampa. Life for the gaucho has changed. Gauchos no longer live out in the open. They live with their families in small houses on *estancias*. Their children go to schools in small towns near the ranches. Not many schools are open for older children, however. They may have to travel a long way to go to school.

Although the gaucho's life is different today, his clothes remain the same. A gaucho still wears baggy pants and sometimes high

Gauchos once lived on the open range. Now they live and work as ranch hands on the fenced lands of the *estancias*.

452

Gauchos show off their famous roping and riding skills at rodeos much like the ones held in the western part of our country.

leather boots. He ties a bright scarf around his neck and wears a hat with a broad brim.

Gauchos still carry a long knife, a **facón** (fah•KOHN). It is tucked into a cloth or leather belt. Gauchos use the *facón* for many things, from cutting rope to slicing beef. No gaucho goes anywhere without his *facón*.

On the saddle of the gaucho's horse is another important tool. It is the **lasso.** The lasso is a rope with a loop tied at the end. When the rope is pulled, the loop gets smaller. Gauchos use the lasso to rope horses or cattle. Like the cowboys of our country, they make roping animals look easy.

A workday starts early for the gauchos. They have saddled their horses by the time the sun comes up. On some days the gauchos **round up** calves for branding. *Rounding up* means herding the animals together. On horseback the gauchos separate a few cattle from the herd. Then the gauchos chase the calves. They throw out their lassos as they ride. When a calf is caught, it is thrown to the ground. Then the calf is branded.

On other days the gauchos round up the cattle to move them to another pasture. Gauchos also check for broken fences and watch for sick cows.

A gaucho chef prepares steaks, ribs, and sausages as part of the menu for a big outdoor feast called an *asado*.

When gauchos are not working, they may get together to sing songs or tell stories. Sometimes they have an **asado** (ah•SAH•doh), or barbecue. At an *asado* guests often dine on a whole cow! The beef is roasted over an open pit. *Asados* have been a custom since the early days of the huge *estancias*.

If you were invited to an *asado*, you might hear the guests talk about how the pampa has changed. There are more *estancias* now, but they are smaller. Roads, railroads, and highways crisscross the pampa. Gaucho families are changing, too. In the past a son would become a gaucho like his father. Fewer choose this life now. Many children from gaucho families leave the *estan-cia*. They go to Buenos Aires to find jobs. They are still proud of their past, though.

Yet some things have not changed on the pampa. The grand houses of the old *estancias* remain. So do many customs of the early Spanish settlers. The guachos remain, too. They still ride proudly across the wide pampa.

Reading Check

1. What is a gaucho's job?
2. What animal is most important to the gaucho?
3. How did refrigerated railroad cars change the way gauchos worked?

Think Beyond Why do you think there are fewer gauchos today than in the past?

454

People MAKE HISTORY

José Hernández
1834–1886

▶▶▶▶▶▶▶▶▶▶▶▶▶▶▶▶▶

José Hernández grew up on Argentina's pampa. As a young boy, José spent many hours working with gauchos. In the evenings he listened to them sing songs and tell stories.

José and his family lived on an *estancia* not far from Buenos Aires. José never received any formal schooling, but he was determined to learn to read and write. José taught himself to do both. He later became a reporter for two different newspapers.

Although he had moved away from the *estancia,* Hernández never forgot his old friends, the gauchos. He was saddened to learn that their way of life was changing. The railroads were slowly replacing cattle drives, and fences were keeping the gauchos from roaming the wide, open pampa.

Hernández wrote a poem called "The Gaucho Martín Fierro," which describes how the gauchos were mistreated. The poem tells the story of a gaucho named Martín Fierro. In the story Martín Fierro is treated so badly that he becomes an outlaw.

The poem was an immediate success, and it made the gauchos heroes. Once again, people came to respect the gauchos and their work. Hernández went on to become a senator. He served in the congress in Buenos Aires for many years.

Think Beyond Why can literature sometimes be an effective way to get people to change their opinions about something?

The gaucho Martín Fierro

Thinking Back

- More than half of the Earth is plains. The Canadian Plains reach across most of Canada's eastern half. This region's major products are wheat, cattle, and oil.

- The warm, dry plains of Kenya lie near the east coast of Africa. Elephants and other wildlife roam these plains. The Masai are nomads who live on Kenya's plains.

- Many people live and work on the European Plain, which stretches through Europe into Asia. This vast plain includes the steppe and the Ukraine region of the Soviet Union. The Ukraine is sometimes called the Soviet Union's "breadbasket."

- Argentina's pampa is one of the world's largest plains. Much of it is grassland or fields of wheat, corn, and alfalfa. The grasslands and alfalfa crop feed cattle.

- *Estancias* are large ranches on the pampa. Gauchos are ranch hands who work on the *estancias*.

Check for Understanding

Using Words

Copy these sentences. Fill in the blanks with the correct words from the list.

alfalfa	round up
estancia	steppe
gauchos	

1. The drier southern part of the Soviet Union's vast plain is called the _____ .
2. An _____ is a large ranch on Argentina's pampa.
3. A leafy plant used as animal feed is _____ .
4. The ranch hands of Argentina are called _____ .
5. Gauchos on horseback _____ calves for branding.

Reviewing Facts

1. Name two ways in which the Canadian Plains are like our Great Plains.
2. Name two ways in which the plains of Kenya are different from our Interior Plains.
3. Why do most Soviet people live on the European Plain?
4. Why is the pampa good for raising cattle?
5. How do gauchos take care of cattle on *estancias*?

Thinking Critically

1. Gauchos have held on to many of their old ways. Would it be difficult for gauchos to change their lives? Why or why not?
2. To help protect wildlife, the government of Kenya has started parks. Some people want to use this land, though. If you were a leader in Kenya, how would you solve this problem and still protect Kenya's wildlife?

Writing About It

Choose one of the many wild animals that live on the plains of Kenya. Then write a short poem in which you decribe the animal or its life. Illustrate your poem by drawing a picture of the animal.

Practicing Citizenship Skills

Conserving Energy

Copy the sentences that tell ways to conserve energy. Then explain how following these suggestions would save energy.

1. Wear warm clothes instead of turning up the heat.
2. In cold weather, keep the window curtains open at all times.
3. Turn off lights when you leave a room.
4. Throw away cans, bottles, and newspapers.

On Your Own

Social Studies at Home

Think about the things that you can do to conserve energy at home. Then ask family members to suggest some ways in which they, too, can conserve energy. Record all the suggestions on a large piece of paper. Ask permission to hang your paper where it will be seen. For example, you might hang it on the refrigerator door to remind your family to conserve energy.

Read More About It

Canada: Giant Nation of the North by Jane Werner Watson. Garrard Press. Learn all about the land and people of Canada, our largest trading partner.

Growing Up Masai by Tom Shachtman. Macmillan. In this book you will follow two Masai children through their daily routine and learn about their home life.

Once Upon a Horse: A History of Horses—and How They Shaped Our History by Suzanne Jarmain. Lothrop, Lee & Shepard. This book explains how horses were used at different times and places in history.

The Union of Soviet Socialist Republics by Abraham Resnick. Childrens Press. In this book you will discover that the USSR is made up of different regions and peoples.

Protecting the Environment

Today many people all over the world talk about "protecting the environment." What do they mean? What is the "environment"?

We call nature and all its resources our environment. Air, land, water, plants, and animals are parts of our environment. Pollution, however, is a threat to our environment. We must protect our environment from pollution.

Air Pollution

For thousands of years people made fires to cook food and keep warm. The fires sent smoke and dust into the air. There were fewer people then, however, and the air could carry the smoke and dust away.

Several hundred years ago people began building factories.

Air pollution then became much worse. Factories burn large amounts of coal and oil. Burning the coal or the oil sends huge amounts of waste into the air. Inventions like the automobile have added much more pollution to the air. In fact, much of the world's air pollution comes from gases that cars give off.

Air pollution can be dangerous to our health. It can burn our eyes and skin and make us feel dizzy or sleepy. It can make us cough. It can make breathing very difficult.

Water Pollution

Our rivers, lakes, and oceans are not as clean as they once were. Chemicals dumped into our waters have caused most water pollution.

Many factories use water from nearby lakes and rivers to clean and cool machines. Often the used water is dumped back into the lake or the river. Chemicals in the waste water can poison fish and plant life. The used water may also be too hot for many fish. Such hot water kills more than 200 million fish a year.

Oil spills in the oceans cause water pollution. Huge oil tankers carry oil around the world. An accident at sea may spill millions of gallons of oil. An off-shore oil well may leak oil into the water. The water

People are trying to find ways to solve the serious air pollution problems that, in many cases, they themselves cause.

Laws can help protect our water supply from the dangers of pollution.

becomes coated with a layer of oil called an **oil slick.**

Cleaning up the oil can be very difficult. Oil slicks kill fish, birds, seals, and other sea life. They also kill the tiny plants that live on the water's surface. Whales and many other animals depend on these plants for food.

▲ An oil spill made this shoreline in Alaska unsafe for both people and wildlife.

Pittsburgh, Pennsylvania

Years ago pollution was a serious problem in Pittsburgh, Pennsylvania. The giant smokestacks of Pittsburgh's steel mills sent great clouds of black smoke into the air. Burning coal to heat homes added to the pollution. The city's three rivers ran dark and dirty.

Groups of Pittsburgh's citizens decided that something had to be done. The city passed some laws. Factories cleaned up smoke before it went out the chimneys. People stopped burning coal in their homes.

It took many years to make a difference, but little by little the air got better. Today the citizens of Pittsburgh are still working together to clean their city's air.

Lake Erie

Twenty years ago Lake Erie, one of the Great Lakes, was dying. How can a lake die? For many years factories and cities had been dumping their wastes into the lake. The lake became polluted. Many kinds of fish were dying. Swimming in the lake was dangerous to people's health.

People along Lake Erie began to take action. They asked their state governments to pass strong laws against pollution. These laws prevented some of the wastes from entering the lake.

Today Lake Erie is cleaner. More fish live in the lake. People can even swim in Lake Erie now. The lake is not yet as clean as it once was. Still, people working together have made it much better.

What Can You Do?

Cleaning up air and water pollution is expensive. Also it may take several years to see a difference. Sometimes it takes many people working together to get the job done.

Can one person do things to help protect the environment? Yes! Everyone can do his or her part. Each person can help stop pollution in the following ways:

- Conserve, or save, energy. For example, turn off electric lights when you are not using them.

- Put litter into trash cans. Being careful with your own litter will make a great difference.

Because of pollution controls, fishing, boating, and swimming are once again safe activities on Lake Erie.

- Recycle bottles, newspapers, and aluminum and tin cans. Huge amounts of land are used to bury garbage. Recycling helps cut down on a community's garbage. You can make and display posters telling people about your community's recycling center. If your community does not have one, your class may want to find out how to start one.

- Whatever you take into a wilderness area, take out again. Do not bury your garbage.

- With a group of people, work to clean up just one stream or playground in your community. Doing your part helps make your community more pleasant for everyone.

Save energy. ▼

Don't be a litterbug! ▼

Recycle what you can. ▶

Unit Review

Words to Remember

Copy the paragraph that follows. Use the words in the list to complete the sentences.

bamboo   **pampa**
export   **rain forest**
flood plain   **reclaim**
gauchos   **steppe**
nomads   **terraces**

How people make a living often depends on the place in which they live. Few people live in the hot, wet __(1)__ of the Amazon Basin. The groups who do live there grow crops in small fields and hunt. The floods of the Chang Jiang have built up a rich __(2)__. Here farmers grow __(3)__, a tall grass that has many uses. The Swiss mainly raise herds of dairy cattle in the Alps. They __(4)__ much of the cheese they make to other countries. The people of the Andes Mountains grow potatoes on __(5)__ built on the mountain slopes. Desert __(6)__ travel with their herds in search of food and water. On the Israeli kibbutz of Yotvata, people have found ways to grow crops with little water. By doing this, they __(7)__ land from the desert. On the dry __(8)__ of the Soviet Union, people grow wheat. Herds of beef cattle are raised on the __(9)__ of Argentina. Cattle on the *estancias* are cared for by __(10)__.

Focus on Main Ideas

1. Why do so many people live near the world's large rivers?

2. Why is the Chang Jiang important to the Chinese?

3. Give two reasons why mountain regions are difficult places in which to live.

4. What ways of life help people live in the Andes Mountains?

5. What is an ancient way of making a living in the desert? What is a modern way?

6. How have the people of Israel turned some parts of the Negev into fertile farmland?

7. In what ways do people make a living in plains regions? What natural resources help them in their work?

8. How did the gauchos live about 150 years ago? What tools do gauchos still use today that they used long ago?

9. How has the pampa of Argentina changed?

10. Name three ways in which Cuzco, Nanjing, and Buenos Aires are alike. Name three ways in which they are different.

463

Think/Write

You have read about people from different lands. Despite different cultures, how are people alike around the world? Write a paragraph in which you give three or four examples of the things that you have in common with children everywhere.

Activities

1. **Research/Mapmaking** You may want to work in a group of four for this activity. Each person should choose one of these natural features: rivers, mountains, deserts, or plains. Use an almanac or an encyclopedia to find the ten largest examples of the natural feature you choose. Using a different color for each feature, group members should mark and label their ten examples on an outline map of the world. Label the continents and the oceans also.

2. **Research Report** Choose one of the places discussed in this unit. Use encyclopedias and other books in your school's library to find out more about the place. Then write a report about it. In your report, describe any of the place's special customs or celebrations. Also include any unusual or interesting facts about the place. You might want to draw pictures or cut out pictures from old magazines to illustrate your report. Share your report with your class.

Skills Review

1. **Reading Line Graphs**

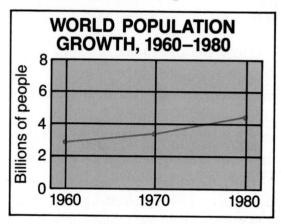

WORLD POPULATION GROWTH, 1960–1980

a. Look at the graph on this page. What does it show?

b. In what year was the population the highest? In what year was the population closest to 3 billion?

2. **Comparing and Contrasting**
Copy each sentence. Next to each one, write *compare* or *contrast*.

a. Buenos Aires is on a plain, but Cuzco is in the mountains.

b. Like Nanjing, Lima is a port city.

c. The Soviet Union, the United States, and Canada raise wheat on their plains.

464

In this unit you have seen how people live in different regions of the world. You have seen that people use their land and natural resources in many different ways. By learning how other people live, we can sometimes learn more about ourselves.

Below are some things you can do to find out more about the people and places of your state.

Learning About History

1. Many city governments have made old buildings into landmarks. They keep other reminders of the past in museums. Pick a large city in your state. Use a library to find out some of the landmarks in this city. Why are they important? Make a catalog of these landmarks. If possible, draw a picture of each one.

2. People have come to our country from all parts of the world. Use the library to find out what countries people in your state have come from. What holidays or customs are celebrated in these countries? Share what you find out with your class.

Learning About People

3. Use a library to find out what famous people have come from your state. Collect some interesting facts about one famous person. Share what you learn about this person with your class.

Learning About Geography

4. Suppose that someone from another country were coming to visit your home. What would you like to tell this person about your school and community? What would you especially like to show this person in your state? How would you make him or her comfortable? Plan a tour of the state for your guest.

5. Choose a mountain range, river, desert, or plain you have read about in this unit. Compare it with a part of your state that is like it. For example, if your state has a large river, you might compare it with the Chang Jiang. Do you live on a plain? Compare ways of farming or ranching in your state with those used on the pampa of Argentina or the European Plain of the Soviet Union.

FOR YOUR REFERENCE

SYMBOLS OF AMERICA

The American Flag

For more than 200 years, the American flag has been a symbol of the people, government, and ideas of our country. Often called the *Stars and Stripes,* the American flag at first had 13 red and white stripes, each standing for one state. There were also 13 white stars on a blue background. Since then a star has been added for every new state to join the country.

Our country's flag should be treated with great respect. There are many rules for making, showing, caring for, and honoring this symbol of freedom. One way we honor our flag and show love for our country is by saying the Pledge of Allegiance.

I pledge allegiance to the flag of the United States of America and to the republic for which it stands, one nation under God, indivisible, with liberty and justice for all.

The National Anthem

Another symbol of our respect for our country is "The Star-Spangled Banner." During the War of 1812 Francis Scott Key, a prisoner of the British, wrote the words to this poem on the back of an envelope.

Key stood on the deck of a ship, watching the English fire rockets and bombs at Fort McHenry near Baltimore, Maryland. At dawn he saw the American flag still waving over the undefeated fort. When Key was set free the next day, he finished the poem. It was printed in a newspaper. Soon people began to sing the poem to a popular English tune.

In 1931 Congress made "The Star-Spangled Banner" our national anthem. It speaks of the fear we feel when our country is in danger. It reminds us of our pride when America's strength carries the nation through.

This flag inspired Francis Scott Key (above) to write our national anthem. The flag may now be seen at the Museum of History and Technology in Washington, D.C.

The Star-Spangled Banner

Oh, say, can you see, by the dawn's
   early light,
What so proudly we hailed at the
   twilight's last gleaming?
Whose broad stripes and bright stars,
   thro' the perilous fight,
O'er the ramparts we watched were so
   gallantly streaming?
And the rockets' red glare,
   the bombs bursting in air
Gave proof through the night that our
   flag was still there.
Oh, say, does that star-spangled
   banner yet wave
O'er the land of the free and the home
   of the brave?

The Liberty Bell

In 1776 a bell was rung in Philadelphia to call people to listen to the Declaration of Independence. America became a free country, and the bell became known as the Liberty Bell. For 60 years the bell was rung from Independence Hall on important days, such as the Fourth of July. Then, the Liberty Bell cracked. Yet the words upon the Liberty Bell still ring out: "PROCLAIM LIBERTY THROUGHOUT ALL THE LAND UNTO ALL THE INHABITANTS THEREOF."

The Statue of Liberty

The beautiful copper Statue of Liberty was given to America by the people of France. It was a gift to honor 100 years of independence. The Statue of Liberty has been and always will be a symbol of freedom to millions of immigrants entering America. They are welcomed by her torch held high and by the words of an American poet, Emma Lazarus, on the base of the statue: . . .Give me your tired, your poor,
Your huddled masses yearning to
breathe free. . .

The Bald Eagle

The majestic bald eagle is America's national bird. It is the eagle's white-feathered head that makes it appear bald. Found only in North America, most bald eagles live in Alaska. Because they are few in number, our national birds are protected from hunters by federal law.

The Capitol

In 1793 President George Washington laid the cornerstone for our national Capitol in Washington, D.C. Congress has met in this building since 1800. Millions of people visit the Capitol each year. Standing in the Great Rotunda under the dome, Americans feel proud of their great history.

National Holidays

Each state in our country decides what holidays to observe. Some special days, such as Arbor Day and Valentine's Day, are popular holidays often observed in school. Our national government has also set aside certain legal holidays for the entire United States.

Martin Luther King, Jr.

New Year's Day (January 1)
Martin Luther King, Jr. Day (3rd Monday in January)
Presidents' Day (3rd Monday in February)
Memorial Day (last Monday in May)
Independence Day (July 4)
Labor Day (1st Monday in September)
Columbus Day (2nd Monday in October)
Veterans Day (November 11)
Thanksgiving (4th Thursday in November)
Christmas Day (December 25)

FACTS ABOUT THE STATES

On the following pages you will find interesting facts about each of the 50 states. Included are the states' abbreviations, nicknames, capitals, and populations. The population figures give the most recent estimates. The outline maps show the states' major rivers and the locations of their capitals. State flags and birds are shown on postage stamps issued by the U.S. Postal Service.

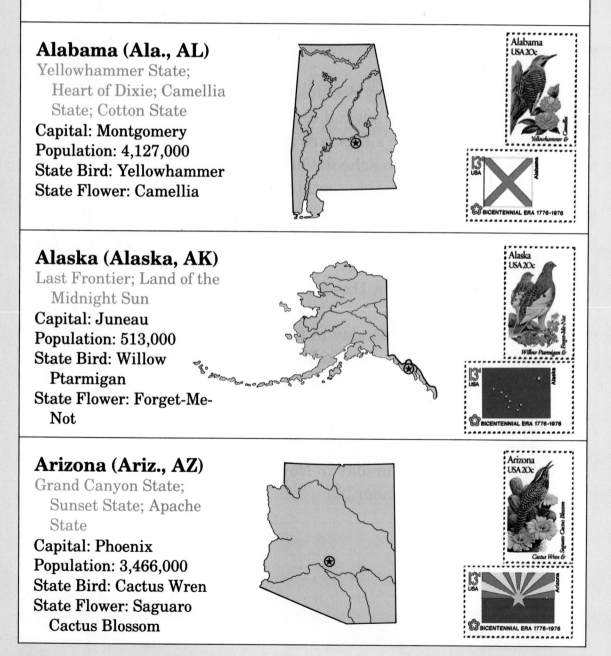

Alabama (Ala., AL)
Yellowhammer State; Heart of Dixie; Camellia State; Cotton State
Capital: Montgomery
Population: 4,127,000
State Bird: Yellowhammer
State Flower: Camellia

Alaska (Alaska, AK)
Last Frontier; Land of the Midnight Sun
Capital: Juneau
Population: 513,000
State Bird: Willow Ptarmigan
State Flower: Forget-Me-Not

Arizona (Ariz., AZ)
Grand Canyon State; Sunset State; Apache State
Capital: Phoenix
Population: 3,466,000
State Bird: Cactus Wren
State Flower: Saguaro Cactus Blossom

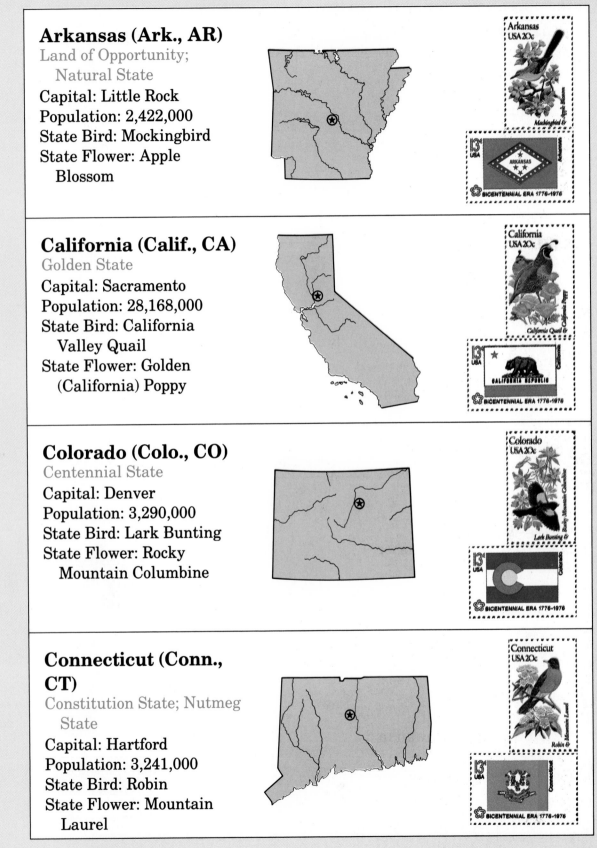

Arkansas (Ark., AR)

Land of Opportunity;
  Natural State

Capital: Little Rock
Population: 2,422,000
State Bird: Mockingbird
State Flower: Apple
  Blossom

California (Calif., CA)

Golden State

Capital: Sacramento
Population: 28,168,000
State Bird: California
  Valley Quail
State Flower: Golden
  (California) Poppy

Colorado (Colo., CO)

Centennial State

Capital: Denver
Population: 3,290,000
State Bird: Lark Bunting
State Flower: Rocky
  Mountain Columbine

Connecticut (Conn., CT)

Constitution State; Nutmeg
  State

Capital: Hartford
Population: 3,241,000
State Bird: Robin
State Flower: Mountain
  Laurel

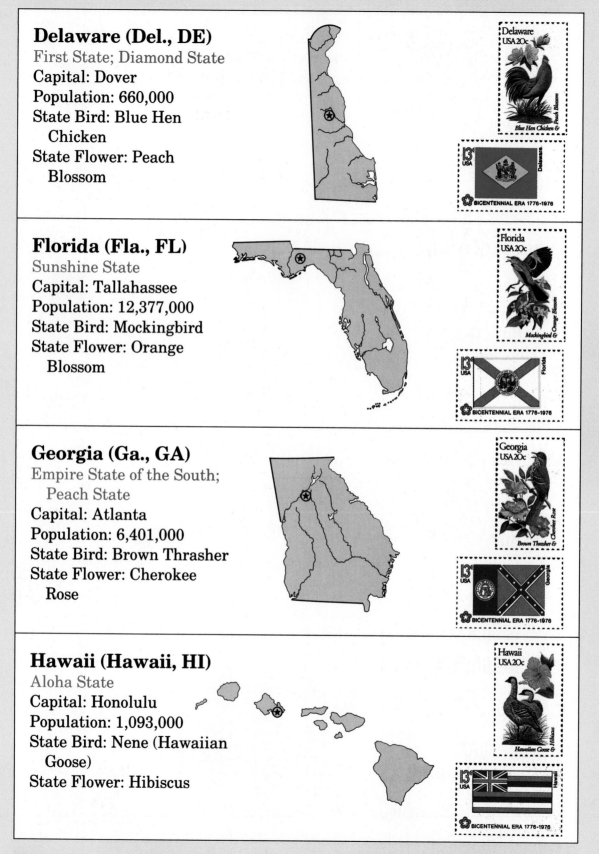

Delaware (Del., DE)
First State; Diamond State
Capital: Dover
Population: 660,000
State Bird: Blue Hen
  Chicken
State Flower: Peach
  Blossom

Florida (Fla., FL)
Sunshine State
Capital: Tallahassee
Population: 12,377,000
State Bird: Mockingbird
State Flower: Orange
  Blossom

Georgia (Ga., GA)
Empire State of the South;
  Peach State
Capital: Atlanta
Population: 6,401,000
State Bird: Brown Thrasher
State Flower: Cherokee
  Rose

Hawaii (Hawaii, HI)
Aloha State
Capital: Honolulu
Population: 1,093,000
State Bird: Nene (Hawaiian
  Goose)
State Flower: Hibiscus

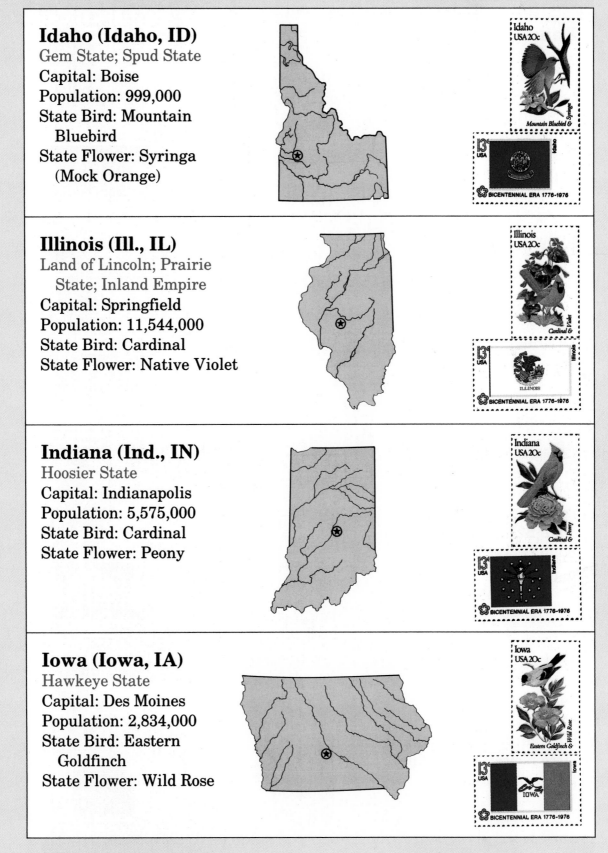

Idaho (Idaho, ID)

Gem State; Spud State

Capital: Boise
Population: 999,000
State Bird: Mountain
   Bluebird
State Flower: Syringa
   (Mock Orange)

Illinois (Ill., IL)

Land of Lincoln; Prairie
   State; Inland Empire
Capital: Springfield
Population: 11,544,000
State Bird: Cardinal
State Flower: Native Violet

Indiana (Ind., IN)

Hoosier State
Capital: Indianapolis
Population: 5,575,000
State Bird: Cardinal
State Flower: Peony

Iowa (Iowa, IA)

Hawkeye State
Capital: Des Moines
Population: 2,834,000
State Bird: Eastern
   Goldfinch
State Flower: Wild Rose

Kansas (Kans., KS)

Sunflower State;
  Jayhawker State
Capital: Topeka
Population: 2,487,000
State Bird: Western
  Meadowlark
State Flower: Sunflower

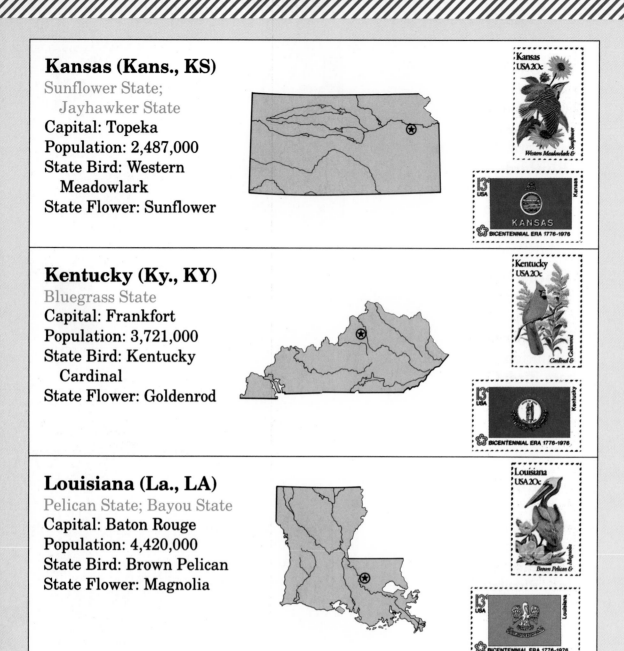

Kentucky (Ky., KY)

Bluegrass State
Capital: Frankfort
Population: 3,721,000
State Bird: Kentucky
  Cardinal
State Flower: Goldenrod

Louisiana (La., LA)

Pelican State; Bayou State
Capital: Baton Rouge
Population: 4,420,000
State Bird: Brown Pelican
State Flower: Magnolia

Maine (Maine, ME)

Pine Tree State
Capital: Augusta
Population: 1,206,000
State Bird: Chickadee
State Flower: White Pine
  Cone and Tassel

Maryland (Md., MD)

Old Line State; Free State
Capital: Annapolis
Population: 4,644,000
State Bird: Baltimore
  Oriole
State Flower: Black-Eyed
  Susan

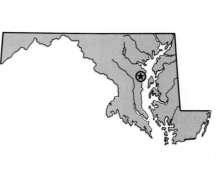

Massachusetts (Mass., MA)

Bay State; Old Colony
Capital: Boston
Population: 5,871,000
State Bird: (Black-Capped)
  Chickadee
State Flower: Mayflower

Michigan (Mich., MI)

Wolverine State; Great
  Lake State; Water
  Wonderland
Capital: Lansing
Population: 9,300,000
State Bird: Robin
State Flower: Apple
  Blossom

Minnesota (Minn., MN)

Land of 10,000 Lakes;
  Gopher State
Capital: St. Paul
Population: 4,306,000
State Bird: Common Loon
State Flower: Pink and
  White (Showy) Lady's
  Slipper

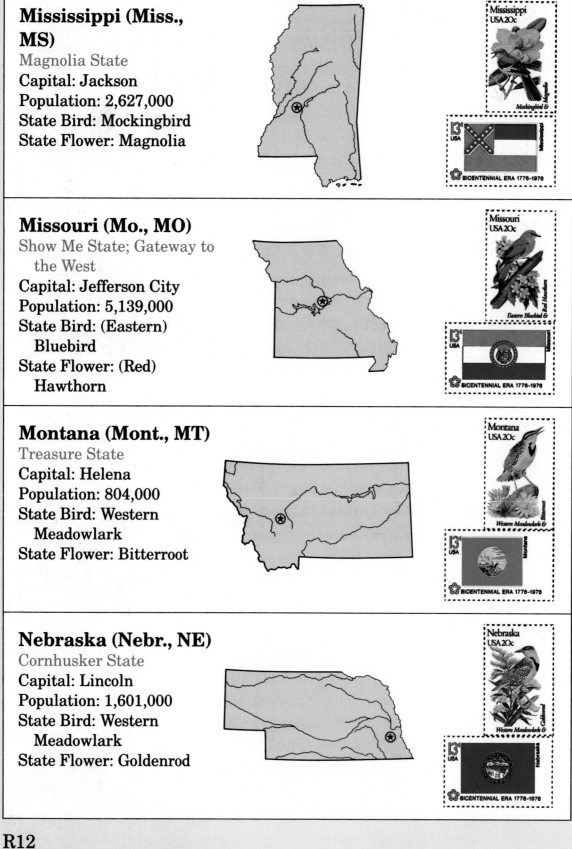

Mississippi (Miss., MS)
Magnolia State
Capital: Jackson
Population: 2,627,000
State Bird: Mockingbird
State Flower: Magnolia

Missouri (Mo., MO)
Show Me State; Gateway to
    the West
Capital: Jefferson City
Population: 5,139,000
State Bird: (Eastern)
    Bluebird
State Flower: (Red)
    Hawthorn

Montana (Mont., MT)
Treasure State
Capital: Helena
Population: 804,000
State Bird: Western
    Meadowlark
State Flower: Bitterroot

Nebraska (Nebr., NE)
Cornhusker State
Capital: Lincoln
Population: 1,601,000
State Bird: Western
    Meadowlark
State Flower: Goldenrod

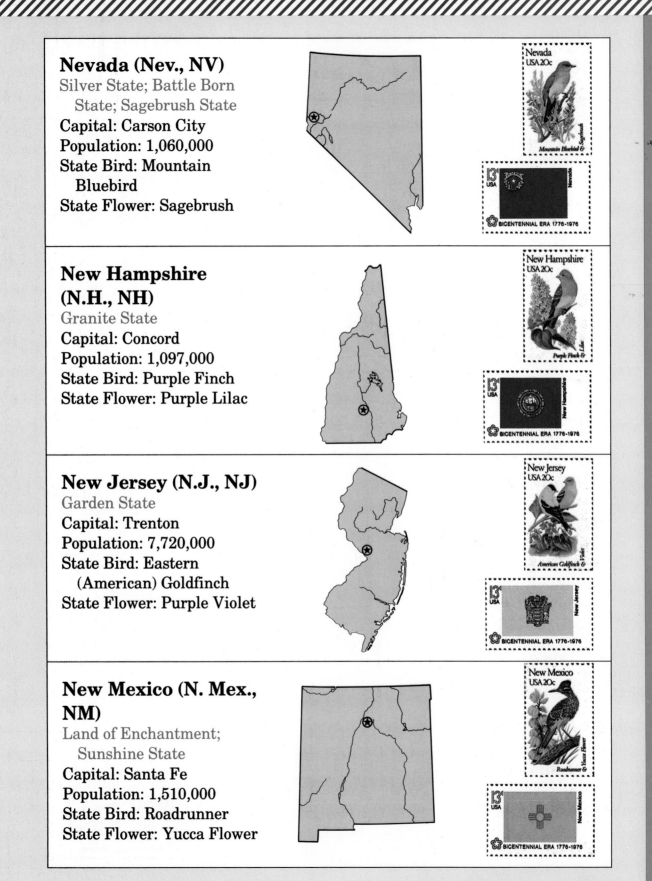

Nevada (Nev., NV)
Silver State; Battle Born
    State; Sagebrush State
Capital: Carson City
Population: 1,060,000
State Bird: Mountain
    Bluebird
State Flower: Sagebrush

New Hampshire (N.H., NH)
Granite State
Capital: Concord
Population: 1,097,000
State Bird: Purple Finch
State Flower: Purple Lilac

New Jersey (N.J., NJ)
Garden State
Capital: Trenton
Population: 7,720,000
State Bird: Eastern
    (American) Goldfinch
State Flower: Purple Violet

New Mexico (N. Mex., NM)
Land of Enchantment;
    Sunshine State
Capital: Santa Fe
Population: 1,510,000
State Bird: Roadrunner
State Flower: Yucca Flower

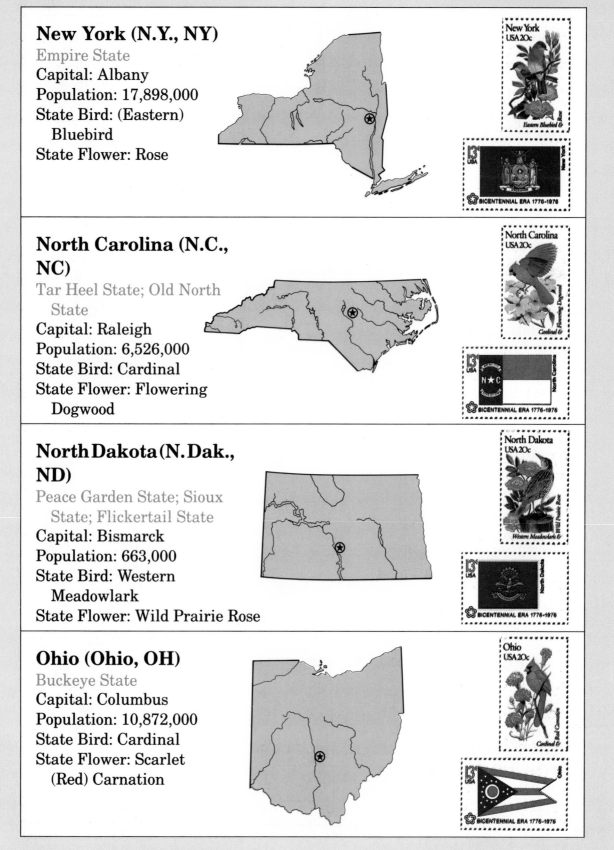

New York (N.Y., NY)

Empire State
Capital: Albany
Population: 17,898,000
State Bird: (Eastern) Bluebird
State Flower: Rose

North Carolina (N.C., NC)

Tar Heel State; Old North State
Capital: Raleigh
Population: 6,526,000
State Bird: Cardinal
State Flower: Flowering Dogwood

North Dakota (N. Dak., ND)

Peace Garden State; Sioux State; Flickertail State
Capital: Bismarck
Population: 663,000
State Bird: Western Meadowlark
State Flower: Wild Prairie Rose

Ohio (Ohio, OH)

Buckeye State
Capital: Columbus
Population: 10,872,000
State Bird: Cardinal
State Flower: Scarlet (Red) Carnation

Oklahoma (Okla., OK)

Sooner State
Capital: Oklahoma City
Population: 3,263,000
State Bird: Scissor-Tailed
Flycatcher
State Flower: Mistletoe

Oregon (Oreg., OR)

Beaver State
Capital: Salem
Population: 2,741,000
State Bird: Western
Meadowlark
State Flower: Oregon
Grape

Pennsylvania (Pa., PA)

Keystone State
Capital: Harrisburg
Population: 12,027,000
State Bird: Ruffed Grouse
State Flower: Mountain
Laurel

Rhode Island (R.I., RI)

Little Rhody; Ocean State
Capital: Providence
Population: 995,000
State Bird: Rhode Island
Red
State Flower: Violet

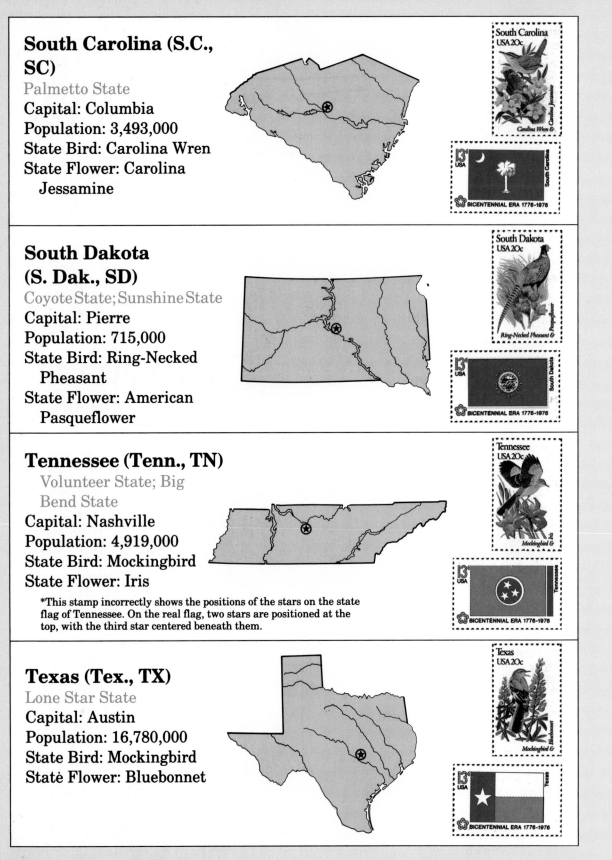

South Carolina (S.C., SC)

Palmetto State
Capital: Columbia
Population: 3,493,000
State Bird: Carolina Wren
State Flower: Carolina
Jessamine

South Dakota (S. Dak., SD)

Coyote State; Sunshine State
Capital: Pierre
Population: 715,000
State Bird: Ring-Necked
Pheasant
State Flower: American
Pasqueflower

Tennessee (Tenn., TN)

Volunteer State; Big
Bend State
Capital: Nashville
Population: 4,919,000
State Bird: Mockingbird
State Flower: Iris

*This stamp incorrectly shows the positions of the stars on the state
flag of Tennessee. On the real flag, two stars are positioned at the
top, with the third star centered beneath them.

Texas (Tex., TX)

Lone Star State
Capital: Austin
Population: 16,780,000
State Bird: Mockingbird
State Flower: Bluebonnet

Utah (Utah, UT)

Beehive State

Capital: Salt Lake City
Population: 1,691,000
State Bird: Sea (California) Gull
State Flower: Sego Lily

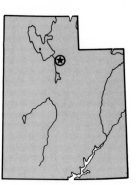

Vermont (Vt., VT)

Green Mountain State

Capital: Montpelier
Population: 556,000
State Bird: Hermit Thrush
State Flower: Red Clover

Virginia (Va., VA)

Old Dominion; Mother of Presidents

Capital: Richmond
Population: 5,996,000
State Bird: Cardinal
State Flower: Flowering Dogwood

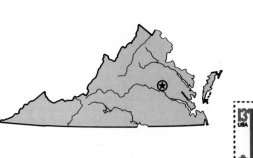

Washington (Wash., WA)

Evergreen State; Chinook State

Capital: Olympia
Population: 4,619,000
State Bird: Willow (American) Goldfinch
State Flower: Coast Rhododendron

West Virginia (W. Va., WV)

Mountain State

Capital: Charleston
Population: 1,884,000
State Bird: Cardinal
State Flower:
   Rhododendron
   (Maximum)

Wisconsin (Wis., WI)

Badger State; America's
   Dairyland

Capital: Madison
Population: 4,858,000
State Bird: Robin
State Flower: Wood Violet

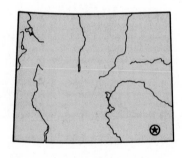

Wyoming (Wyo., WY)

Equality State; Cowboy
   State

Capital: Cheyenne
Population: 471,000
State Bird: Western
   Meadowlark
State Flower: Indian
   Paintbrush

GEOGRAPHIC DICTIONARY

On the following pages are descriptions of some important natural features. Study these pages. Refer to them often as you read.

bay a small area of ocean partly surrounded by land

coast the land next to an ocean

coastal plain low, flat land near an ocean

continent one of the Earth's main areas of land

gulf a large area of ocean partly surrounded by land

harbor a place on a coast where ships can dock safely

island land completely surrounded by water

ocean a large body of salt water

peninsula a piece of land with water on three sides of it

sea a large body of salt water surrounded by land

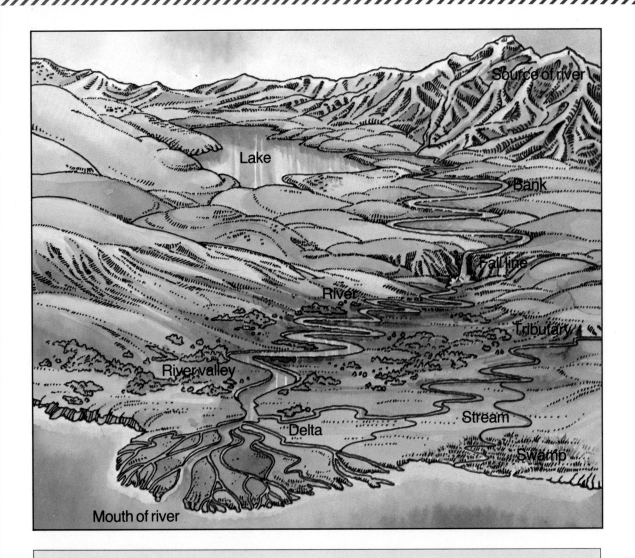

Source of river

Lake

Bank

Fall line

River

Tributary

River valley

Stream

Delta

Swamp

Mouth of river

bank the land on either side of a river

branch a stream or river that flows into a larger one

delta the land formed at the mouth of a river

fall line a place where the height of the land drops suddenly and waterfalls form

lake a body of fresh water or salt water surrounded by land

mouth of river the place where a river empties into a larger body of water

river a large stream of water

river basin all the land drained by a river and its branches

river valley the low land through which a river flows

source of river the place where a river begins

stream a small body of running water

swamp low, wet land

tributary a stream or river that flows into a larger one

waterway a body of water that ships can use

basin a low, bowl-shaped area

canyon a narrow valley with high, steep sides

cliff a high, steep wall of rock

desert dry land where few plants grow

foothill a low hill at the base of a mountain

hill a small, raised part of the land, lower than a mountain

mesa a flat-topped hill with steep sides, common in dry areas

mountain a large, high part of the land with steep sides

mountain range a group or chain of mountains

peak the pointed top of a mountain

plain a large area of flat or gently rolling land

plateau an area of high, flat land

sand dune a hill of sand piled up by the wind

slope the side of a mountain or hill

valley low land between mountains or hills

volcano an opening in the Earth that throws out melted rock and gases

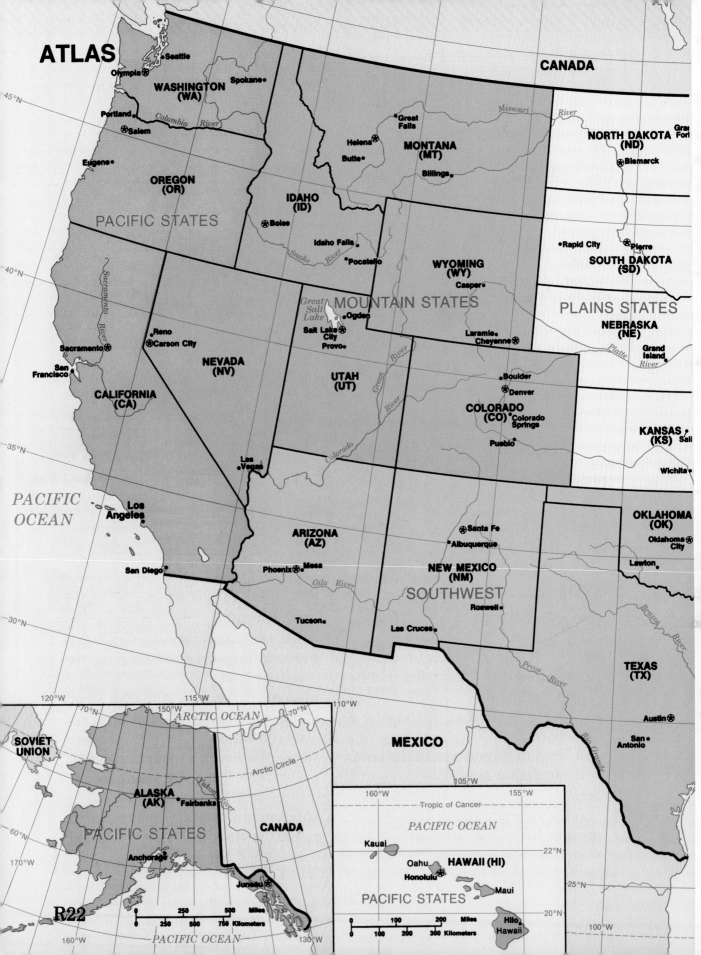

ATLAS

CANADA

45°N

WASHINGTON (WA)
- •Seattle
- Olympia⊛
- Spokane•
- •Portland
- Salem⊛
- Eugene•

Columbia River

OREGON (OR)

PACIFIC STATES

40°N

IDAHO (ID)
- Boise⊛
- Idaho Falls•
- •Pocatello

Snake River

MONTANA (MT)
- •Great Falls
- Helena⊛
- Butte•
- Billings•

Missouri River

NORTH DAKOTA (ND)
- Grand Forks
- Bismarck⊛

WYOMING (WY)
- Casper•
- Laramie•
- Cheyenne⊛

SOUTH DAKOTA (SD)
- •Rapid City
- Pierre⊛

PLAINS STATES

NEBRASKA (NE)
- Grand Island•

Platte River

35°N

MOUNTAIN STATES

Great Salt Lake
- •Ogden
- Salt Lake City⊛
- Provo•

NEVADA (NV)
- •Reno
- ⊛Carson City
- Sacramento⊛
- San Francisco•

Sacramento River

UTAH (UT)

Green River

COLORADO (CO)
- •Boulder
- ⊛Denver
- •Colorado Springs
- Pueblo•

KANSAS (KS)
- •Salina
- Wichita•

CALIFORNIA (CA)
- Los Angeles•
- •Las Vegas

Colorado River

PACIFIC OCEAN

ARIZONA (AZ)
- Phoenix⊛•Mesa
- Tucson•

Gila River

San Diego•

30°N

NEW MEXICO (NM)
- ⊛Santa Fe
- •Albuquerque
- Roswell•
- Las Cruces•

SOUTHWEST

OKLAHOMA (OK)
- Oklahoma City⊛
- Lawton•

MEXICO

Pecos River

TEXAS (TX)
- Austin⊛
- San Antonio•

Rio Grande

Brazos River

120°W · 115°W · 110°W · 105°W · 100°W

70°N

ARCTIC OCEAN

SOVIET UNION

Arctic Circle

ALASKA (AK)
- •Fairbanks
- Anchorage•
- Juneau⊛

Yukon River

PACIFIC STATES

CANADA

60°N

R22

170°W · 160°W · 150°W · 130°W

0 ___ 250 ___ 500 Miles
0 __ 250 __ 500 __ 750 Kilometers

PACIFIC OCEAN

160°W · 155°W

Tropic of Cancer

PACIFIC OCEAN

- Kauai
- Oahu
- Honolulu⊛
- Maui
- Hilo Hawaii

HAWAII (HI)

22°N

25°N

20°N

PACIFIC STATES

0 ___ 100 ___ 200 Miles
0 __ 100 __ 200 __ 300 Kilometers

UNITED STATES OF AMERICA: THE LAND

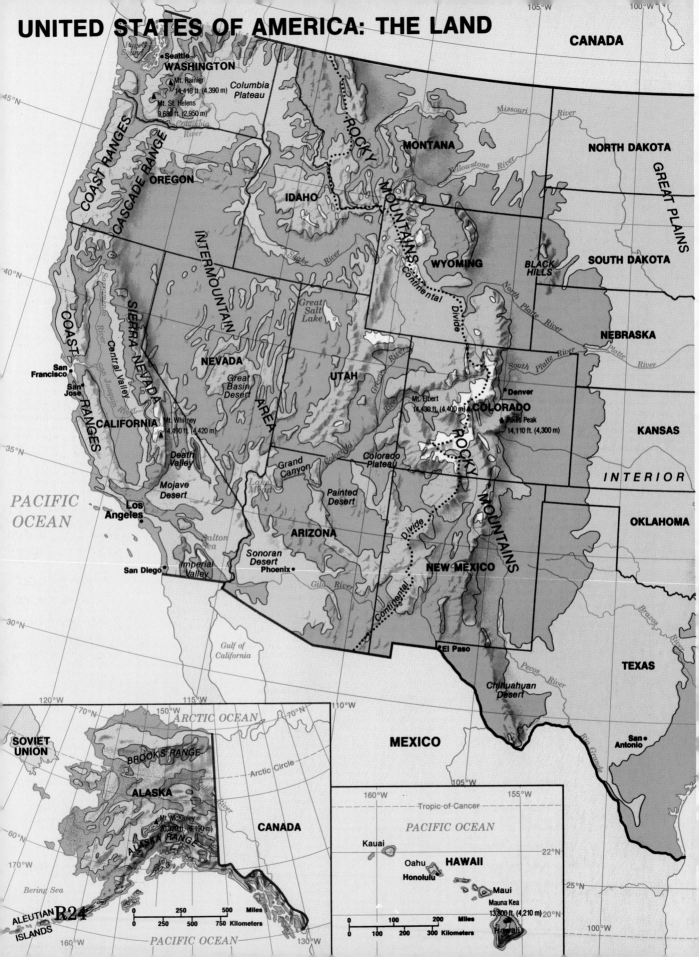

CANADA

WASHINGTON
Seattle
Puget Sound
▲ Mt. Rainier
14,410 ft. (4,390 m)
▲ Mt. St. Helens
9,680 ft. (2,950 m)

Columbia Plateau

Columbia River

COAST RANGES

CASCADE RANGE

OREGON

IDAHO

Snake River

MONTANA

ROCKY MOUNTAINS

Missouri River

Yellowstone River

WYOMING

Continental Divide

NORTH DAKOTA

GREAT PLAINS

SOUTH DAKOTA

BLACK HILLS

INTERMOUNTAIN

Great Salt Lake

NEVADA

Great Basin Desert

AREA

UTAH

Green River

Colorado River

COLORADO

Denver ●
Mt. Elbert
14,430 ft. (4,400 m) ▲
▲ Pikes Peak
14,110 ft. (4,300 m)

North Platte River

South Platte River

NEBRASKA

Platte River

KANSAS

SIERRA NEVADA

Sacramento River

Central Valley

San Joaquin River

San Francisco ●
San Jose ●

CALIFORNIA

COAST RANGES

▲ Mt. Whitney
14,490 ft. (4,420 m)

Death Valley

Mojave Desert

Los Angeles ●

San Diego ●

Imperial Valley

Salton Sea

Grand Canyon

Lake Mead

Colorado River

Painted Desert

Colorado Plateau

ROCKY MOUNTAINS

Divide

Continental Divide

INTERIOR

OKLAHOMA

ARIZONA

Sonoran Desert

Phoenix ●

Gila River

NEW MEXICO

El Paso ●

Pecos River

TEXAS

Brazos River

San Antonio ●

Chihuahuan Desert

PACIFIC OCEAN

Gulf of California

Rio Grande

MEXICO

45°N
40°N
35°N
30°N

120°W
115°W
110°W
105°W
100°W

SOVIET UNION

ARCTIC OCEAN

BROOKS RANGE

Arctic Circle

ALASKA

ALASKA RANGE

▲ Mt. McKinley
20,320 ft. (6,190 m)

Yukon River

CANADA

Bering Sea

ALEUTIAN ISLANDS

R24

PACIFIC OCEAN

0 250 500 Miles
0 250 500 750 Kilometers

70°N
60°N

170°W
160°W
150°W
130°W

Tropic of Cancer

PACIFIC OCEAN

Kauai

Oahu
Honolulu ●

HAWAII

Maui

Mauna Kea
13,800 ft. (4,210 m)

Hawaii

22°N
25°N
20°N

160°W
155°W

0 100 200 Miles
0 100 200 300 Kilometers

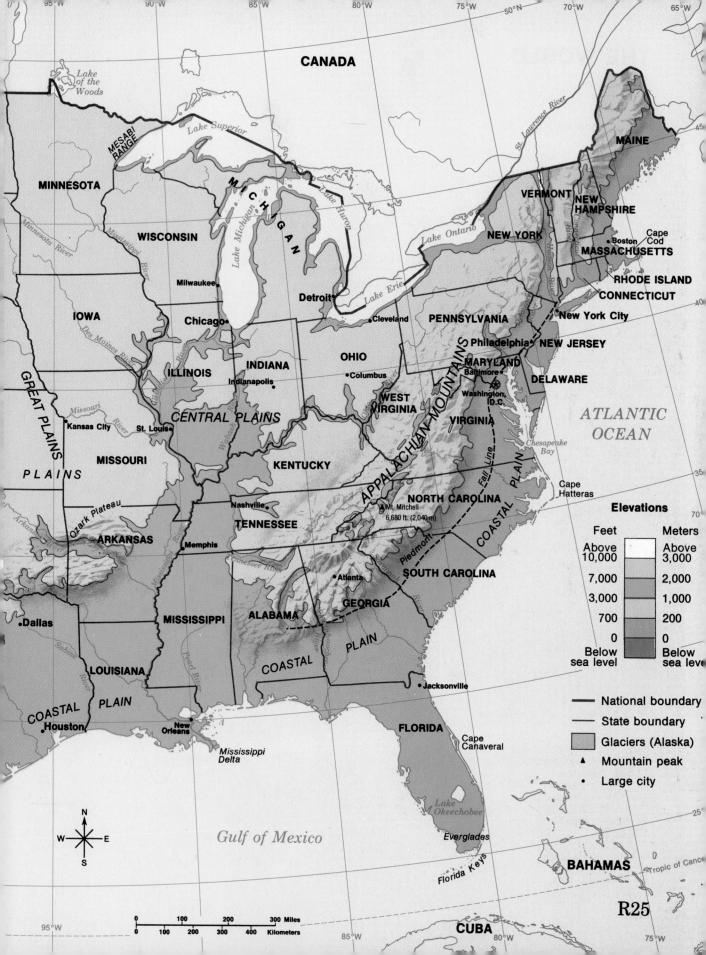

THE WORLD

—— National boundary

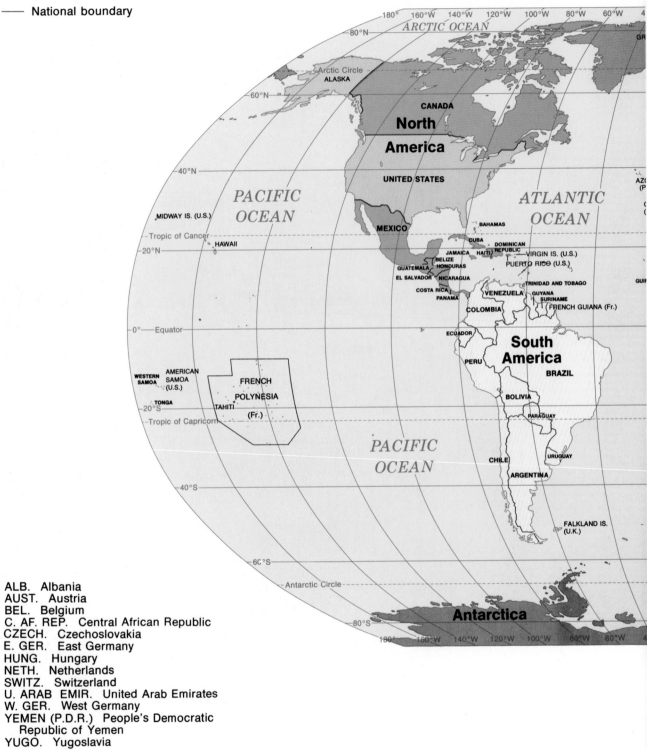

ALB. Albania
AUST. Austria
BEL. Belgium
C. AF. REP. Central African Republic
CZECH. Czechoslovakia
E. GER. East Germany
HUNG. Hungary
NETH. Netherlands
SWITZ. Switzerland
U. ARAB EMIR. United Arab Emirates
W. GER. West Germany
YEMEN (P.D.R.) People's Democratic
   Republic of Yemen
YUGO. Yugoslavia

ARCTIC OCEAN

40°W 20°W 0° 20°E 40°E 60°E 80°E 100°E 120°E 140°E 160°E 180°

80°N

GREENLAND
(Den.)

Arctic Circle

60°N

ICELAND

NORWAY
SWEDEN
FINLAND

UNITED
KINGDOM
England
IRELAND

SOVIET UNION (USSR)

DENMARK
NETH.
BEL.
W. GER.
E. GER.
POLAND
CZECH.
Europe
HUNG.
ROMANIA
YUGO.
BULGARIA
ALB.
GREECE

MONGOLIA

Asia

40°N

N. KOREA
S. KOREA

JAPAN

FRANCE
SWITZ.
AUST.
ITALY

SPAIN
PORTUGAL

AZORES
(Port.)

CANARY IS.
(Spain)

WESTERN
SAHARA
(Morocco)

MOROCCO

TURKEY

TUNISIA

ALGERIA

LIBYA

EGYPT

LEBANON
ISRAEL
JORDAN

SYRIA
IRAQ
KUWAIT
QATAR

IRAN

AFGHANISTAN

PAKISTAN

NEPAL

BHUTAN

CHINA

INDIA

BANGLADESH

BURMA
(Myanmar)

TAIWAN

Tropic of Cancer

WAKE I.
(U.S.)

20°N

SAUDI
ARABIA

U. ARAB EMIR.

OMAN

MARIANA IS. (U.S.)

GUAM (U.S.)

TRUST
TERRITORY
OF THE
PACIFIC ISLANDS
(U.S.) MARSHALL IS.

MAURITANIA

SENEGAL
GAMBIA
GUINEA-BISSAU
SIERRA LEONE
LIBERIA

MALI

GUINEA
IVORY
COAST
GHANA

BURKINA
FASO

Africa

NIGER

NIGERIA

BENIN
TOGO

CAMEROON

CHAD

C. AF. REP.

SUDAN

YEMEN

YEMEN
(P.D.R.)

DJIBOUTI

ETHIOPIA

SOMALIA

THAILAND

LAOS

VIETNAM

CAMBODIA

PHILIPPINES

SRI LANKA

MALDIVES

SEYCHELLES

BRUNEI
MALAYSIA
SINGAPORE

CAROLINE IS.

Equator 0°

UGANDA

KENYA

CONGO

GABON

RWANDA

BURUNDI

ZAIRE

TANZANIA

INDONESIA

PAPUA
NEW
GUINEA

SOLOMON
ISLANDS

ANGOLA

MALAWI

ZAMBIA

COMOROS

INDIAN
OCEAN

FIJI

ATLANTIC
OCEAN

NAMIBIA

ZIMBABWE

MOZAMBIQUE

BOTSWANA

SWAZILAND

SOUTH
AFRICA

LESOTHO

MADAGASCAR

MAURITIUS

20°S

Australia

Tropic of Capricorn

N
W   E
S

NEW
ZEALAND

Prime Meridian

60°S

Antarctic Circle

80°S

Antarctica

40°W 20°W 0° 20°E 40°E 60°E 80°E 100°E 120°E 140°E 160°E 180°

0   500   1,000 1,500 2,000 Miles

0   1,000   2,000   Kilometers

R27

THE WORLD: MOUNTAINS, RIVERS, DESERTS

Elevations

Feet		Meters
Above 10,000		Above 3,000
7,000		2,000
3,000		1,000
700		200
0		0
Below sea level		Below sea level

—— National boundary

------ Disputed or undefined boundary

Ice pack

▲ Mountain peak

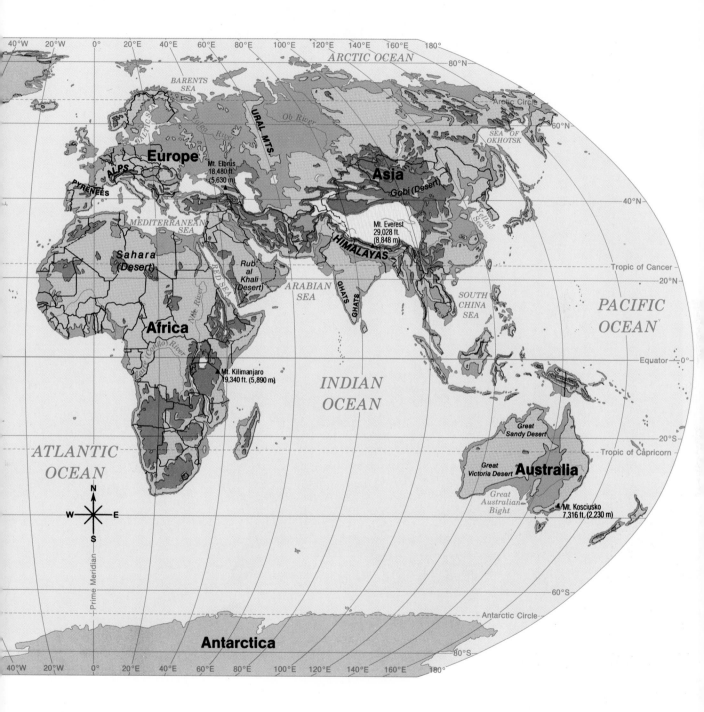

ARCTIC OCEAN

80°N

BARENTS
SEA

60°N

Ob River

Volga River

URAL MTS.

SEA OF
OKHOTSK

Arctic Circle

Europe

Mt. Elbrus
18,480 ft.
(5,630 m)

Asia

Gobi (Desert)

40°N

ALPS

PYRENEES

Mt. Everest
29,028 ft.
(8,848 m)

HIMALAYAS

Yellow Sea

MEDITERRANEAN
SEA

Sahara
(Desert)

Tropic of Cancer

20°N

Rub
al
Khali
(Desert)

RED SEA

ARABIAN
SEA

GHATS

GHATS

SOUTH
CHINA
SEA

**PACIFIC
OCEAN**

Nile River

Africa

Zaire (Congo) River

Mt. Kilimanjaro
19,340 ft. (5,890 m)

Equator

0°

**INDIAN
OCEAN**

**ATLANTIC
OCEAN**

Great
Sandy Desert

20°S

Great
Victoria Desert

Australia

Tropic of Capricorn

Great
Australian
Bight

Mt. Kosciusko
7,316 ft. (2,230 m)

N
W E
S

Prime Meridian

60°S

Antarctic Circle

80°S

Antarctica

40°W 20°W 0° 20°E 40°E 60°E 80°E 100°E 120°E 140°E 160°E 180°

| 0 | 500 | 1,000 | 1,500 | 2,000 Miles |
| 0 | 1,000 | 2,000 | Kilometers |

NORTH AMERICA

Europe

Asia

ARCTIC OCEAN

Greenland Sea

Greenland

Bering Strait

Bering Sea

Beaufort Sea

Baffin Bay

Yukon

Mt. McKinley
20,320 ft.
(6,194 m)

ROCKY

Gulf of Alaska

COAST MOUNTAINS

Hudson Strait

Labrador Sea

Hudson Bay

Canadian   Shield

Gulf of St. Lawrence

MOUNTAINS

Great

Lake Superior

St. Lawrence River

Bay of Fundy

ATLANTIC

Plains

Lake Huron

OCEAN

Great Salt Lake

Missouri

Lake Michigan

Lake Ontario

River

Mt. Whitney
14,494 ft.
(4,418 m)

Great Basin

Pikes Peak
14,110 ft.
(4,301 m)

River

Lake Erie

APPALACHIAN MTNS.

Death Valley
-282 ft.
(-86 m)

Ozark Plateau

Ohio

River

Plain

Mississippi River

Coastal

Tropic of Cancer

Gulf of California

SIERRA

SIERRA MADRE ORIENTAL

Rio Grande

Gulf of Mexico

Hispaniola

MADRE

OCCIDENTAL

Citlaltépetl
18,700 ft. (5,700 m.)

Caribbean   Sea

PACIFIC

Panama Canal

OCEAN

Lake Nicaragua

South

America

───── International boundary

▲ Mountain peak

| 0 | 300 | 600 | Miles |
| 0 | 300 | 600 | 900 | Kilometers |

Equator

N
W   E
S

R30

SOUTH AMERICA

Caribbean Sea

ATLANTIC

OCEAN

ANDES

Orinoco River

Guiana

Highlands

Equator

Amazon

Amazon River

Basin

PACIFIC

Lake Titicaca

ANDES MOUNTAINS

Mato Grosso

Plateau

Brazilian Highlands

São Francisco

River

OCEAN

Atacama Desert

Tropic of Capricorn

Salado R.

Paraguay River

ATLANTIC

Mt. Aconcagua
22,840 ft. (6,960 m)
(highest point in S. America)

P a m p a s

Uruguay River

OCEAN

ANDES

Valdés Peninsula
(lowest point in S. America)

————— International boundary

▲ Mountain peak

N

W   E

S

| 0 | 250 | 500 | Miles |
| 0 | 250 | 500 | 750 | Kilometers |

R31

Cape Horn
Drake Passage

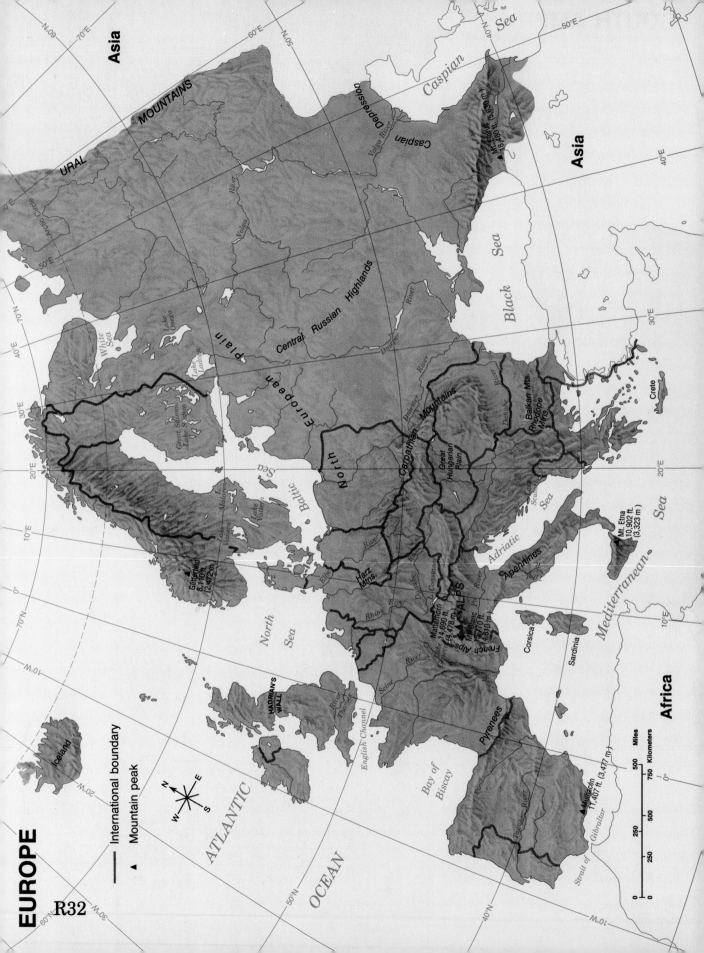

EUROPE

R32

— International boundary
▲ Mountain peak

Asia

Asia

Africa

URAL MOUNTAINS

Volga River

Caspian Depression

Mt. Elbrus (5,630 m)
18,460 ft.

Caspian Sea

Black Sea

Crete

White Sea

Lake Onega

Lake Ladoga

Central Russian Highlands

European Plain

Dnepr River

Volga River

Great Saimaa Lake System

Carpathian Mountains

Balkan Mts.

Rhodope Mtns.

Great Hungarian Plain

Danube River

Lake Scutari

North Sea

Baltic Sea

L. Mälaren

Lake Vänern

Lake Vättern

Elbe River

Harz Mtns.

Rhine River

Oder River

L. Constance

Adriatic Sea

Apennines

Glittertind 8,110 ft. (2,472 m)

Mt. Etna 10,902 ft. (3,323 m)

Mediterranean Sea

Matterhorn 14,690 ft. (4,478 m)

ALPS

Mt. Blanc 15,770 ft. (4,810 m)

French Alps

Corsica

Sardinia

Rhine River

Danube River

Seine River

English Channel

HADRIAN'S WALL

River Thames

Iceland

Bay of Biscay

Pyrenees

Mulhacén 11,407 ft. (3,477 m)

Strait of Gibraltar

Tagus River

North Sea

ATLANTIC

OCEAN

N
E
W
S

Miles
0 250 500
Kilometers
0 250 500 750

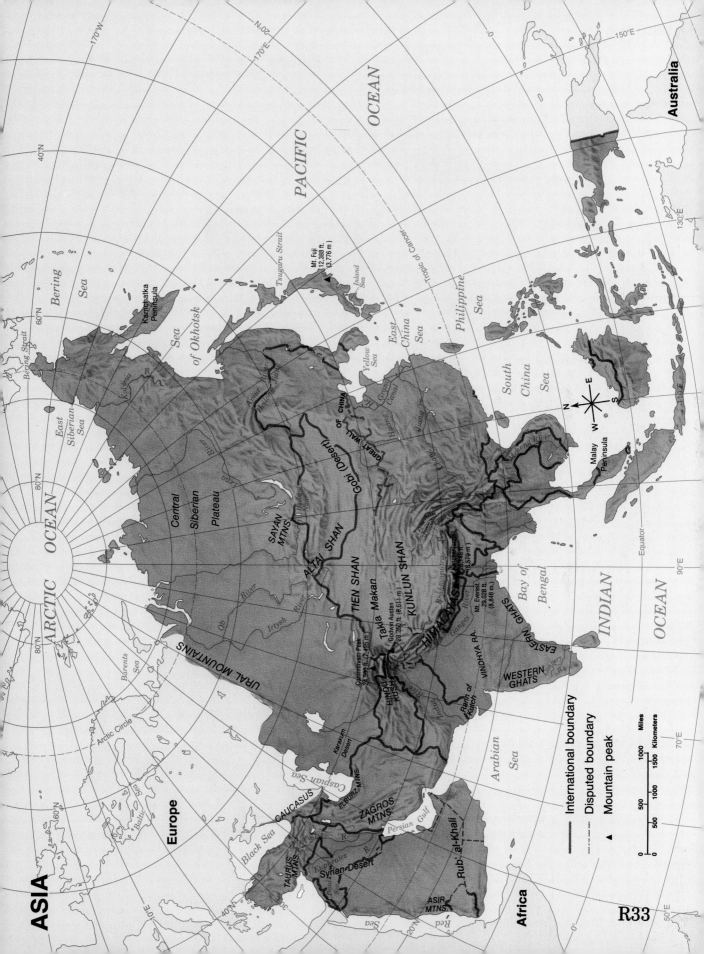

ASIA

Europe

Africa

Australia

ARCTIC OCEAN

PACIFIC OCEAN

INDIAN OCEAN

Bering Sea

Sea of Okhotsk

Bering Strait

East Siberian Sea

Kamchatka Peninsula

Kolyma R.

Lena River

Amur River

Ob River

Irtysh River

Yenisey River

Central Siberian Plateau

SAYAN MTNS.

ALTAI SHAN

TIEN SHAN

URAL MOUNTAINS

Gobi (Desert)

GREAT WALL OF CHINA

Yellow Sea

East China Sea

Philippine Sea

South China Sea

Tsugaru Strait

Inland Sea

Mt. Fuji
12,388 ft.
(3,776 m)

Huang (Yellow) River

Grand Canal

Chang (Yangtze) River

Mekong River

Takla Makan

KUNLUN SHAN

Communism Peak
24,590 ft. (7,495 m)

Godwin Austen
28,250 ft. (8,611 m)

HIMALAYAS

Mt. Everest
29,028 ft.
(8,848 m)

Kanchenjunga
28,146 ft.
(8,579 m)

HINDU KUSH

Brahmaputra River

Ganges River

VINDHYA RA.

EASTERN GHATS

WESTERN GHATS

Indus River

Rann of Kutch

Bay of Bengal

Arabian Sea

Malay Peninsula

Karakum Desert

Caspian Sea

CAUCASUS

ELBURZ MTNS.

ZAGROS MTNS.

Persian Gulf

TAURUS MTNS.

Syrian Desert

Euphrates R.

Tigris R.

Rub' al-Khali

ASIR MTNS.

Red Sea

Black Sea

Baltic Sea

Bärents Sea

Arctic Circle

Tropic of Cancer

Equator

N
E
S
W

Legend

— International boundary

—·— Disputed boundary

▲ Mountain peak

Miles
0   500   1000

Kilometers
0   500   1000   1500

R33

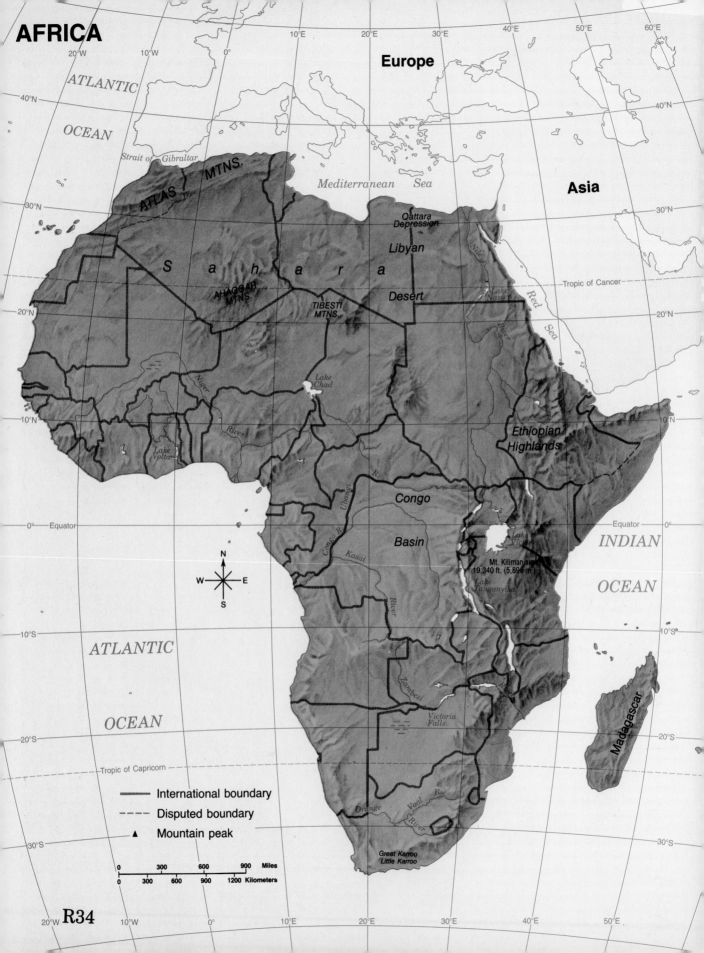

AFRICA

20°W   10°W   0°   10°E   20°E   30°E   40°E   50°E   60°E

Europe

Asia

ATLANTIC

OCEAN

40°N

Strait of Gibraltar

Mediterranean   Sea

30°N

ATLAS   MTNS.

*Qattara
Depression*

Libyan

S   a   h   a   r   a

AHAGGAR
MTNS.

TIBESTI
MTNS.

Desert

Tropic of Cancer

20°N

Nile

*Lake
Nasser*

River

Red Sea

*Lake
Chad*

10°N

Niger

River

*Ethiopian
Highlands*

*Lake
Volta*

Ubangi

Congo

R.

Congo R.

Basin

Kasai

*Lake
Victoria*

Equator   0°   Equator

INDIAN

*Mt. Kilimanjaro
19,340 ft. (5,890 m)*

ATLANTIC

River

*Lake
Tanganyika*

OCEAN

10°S

Madagascar

OCEAN

Zambezi

River

*Victoria
Falls*

20°S

Tropic of Capricorn

— — — International boundary

- - - - Disputed boundary

▲ Mountain peak

Orange

Vaal

R.

River

30°S

*Great Karroo
Little Karroo*

| 0 | 300 | 600 | 900 | Miles |
| 0 | 300 | 600 | 900 | 1200 | Kilometers |

20°W   R34   10°W   0°   10°E   20°E   30°E   40°E   50°E

AUSTRALIA

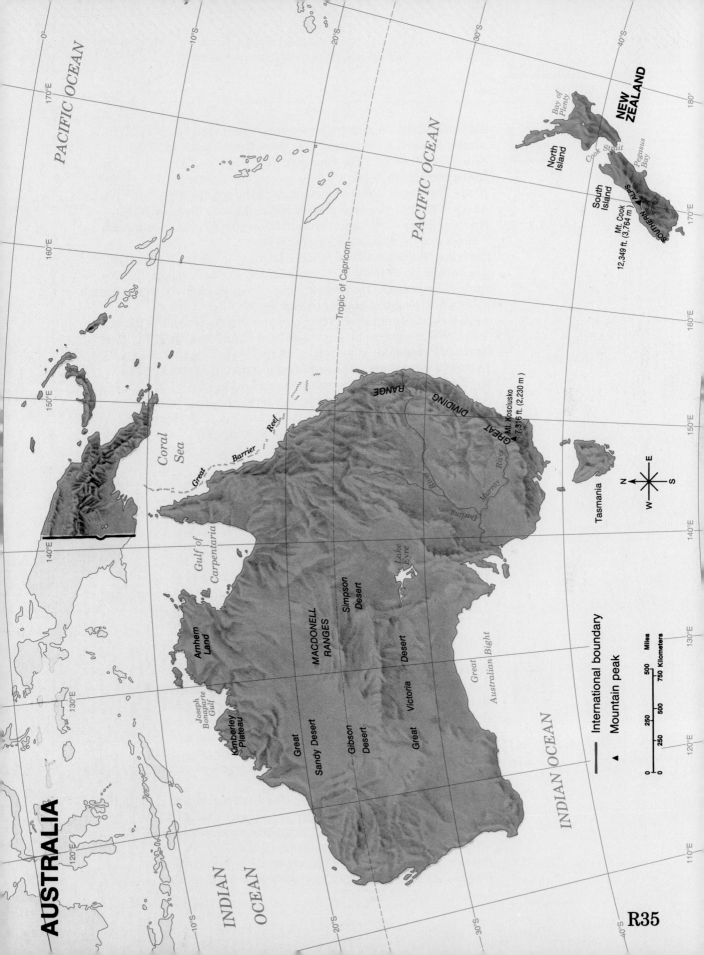

PACIFIC OCEAN

PACIFIC OCEAN

NEW ZEALAND

Bay of Plenty

North Island

Cook Strait

South Island

Pegasus Bay

SOUTHERN ALPS

Mt. Cook
12,349 ft. (3,764 m)

INDIAN OCEAN

INDIAN OCEAN

Coral Sea

Great Barrier Reef

Gulf of Carpentaria

GREAT DIVIDING RANGE

Mt. Kosciusko
7,316 ft. (2,230 m)

Murray River

Darling River

Tasmania

Lake Eyre

Simpson Desert

MACDONELL RANGES

Great Sandy Desert

Gibson Desert

Great Victoria Desert

Arnhem Land

Joseph Bonaparte Gulf

Kimberley Plateau

Great Australian Bight

Tropic of Capricorn

N
W E
S

International boundary
▲ Mountain peak

Miles
0   250   500
0 250 500 750 Kilometers

R35

Alabama River   A river in the southeastern United States. (p. 77)
Alaska Range   A mountain range in southern Alaska. (p. 290)
Albany (43°N/74°W)   The capital of New York. (p. 154)
Albuquerque (35°N/107°W)   The largest city in New Mexico. (p. 244)
Alps   The largest group of mountains in Europe. (p. 398)
Amazon Basin   The area drained by the Amazon River. (p. R31)
Amazon River   The largest river in the world; found in South America; flows into the Atlantic Ocean. (p. 374)
American Samoa   A United States territory in the Pacific. (p. R16)
Anchorage (61°N/150°W)   Alaska's largest city and seaport. (p. 290)
Andes Mountains   The longest group of mountains in the world; stretch the whole length of South America. (p. 398)
Appalachian Mountains   The mountains that cover much of the eastern United States; begin in Canada and end in Alabama. (p. 39)
Arabian Peninsula   A peninsula located east of the Red Sea. (p. 418)
Arctic Coastal Plain   The northernmost part of Alaska. (p. 290)
Arctic Ocean   The northernmost ocean. (p. 7)
Arecibo (18°N/67°W)   A port city in Puerto Rico. (p. 316)
Arkansas River   A tributary of the Mississippi River; begins in central Colorado and ends at the Mississippi River. (p. 39)
Aspen (39°N/107°W)   A town and ski resort in western Colorado. (p. 266)
Atacama Desert   A desert on the west coast of South America. (p. 418)
Atlanta (34°N/84°W)   Georgia's capital and largest city. (p. 177)
Atlantic Ocean   The body of water that separates North and South America from Europe and Africa. (p. 7)
Atlas Mountains   The mountains that stretch across northwestern Africa. (p. 398)
Austin (30°N/98°W)   The capital of Texas. (p. 244)
Australian Desert   The name for the deserts that cover nearly half of Australia; gets about 5 inches (13 cm) of rain a year. (p. 418)

Badlands   An area of dry land in South Dakota. (p. 222)
Baltimore (39°N/77°W)   A large port city in Maryland. (p. 154)
Baton Rouge (30°N/91°W)   The capital of Louisiana. (p. 177)
Beijing (40°N/116°E)   The capital of China. (p. 382)
Birmingham (34°N/87°W)   An industrial city in Alabama. (p. 177)
Black Hills   A group of mountains in South Dakota. (p. 222)
Blue Ridge Mountains   The eastern and southern part of the Appalachian Mountains. (p. 177)
Boston (42°N/71°W)   Massachusetts's capital and largest city. (p. 154)
Brooks Range   A mountain range in northern Alaska. (p. 290)
Bryce Canyon National Park   A national park in southern Utah; noted for its wind-carved rock formations. (p. 266)
Buenos Aires (35°S/58°W)   The capital of Argentina. (p. 447)
Buffalo (43°N/79°W)   A city in western New York. (p. 154)

Cairo   **Detroit**

Cairo (37°N/89°W)   A city in southwestern Illinois. (p. 77)

Canadian Plains   The northern part of the Interior Plains. (p. 438)

Caribbean Sea   A part of the Atlantic Ocean; located southeast of Florida. (p. R28)

Carlsbad Caverns National Park   A national park in southeastern New Mexico; noted for its large caves. (p. 244)

Cascade Range   A mountain range in the western United States; extends north from California through Oregon and Washington. (p. 38)

Central Plains   The eastern part of the Interior Plains. (p. 127)

Central Valley   A large valley in central California. (p. 38)

Chang Jiang   China's longest river and the third-largest river in the world; links the interior of China with the Pacific Ocean. (p. 375)

Charlotte (35°N/81°W)   A city in North Carolina. (p. 177)

Chesapeake Bay   A large bay of the Atlantic Ocean; partly surrounded by Virginia and Maryland. (p. 154)

Chicago (42°N/88°W)   The largest city in Illinois. (p. 199)

Chihuahuan Desert   A part of the North American Desert; located in New Mexico and Texas. (p. 110)

Cincinnati (39°N/85°W)   A large city in southern Ohio. (p. 199)

Coast Ranges   The mountains that extend north and south along the Pacific coast of the United States; get heavy rainfall each year. (p. 38)

Coastal Plain   One of two major plains in the United States; located along the coasts of the Atlantic Ocean and the Gulf of Mexico. (p. 38)

Colorado Plateau   A plateau in the southwestern United States; covers most of northern New Mexico and Arizona. (p. R24)

Colorado River   A river in the southwestern United States. (p. 77)

Columbia Plateau   A plateau east of the Cascade Range. (p. R24)

Columbia River   A river in the Pacific Northwest. (p. 77)

Connecticut River   A river in the northeastern United States. (p. 154)

Continental Divide   The imaginary line that runs along the highest points of the Rocky Mountains; separates rivers that flow west from those that flow east. (p. 266)

Corn Belt   The part of the Central Plains where farmers grow large corn crops. (p. 133)

Cuzco (14°S/72°W)   A city high in the Andes Mountains in Peru. (p. 408)

Dallas (33°N/97°W)   A large city in Texas. (p. 244)

Death Valley   A valley in the Mojave Desert in California; the lowest point in the Western Hemisphere. (p. 110)

Delaware Bay   A bay of the Atlantic Ocean; separates New Jersey and Delaware. (p. 154)

Delaware River   A river in the northeastern United States. (p. 154)

Denver (40°N/105°W)   Colorado's capital and largest city. (p. 266)

Des Moines (42°N/94°W)   Iowa's capital and largest city. (p. 222)

Detroit (42°N/83°W)   The largest city in Michigan. (p. 199)

East China Sea   A part of the Pacific Ocean; extends from Japan to the southern end of the Malay Peninsula, north of Taiwan. (p. 382)

European Plain   A large plain that covers more than half of the Soviet Union; located mostly in Europe but stretches into Asia. (p. 438)

Everglades National Park   A national park and swamp in Florida. (p. 177)

Fairbanks (65°N/148°W)   A city in central Alaska. (p. 290)

Fall Line   An imaginary line that runs between the Appalachian Mountains and the Coastal Plain; the land drops suddenly along the Fall Line, and rivers there form waterfalls. (p. 127)

Florida Bay   The body of water between the southern tip of Florida and the Florida Keys. (p. 177)

Gobi   A desert in Asia; located in Mongolia and China. (p. 418)

Grand Canal   A canal in northeastern China. (p. 382)

Grand Canyon   A canyon in Arizona; formed by the Colorado River. (p. 77)

Grand Coulee Dam (48°N/119°W)   The most important electric power plant in the United States; located on the Columbia River. (p. 77)

Great Basin   An area of low, dry land in the western United States; located in the Intermountain area. (p. 38)

Great Basin Desert   The largest of the North American deserts; located between the Sierra Nevada and the Rocky Mountains. (p. 110)

Great Lakes   The world's largest group of freshwater lakes. (p. 39)

Great Plains   The western part of the Interior Plains. (p. 127)

Great Salt Lake (41°N/112°W)   The largest lake in the Great Basin; located in Utah. (p. 38)

Great Smoky Mountains   A part of the Appalachian Mountains; extend along the North Carolina–Tennessee border. (p. 177)

Greenland   The largest island in the world. (p. 159)

Guam   A United States territory in the Pacific. (p. R17)

Gulf of Mexico   A part of the Atlantic Ocean; borders the Texas, Louisiana, Mississippi, Alabama, and Florida coasts. (p. 36)

Himalayas   The highest mountains in the world; separate China from India; Mt. Everest, the world's highest mountain, is found here. (p. 398)

Hollywood (34°N/118°W)   A city in California. (p. 304)

Honolulu (21°N/158°W)   The capital and largest city of Hawaii. (p. 295)

Hoover Dam   A dam on the Colorado River; forms Lake Mead. (p. 244)

Houston (30°N/95°W)   The largest city in Texas. (p. 244)

Houston Ship Channel   A narrow, deep waterway that connects Houston, Texas, with the Gulf of Mexico. (p. 244)

Huang He   The second-largest river in China. (p. 375)

Hudson River   A large river in New York. (p. 154)

Illinois Waterway   The waterway that connects Lake Michigan with the Illinois River, and then with the Mississippi River. (p. 199)

Imperial Valley   A valley in southern California. (p. 110)

Indian Ocean   The body of water that separates Africa, Asia, Antarctica, and Australia. (p. 7)

Indianapolis (40°N/86°W)   Indiana's capital and largest city. (p. 199)

Interior Plains   One of two major plains in the United States; located between the Appalachian Mountains and the Rocky Mountains; divided into the Central Plains and the Great Plains. (p. 39)

Jamestown (37°N/77°W)   The first successful English settlement in North America; located in what is now the state of Virginia. (p. 177)

Juneau (58°N/134°W)   The capital of Alaska. (p. 290)

Kansas City (39°N/95°W)   A city in Missouri. (p. 222)

King's Canyon National Park   A national park in the Sierra Nevada of California; known for its giant sequoia trees. (p. 304)

Lake Champlain   A large lake located on the New York–Vermont border. (p. 154)

Lake Erie   The fourth largest of the Great Lakes. (p. 39)

Lake Huron   The second largest of the Great Lakes. (p. 39)

Lake Michigan   The third largest of the Great Lakes; the only one of the Great Lakes located totally within the United States. (p. 39)

Lake Okeechobee   The largest lake in the southeastern United States; located in central Florida. (p. R25)

Lake Ontario   The smallest of the Great Lakes. (p. 39)

Lake Pontchartrain   A lake in southeastern Louisiana. (p. 71)

Lake Superior   The largest of the Great Lakes. (p. 39)

Lake Victoria   A large lake in central Africa. (p. R34)

Leadville (39°N/106°W)   A town in Colorado. (p. 266)

Lima (12°S/77°W)   The capital of Peru; founded by Pizarro. (p. 408)

Little Bighorn River   A river in Wyoming and Montana. (p. 266)

Los Angeles (34°N/118°W)   The largest city in California. (p. 304)

Machu Picchu   The ruins of an ancient city high in the Andes Mountains in Peru; built by the Incas. (p. 408)

Mammoth Cave National Park   A national park in southwestern Kentucky; noted for its unusual caves. (p. 177)

Massachusetts Bay   A bay of the Atlantic Ocean; extends along the east coast of Massachusetts from Cape Ann to Cape Cod. (p. 154)

Mauna Kea   A volcano on the island of Hawaii. (p. 295)

Mediterranean Sea   A body of water surrounded by Europe, Asia, and Africa; connected to the Atlantic Ocean and the Black Sea. (p. R29)

Memphis (35°N/90°W)   A city in Tennessee. (p. 177)

Mesabi Range   An area of low hills in northern Minnesota. (p.199)

Miami (26°N/80°W)   A city in southern Florida. (p. 177)

Midway Islands   A United States territory in the Pacific. (p. R26)

Milwaukee (43°N/88°W)   The largest city in Wisconsin. (p. 199)

Minneapolis (45°N/93°W)   The largest city in Minnesota. (p. 199)

Mississippi River   The longest river in the United States. (p. 77)

Missouri River   A major tributary of the Mississippi. (p. 77)

Mobile (31°N/88°W)   A city and major port in Alabama. (p. 177)

Mojave Desert   One of the four North American deserts; located south of the Sierra Nevada in southern California. (p. 110)

Mt. Everest (28°N/87°E)   The highest mountain in the world; found in the Himalayas. (p. R33)

Mt. Fuji (Fujiyama) (35°N/138°E)   A volcano in Japan. (p. R33)

Mt. McKinley (64°N/150°W)   North America's highest mountain; found in the Alaska Range. (p. 290)

Mt. Rainier (47°N/122°W)   The highest point in Washington State; the highest point in the Cascade Range. (p. 299)

Mt. Rushmore (44°N/103°W)   A mountain in the Black Hills of South Dakota; Mt. Rushmore National Memorial is found here. (p. 222)

Mt. St. Helens (46°N/122°W)   An active volcano in southern Washington State. (p. 299)

Mt. Waialeale (22°N/160°W)   A mountain on the island of Kauai, Hawaii; the wettest spot in the world. (p. 295)

Mt. Whitney (37°N/118°W)   The highest mountain in California. (p. 304)

Nanjing (32°N/120°E)   A port on the Chang Jiang in China. (p. 382)

Negev   A desert in southern Israel. (p. 425)

New Orleans (30°N/90°W)   A major port in the United States and the largest city in Louisiana; located on the Mississippi River. (p. 177)

New York City (41°N/74°W)   A major port and the largest city in the United States; located at the mouth of the Hudson River. (p. 154)

New York State Barge Canal System   A system of four canals built to move freight across the state of New York; links the Great Lakes with the Hudson River and the Atlantic Ocean. (p. 154)

Newfoundland   An island off the east coast of Canada. (p. 90)

Niagara Falls   The large waterfalls on the Niagara River. (p. 154)

Nile River   The longest river in the world; forms in central Africa and flows north to the Mediterranean Sea. (p. 375)

Norfolk (37°N/76°W)   A port city in Virginia. (p. 177)

North American Desert   A large desert in the western United States; divided into four major areas—the Great Basin Desert, the Mojave Desert, the Sonoran Desert, and the Chihuahuan Desert. (p. 418)

North Pole   The northernmost point on the Earth. (p. 5)

North Sea   A part of the Atlantic Ocean; located east of Great Britain and west of Denmark; the Rhine River empties into it. (p. R32)

Ohio River A major tributary of the Mississippi. (p. 77)
Omaha (41°N/96°W) The largest city in Nebraska. (p. 222)

Pacific Ocean The largest body of water on the Earth. (p. 7)
Painted Desert A desert in northwestern Arizona. (p. 244)
Patagonia A large, dry plateau in southern Argentina. (p. 447)
Pearl River A river in the southeastern United States. (p. 71)
Persian Gulf The body of water on the eastern side of the Arabian Peninsula. (p. R33)
Petrified Forest National Park A national park in Arizona; on the ground lie logs from ancient forests that have turned to stone. (p. 244)
Philadelphia (40°N/75°W) The largest city in Pennsylvania. (p. 154)
Phoenix (33°N/112°W) Arizona's capital and largest city. (p. 244)
Pikes Peak (39°N/105°W) A mountain peak in the Rocky Mountains; named for Zebulon Pike. (p. 266)
Pittsburgh (40°N/80°W) A city in Pennsylvania; the Allegheny and Monongahela rivers meet here to form the Ohio River. (p. 154)
Platte River A tributary of the Missouri River. (p. 266)
Plymouth (41°N/72°W) A city in Massachusetts; the site of the first settlement built by the Pilgrims. (p. 154)
Ponce (18°N/67°W) A city on the southern coast of Puerto Rico. (p. 316)
Portland (46°N/123°W) The largest city in Oregon. (p. 299)
Potomac River A river on the Coastal Plain of the United States; Washington, D.C., is found on this river. (p. 39)
Pueblo (38°N/105°W) A city in Colorado. (p. 266)
Puerto Rico A commonwealth of the United States; located southeast of Florida in the Caribbean Sea. (p. 316)
Puget Sound A part of the Pacific Ocean; Seattle, Washington, is located on this body of water. (p. 299)

Red River A tributary of the Mississippi River. (p. 77)
Red Sea A sea between the Arabian Peninsula and Africa. (p. R33)
Rhine River The most important waterway in Europe. (p. 375)
Rio Grande The river that forms the Texas–Mexico border. (p. 36)
Rocky Mountains The mountains that cover much of the western United States; begin in Alaska and end in New Mexico. (p. 38)
Rub' al Khali A desert on the Arabian Peninsula. (p. R29)

Sabine River A river in Texas. (p. 77)
Sacramento (39°N/121°W) The capital of California. (p. 304)
Sacramento River A river in California. (p. 77)
Sahara The world's largest desert; located in Africa. (p. 418)
St. Lawrence River The river that flows from the Great Lakes to the Atlantic Ocean; forms part of the U.S.–Canada border. (p. 36)

St. Lawrence Seaway   A series of canals on the St. Lawrence River; allows ships to travel from the Atlantic to the Great Lakes. (p. 79)

St. Louis (39°N/90°W)   The largest city in Missouri. (p. 222)

Salado River   The only large river on the pampa in Argentina. (p. 447)

Salt Lake City (41°N/112°W)   Utah's capital and largest city. (p. 266)

Salton Sea   A desert lake in southern California. (p. 304)

San Antonio (29°N/98°W)   A city in central Texas. (p. 244)

San Diego (33°N/117°W)   A city in southern California. (p. 304)

San Francisco (38°N/122°W)   A city in northern California. (p. 304)

San Francisco Bay   A part of the Pacific Ocean; San Francisco is located on this large bay in northern California. (p. 304)

San Joaquin River   A river in California. (p. 304)

San Jose (37°N/122°W)   A city in northern California. (p. 304)

San Juan (18°N/66°W)   Puerto Rico's capital and largest city. (p. 316)

Santa Fe (36°N/106°W)   The capital of New Mexico; the oldest capital city in the United States. (p. 244)

Savannah River   A river in the southeastern United States. (p. 39)

Sea of Galilee   A freshwater lake in northeastern Israel. (p. 425)

Seattle (48°N/122°W)   The largest city in Washington State. (p. 299)

Shanghai (32°N/122°E)   A port and the largest city in China. (p. 382)

Sierra Nevada   A high mountain range located east of the Coast Ranges in California. (p. 38)

Snake River   A river in the Pacific Northwest. (p. 77)

Sonoran Desert   A part of the North American Desert; located in southwestern Arizona. (p. 110)

South Pole   The southernmost point on the Earth. (p. 5)

Springfield (40°N/90°W)   The capital of Illinois. (p. 199)

Sun Valley (44°N/114°W)   A town in central Idaho. (p. 266)

Sutter's Mill (38°N/122°W)   A sawmill in northern California; gold was discovered there in 1848. (p. 304)

Syracuse (43°N/76°W)   A city in central New York. (p. 154)

Tel Aviv (32°N/35°E)   A large city in Israel. (p. 425)

Tennessee River   A river in the southeastern United States. (p. 39)

Tulsa (36°N/96°W)   A large city in Oklahoma. (p. 244)

Ural Mountains   The low mountains in the Soviet Union that separate Europe and Asia. (p. 398)

Valley Forge (40°N/76°W)   A city in Pennsylvania; George Washington and the American army spent the winter of 1777 here. (p. 154)

Virgin Islands   A group of islands in the Caribbean Sea that are United States territories. (p. R26)

Virginia Beach (37°N/76°W)   A city and ocean resort in Virginia. (p. 177)

Volga River   The longest river in Europe; located in the Soviet Union east of the Ural Mountains. (p. 375)

Wake Island   A United States territory in the Pacific. (p. R27)

Washington, D.C. (39°N/77°W)   The capital of the United States; located on the Potomac River; not in any state but in the District of Columbia. (p. 39)

Wheat Belt   The part of the Great Plains where farmers grow large wheat crops; much of our nation's wheat is grown here. (p. 133)

Wichita (38°N/97°W)   A city in Kansas. (p. 222)

Williamsburg (37°N/77°W)   A city in Virginia; historic area has been restored to look the way it did in the 1700s. (p. 177)

Wind River Indian Reservation   A reservation in Wyoming. (p. 266)

Yellowstone National Park   A national park in Wyoming; the oldest national park in the United States; known for its geysers, such as Old Faithful. (p. 266)

Yosemite National Park   A national park in central California; noted for its high waterfalls and giant sequoias. (p. 304)

Yotvata (30°N/35°E)   A kibbutz in the Negev in Israel. (p. 425)

Yukon River   A large river in Alaska and Canada. (p. 290)

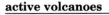

Glossary

GLOSSARY • GLOSSARY • GLOSSARY • GLOSSARY • GLOSSAF

active volcanoes   border

This glossary contains important social studies words and their definitions. Each
word is respelled as it would be in a dictionary. When you see this mark ' after a
syllable, pronounce that syllable with more force than the other syllables. The page
number at the end of the definition tells where to find the word in your book.

add, āce, câre, pälm; end, ēqual; it, īce; odd, ōpen, ôrder; tŏŏk, pōōl; up, bûrn; yŏŏ as u
in *fuse;* oil; pout; ə as a in *above,* e in *sicken,* i in *possible,* o in *melon,* u in *circus;*
check; ring; thin; this; zh as in *vision.*

A

active volcanoes (ak′tiv vol·kā′nōz)   Volcanoes that are erupting or are
  likely to erupt. (p. 401)
adobe (ə·dō′bē)   The sun-dried clay bricks used to build pueblos. (p. 258)
alfalfa (al·fal′fə)   A leafy plant grown as cattle feed. (p. 448)
altitude (al′tə·tŏŏd)   The elevation, or height, of a mountain. (p. 91)
aluminum (ə·lōō′mə·nəm)   A lightweight metal. (p. 302)
amendments (ə·mend′mənts)   Changes to the Constitution. (p. 358)
American Revolution (ə·mer′ə·kən rev·ə·lōō′shən)   The war in which
  American colonists won their freedom from England. (p. 162)
ancestors (an′ses·tərz)   Early family members. (p. 18)
architects (är′kə·tektz)   People who make plans for a building. (p. 212)
arctic (är′tik)   Having a cold climate. (p. 380)
area (âr′ē·ə)   The amount of land. (p. 121)
asado (ä·sä′dō)   A barbecue in Argentina. (p. 454)
assembly line (ə·sem′blē līn)   A moving belt on which a product is
  carried through an assembly plant. (p. 210)
assembly plant (ə·sem′blē plant)   A factory in which all the parts of a
  product are assembled, or put together. (p. 210)
axis (ak′səs)   The imaginary line around which the Earth turns. The line
  runs from the North Pole to the South Pole. (p. 378)

B

balsa (bôl′sə)   A soft wood that is easy to carve. (p. 308)
bamboo (bam·bōō′)   A fast-growing, giant grass. (p. 384)
banks (bangks)   The land on both sides of a stream or river. (p. 68)
barges (bär′jəz)   Flat-bottomed boats that are pushed by tugboats. (p. 77)
barrier (bar′ē·ər)   Something that blocks the way. (p. 94)
barrio (bär′rē·ō)   A Spanish-speaking neighborhood. (p. 341)
bartering (bär′tər·ing)   Trading for goods. (p. 202)
basin (bā′sən)   A low, bowl-shaped land. (p. 41)
bay (bā)   A body of water that is partly surrounded by land. (p. 155)
Bill of Rights (bil uv rīts)   The first ten amendments to the Constitution,
  which list our basic rights and freedoms. (p. 358)
bison (bī′sən)   Buffalo. (p. 228)
blacksmith (blak′smith)   A person who works with iron by heating it
  and hammering it into useful shapes. (p. 136)
blizzard (bliz′ərd)   A heavy snowstorm with strong, freezing winds.
  (p. 224)
bodies of water (bod′ēz uv wô′tər)   Rivers, lakes, and oceans. (p. 4)
border (bôr′dər)   The outside edge of a place. (p. 9)

R44

boundary   **conservation**

boundary (boun'də·rē *or* boun'drē)   The border of a place. (p. 35)

branch (branch)   1. A smaller river or stream that joins a larger river; also called a tributary. (p. 68)   2. One of the three main parts of the government. (p. 349)

brand (brand)   To mark calves to show who owns them. (p. 101)

broadleaf (brôd'lēf)   A kind of tree with wide, flat leaves that often are shed in the fall. (p. 157)

cactus (kak'təs)   A desert plant with sharp spines that stores water in its thick, fleshy stem. (p. 111)

calligraphy (kə·lig'rə·fē)   A beautiful way of writing. (p. 393)

canal (kə·nal')   A waterway built by people. (p. 118)

canyon (kan'yən)   A narrow valley with steep sides. (p. 41)

capital (kap'ə·təl)   A city where leaders make laws. (p. 37)

caravan (kar'ə·van)   A group of desert travelers. (p. 423)

cardinal directions (kär'də·nəl di·rek'shənz)   The four main directions: north, south, east, and west. (p. 10)

century (sen'chə·rē)   A period of 100 years. (p. 165)

chaff (chaf)   The outside covering of a grain of wheat. (p. 233)

chuña (chōō'nya)   A meal ground from dried potatoes. (p. 404)

citizen (sit'ə·zən)   A member of a community, state, or nation. (p. 1)

city manager (sit'ē man'ij·ər)   The head of the local executive branch of government. (p. 356)

Civil War (siv'əl wôr)   The war fought between the Northern and Southern states after the Southern states voted to break away from the United States and form their own government. (p. 205)

climate (klī'mət)   The weather a place has year after year. (p. 4)

climate zones (klī'mət zōnz)   The wide areas of similar climates that circle the Earth. (p. 380)

cloudburst (kloud'bûrst)   A sudden hard rain. (p. 246)

coast (kōst)   The land next to an ocean. (p. 37)

coke (kōk)   A fuel made from coal. (p. 209)

colonies (kol'ə·nēz)   Places that are ruled by another country. (p. 161)

combine (kom'bīn)   A machine that cuts and threshes wheat. (p. 233)

commonwealth (kom'ən·welth)   A territory that governs itself. (p. 315)

communication (kə·myōō·nə·kā'shən)   The way in which people send and receive messages. (p. 333)

comparison shopping (kəm·par'ə·sən shop'ing)   Comparing the quality and prices of a product before making a purchase. (p. 328)

compass rose (kum'pəs rōz)   A drawing, on a map, that shows directions. (p. 12)

competition (kom·pə·tish'ən)   A contest between producers to get more customers. (p. 338)

Congress (kong'gris)   The lawmaking branch of the federal government. (p. 350)

conservation (kon·sər·vā'shən)   Saving something by using it wisely. (p. 102)

R45

conserve   **elected**

conserve (kən·sûrv′)   To save or keep from being used up. (p. 444)

Constitution (kon·stə·tōō′shən)   The document that contains our country's most important laws and that gives the plan for our federal government. (p. 349)

construction (kən·struk′shən)   The act of building. (p. 212)

consumers (kən·sōō′mərz)   People who spend money to buy the things they need or want. (p. 326)

continents (kon′tə·nənts)   Earth's seven main land areas. (p. 7)

cost (kôst)   The money spent to make a product. (p. 327)

council (koun′səl)   The lawmaking branch of a local government. (p. 356)

county (koun′tē)   A part of a state that has its own government. (p. 237)

county seat (koun′tē sēt)   A town or city that is the center of government for a county. (p. 236)

courts (kôrts)   The branch of government that makes sure that laws are applied fairly and that decides how people who break laws should be punished. (p. 351)

crater (krā′tər)   The opening in the top of a volcano. (p. 401)

crude oil (krōōd oil)   The name for oil when it is pumped from the earth and before it is turned into gasoline or other products. (p. 189)

culture (kul′chər)   A way of life. (p. 27)

current (kûr′ənt)   A river's flow. (p. 82)

customs (kus′təmz)   Special ways of doing things. (p. 17)

dams (damz)   Walls built across rivers to hold back water and store it for drinking and irrigation. (p. 73)

Declaration of Independence (dek·lə·rā′shən uv in·di·pen′dəns)   The document written to explain why the colonies wanted independence from England. (p. 182)

delta (del′tə)   Land formed by silt built up at a river's mouth. (p. 72)

democracy (di·mäk′rə·sē)   A belief that people are free to make choices about their lives. (p. 26)

desert (dez′ərt)   An area where the land is mostly dry. (p. 41)

dikes (dīks)   Banks built along rivers to help stop flooding. (p. 73)

distance scale (dis′təns skāl)   The part of a map that shows that a certain length stands for some longer, real distance on the Earth. (p. 10)

Douglas fir (dug′ləs fûr)   A kind of pine tree that grows in many parts of the West. It is the region's most valuable tree. (p. 280)

downstream (doun′strēm′)   Toward a river's mouth. (p. 85)

drains (drānz)   Carries water away from. (p. 68)

drought (drout)   A time of little or no rainfall. (p. 134)

dugout (dug′out)   A house dug into a hillside. (p. 231)

economy (i·kon′ə·mē)   The way in which a country provides and uses goods and services. (p. 338)

elected (i·lekt′əd)   To be choosen by vote. (p. 205)

elevation (el·ə·vā′shən)   The height of the land. (p. 84)

energy (en′ər·jē)   The power that makes things work. (p. 353)

environment (in·vī′rən·mənt)   Surroundings. (p. 247)

equator (i·kwā′tər)   The make-believe line that circles the Earth halfway between the North Pole and the South Pole. (p. 5)

erode (i·rōd′)   To wear away the Earth's surface. (p. 72)

erosion (i·rō′zhən)   The slow wearing away of large areas of land. (p. 72)

estancias (is·tän′sē·əz)   Large ranches on the pampa. (p. 449)

evaporate (i·vap′ə·rāt)   To dry up. (p. 109)

executive branch (ig·zek′yə·tiv branch)   The branch of government that makes sure the laws are carried out. (p. 351)

export (ik·spôrt *or* eks′pôrt)   To send something to another country to be sold. (p. 399)

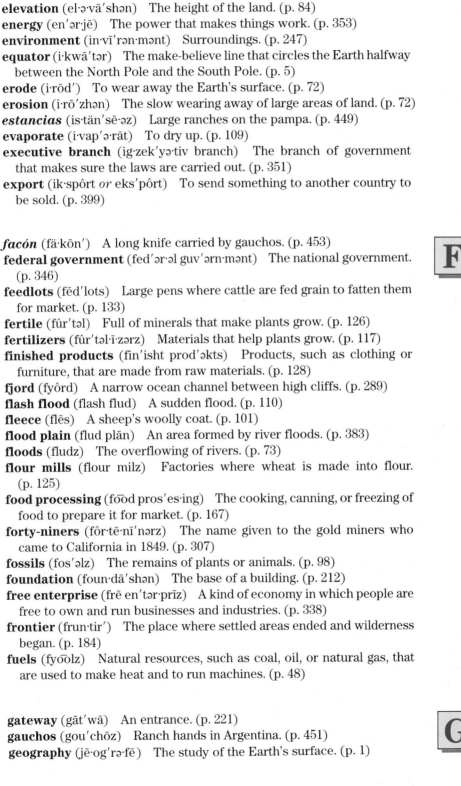

facón (fä·kōn′)   A long knife carried by gauchos. (p. 453)

federal government (fed′ər·əl guv′ərn·mənt)   The national government. (p. 346)

feedlots (fēd′lots)   Large pens where cattle are fed grain to fatten them for market. (p. 133)

fertile (fûr′təl)   Full of minerals that make plants grow. (p. 126)

fertilizers (fûr′təl·i·zərz)   Materials that help plants grow. (p. 117)

finished products (fin′isht prod′əkts)   Products, such as clothing or furniture, that are made from raw materials. (p. 128)

fjord (fyôrd)   A narrow ocean channel between high cliffs. (p. 289)

flash flood (flash flud)   A sudden flood. (p. 110)

fleece (flēs)   A sheep's woolly coat. (p. 101)

flood plain (flud plān)   An area formed by river floods. (p. 383)

floods (fludz)   The overflowing of rivers. (p. 73)

flour mills (flour milz)   Factories where wheat is made into flour. (p. 125)

food processing (fōod pros′es·ing)   The cooking, canning, or freezing of food to prepare it for market. (p. 167)

forty-niners (fôr·tē·nī′nərz)   The name given to the gold miners who came to California in 1849. (p. 307)

fossils (fos′əlz)   The remains of plants or animals. (p. 98)

foundation (foun·dā′shən)   The base of a building. (p. 212)

free enterprise (frē en′tər·prīz)   A kind of economy in which people are free to own and run businesses and industries. (p. 338)

frontier (frun·tir′)   The place where settled areas ended and wilderness began. (p. 184)

fuels (fyōolz)   Natural resources, such as coal, oil, or natural gas, that are used to make heat and to run machines. (p. 48)

gateway (gāt′wā)   An entrance. (p. 221)

gauchos (gou′chōz)   Ranch hands in Argentina. (p. 451)

geography (jē·og′rə·fē)   The study of the Earth's surface. (p. 1)

geysers (gī′zərz)   Springs of water that shoot jets of steam and hot water into the air. (p. 277)

glaciers (glā′shərz)   Large masses of ice that move slowly. (p. 153)

globe (glōb)   A model of the Earth. (p. 5)

Gold Rush (gōld rush)   The name given to the time in history during which thousands of people went to California in search of gold. (p. 306)

goods (goͮodz)   Things that people buy and sell. (p. 23)

government (guv′ərn·mənt)   A group of people who lead a city, a state, or a country. (p. 26)

governor (guv′ər·nər)   The head of the state executive branch. (p. 355)

grain elevators (grān el′ə·vā·tərz)   Tall towers that store grain. (p. 232)

graze (grāz)   To feed on grass. (p. 101)

groundwater (ground′wô·tər)   The water beneath the Earth's surface. (p. 224)

growing season (grō′ing sē′zən)   The time when the weather is warm enough for plants to grow. (p. 47)

guarantee (gar·ən·tē′)   A promise that a product will work. (p. 330)

hailstorms (hāl′stôrmz)   Storms that drop pieces of ice. (p. 225)

harbor (här′bər)   A place where ships can dock safely. (p. 39)

harvest (här′vəst)   To gather crops. (p. 207)

hemisphere (hem′ə·sfir)   Half of a sphere, such as a ball or globe. (p. 5)

heritage (her′ə·tij)   Something, such as a way of life or a belief, handed down from the past. (p. 27)

history (his′tə·rē)   The past. (p. 160)

House of Representatives (hous uv rep·ri·zen′tə·tivz)   One group of Congress, the lawmaking branch of the federal government. (p. 350)

humid (hyoͮo′mid)   Having a lot of moisture. (p. 156)

hurricane (hûr′ə·kān)   A fierce, driving storm with heavy winds and rains. (p. 316)

immigrants (im′ə·grənts)   People who come from other countries to live in a new country. (p. 17)

import (im′pôrt)   To bring something into a country for sale. (p. 398)

industrialized (in·dus′trē·əl·īzd)   Made to have many industries. (p. 334)

industries (in′dəs·trēz)   Kinds of manufacturing. (p. 78)

ingots (ing′gəts)   Blocks of steel formed from molten steel. (p. 210)

interdependence (in·tər·də·pen′dəns)   The dependence of people or regions on one another for products or services. (p. 327)

intermediate directions (in·tər·mē′dē·it di·rek′shənz)   The four directions between the cardinal directions: northeast, southeast, southwest, and northwest. (p. 12)

irrigation (ir·ə·gā′shən)   Bringing water to dry areas. (p. 48)

junks (jungks)   Light boats with tall square sails. (p. 385)

kibbutz (kib·o͞ots′) A kind of farming settlement in Israel where the members own the land together and share the work. (p. 430)

labor (lā′bər) Work. (p. 326)

landforms (land′fôrmz) The shapes of the land. (p. 4)

lasso (las′ō) A rope with a loop tied at the end. (p. 453)

lava (lä′və) Melted rock that flows from a volcano. (p. 89)

laws (lôz) Rules that all must follow. (p. 26)

legends (lej′ənds) Stories, which may or may not be true, that have come down from earlier times. (p. 129)

legislature (lej′is·lā·chər) The lawmaking branch of a state government. (p. 355)

lines of latitude (līnz uv lat′ə·to͞od) The lines on a map or globe that go from east to west; also called parallels. (p. 95)

lines of longitude (līnz uv lon′jə·to͞od) The lines on a map or globe that run from the North Pole to the South Pole; also called meridians. (p. 96)

llama (lä′mə) An animal of the Andes that looks somewhat like a camel without a hump. Its wool is used for clothing and blankets. (p. 405)

local government (lō′kəl guv′ərn·mənt) The government of a city or community. (p. 346)

location (lō·kā′shən) Where a place is on Earth. (p. 211)

Lower 48 (lō′ər 48) The name given to the 48 states of the United States that touch one another. (p. 291)

lumberjacks (lum′bər·jaks) People who cut down trees. (p. 283)

luxury (luk′shər·ē) Something expensive that only a few people can afford. (p. 388)

majority rule (mə·jôr′ə·tē ro͞ol) A way of deciding something by which whoever or whatever gets the most votes wins. (p. 345)

manufacturing (man·yə·fak′chər·ing) The making of goods. (p. 23)

map (map) A drawing of a place. (p. 6)

map key (map kē) The part of a map that shows the symbols used and tells what each symbol means. (p. 9)

Mardi Gras (mär′dē grä′) A carnival held in New Orleans. (p. 192)

Mayflower (mā′flou·ər) The name of the ship that brought the Pilgrims to America. (p. 160)

mayor (mā′ər) The head of the local government's executive branch. (p. 356)

meat-packing plants (mēt′pak·ing plants) Factories that process meat for market or that manufacture meat products, such as hot dogs and cold cuts. (p. 235)

mesas (mā′səz) Flat-topped hills. (p. 244)

mesquite (mes·kēt′) A treelike desert bush with long roots. (p. 112)

metropolitan area (met·rə·pol′ə·tən âr′ē·ə) An area that includes a large city and the smaller cities near it. (p. 211)

R49

minerals   **paniolos**

minerals (min′ər·əlz)   Natural resources, such as sand, stone, and iron, that are used to make machines and buildings. (p. 48)

missions (mish′ənz)   Churches and schools started by priests in Spanish colonies. (p. 249)

moisture (mois′chər)   A small amount of water; dampness. (p. 93)

monument (mon′yə·mənt)   Something that is built to remind people of the past. (p. 221)

moshav (mō·shäv′)   A kind of farming settlement in Israel where each family owns a part of the land. (p. 430)

mountain ranges (moun′tən rān′·jəz)   Chains of mountains. (p. 91)

mouth (mouth)   The place where a river empties into the ocean. (p. 69)

municipal court (myōō·nis′ə·pəl kôrt)   The kind of court that judges people accused of breaking city laws. (p. 356)

musher (mush′ər)   The driver of a dogsled team. (p. 44)

nation (nā′shən)   A country. (p. 17)

national parks (na′shən·əl pärks)   The parks that are maintained by the national government. (p. 102)

natural features (nach′ər·əl fē′chərz)   The things on the Earth, such as landforms, bodies of water, climate, and resources, that have not been made by humans. (p. 4)

natural region (nach′ər·əl rē′jən) A large area that has one major kind of natural feature, such as mountains or plains. (p. 65)

natural resources (nach′ər·əl ri·sôr′səz)   The things in nature that people can use. (p. 4)

navigate (nav′ə·gāt)   To find one's way on an ocean or sea. (p. 163)

needleleaf (nēd′əl·lēf)   A kind of tree with long, sharp leaves that often stay green all year. (p. 157)

nomads (nō′madz)   People who do not have one home but move from place to place. (p. 419)

nonrenewable resource (non·ri·nōō′ə·bəl ri·sôrs′)   A resource that cannot be remade by nature or by people. (p. 420)

oasis (ō·ā′səs)   A desert place with water. (p. 419)

offshore wells (of·shôr′ welz)   Wells off the coast, where oil is pumped from under the ocean floor. (p. 254)

oil slick (oil slik)   The layer of oil that coats the water after an oil spill. (p. 460)

open-pit mines (ō′pən pit mīnz)   Mines in which giant machines dig ore from deep, open holes in the ground. (p. 208)

ore (ôr)   A rock that has a mineral in it. (p. 157)

outback (out′bak)   Another name for the Australian Desert. (p. 423)

paddies (pad′ēz)   Rice fields. (p. 383)

pampa (pam′pə)   A large grassland. (p. 447)

paniolos (pan·ē·ō′lōz)   Hawaiian cowboys. (p. 297)

passes   **region**

passes (pas′əz) Low areas between mountains. (p. 94)

peaks (pēks) The tops of mountains. (p. 90)

peninsula (pə·nin′sə·lə) Land with water on three sides of it. (p. 175)

petrified (pet′rə·fīd) Turned to stone. (p. 113)

pioneers (pī·ə·nirz′) The first people to settle in a new place. (p. 204)

plain (plān) A large area of flat, low land. (p. 37)

plantations (plan·tā′shənz) Huge farms on the Coastal Plain in early America. (p. 181)

plateau (pla·tō′) An area of high, flat land, like a table. (p. 41)

plaza (plä′zə) A public square. (p. 249)

polluted (pə·lo͞ot′əd) dirty; unclean. (p. 74)

poncho (pon′chō) A blanket with a hole in the middle that slips over the wearer's head. (p. 405)

population (pop·yə·lā′shən) The number of people who live in a place. (p. 121)

port (pôrt) A city with a harbor. (p. 78)

poultry (pōl′trē) Chickens and turkeys. (p. 168)

prairie (prâr′ē) Another name for the Central Plains. (p. 130)

precipitation (pri·sip·ə·tā′shən) Rain or snow. (p. 46)

preserve (pri·zûrv′) To keep for future use. (p. 231)

President (prez′ə·dənt) The head of the executive branch of the federal government. (p. 351)

producers (prə·do͞o′sərz) People who make goods or provide services. (p. 326)

products (prod′əkts) Things that people make, or get from nature. (p. 48)

profit (prof′ət) The money that is left over after a product is sold and the costs of making it are paid. (p. 327)

pueblos (pweb′lōz) Indian dwellings built on the sides of cliffs. (p. 258)

pulp (pulp) Ground-up wood used to make paper. (p. 190)

quality (kwol′ə·tē) How good a product is. (p. 328)

rain forest (rān fôr′əst) A wet area where trees, vines, and other plants grow close together. (p. 376)

range (rānj) Grassland where animals graze, or eat. (p. 101)

raw materials (rô mə·tir′ē·əlz) Materials, such as wool, cotton, wood, and oil, that are used to make products. (p. 128)

reclaim (ri·klām′) To take back. (p. 427)

recreation (rek·rē·ā′shən) Things people do for enjoyment. (p. 102)

recycle (rē·sī′kəl) To use materials again. (p. 445)

redwoods (red′wo͝odz) The very tall evergreen trees that grow in northern California. (p. 304)

refineries (ri·fī′nər·ēz) Factories that change crude oil into gasoline and heating oil. (p. 189)

region (rē′jən) An area with many things in common. (p. 1)

R51

represent (rep·ri·zent′) To act or speak for the people. (p. 346)

republic (ri·pub′lik) A kind of government in which the people are free to elect, or choose, their leaders. (p. 26)

research (ri·sûrch′) Using books and other sources to find out facts and information. (p. 63)

reservoir (rez′ər·vwär) A lake that stores water held back by a dam. (p. 253)

responsibilities (ri·spon·sə·bil′ə·tēz) Things a person should do. (p. 27)

responsibility system (ri·spon·sə·bil′ə·tē sis′təm) The economic system in China in which each farmer is expected to grow a certain amount of crops, and each factory is expected to produce a certain amount of goods. (p. 391)

restore (ri·stôr′) To rebuild. (p. 155)

rights (rīts) Freedoms. (p. 27)

river basin (riv′ər bā′sən) The area of land drained by a river and its branches. (p. 68)

river valley (riv′ər val′ē) The low land through which a river flows. (p. 155)

riverbed (riv′ər·bed) The bottom of the path of a river. (p. 68)

round up (round up) To herd animals together. (p. 453)

ruins (rōō′ənz) The remains of destroyed buildings and communities. (p. 259)

saguaro cactus (sə·gwä′rō kak′təs) The largest kind of cactus in the Sonoran Desert. (p. 245)

salmon (sam′ən) A fish that lives in coastal waters. (p. 289)

sampan (sam′pan) A type of fishing or cargo boat in China. (p. 385)

sand dunes (sand dōōnz′) Rounded piles of sand found in deserts. (p. 110)

sandbars (sand′bärz) Low mounds of sand in a river. (p. 68)

sawmills (sô′milz) Buildings where logs are cut into lumber. (p. 125)

sculptor (skulp′tər) An artist who shapes figures out of stone, metal, wood, or some other material. (p. 226)

sea level (sē lev′əl) The level of the surface of the ocean. The height of land is measured from sea level. (p. 46)

self-government (self·guv′ərn·mənt) The ruling of a country by its own people. (p. 349)

self-sufficient (self·sə·fish′ənt) Able to provide for all of one's needs without help. (p. 325)

Senate (sen′it) One of the two groups of Congress, the lawmaking branch of the federal government. (p. 350)

sequoias (si·kwoi′əz) Huge trees that grow in the Sierra Nevada. (p. 305)

service (sûr′vəs) An activity that people do for others. (p. 23)

shear (shir) To cut a sheep's fleece. (p. 101)

shoots (shōōts) The young, tender branches of a plant. (p. 384)

silkworm (silk′wûrm) A kind of caterpillar that spins silk. (p. 384)

silt (silt) The soil washed into and carried by a river. (p. 68)

skyscrapers (skī′skrā·pərz)   Tall buildings. (p. 37)

slave (slāv)   A person owned by another person. (p. 19)

slavery (slā′vər·ē)   The owning of slaves. (p. 19)

slough (slōo)   A marshy field of tall, dry grass. (p. 191)

society (sə·sī′ə·tē)   A group of people who share many things in common. (p. 325)

sod (sod)   A layer of grass-covered earth. (p. 231)

solar cells (sō′lər selz)   Batteries that turn sunlight directly into electricity. (p. 433)

solar energy (sō′lər en′ər·jē)   Power made from sunlight. (p. 433)

source (sôrs)   The place where a river begins. (p. 67)

soybean (soi′bēn)   A small bean used in many foods. (p. 188)

space probes (spās prōbz)   Spacecraft that explore our solar system. (p. 433)

spawn (spôn)   To lay eggs in pools of water. (p. 301)

specialization (spesh·ə·lə·zā′shən)   Doing only one kind of job. (p. 326)

sphere (sfir)   A ball. (p. 5)

spring wheat (spring wēt)   The kind of wheat that grows in the northern Great Plains. (p. 233)

stampede (stam·pēd′)   A sudden rushing off of a herd. (p. 252)

standard of living (stan′dərd uv liv′ing)   A measure of how well people live in a country. (p. 339)

state government (stāt guv′ərn·mənt)   The government of a state. (p. 346)

state parks (stāt pärks)   The parks that are maintained by state governments. (p. 102)

stations (stā′shənz)   Large ranches in Australia. (p. 422)

steel mills (stēl milz)   Factories where steel is made. (p. 78)

steppe (step)   A grassy plain; a grassland of the Soviet Union. (p. 440)

sugar beet (shŏŏg′ər bēt)   A beet from which sugar is made. (p. 278)

sugarcane (shŏŏg′ər·kān)   A grass from which sugar is made. (p. 187)

Supreme Court (sə·prēm′ kôrt)   The most important court in the federal government. (p. 351)

swamp (swomp)   A low, wet land. (p. 98)

symbol (sim′bəl)   Something that stands for something else. (p. 8)

taxes (tak′sez)   The money that government collects from people. (p. 357)

technology (tek·nol′ə·jē)   The building, using, repairing, and improving of modern machines. (p. 334)

temperate (tem′pər·it)   Having a mild climate. (p. 380)

temperature (tem′pər·ə·chər)   How warm or cold a place is. (p. 46)

terrace (ter′əs)   A flat shelf dug out of a mountainside. (p. 404)

territory (ter′ə·tôr·ē)   A place governed by another nation. (p. 315)

textiles (teks′tīlz)   Cloth. (p. 188)

thresh (thresh)   To separate the wheat from its chaff. (p. 233)

tidal waves (tīd′əl wāvz)   Very high ocean waves. (p. 401)

time zone   **yucca**

time zone (tīm zōn)   An area where people use the same time. (p. 336)

timeline (tīm′līn)   A line showing the important events of a certain period of time. The events are marked in order on the timeline. (p. 164)

tornado (tôr·nā′dō)   A tall, dry funnel of whirling wind. (p. 224)

tourism (tŏŏr′iz·əm)   The selling of goods and services to tourists. (p. 190)

tourists (tŏŏr′ists)   Visitors to a place. (p. 190)

trade (trād)   The buying and selling of goods. (p. 169)

transportation (trans′pər·tā·shən)   The moving of people and things from place to place. (p. 82)

trawler (trô′lər)   A fishing boat. (p. 166)

treaty (trē′tē)   A written agreement. (p. 230)

tributary (trib′yə·ter·ē)   A smaller stream or river that joins a larger river; also called a branch. (p. 68)

tropics (trop′iks)   The warm climate zones between the equator and tropic lines. (p. 380)

tundra (tun′drə)   Flat, treeless land that stays frozen most of the year. (p. 290)

upstream (up′strēm)   Against the flow of a river. (p. 85)

U.S. Mint (yōō es mint)   An agency of the United States government that manufactures money. (p. 279)

volcano (vol·kā′nō)   A crack in the Earth's surface through which hot, melted rock, called lava, comes. Lava builds up around the crack over many years and forms a cone-shaped mountain. (p. 89)

volunteers (vol·ən·tirz)   People who work for no pay. (p. 282)

voting (vōt′ing)   Choosing a leader. (p. 26)

wage (wāj)   The money paid for work. (p. 326)

water power (wô′tər pou′ər)   The power produced by rushing water, put to use to spin a wheel in a machine that makes electricity. (p. 74)

waterway (wô′tər·wā)   A body of water that ships can use. (p. 77)

wharf (wôrf)   A platform built along a shore where ships can load and unload cargo. (p. 391)

wilderness (wil′dər·nis)   Land on which people do not live. (p. 43)

windmills (wind′milz)   Wind-powered machines, with wide blades set in the shape of a wheel, that are used to drive pumps. (p. 224)

winter wheat (win′tər wēt)   The kind of wheat that grows in the southern Great Plains. It is planted in the fall. (p. 233)

yak (yak)   A large animal of the Himalayas. (p. 400)

yucca (yuk′ə)   A desert plant with long, pointed leaves. (p. 245)

Page references for illustrations are set in boldfaced italics.

Jobs   **Miami, Florida**

Key: (t) top, (b) bottom, (l) left, (r) right, (c) center.

Photographs

Front Cover(t), Four By Five; Front Cover(b), Four By Five; Back Cover, Four By Five; iv(t), C. Motisher/H. Armstrong Roberts; iv(b), HBJ Photo/David Lavine; v, Peter Beck/TSW/After-Image; vi(t), Ric Ergenbright/West Light; vi(b), Living History Farms, Des Moines, IA; vii, Robert Kristofik/The Image Bank; viii(t), Lon Jacobs, Jr./Grant Heilman Photography; viii(b), Grant Heilman Photography; ix(t), Larry Lee/West Light; ix(b), John P. Kelly/The Image Bank; x(t), Jack Fields/TSW/After-Image; x(b), National Cowboy Hall of Fame, Oklahoma City, OK; xi(t), E.R. Degginger/H. Armstrong Roberts; xi(b), HBJ Photo; xii(t), Farrell Grehan/Photo Researchers; xii(b), Bruno Barbey/Magnum Photos; xiii, William and Marcia Long/Photo Researchers; xiv, Jim Pickerell/FPG; xviii, Tom Padgitt/Berg & Assoc.

CHAPTER 1: 3, HBJ Photo/Alec Duncan; 4, Phil Degginger; 8, Grant Heilman Photography; 14-15, H. Armstrong Roberts; 16, Dennis Hallinan/FPG; 20, David Burnett/Contact; 21, HBJ Photo; 22(t), Porterfield-Chickering/Photo Researchers; 22(b), D.P. Hershkowitz/Bruce Coleman, Inc.; 23(l), Robert Ashe/Stock Imagery; 23(r), John Colwell/Grant Heilman Photography; 24, Tom Zimberoff/Sygma; 25, Jim Pickerell/FPG; 26, Mike Powell/Woodfin Camp & Assoc.; 27, HBJ Photo/David Lavine; 28(t), © Harry Benson; 28(b), © Harry Benson; 30, HBJ Photo/Elliott Varner Smith.

CHAPTER 2: 34, T. Kitchin/Tom Stack & Assoc.; 40, Artstreet; 41, C. Motisher/H. Armstrong Roberts; 42(l), John Elk III; 42(r), M.W. Grosnick/Bruce Coleman, Inc.; 43, Nicholas Devore III/Bruce Coleman, Inc.; 44(t), Mark Newman/Tom Stack & Assoc.; 44(b), Christopher Arend/AllStock; 45, Clark Mishler/AllStock; 47, Milt & Joan Mann/Cameramann International; 49(tl), Richard W. Tolbert/TSW/After-Image; 49(tr), Al Stephenson/Woodfin Camp & Assoc.; 49(b), Tom Tracy; 50(t), Culver Pictures; 50(b), Hal Clason M. Photography/Tom Stack & Assoc.; 64-65, Melinda Berge/DRK Photo.

CHAPTER 3: 66, M. Thonig/H. Armstrong Roberts; 68, Farrell Grehan/Photo Researchers; 69(tl), Grant Heilman Photography; 69(tr), J. Urwiller/H. Armstrong Roberts; 69(b), Jay Maisel/The Image Bank; 72, Bill Barksdale; 73, Keith Gunnar/Bruce Coleman, Inc.; 75, T. Kitchin/Tom Stack & Assoc.; 76, Peter Beck/TSW/After-Image; 77, Stacy Pick/Stock, Boston; 78, Milt & Joan Mann/Cameramann International; 80, Alex Webb/Magnum Photos; 81, Earl Roberge/Photo Researchers; 82, Nancy Creedman; 83(t), Culver Pictures; 83(b), The Granger Collection.

CHAPTER 4: 88, Four By Five; 91(l), Grant Heilman Photography; 91(r), Ron Thomas/FPG; 92(t), Colorado Historical Society; 92(b), Colorado Historical Society; 99(tl), Craig Aurness/West Light; 99(bl), Eric Kroll/Taurus Photos; 99(r), Phil Degginger/Bruce Coleman, Inc.; 101, Russ Lamb/H. Armstrong Roberts; 102, Bob Winsett/Tom Stack & Assoc.; 103(t), HBJ Photo/Maria Paraskevas; 103(b), HBJ Photo/Maria Paraskevas; 104, HBJ Photo.

CHAPTER 5: 108, Mike Price/Bruce Coleman, Inc.; 111(t), Ric Ergenbright/West Light; 111(b), Katherine S. Thomas/Taurus Photos; 112(l), Runk/Schoenberger/Grant Heilman Photography; 112(r), Tom McHugh/Photo Researchers; 113, Spencer Swanger/Tom Stack & Assoc.; 116, Rick Stockton/FPG; 117, Manuel Grossberg/Photo Researchers; 118, Bill Ross/West Light; 119(t), courtesy, Museum of New Mexico; 119(b), courtesy, Museum of New Mexico.

CHAPTER 6: 124, Tom Bean/DRK Photo; 126, Bob Brudd/TSW/Click, Chicago; 128, Milt & Joan Mann/Cameramann International; 129, C.C. Lockwood/Cactus Clyde Productions; 131(t), John Zoiner/International Stock Photo; 131(b), Lynn M. Stone/Bruce Coleman, Inc.; 134(l), Grant Heilman Photography; 134(r), Living History Farms, Des Moines, IA; 135, Grant Heilman Photography; 136(t), The Bettmann Archive; 136(b), John Deere; 137, HBJ Photo/Elliott Varner Smith; 138, HBJ Photo/Elliott Varner Smith; 142(t), Office of Tourism Development, Frankfort, KY; 142(b), The Thomas Gilcrease Institute of American History & Art, Tulsa, OK.

CHAPTER 7: 150-151, David Stoecklein/The Stock Market; 152, Michael George/Bruce Coleman, Inc.; 155, Robert Kristofik/The Image Bank; 156, Sepp Seitz/Woodfin Camp & Assoc.; 157(t), Douglas Kirkland/Contact; 157(b), W.H. Clark/H. Armstrong Roberts; 158, Ellis Herwig/Stock, Boston; 162, The Bettmann Archive; 163, Mark Sexton/Peabody Museum of Salem, watercolor by J.E. Toulza, Vietor Collection; 166, Smallman/International Stock Photo; 167, Costa Manos/Magnum Photos; 168(l), Cary Wolinsky/Stock, Boston; 168(r), Dan Budnik/Woodfin Camp & Assoc.; 169, Delaware River Port Authority; 170, Cary Wolinsky/Stock, Boston; 171(t), Werner Wolff/Black Star; 171(b), UPI/Bettmann Newsphotos.

CHAPTER 8: 174, NASA/The Picture Cube; 176, The Wilbur Kurtz Collection/Atlanta Historical Society; 178, Paul Dix/TSW/After-Image; 179(l), Jack Fields/TSW/After-Image; 179(r), Chuck Fishman/Contact/Woodfin Camp & Assoc.; 181, Bob Glander/Shostal Assoc.; 182, © J L G Ferris/Archives of '76/Bay Village, OH; 183(l), Art Collection of the Union League of Philadelphia; 183(r), Independence National Historical Park Collection; 184, The Granger Collection; 187, Alan Pitcairn/Grant Heilman Photography; 188, Eric Kroll/Grant Heilman Photography; 189(tl), Bruce Roberts/Photo Researchers; 189(bl), Donald Smetzer/TSW/Click, Chicago; 189(r), C.B. Jones/Taurus Photos; 190, Edith G. Haun/Stock, Boston; 191(l), James H. Carmichael/Bruce Coleman, Inc.; 191(r), M.P.L. Fodgen/Bruce Coleman, Inc.; 192, Momatiuk/Eastcott 1981/Woodfin Camp & Assoc.; 193(t), National Portrait Gallery; 193(b), National Portrait Gallery.

CHAPTER 9: 196, Tom Tracy/The Photo File; 197, Grant Heilman Photography; 198, Grant Heilman Photography; 200(t), John Elk III; 200(b), Milt & Joan Mann/Cameramann International; 203(t), Architect of the Capitol; 204, Lou Jacobs, Jr./Grant Heilman Photography; 205, Library of Congress; 206(t), Historical Picture Service; 206(b), Historical Picture Service; 208, Owen Franken/Stock, Boston; 209, H. Armstrong Roberts; 210(tl), Donald Dietz/Stock, Boston; 210(bl), Milt & Joan Mann/Cameramann International; 210(r), J. Howard/FPG; 211, Grant Heilman Photography; 212, The Granger Collection; 213, Frank Cezus/TSW/Click, Chicago; 214(l), Christopher Springman/TSW/After-Image; 214(r), Michael Philip Manheim/TSW/After-Image; 215, Santi Visalli/The Image Bank.

CHAPTER 10: 220, Gary Withey/Bruce Coleman, Inc.; 221, Frank Siteman/Taurus Photos; 223, Grant Heilman Photography; 224, Grant Heilman/Grant Heilman Photography; 225, E.R. Degginger/Bruce Coleman, Inc.; 226(t), The Bettmann Archive; 226(b), The Bettmann Archive; 228, National Museum of American Art, Smithsonian Institution, gift of Mrs. Joseph Harrison, Jr., BLACK ROCK, A TWO KETTLE CHIEF, George Catlin; 229, Smithsonian Institution, HELD UP, N.H. Trotter; 231, Solomon D. Butcher Collection/Nebraska State Historical Society; 232, Larry Lee/West Light; 233, Chuck O'Rear/West Light; 235, Fred Leavitt/TSW/Click, Chicago; 236, HBJ Photo/Alec Duncan; 237, Cy Furlan/Berg & Assoc.; 238, HBJ Photo/Alec Duncan.

CHAPTER 11: 242, David Ball/The Picture Cube; 245(t), John Running/Stock, Boston; 245(b), Manley Photos/Shostal Assoc.; 246, Joe Munro/Photo Researchers; 247, David C. London/Tom Stack & Assoc.; 251, International Museum of Photography at George Eastman House; 252, The Granger Collection; 253, Manley Photos/Shostal Assoc.; 254, Owen Franken/Stock, Boston; 256, Adam Woodfitt/Woodfin Camp & Assoc.; 257(t), Michael Freeman/Bruce Coleman, Inc.; 257(b), HBJ Photo/Alec Duncan; 258, Ethan Hoffman/Archive; 259(t), Culver Pictures; 259(b), Culver Pictures.

CHAPTER 12: 264, Robert Ashe/Stock Imagery; 267, Steve Solum/Bruce Coleman, Inc.; 268(l), Tom Stack & Assoc.; 268(r), Grant Heilman Photography; 269(l), E.R. Degginger; 269(r), Larry Ulrich/DRK Photo; 270(t), HBJ Photo/Elliott Varner Smith; 270(b), HBJ Photo/Elliott Varner Smith; 271, HBJ Photo/Elliott Varner Smith; 276(t), State Historical Society of Colorado (HBJ Photo); 276(b), Frank Leslie's Illustrated Newspaper, May 24, 1879, reproduced from the collections of the Library of Congress; 277, John Elk III; 278, James H. Karales/Peter Arnold, Inc.; 279, Peter Menzel; 280, John P. Kelly/The Image Bank; 281(l), HBJ Photo/Alec Duncan; 281(r), HBJ Photo/Alec Duncan; 282(t), HBJ Photo/Alec Duncan; 282(b), HBJ Photo/Alec Duncan.

CHAPTER 13: 288, Charles A. Mauzy/AllStock; 291(l), George Herbert/Woodfin Camp & Assoc.; 291(r), Peter Menzel; 292(tl), John L. Marshall/TSW/After-Image; 292(tr), Stephen J. Kraseman/Peter Arnold, Inc.; 292(b), Steve McCutcheon; 293, Steve McCutcheon; 294, Jack Fields/TSW/After-Image; 296(t), Milt & Joan Mann/Cameramann International; 296(bl), Milt & Joan Mann/Cameramann International; 296(br), Gary Hofheimer; 297, Holly Reckford/TSW/After-Image; 298(t), The Granger Collection; 298(b), The Granger Collection; 300(l), Craig Aurness/West Light; 300(r), Cary Wolinsky/Stock, Boston; 301, Windsor Publications/FPG; 302, Tom Tracy; 304, Tom Tracy; 305, Bob & Clara Calhoun/Bruce Coleman, Inc.; 306, National Cowboy Hall of Fame, Oklahoma City, OK; 307, United States Borax & Chemical Corporation; 308, Kit Hedman; 309(l), HBJ Photo/John Green; 309(r), HBJ Photo/John Green; 310, Garry Gay/The Image Bank; 311(l), Michael George/Bruce Coleman, Inc.; 311(r), HBJ Photo/Rick Der; 318(t), Robert Frerck/Woodfin Camp & Assoc.; 318(b), Commonwealth of Puerto Rico Tourism Co.; 322-323, Uniphoto/Bruce Coleman, Inc.

CHAPTER 14: 324, Ron Ruhoff/Stock Imagery; 326(l), HBJ Photo/Elliott Varner Smith; 326(r), HBJ Photo/Elliott Varner Smith; 327, Patti McConville/The Image Bank; 328, HBJ Photo/Elliott Varner Smith; 330, HBJ Photo/Elliott Varner Smith; 331, Photri; 335, Ken Biggs/TSW/After-Image; 337(l), Tom Bross/Stock, Boston; 337(r), HBJ Photo; 339, HBJ Photo; 340, Claude Urraca/Sygma; 341(t), John Grossman; 341(b), John Grossman.

CHAPTER 15: 344, H.G. Ross/H. Armstrong Roberts; 346, HBJ Photo/Elliott Varner Smith; 348, HBJ Photo/Elliott Varner Smith; 350, R. Maiman/Sygma; 352(t), The Granger Collection; 352(b), Architect of the Capitol, Washington, D.C.; 354, HBJ Photo/Elliott Varner Smith; 355, E.R. Degginger/H. Armstrong Roberts; 356, William Hubbell/Woodfin Camp & Assoc.; 357, HBJ Photo; 358(t), Larry Downing/Woodfin Camp & Assoc.; 358(b), Jeffrey W. Myers/Nawrocki Stock Photo; 359(tl), Gabe Palmer/Mugshots/TSW/After-Image; 359(bl), HBJ Photo/Rodney Jones; 359(r), Chad Slattery/TSW/After-Image; 370-371, Guido Alberto Rossi/The Image Bank.

CHAPTER 16: 372, J.C. Carlton/Bruce Coleman, Inc.; 374(l), E. Streichan/Shostal Assoc.; 374(r), Albert J. Gordon/TSW/After-Image; 376, Farrell Grehan/Photo Researchers; 377, Martin Rogers/Stock, Boston; 382, Herman Wong; 383(t), Audrey Topping/Photo Researchers; 383(b), Grant V. Faint/The Image Bank; 384(t), Bill Gillette/Stock, Boston; 384(b), Kit Luce/International Stock Photo; 385(l), Dallas & John Heaton/Uniphoto; 385(r), Susan Pierres/Peter Arnold, Inc.; 386, Bob Davis/Woodfin Camp & Assoc.; 387(t), Ru Chih Chow Huang; 387(b), Ru Chih Chow Huang; 388, China Pictorial Magazine; 389, Art Brown/TSW/Click, Chicago; 390, Art Brown/TSW/Click, Chicago; 391, Bruno Barbey/Magnum Photos; 392, D. Waugh/Peter Arnold, Inc.; 393, Richard Balzer/Stock, Boston.

CHAPTER 17: 396, Four By Five/SuperStock; 398, John Elk III; 399(l), Martine Franck/Magnum Photos; 399(r), Bruno Barbey/Magnum Photos; 400, Craig Aurness/Woodfin Camp & Assoc.; 401, Phil Degginger/Color-Pic; 403, Shostal Assoc.; 404, Moss Henry; 405(l), Ira Kirschenbaum/Stock, Boston; 405(r), L.L.T. Rhodes/Taurus Photos; 406, Jacques Jangou/Peter Arnold, Inc.; 407(t), "Portrait of Athahualpa, 14th Century Inca" by unidentified artist, courtesy of the New York Historical Society; 407(b), "Portrait of Athahualpa, 14th Century Inca" by unidentified artist, courtesy of the New York Historical Society; 409(tl), Steve Vidler/Leo deWys, Inc.; 409(b), Elliott Varner Smith; 410, Moss Henry; 411, Manley Photo/Shostal Assoc.

CHAPTER 18: 416, Shostal Assoc.; 418, John Elk III; 419, Giorgo Gualco/Bruce Coleman, Inc.; 420(l), Burnett H. Moddy/Bruce Coleman, Inc.; 420(r), Harvey Lloyd/The Image Bank; 422(l), George Holton/Photo Researchers; 422(r), Howard Sochurek/Woodfin Camp & Assoc.; 423(t), Rick Smolan; 423(b), Rick Smolan; 424, Fred Mayer/Woodfin Camp & Assoc.; 425, Alan Reininger/Contact; 426(l), Bill Apton; 426(r), Bill Apton; 427, Bill Apton; 428(l), John Elk III; 428(r), Fred Mayer/Woodfin Camp & Assoc.; 431, Motke Avivi, Kibbutz Yotvata; 432(tl), Motke Avivi, Kibbutz Yotvata; 432(tr), Motke Avivi, Kibbutz Yotvata; 432(bl), Motke Avivi, Kibbutz Yotvata; 432(br), Motke Avivi, Kibbutz Yotvata; 433, James H. Simon/The Picture Cube.

CHAPTER 19: 436, D & J Heaton/TSW/After-Image; 438, George Hunter/FPG; 439(l), Cameramann International; 439(r), William and Marcia Levy/Photo Researchers; 440, Marc and Evelyne Bernheim/Woodfin Camp & Assoc.; 441(l), TASS/Sovfoto; 441(r), TASS/Sovfoto; 442, TASS/Sovfoto; 443, E.R. Degginger; 444, Alec Duncan; 445(l), HBJ Photo; 445(r), HBJ Photo/Tom Tracy; 446, Jen and Des Barlett/Bruce Coleman, Inc.; 447, Woodfin Camp & Assoc.; 448, Leo Hertzel; 449, Leo Hertzel; 450, Leo Hertzel; 451(l), Leo Hertzel; 451(r), Leo Hertzel; 452, Rene Burri/Magnum Photos; 453, Leo Hertzel; 454, Leo Hertzel; 455(t), Benson Latin American Collection/University of Texas at Austin; 455(b), Benson Latin American Collection/University of Texas at Austin; 458(t), Grant Heilman Photography; 458(b), Jim Pickerell/TSW/Click, Chicago; 459(t), Tom Stack & Assoc.; 459(b), Eric Kroll/Taurus Photos; 460, Mark Newman/Tom Stack & Assoc.; 461, Hamilton & Hamilton/TSW/Click, Chicago; 462(l), HBJ Photo/Alec Duncan; 462(tr), HBJ Photo/Elliott Varner Smith; 462(br), HBJ Photo/Elliott Varner Smith.

FOR YOUR REFERENCE: 466-R1, Gabe Palmer/The Stock Market; R3(t), The Granger Collection; R3(b), HBJ Photo; R4(t), Norman D. Tomalin/Bruce Coleman, Inc.; R4(c), Steve Elmore/Tom Stack & Assoc.; R4(b), Leonard Lee Rue III/Bruce Coleman, Inc.; R5(t), SuperStock; R5(b), Flip Schalpe/Black Star; R6-R18(all), United States Postal Service.

Illustrations

Lynn Uhde Adams: 216. Jane Heaphy: 9, 315. Intergraphics: 42, 46, 70, 74, 79, 94, 95, 96, 104, 105, 114, 115, 120, 121, 123, 126, 148, 164, 165, 213, 217, 248, 255, 329, 347, 351, 353, 368, 378, 379, 380, 412(l), 412(r), 413, 464, R19, R20, R21. Aline Ordman: 275, 317. Jim Pearson: 239, 250, 260. Julie Peterson: 29, 31. Tom Powers: 58, 59, 60. Charles Scogins: 18, 161, 203, 273. Brad Strode: 283.

Maps

R. R. Donnelley Cartographic Services: 7, 13, 19, 36, 38-39, 51, 52, 53, 54, 55, 62, 71, 77, 84, 90, 97, 100, 110, 127, 132, 133, 154, 159, 177, 222, 244, 266, 274, 290, 295, 299, 304, 312, 316, 332, 333, 336, 374-375, 382, 398, 408, 425, 438, 447, R22-R35.

A 0
B 1
C 2
D 3
E 4
F 5
G 6
H 7
I 8
J 9